With Best Wishes
Evelyn E Atkins

Our Cornish Island

Omnibus Edition

by

Evelyn E Atkins

Fowey Rare Books

Published by Fowey Rare Books
4 South Street, Fowey, Cornwall PL23 1AR. UK.

"We Bought an Island"
First Published George G Harrap 1976
"Tales from our Cornish Island"
First Published George G Harrap 1986

Omnibus Edition First Published 1995

ISBN 1 899526 40 4

Typeset and printed by
Alexander Associates
Fowey PL23 1AR. UK.

TALES FROM OUR CORNISH ISLAND

Everybody dreams of escaping from it all to a peaceful, private island of their own. But for most people escape remains just that, a dream, a fantasy. Evelyn Atkins and her sister, Babs, dreamed like everybody else, but they chased their dream and on 13th February 1965 they spent their first night on St George's Island off Looe in Cornwall.

Evelyn Atkins told the story of how they became the owners of the island in "WE BOUGHT AN ISLAND". In the sequel "TALES FROM OUR CORNISH IS-LAND" she describes the adventures and excitements, hazards and challenges of everyday life on a remote island.

As the author says, once 'you have been touched by "island fever" you have been inoculated for life against the hazards which will surely beset you' and this book is a testament to her continuing delight in her island home.

About the Author

Evelyn Atkins, as well as working for many years for ICI, was actively involved in mountaineering, various sports, including small-bore shooting (she is a mastershot and has represented Surrey at Bisley), photography and music. During the war she was an officer with the WRNS. Her time is now taken up by pottery but, with her sister, Babs - who retired in 1977 from her position as Senior Mistress at Looe Secondary School she also shares an interest in woodcarving, gardening, cooking, beekeeping and making (and drinking) wine.

Praise for WE BOUGHT AN ISLAND

'A delightful story of what happened when the Misses Atkins did what everyone dreams of doing'

Daily Mail

'It takes pluck, optimism and a sense of humour to leave a pleasant house and a circle of friends in suburban Surrey and decamp to an unpeopled island off the coast of Cornwall. Fortunately this sturdy pair had plenty of the right qualities. Here is their engaging account of how they turned dream into reality'

Sunday Telegraph

'Against formidable odds, physically and financially, the dream was realised and this interesting and easily-read book unfolds the tale'

Yorkshire Post

'The age of chivalry is dead, but the time of adventure is not yet past. Miss Atkins' writing is lively, but never lush, plain but never humdrum'

Daily Telegraph

Publisher's Note

The close of the twentieth century doesn't seem to be bringing the world any nearer to a more satisfying lifestyle for the majority of the population, and most of us are having to deal with an increasing bureaucracy, polution, clogged-up motorways, inflation, higher crime levels, ever increasing commercialisation . . .

As an antidote therefore, we are particularly pleased to publish this omnibus edition of the two books about St George's Island off the south coast of Cornwall, **"We Bought an Island"** and **"Tales From Our Cornish Island"**. Refreshingly written by Evelyn Atkins (Attie, to her friends - which you will be, if you visit the island) these famous stories demonstrate many of the best traits of this nation's inherent characteristics. Attie and her sister Babs, have lived on the island now for thirty years and continue to provide visitors with old-world charm and a delightful welcome to their home.

It is worth pointing out that most visitors arrive during the spring and summer months and carry away idyllic memories of their short time on the island. However, there are many practicalities that can easily escape ones notice, by the very nature of the surroundings and the warmth of the hosts. There are no mainland services on the island and the fresh water supply is only sufficient for drinking and cooking purposes. Rain water is carefully collected for washing, and sea water is pumped up for flushing toilets. Electricity has to be generated and requires two hefty diesel engines with their own building and which require fuel oil to drive them, that has to be shipped from Looe, at a time to coincide with the availability of able-bodied *voluntary helpers*, who can haul the drums up the beach to the pumping station. The telephone is a *Mobile* - a simple enough solution one might think - but even this causes some headaches as the rechargeable batteries are subject to the vagaries of the generators. The most pressing consideration however, is the weather. Easterly winds of even quite average force for most nautical types, bar anyone leaving Looe Harbour and any rough seas prevent boats landing on the island, and therefore the winter months can leave the sisters isolated for long periods and it is an imperative that sufficient stores are in place for these times. Finding the funds to keep the island open for visitors is an on-going juggling act and without the sisters' dedication and willingness to sink their all (including their pensions) into the island, we would be without the simple joy of being able to visit them.

None of the foregoing phases our hosts one jot - they just get on with dealing with whatever problems arise without a murmur of irritation. They do have a lot of friends and voluntary helpers who willingly spend their own holidays working on the island, enabling most of the rest of us to soak up the glorious ambience and peacefulness of their home but, without their own fortitude and resilience, great good humour and empathy with people, we would not be in the very fortunate position of saying "we are friends and island lovers". Long may they thrive to enrich our lives.

Fowey,May 1995.

Book 1

Contents "We Bought An Island"

Book 2

Contents "Tales From Our Cornish Island"

Prologue

Island For Sale—off the Scottish coast—£30. It seemed the answer to a dream. A dream shared by many apparently, because although I wrote by return it was already sold.

What is this fascination about islands? Is it perhaps some half remembered magic of childhood that we take with us into adult life? Dreams of a treasure island where one can live an adventurous life in a glorious sunlit land teeming with cockatoos, luscious fruits and coconuts, bordering on a golden strand leading to an ever blue sparkling sea. Maybe it is just the hope that if only we could cut ourselves off from the mainstream of life all problems would be resolved, all frustrations would melt away.

Perhaps it was just as well that this particular island was already sold. At the time I was 19 and would have been hard put to find 30/– let alone £30.

It was a bitter disappointment nevertheless. I had just returned from a holiday in the Isle of Wight. To this day I can remember the breathtaking moment when I climbed to the top of Boniface Downs above Ventnor. Below, the blue sea shimmered in the sunshine; above, as far as the eye could see, the island was encircled by golden banks of cumulus clouds. It was as though the island had been crowned with a golden diadem. The magic of that moment was enhanced by the feeling of complete isolation, a sense of detachment from the world. As I stood entranced I wished a wish that one day I would come to live on an island, an island of my very own.

Decades were to pass. Decades during which holidays were spent visiting islands and climbing their cousins the mountains. The names chime like chords in one's memory: Skye, the Cuillins, Striding Edge, Ben Nevis, Wildspitz, the Wetterhorn, Zugspitzl. Wild, lonely places. Often one slept above the clouds.

Then came a holiday that triggered off a chain reaction of events that led eventually to the realisation of that youthful dream.

The holiday was spent in Wales. The first significant feature was that my sister Roselyn (Babs to the family) and I visited Caldy Island off the Pembrokeshire coast. During our early years Babs, the baby of the family, and I were in effect a generation apart. With the passage of time she had caught up, so to speak. Together we were enchanted by Caldy and the apparent idyll of island life. So much so that later, after our return from holiday, when St Catherine's Rock, a once fortified and now inhabited rock cum island, was up for sale, we contemplated buying it. We dropped the idea not because the price was beyond our means, which it was by many thousands of pounds, but because we said, dismissing the idea disdainfully, "It is too near the mainland." In fact it lies just off Tenby and one can cross by foot in a matter of minutes at low tide.

Now, nevertheless, there were two of us with incipient island fever.

The second event which we had no way of knowing would have such far-reaching effects on both our lives and careers was in the nature of a disaster. Slipping on a steep cliff I broke both the bones in my right leg. After a week in hospital in Wales and a further four months in plaster and still partly immobilised I returned to full time work, travelling each day in the rush hour from Surrey to a hectic job in the Staff Department of the Head Office of I.C.I. in London. Walking was still painful a year later. I never really picked up; a breakdown in general health resulted. Following a three month's illness I retired early.

It was during an additional eight month's sick leave I was generously given by I.C.I. that I made plans that, modest though they were, led by a chain of extraordinary chances to our becoming the owners of our very own island.

It is at this point therefore that the tale really begins.

Chapter 1
The scene is set

One advantage of early retirement is that one is still young enough to consider another career. One not so demanding, minus the stresses and strains of commuting to London and dealing with people and problems. Preferably one as far away from a telephone as possible.

Pottery perhaps. The thought of sitting in a world of one's own and throwing masterpieces to the rhythmic whirring of the wheel has a compulsive appeal. To fashion pots from clay with one's own hands, as had been done since time immemorial, would be creative, therapeutic and fulfilling. I couldn't wait. The fact that every activity makes demands and has its own frustrations and disappointments conveniently eluded me. I was all set to join the immortals—a Bernadette Leach at least.

Keeping to a well tried philosophy of last things first, a belief that if you keep your sights on the ends the ways and means would take care of themselves, I set about acquiring a kiln. After all you do not take up cooking unless you have an oven, so it seemed a reasonable idea. Nevertheless there was a certain amount of astonishment when I asked for an electric kiln as one of my retirement gifts from I.C.I. At the end of my sick leave I went up to the office to have it presented to me, in token, as it was too heavy for anyone to move except Pickford's. Everyone thought I looked much better in health. They also thought that I would need to be.

Next I booked in for a residential course in pottery with John Shelly, who at that time, with his wife Elizabeth, ran one week courses at their lovely 9th-century Manor home near Totnes in Devon.

Babs, like a star character in a play who performs off stage during the opening scenes then makes a telling and dramatic entrance later as the plot unfolds, on a lovely day in June deposited me by car at the gates of the manor.

There were eight others on the course all at different stages of ability. I was the only raw beginner. John Shelly, a tall intellectual, ascetic looking man had an impressive personality. Obviously believing in pushing people in off the deep end, he had us all throwing on the wheel at the very first lesson. I was absolutely terrified and clung to my lump of clay for dear life.

"Kick harder! Harder!" he commanded as he towered over me. I kicked as though I were in training for the World Cup at least. Desperately I hung on to the clay. It was my anchor. Without it I felt I might have taken a header through the nearest window as my leg zoomed back and forth.

"Harder! Harder! HARDER!" he ordered on the second and again on the third visit to my wheel. I kicked until my newly mended leg had no feeling left in it at all. I thought it had dropped off. Next time round he called over his wife Elizabeth, a sweet charming lady. "She's come to stick my leg on again," I thought hopefully.

"Look!" said John "A pot first time!" And there quite unbelievably, clasped between my hands was a pot.

"Most beginners' first efforts land on the ceiling," he said kindly. "You have very good hand control." Personally I thought then as I still think today that, apart from the sheer terror that made me cling on to the lump of clay, John Shelly hypnotised me into making it. I still have that pot and it has a place of honour as a symbol of the start of the adventures that led us to our island home.

Because of that first lucky effort John made me practise throwing until every bone in my body ached. I used to crawl into bed every night feeling like a penitent of old. My bedroom added to the illusion. Bare but for essential furniture, plain or white wood, the room with its stone walls whitewashed breathed the atmosphere of its 1000-year-old history. It could have been a monk's cell. A lucky monk nevertheless for the room was large and had a view of the mellowed courtyard and the beautiful Devon countryside beyond.

On the fourth day I tottered down to the pottery and climbed on to the wheel once more to force my aching limbs to set it in motion. I was thinking despondently "This must be what they meant by being broken on the wheel," when John loomed up from behind.

"You could become a very good potter," he smiled encouragingly. "When you leave here you must go to a good Art School as soon as possible. It will take years of hard practice, but you can do it."

That was enough for me. Forgetting my aching limbs and, conveniently, the years bit, I rushed off to the others on the course and announced that I intended to have a pottery of my own in the West Country, "residential, rather on these lines," I said grandly, waving my arms at the manor in general. That night over drinks in the local and not a bit put off by the fact that I had only four days of potting behind me they all clamoured to give me their addresses. "Just what is wanted," said one. "Somewhere one can holiday with the family and yet be able to pot." I still have those addresses but alas! they are hidden in a welter of papers stowed away somewhere on the island. Bill and Joyce Adams were two on the course with whom I became friendly. They have actually been here and previously were in on some of the dramatic moves. The others if they remember and ever read this will know that I did not break faith. Maybe one day they will get a surprise reminder from the past. Little did I think as we sipped our drinks that within 18 months I would indeed have my own pottery, in the West Country, on an island lived on by monks at the same time, give or take a hundred years, as John's Manor house first began its history. I did not tell John or Elizabeth of my plan. I felt sure he would not approve of running before one can kick. Nevertheless they have both been here twice and given their benediction. I shall always be grateful to John for his encouragement and his help in getting me over those first seemingly unsurmountable hurdles.

Back in Surrey I waited impatiently for the Autumn term at Epsom School of Art to begin. Meantime accidentally I found myself with a job—and a spare time occupation. Both these, too, were destined to have an effect on the future.

One day I went to the local post office-cum-stores to buy (a) a postage stamp (b) to enquire about joining the local National Savings Group so that I could continue with the regular savings scheme that we had *had* in the office and (c) to buy stamps to put on my National Insurance Card. All very straightforward it would appear. Certainly I found myself in possession of a postage stamp without any difficulty at all. It is said that some people are incident prone. Regrettably I fear that I come into this category. In no time at all the orderly queue in that tiny little post office/shop turned into a public meeting and it appeared to centre around me. In less time than it takes to recount the incident I found myself agreeing to be in charge of a Street National Savings Group. I was introduced to a Committee member who was present, the queue quietly reformed and I left an all but signed up member ready to "Fight in the Streets".

The case of the Insurance stamp became even more involved. For this apparently I had to apply at the Labour Exchange down in Epsom. Here I did my best to explain that I wished to buy an Insurance stamp. "No" I was told, they bought the stamp for me. "How kind!" I thought, handing over my card as requested. And that was that. So I thought. Later that day a pleasant female voice informed me on the telephone that she had found a job for me—typing and in charge of accounts. Panic gripped me. "Typing, accounts," I stuttered. "I am no good at all at those. In any case I don't actually want a job." Indeed I did not. For years I had been in charge of a large busy staff section, working early and late, chasing or being chased by people and papers, and baulked at every turn by the insistent and jangling demands of that torture, the telephone. In my spare time among many other activities I did freelance photography for the Publicity Department and as I did my own processing I frequently worked in my darkroom until 2 a.m. or 4 a.m. to meet the going to press deadline. I had had work. Now, fortified by eight months sick leave, all I wished to be was a potter. The helpful girl on the other end of the line explained; apparently I was now on their books and would be in receipt of Unemployment Benefit. Being offered a job was part of the arrangement.

"Well," I hedged, as she was being so kind and helpful, "perhaps a part time one then." That didn't count. It was arranged that I should go and see them again to sort it all out.

The next time I was in Epsom I called in. Proceeded by an elegant looking female trailing three dogs and smoking through a long cigarette holder I took my turn at the counter. "Sign please," said the clerk. Obediently I did so. "Nothing this week." he said and gave me £5. "But . . ." I started to say. "Come again next Wednesday," he added dealing once more with the elegant female who was still around. I looked at the notes. "Nothing!" I muttered to myself. I didn't understand at all.

The following Wednesday the same thing happened. I decided to resign. Babs was on school holiday and we intended to go off to the West country for a few weeks so the next Wednesday I stepped firmly up to the counter.

"I am leaving," I announced in a clear voice "I am going on holiday."

"Sign, please." said the clerk.

"For three weeks at least." I continued. The clerk looked up.

"Just leave us your holiday address."

"I haven't got one."

"Well send it as soon as you have in case anything turns up" he said, handing me a wad of notes. I felt trapped. I was a member of the Labour Exchange for life.

Soon after our return from holiday the girl with the helpful voice rang up again.

"We have just the job for you," she said "part-time receptionist at Halls, the coal merchants in Epsom."

"Ooh!" I quavered. "I don't think I would be any good at that. I don't know anything at all about nutty slack and that kind of thing. In any case receptionists are always young and blond, young anyway." "Well at least go and see them," she said. "It's *part time*" she urged. Thinking of all those wads of notes they had given me I could not but agree.

An appointment was made for me to see the Manager the next morning. To my great surprise I was engaged as part time receptionist starting on the following day.

The duties entailed taking orders from customers, dealing with their queries, and taking payment for their bills in person or by post. If the former, payment was made by cash or cheque. Everything had to be balanced up before the office closed for lunch and left, at 1 p.m. As customers came in right up to 1 o'clock waving money and bills, balancing up was quite a headache, especially as the chief clerk waited patiently at the door, keys a-dangling, to lock up before going to lunch. The telephonist whose switchboard was in a little cubby hole leading from the reception office was a particular comfort. Out of sight of the customers she would encourage me with sign language. I certainly needed moral support. For one thing I was not used to handling cash. My salary had always been paid into a bank account. Consequently I was in the habit of paying by cheque whenever possible. Cash transactions I did by weight—that is, I would hand over a note and if the weight of the change felt about right I accepted it. Now, as it was the firm's or other people's money, I had to be most meticulous. To count out change *and* keep up a pleasant conversation needed a dexterity of mind that eluded me. My friend in the cubby hole used to dissolve into laughter at my efforts to combine repartee and arithmetic. Mr Samuels, the General Manager who had engaged me, was very kind. A charming man, he did not criticize and there was never any unpleasantness if I were down on the day's takings nor if I made a bit for the firm.

Another problem was dealing with customer's complaints. If necessary the manager could always be called to deal with them, but it did seem that it was up to me to act as first line of defence.

One day a man strode in and brandished a shovelful of coal under my nose.

"Look at this!" he cried threateningly. "Do you call this coal? It won't burn at all, it only smoulders."

Not knowing what to do or say I gazed intently at the shovel hoping he would not throw the contents in my face. Suddenly I had an idea. "I expect your chimney needs sweeping," I said brightly. Wavering the shovel he stopped short, nonplussed.

"Perhaps you are right," he muttered. And to my intense relief he strode out again, shovel and all.

A few days later he was back. This time he brandished a bunch of flowers under my nose and presented them to me.

"You were right," he said, "my chimney *does* need sweeping." He called in several times after that to tell me the state of his chimney and he was always welcome because unwittingly he had provided me with a useful weapon in my verbal armoury. From then on "Your chimney needs sweeping" was my stock answer to similar complaints. It worked like a charm every time. In fact it had to be true for all the domestic fuels were tried out in the stove in my office. I soon came to know which burnt best, brightest or longest.

It was tricky though when customers complained of short weight. One man actually weighed every bit of coal from a one ton delivery on his bathroom scales, or so he said, to find that it was a few pounds short. It must have taken him a week at least. This gave me an idea.

"It has been belting with rain for weeks now," I reminded him. "The coal would get very wet standing out here in the yard when it was weighed. It would be dry and therefore lighter by the time you had finished weighing it." I called the manager nevertheless, as I always did for short weight complaints. This was dangerous ground and there could be far reaching repercussions.

My friend, the telephonist, said she enjoyed being on the same "watch" with me; she reckoned it was free entertainment.

I found coal fascinating. My knowledge was increased by a conducted tour of the heaps in the yard by the manager, some gleaming like black diamonds, and I just about knew the finer distinctions between Kitchen Nuts, Cobs, Derby Brights, Phurnacite and the rest when came enrolment day at the Art School.

With it came a severe set back to my plans. On the blackboard in the enrolment room were the fateful words "Pottery Classes FULL UP".

8

Going up to the desk I explained how important it was. Yes, they quite understood. Yes, they had heard of John Shelly, but it was out of the question: the classes were booked *for two years ahead.* The room was milling with frustrated would-be potters. A feeling of utter despair engulfed me and I was about to plough my way out through the shuntering throng when suddenly I saw at the bottom of the blackboard "Teachers' Class—1 vacancy." I fought my way back to the enrolment desk.

"Do you have to be a teacher of pottery to get into that?" I asked.

"No, you just have to be a teacher."

"Any kind of teacher?"

"Yes, any kind of teacher."

"In that case may I enrol my sister?"

"Certainly you can do that." And so I did.

Babs took it very philosophically.

"You must go," I implored, "and do your best to get me in when once you are there. It is my only hope."

She agreed although goodness knows she had little enough spare time to give to a wild goose chase. As Deputy Head of a new school which she and the Headmaster had started from scratch she had a lot on her plate. It was now a school of 1000 pupils and 46 staff. As well as being Headmistress to the girls she had recently had to take over the entire responsibility for the school due to the serious illness of the headmaster. Combining both jobs without a deputy to help *her* for two periods of six months was a great strain on her time and energy. As Careers teacher also she had organised a Careers Exhibition and for good measure a Leisure Exhibition that embraced the countryside for miles around. These exhibitions incidentally were so successful and had such appeal that one felt like going in for every activity on show. In fact it was through these exhibitions that I took up printing and bee-keeping, both of which have become rewarding parts of our lives on the island.

Any spare time Babs had was given to serving on N.U.T. Committees, organising parties and fetes in aid of Teachers' Charities, and taking part in or running the multifarious activities that take place outside of school hours. If at this particular point in time she was acting "off stage" as far as this tale is concerned she was certainly giving a marathon performance in her own particular sphere. Nevertheless she made a brief but telling entrance "on stage" by actually joining the pottery class as requested. Every week I eagerly awaited her return hoping that she had managed to enrol me. Each time she asked "Can my sister join too?" The answer was always the same: "No! it is impossible. The Office would never agree—the class is for teachers only." Each week my hopes were dashed to the ground once more. Then on the fourth week Babs burst in. "I've done it—you are in!" She had had an inspiration. "My sister *is* a teacher," she told Mrs O'Neill who was in charge of the class, "she teaches winemaking at an Evening Institute."

It was a fact. At one of Babs' private charity parties as an ardent winemaker I had apparently promised a friend of Babs, Ken Longley, who was Head of an Evening Institute that I would give a series of lectures in the coming term. I must have been an ardent wine imbiber too that evening because I had no recollection whatever of making any such promise and to this day the incident remains a complete blank. Nevertheless a letter officially appointing me arrived in due course from the Surrey Education Committee. Consequently every Tuesday evening for the last few weeks Babs had transported me plus all my equipment to this Evening Institute in darkest Surrey. There in the Domestic Science room I set up jars of wine, buckets, hydrometer and all the paraphernalia of this fascinating craft. With the room suitably labelled "WINEMAKING FOR BEGINNERS" I then proceeded to lecture and demonstrate to a class composed entirely of men. Bless them! they too must take their anonymous bow with Ken Longley for not only did they bring me samples of their but three week young wine to try, and much more acceptable I have to confess, the gift of a sack of pears, but their presence bestowed on me the accolade of teacher. For this magic word admitted me into what I had by now come to regard as the holy of holies—The Teachers' Pottery Class, Epsom School of Art.

Babs, her part done, thankfully returned to her busy life, merely adding the chore of ferrying me plus loads of clay and wet pots on Thursday nights to the Tuesday load-up to the winemaking class. How she fitted me in with all her commitments I shall never know. No doubt she felt she was performing a public service in keeping me quiet.

The pottery class was obviously full of geniuses. Gorgeous pots rose as if by magic under the hands of dedicated females. As they bowed as in supplication over their potter's wheels the air was filled with the sound of slapping clay and whirring wheels. At intervals one of these nun-like creatures arose, and, as with a votive offering in outstretched hands, would advance to the High Priestess bearing her work of art. This appeared to be a closed order, for very little speech accompanied the ritual. A few signs of benediction, an occasional censure, and the suppliant returned to her wheel elated or chastened accordingly.

Presently the High Priestess was joined by the High Priest and together they made a tour of the bowed figures, presumably to bestow a blessing, judging by the air of uplift that followed in their wake. Allow me to introduce Dennis O'Neill, Head of the Pottery School and his wife An, in charge of the teachers' class. Both were destined to play an important part in our saga. That was in the future. At the time I doubted whether I would ever become a member of that hallowed circle. With just one week's pottery to my credit and a mythical academic title I felt an uneasy novitiate; the possibility of excommunication a nagging fear. I need not have worried. Potters are a dedicated lot but ever ready to help and encourage their less expert members. Certainly I have always found this to be so. Soon under the patient guidance of An O'Neill I too was happily slapping clay and had the infinite satisfaction of again feeling wet clay rising under my hands on the spinning wheel to form that glorious bit of magic—a pot.

After a few weeks it seemed to me that the time was ripe to start looking for somewhere to have my own pottery. After all, I did have my own kiln. No matter that it takes years to become a fully fledged potter. With eyes firmly fixed on the distant goal it was not temerity or an exaggerated belief in my ability that made me think that I could overcome the intervening hurdles in record time; I merely ignored the possibility of their existence. Furthermore, life was beginning to crowd in on me again.

The National Savings Group which I had so impetuously joined was taking up an increasing amount of time. My "parish" was a street that consisted in the main of professional middle class members, who for reasons of health, age or young children, were housebound and consequently they welcomed the weekly visit. Their cares inevitably became my cares. In addition I had been asked to help canvass for new members in order to form more street groups. At first I felt it was a bit presumptuous to knock on people's doors and persuade them to save their money. One could not even say there was a war on and therefore it was a public duty. I had fallen into the National Savings Scheme so haphazardly on that eventual day when I had gone into the Post Office merely to buy a stamp that I was not sure exactly *why* we wanted people to save if they hadn't thought of doing it themselves. Soon, however, I had got caught up in the spirit of it all and felt it was a "GOOD THING".

It became quite a challenge to knock on a door and in that split second when it opened, try to get across the fact that you were not selling something or about to clonk the occupant on the head. It was surprising how well one was received and quite a number joined. At the end of each road we compared notes and there was keen rivalry as to who had bagged the most. Some of the houses we visited stood in their own grounds. I often wondered why their occupants whose husbands might have been stockbrokers and certainly were very well heeled did not tell us in no uncertain manner to save our time instead of telling them to save their money. They never did.

Quite suddenly I found myself a delegate at the National Conference at Folkestone and at the next meeting of the District committee was expected to stand up in the Council Chamber and make a report on it. How appropriate the saying "Great oaks from little acorns grow!"

The wine-making classes, photography, and for some inexplicable reason, a refresher course in German, wood-carving, and some political activity locally also made inroads on precious time and energy.

The main demands were, of course, those of the part-time receptionist's job. This frequently became full time as autumn colds and sickness hit the staff. Another pressing problem was that in spite of my somewhat unorthodox approach to customers I had, after a visit from one of the directors, been invited to become a member of the permanent staff, full time. Mr Samuels, the General Manager, had been so kind that it was going to be difficult to say "No".

There was yet another reason why it seemed propitious to move on. It can best be described as "The Case of the Bank Manager and the Bookshop." Like many other incidents it started in an unexceptional way. That is, someone came knocking on the door on behalf of Encyclopaedia Britannica. There was nothing extraordinary about that. Young men in their droves at this very moment must be knocking on doors all over the country on behalf of some encyclopaedia or other, but I am willing to wager that none of them has had such an unusual outcome as this one. Ever since Mother had helped me to buy a copy of Arthur Mee's Children's Encyclopaedia when I first earned the princely sum of £1.5s (£1.25) per week I had aspired to owning this one some day. With my retirement "lump sum" still burning in my pocket what better use for it than to spend a part on achieving this ambition?

"Come right in," I said. "I will have a set."

The young American was so astounded at making this lightning sale without any sales talk on his part at all that, deciding probably that I was not getting my money's worth in that direction, he gave me an excellent after sales service instead. Soon he got to calling in any time he was passing. He was mad keen on fast cars, and was always trading in the current car for an even longer, lower and faster one. He would call in and invite me for a spin in his latest model. It was quite terrifying. We would zoom off towards the Downs reaching 100 m.p.h. from scratch in about two seconds flat. While I clutched my stomach to stop it from shooting up like a lift and taking off for a solo flight of its own over the Downs, he would glance down at me and say proudly "Isn't she *great*?" To escape from this ordeal one evening I asked him in for a coffee instead. Babs was out as usual at one of her many activities. I told him of my plan for having a pottery in the West Country. "Gee!" he drawled, glancing round admiringly at our overspilling bookcases everywhere, "You don't want to waste your time on pottery. You should have a bookshop." He began to warm to the idea, and I got the impression that if it were not for fast cars he would have a bookshop himself. After that, every time he called he was full of this bookshop idea. "It would take a lot of capital," I objected, trying to fob him off. Because I liked buying books it did not necessarily follow that I would enjoy selling them. In fact the reverse would most likely be true, and I could imagine myself glaring at a customer I did not fancy wanting to buy one of my favourite books.

"No problem," he said, "I know a bank manager who will lend you the money. I will get him to call on you." With that he was off like a shot and made an appointment for the very next day.

Babs did not like the sound of any of this at all. So far she had not met my young American friend, and she thought that in some way I was being "got at". I did not quite see how. I had already bought his Encyclopaedia; he did not sell to shops and he was getting someone to lend *me* the money, not persuading me to invest any. It had not struck me as at all odd as I was used to these instant and unlikely "friendships". Only a few weeks earlier I had been to the Photographic Exhibition at Earl's Court. It was an enormous Exhibition with masses of people seething about. I no sooner entered and made a bee line for the Rolleiflex Stand in the Main Hall when a young fellow, a visitor also, spoke to me and in no time at all we were discussing the comparative merits of the different Rollei models. He then suggested that we spend the day together touring the exhibition. This we did all day until closing time. We had lunch together, each paying our own share, although he did at intervals buy me tea or coffee. He was starting a new job the next day down in Somerset, something to do with chemical research, and he was keen to discuss his prospects at what was really the beginning of his career. I told him too of my new "career" as a potter in the West Country and we had a really enjoyable day bound together by our common interest in photography. When closing time came we solemnly shook hands with each other he thanked me for my company and, wishing each other success in our respective enterprises, we went our separate ways. Ships that pass in the night. Why not?

Thinking it over however it did seem a little strange that a Bank Manager should call at one's home to offer a loan. Perhaps if you were a Paul Getty you might expect it, for it is a commonly held opinion and possibly a true one that you can always borrow money if you do not need it, but for those who have none there is no way. I was not a customer of this particular bank and it was in any case in a town several miles away from our nearest village or town, quite a journey for the Manager to make.

By the following lunchtime after leaving the office I was convinced I was being conned, or something even more sinister. The appointment was for 3 o'clock. By 2.30 I had arrived at the conclusion that the gang, for surely there would be an offshoot of the Mafia behind this, had, through their "front" man, decided that the bookcases would slide back to reveal hidden safes, as in the best thriller films. Anyone, they would reason, who bought an expensive set of encyclopaedias in ten seconds flat and proposed to buy property in the West Country to house a pottery must be well heeled. My young friend had cased the joint and now the gang headed by the supposed bank manager would muscle in for the crunch.

How would I defend myself? Not being a karate, kung-fu or even a judo expert the choice was limited. I no longer possessed a rifle from shooting days and was only accustomed to target shooting anyway. What about the old stand-by, pepper? You just threw it in the face of your assailants and while they were choking in agony dialled 999 and a Panda car would skid outside to a sickening halt and disgorge a posse of policemen who would whip the villains into handcuffs before they could sneeze "Atishoo." I fetched the pepper pot and put it in a handy place on the window sill by the front door. But wait! In this democratic country is it not illegal to carry an offensive weapon, or anything of a harmful nature even if it is intended only as a means of self protection? Better play safe and keep within the law. Regretfully I put the pepper pot back, then got it out again and cunningly put it in a strategic position on the sideboard. "It was the first thing that came to hand m'lud," I would state in court. "You showed great presence of mind," the Judge would say. "If more citizens acted like this there would soon be no criminals left."

As the villains were being led below to serve stiff prison sentences the doorbell rang and I nearly jumped out of my skin. I opened the door to find a very smart middle-aged gentleman standing there wearing a Homburg hat, gloves, and carrying a briefcase under his arm—just like a bank manager in fact. "A trick of the trade," I thought. After all, he would not come dressed like Bill Sykes complete with jemmy and a bag of tools.

"Come in!" I said cordially, trying to stop my voice from quavering. He came in and sat down. He was really most friendly and disarming. "Wait for it!" I said to myself. "This is just the softening up process." Nevertheless the conversation went along on most conventional lines. He took papers out of his case and asked me some ordinary straightforward questions. "Only a con trick after all then," I told myself, perhaps a little disappointed that I would not have the opportunity to thwart dastardly deeds with a simple culinary device. Yes, he would lend *me* the money, how much would I require? "It really depends," I hedged, "on the price of a suitable property", not daring to let on that I did not actually want a bookshop at all, but a pottery. "You will need stock, of course," he said, "and I feel that I really must give you a word of warning. You need a great deal of experience to know in advance what books will sell. Salesmen will try to convince you that what they are trying to sell will become bestsellers. If you haven't a nose for these things you could find yourself stocked up with a lot of white elephants. Unlike most other commodities you could find that you have a lot of capital tied up in something that will never sell."

"Well!" I thought, "this is the con trick to out-con all con tricks. Lull me into a false sense of security by giving me what was obviously very sound advice—just the sort of advice in fact that you would expect from a bank manager. The crunch will come later." Unexpectedly the crunch did not come by the time he rose to leave. "I will back you," he said handing me his card "but think very carefully and remember that though our young friend means well he is very impetuous. Ring me if you want any further advice and let me know when you find suitable premises."

After he had gone I glanced at his card. He was, it stated, the manager of a branch of one of the Big Five, in a very large town indeed. It sounded an important branch but if of course I rang the number I should get through to some back room of one of the gang. "I am really being set up," I muttered to myself. "I am now a sitting target, just ready for picking off." Just what I was being set up for I could not guess. Not the books obviously and my "lump sum" would hardly have the allure of a golden handshake of one of the Princes of Industry. It must be that my style of living gave the impression that I had hidden resources and I had been carefully cultivated until I was ripe for the picking. Well, I would soon find out. Tomorrow when the banks would be open again I would telephone, not the number on the card, but the one given in the telephone book for the branch shown on the card—if such a branch existed.

When Babs arrived home she was very worried indeed. "I don't see why. I haven't committed myself to anything," I explained, "and he actually offered to lend me money." She was much relieved to know that I intended ringing the bank and our suspicions being confirmed that would be the end of the matter.

The next day I looked up the Bank in the telephone directory and found surprisingly that the branch really existed, but I was astonished to find that the number was the same as that on the business card. I had intended enquiring about opening an account when I spoke to the real manager as I had to have some pretext for calling him; intending to move to the district or some such tale.

I called the number and asked to speak to the manager. When he came on the line he was the very same man who had called on me yesterday. Quickly I thought up some query arising out of our conversation of the day before. Courteously he advised me, again offered his help and we rang off. It was absolutely incredible. He really was a bank manager and the whole affair genuine. Babs could not believe it either and gave me a very strange look indeed. Later in our saga I dropped a note to him explaining that instead of a bookshop we had bought an island. I have often wondered what he thought about this and how we could find the money for an island if we needed a loan for a bookshop. Since that incident I have never really been able to look a pepper pot in the face either.

The next day my young American friend called round cock-a-hoop. "Now we must find you an estate agent," he enthused. "I think I know just the man—I will get him to call on you." "Don't do that," I said faintly, "get him to ring me instead." This he did and it was just as well for his journey to see me would have been even longer than the bank manager's. I explained that I was really looking for property that would serve as a pottery or a bookshop, and in the West Country. He sounded rather puzzled, as well he might, but promised to keep a look out for me.

One way and another my affairs were getting involved, and the only way was to escape away from them. It was fortuitous therefore that Babs was just about to start her week's half term holiday, due the last week in October. During our holiday in Cornwall in August we had both decided that we would dearly love to live there. We had toured around looking at properties for sale. None was suitable. They were either crumbling mansions or derelict shells of cottages. Any dwelling that looked structurally sound and attractive turned out to be a guest house being sold as a "going concern" with a corresponding high price. Now on the first Sunday of her holiday we suddenly decided just half an hour before the post was due to go to write off to as many estate agents as possible in the time, asking for details of cottages for sale, preferably for £500 or under. With Sunday papers and guide books for reference, typewriter and carbons for speed, we managed to write to twenty-one and caught the post as the box was being emptied. I optimistically hoped that I could get time off so that we could leave Thursday lunchtime for a long weekend with as many replies as we had received by then.

Monday morning I presented myself to the chief clerk and asked if my part-time could be arranged so that I could leave at midday Thursday for the weekend. I would work full-time until then I obligingly added. He looked dubious and started to shake his head.

"It would still be part-time," I pointed out with what I considered was impeccable logic as though that was the crux of the matter. "More than part-time, in fact. I shall be working three and a half days and only having two off." This must have carried some weight because he agreed to see what he could arrange. Luckily no one was off sick and my colleagues were more than willing to help us with our venture and swop duties. And so it was arranged.

Chapter 2

Enter Fairy Godmother and
Knight in Shining Armour

At 1 o'clock on Thursday the last day of October Babs called for me at the office and we set off armed with a sheaf of papers from estate agents and accompanied by our constant companion Toby, our smooth haired fox terrier. By 7 p.m. on a pitch dark night we had just left Plymouth and crossed the Tamar bridge into Cornwall when gale warnings were given out on the radio, as by the light of a torch I put all the agents' papers in geographical order. The nearest cottage for sale was in West Looe, just 19 miles into Cornwall. Presently we drew up outside the Copley Arms at Hessenford. Bathed in a glow of mellow light in the darkness the inn bade us welcome. We were actually halfway out of the car when one of those momentous decisions was made, trivial at the time but so far reaching in its repercussions that one can only think that Fate or some unseen power does take a hand in one's affairs.

"Let's go on to Looe and find somewhere there to stay," I remember saying. We both agreed it would be more fun to wake up by the sea. If we had stayed at Hessenford the chances are that we would have kept on the main road and by-passed Looe the next day, for there was only one cottage on our list in that part of Cornwall. The majority were much farther west and, as we only had Friday and Saturday before returning on Sunday, time was an important factor.

Neither of us had been to Looe before. We were enchanted with it the moment we crossed the bridge over the river from East to West Looe. Reflected in the river the harbour lights sparkled like a fairyland of stars on that wild October night. A "VACANCIES" sign hung invitingly from the window of The Harbour Moon, the first inn we came to along the quayside. Unfortunately as we walked up to the door the notice was taken down. We were not the only travellers abroad that night.

The proprietor was very sorry but no other rooms were open at that time of year. However he kindly telephoned a friend who appeared almost

18

at once, to lead us by car to his guest house. This was perched at the top of Shutta, a valley leading high up in the hills above Looe. The house could only be approached by driving the car for the last hundred yards in reverse. The lane was narrow and twisted upwards at a gradient of at least 1 in 4. To get into the driveway Babs had to shunt to and fro and finally reverse up and round an enormous tree—all this in the pitch dark. It was as well Babs is a good and experienced driver as it was some hazard to cope with at the end of a 240 miles journey. We realised now why our host had arrived so quickly down in Looe: he probably shot down from top to bottom in a nose dive. Our host, too, plays a small but important part and is in our *Dramatis Personae*, for as a baker's roundsman in the close season he not only knew the cottage we had come to view but the lady who owned it. What is more, he offered to take us there in the morning.

The cottage proved to be one of two nestling against each other in a minute cobbled courtyard. The walls were whitewashed and flowers were still in bloom round the horsebox-type door. It looked idyllic. The upper part of the door opened to reveal the top half of a lady to whom our host introduced us and then departed from us and from this tale.

"Are you sure it is not the one next door you want to see?" she asked. Astonished that both should be for sale, we mentally bought that one too, for we knew that we need go no further, need look at no more cottages. This was it. We had not actually crossed the threshold, indeed we had as yet only met the top half of the owner when we made this joint but so far unspoken decision. Whatever snags there were they would be overcome.

Oak-beamed with "two up and one down" it seemed a dream of a fisherman's cottage. It was to be sold freehold, and, for preference furnished. As the furniture included a new cooker, new radiogram, and money-consuming items like cutlery and china for hardly any difference in the asking price, we opted for that. For good measure the owner impulsively threw in her beautiful collection of horse brasses as she said she knew we would take good care of them. We did not quibble over the price, nor ask why she was leaving. In ten minutes flat from crossing the threshold we agreed to buy. We raced over to Hicks the estate agent in East Looe, paid the deposit and considered that as far as these things go the cottage was ours. We also asked him to arrange a survey in case any structural repairs were necessary, but in order not to hold up proceedings did not make it a condition of purchase. Armed with an order to view the adjoining cottage, which was empty, we dashed back to West Looe.

This cottage was completely bare; damp patches showed everywhere and plaster flaked off the walls and ceilings in huge chunks. This was a "one up, one down" although the landing had been partitioned off to make an extra minute bunk room. Downstairs the floor was stone-flagged; oak posts supported the oak-beamed ceiling; upstairs the walls of the bedroom were panelled. We looked at each other.

"Ideal for a pottery," we said simultaneously. "Downstairs for kiln and wheel, upstairs for storage."

So within hours of setting foot in Cornwall and just four months since John Shelly's pottery course we were virtually the owners of two cottages, one of which was the pottery designate. The prices were within our reach for this was 1963 before gazumping and rocketing prices, and the first cottage had been reduced in price as the summer season was well past. I still had most of the "lump sum" acquired on retirement and we also had a legacy from an aunt. This seemed an excellent use for both. By buying the two cottages we had, too, acquired the privacy of the courtyard. Looe is very hilly, rising steeply from both sides of the river. The "pottery" cottage, No 1 Bassett Court, is literally built into the side of a hill. The terrace and garden of our nearest neighbour is on a level with our roof, the sub-strata forming the fourth wall of our cottage. This accounts for the damp for which there seems to be no solution. Its unique placement has the advantage that Mr and Mrs Vague, who abutt us, keep a kindly eye on our roof and tell Babs when the guttering is blocked, a tile is missing, or the chimney needs repointing. This was to be all in the future. At that time all we knew was that we were on the level—a great advantage in hilly Looe—about 100 yards from the quayside and, rather temptingly, some fifteen yards from *The Jolly Sailor*, a sixteenth-century inn. Later we discovered that both cottages were reputed to be as old as *The Jolly Sailor*. There may be some truth in this for as I write they have both been designated as of historical and architectural interest. We had, of course, taken a chance in buying without a survey or search. The fact that both cottages were for sale independently might have signified that they were due for demolition or some other fate. Luckily for us it was pure coincidence that No 1 was also up for sale at the end of the summer letting season, for which purpose it had been used.

So jubilant were we with our rare good luck in finding our dream cottage, and unexpectedly doubling up on it, right at the start of our quest, that we were undeterred by the fact that during our to-ing and fro-ing between the cottages and the estate agent the river had overflowed its banks and swept up the street to within yards of *The Jolly Sailor* and perilously near our future abode. But for the railing there was no way of knowing where river and street ended or began. At the quayside cars and boats lay side by side in deep water. All the cottages leading to the river and those along the quayside had stormboards up, so the flooding appeared to be a usual occurrence. On the second trip back from the agent the road running alongside the river was completely submerged and we could only reach the cottage by nosing the car through flood water by narrow back streets. No one seemed to be worried by this state of affairs so we were prepared to do likewise. The cause of all this apparently was a combination of heavy rain from the south-west gale and an exceptionally high tide with which the manholes could not cope.

Mr Hicks introduced us to Mr Nancollas the surveyor and estate agent on our side of the river. It was he who was to make the survey as it would have been unethical for Mr Hicks, the agent responsible for the sale, to have done so himself. At the same time we arranged with Mr Nancollas for an application to be made for planning permission for No 1 Bassett Court for use as a pottery as soon as the purchasing formalities were completed. So, incredibly, within 24 hours of leaving, not only was our mission achieved but we had an embryo pottery thrown in for good measure.

Back at the Art School I diffidently told Mrs O'Neill about the cottage and that it was going to be a pottery. She did not turn a hair at what must have been a startling piece of news from her newest and rawest pupil. Indeed she was as delighted as we were when eventually unconditional planning permission was granted for the pottery. In fact both she and her husband did all they could to teach me as much as possible and introduced me to the mysteries of glaze making, a facet of pottery not usually covered in evening or part-time classes, and explained other technicalities that I would need to know, but which in my ignorance I did not even know existed.

Christmas, which followed only a few weeks later, saw us heading once more for Cornwall; this time to spend the holiday for the first time in our new little home, which we were now pleased to have bought already furnished. The kindly Mr Hicks had booked us into the Hannafore Point Hotel for lunch and dinner on Christmas Day, so, the festivities taken care of, we arrived at the cottage laden with gallons of paint, turps, paint brushes, cleaning materials and overalls as well as linen, Christmas presents, cards and a store of home-made wine.

It was exciting to wake up to the sound of strange footsteps on the cobbles and hear voices calling to each other in their rich Cornish tongue across Market Square. Our courtyard led into Market Square which is not square at all and is so tiny that occupants hold conversations with each other from opposite bedroom windows and doorways. Sometimes a fisherman's wife with perhaps a freshly baked long loaf under her arm, reminiscent of Brittany, would join in, so too would a fisherman on his way to his boat in the river. The whole effect was like a stage-set in a musical comedy or operetta, and as colourful. One would not be surprised if a window were to be flung open in one of the pink or whitewashed cottages perched on the hillside and a face appear to burst into an impassioned aria, or a chorus of fishermen were to march out of *The Jolly Sailor* singing excerpts from *The Pirates of Penzance*. It would not be surprising at all, for the Cornish are very musical and the Looe Singers or "Pennylanders" are a nationally known choir and have a delightfully sung record to their credit.

On one side of our courtyard entrance is a minute cottage owned by the West Looe Town Trust and used as a store. On the other side of the entrance is a mounting block from the days of horsemen, for the cottage flanking us on that side and facing Market Square used to be an inn called "The Cornish Arms". In the courtyard opposite our two cottages is a kind of outhouse which was used at that time as a milk store. In the centre of the Square is an hexagonal shaped structure once the market house, hence the name. It is at present a greengrocer's shop owned by another Shelley, Paul; he later was to become one of our *Dramatis Personae*.

We actually had a party in the cottage on Boxing Day. Our niece, whose folk on that side of the family are Devonians, and her husband who is also from Devon, although of Cornish extraction with the unmistakable Cornish name of Penhaligon, called over to spend the day with us from Devon where they were spending the holiday with her mother Molly, our brother Willie's widow. Even this meeting had a portent of our future. They brought with them another relative who was a young Cornish teacher and a friend of his, a girl from the Falkland Islands. We listened enthralled to tales of the Falkland Islands. Islands! islands! how we still dreamed of them. A short time after we were very thrilled when Molly herself came and spent a few days with us.

The rest of the holiday we spent painting in the "pottery" far into the night. After a long painting session we took Toby for a walk for a breath of fresh air, and were amazed to find the river over at East Looe ablaze with lights at 2 a.m. as the fishermen unloaded their catch from the luggers. In daytime with their many coloured sails they make a picturesque sight as they ride at anchor alongside the quay waiting for the tide to take them to sea once more.

Before returning to Surrey we contacted builders, a plumber and the Electricity Board, for there were improvements we wanted to make. We planned to have the plumbing altered in both cottages; washbasins with hot and cold installed in the bedrooms and in the inside lavatory in our No 2 residence. No 1, the "pottery", had an outside lavatory which for its purpose was enormous. As this actually adjoined the cottage we intended to convert it into a bathroom with washbasin and overhead heater. Both cottages were to have airing cupboards with immersion heaters for we had, after all, decided to keep the bedroom of the pottery as such instead of using it as a store for clay, glazes, etc. The reason was that our decorating and cleaning up of the panelling revealed it as an attractive room with possibilities. The "bunk room" would now be the store. We also arranged to have more light and power points.

Most of this was achieved by our next visit at the Easter holiday, but the decorating which we were doing ourselves went on interminably because the plaster pulled off in lumps with every brushful of paint like encrustments of stale cake icing. The whole lot really needed stripping back. Who knows what we should have found under the layers that had accumulated over the years, maybe centuries—perhaps a hidden room or some Elizabethan carvings? We had neither the time nor resources to find out, but eventually with the help of some size and five coats of paint the walls began to look quite presentable.

At Whitsun we were joined by two very good friends of ours, Bill and Marjorie Buck, both fervent do-it-yourselfers, who came down to lend us a hand and give us, we hoped, some of the benefit of their experience. Bill's forte was laying carpets and this he did with great expertise in spite of undulating walls and narrow twisting stairs.

The bedroom above the pottery in No 1, with its soft lighting, panelled walls and thick carpeting, now had an air of old-world luxury, invitingly comfortable for a weary potter to rest aching limbs. Perhaps it had become an incongruous appendage to a pottery, for many pottery workshops often resemble a bricklayer's yard. First it would need a bed. This was easier said than done for the window was too small and the stairs too narrow to allow the passage of a bed, double or even single. However, we reasoned, there must be a solution, for the room had always been used as a bedroom. In fact, we were under the impression that half the population of West Looe had been born in that room, for within weeks of our arrival we met at least three people who claimed that distinction for themselves or for an aunt or grandfather. An examination of the bed in No 2, which of course was part of the furniture that went with that cottage, solved the problem. This, although it was a traditional double bed with solid wooden framework, was hinged and so folded up for removal purposes. Later we were able to pick one up at one of the fortnightly auction sales held alternatively by Mr Hicks in East Looe and Nancollas and Lampshire in West Looe.

Bill, inspired by all the winemaking he had seen and sampled at our home, had recently taken it up himself. Between us we had quite a few bottles, so to celebrate the progress of the work in the cottages and the departure home of Bill and Marjorie the next day we decided on the spur of the moment around midnight to have a party. There was wine in plenty. In fact "Have wine—will travel," could have been one of our mottos for we rarely seemed to go on our journeys without some stowed away in our baggage. Food was the problem. We had nothing that would contribute to party "eats" except a packet of aspic. Chicken in aspic would be ideal if only we had the chicken.

This reminded us of an incident which Babs now related. When we first stayed at the cottage we needed to go out on a food shopping expedition. With our urban/rural background where shopping entailed a car ride into the nearest village or town or a 20 minute walk to the nearest row of shops we now proceeded to damp down the fire, dress up for all the rigours of weather that we might meet, put Toby on his lead, lock up and set forth with our shopping baskets for the forage. In five minutes flat, Babs told them, we were back, our baskets laden with food for the whole weekend.

"West Looe," we boasted "has every kind of shop you need literally within yards of the cottage, *and*, as each one is a family concern, you get personal service thrown in."

"Even your marvellous Toy Town couldn't produce chicken at this time of night though," said Marjorie, slightly aggrieved at the prospect of returning to the land of supermarkets and stores on the morrow.

"You never can tell," I said, accepting the challenge and with optimism raised to a high level by wine made from Surrey's best elderflowers I plunged out into the night. I do not know who was the most amazed when a few minutes later I returned with a leg of chicken in one hand and a cucumber and tomato in the other. By sheer luck a little café in the square had its lights on as its owner was still clearing up. In response to my frantic gesticulations at the window he opened the door to let me in, and probably relieved to find that he had no drama on his hands, kindly allowed me these items from his showcase. Was it mere coincidence, I wondered, that the name of the café was *The Witches' Cauldron*?

Marjorie was convinced that there was magic in the air and was more gloomy than ever at the thought of leaving tomorrow. There certainly was magic about as the next day was to prove.

In the morning, exhilarated by these events and not at all deflated by the fact that we did not actually have chicken in aspic as it did not set in time, I was up and out by 6 a.m. to take Toby for a walk. Although we had now stayed in the cottage several times we had been too busy decorating to explore and had not as yet seen the sea in spite of the fact that it had been our *raison d'être* for the coming to Looe in the first place. West Looe is separated from the sea front at Hannafore by steep downs and can be reached by a hilly motor road or an even hillier path, but this we did not know at that time.

On this fine May morning I proposed to cross the river and climb the Downs above East Looe to get a panoramic view of West Looe and, I hoped, at last a glimpse of the sea. East Looe Downs proved to be more built up on than I had anticipated and for some time we climbed and walked along made-up roads, rows of modern houses blocking out any view there might have been. At last a field appeared between the houses and, anxious to get grass under our feet and paws, we looked for a way in. To our delight there was a stile and a public footpath beyond. This led directly to an open meadow where sheep grazed and this sloped down the cliffs on the seaward side of East Looe.

Below at last was the sea shimmering in the early morning sunlight, but what riveted my gaze in spellbound astonishment was what I thought at first must be a mirage. There, beyond Hannafore, rising like a lost Atlantis out of the mist, was an island. Tender and green in the soft morning light it looked infinitely alluring as the mists melted in the rays of the rising sun. Enchanted, I took a photograph although I knew that no camera could capture the evanescent quality of the light or the magic of that moment of discovery.

I *had* to get back as quickly as I could to tell Babs. With Toby trotting by my side I hurtled down through farmland, and almost toppled over a fence down into Looe, then ran pausing for breath at intervals across the bridge down the quayside and so back to the cottage. Over breakfast we could talk of nothing else for we realised that as the island was only hidden from our sight by West Looe Downs, it was excitingly near.

Having waved Bill and Marjorie on their reluctant way Babs and I found the path that climbed up the side of the Downs above the harbour and, passing cottages and houses perched precariously above and below us, came down the other side to Hannafore. There, dominating the view, was the island. Less than a mile away it looked tantalisingly close yet with the sea between, elusively remote. Rising gracefully to the sky it looked like the tip of a submerged mountain. It seemed another world. Did anyone live there? We could see a cottage nestling in the woods below the slope of the summit and a house and a low building on the distant headland where the eastern tip ran down to the sea. How to set foot on the island? for that we must surely do. The answers to these questions would have to wait until we came down again in August for alas! we too had to return to Surrey the next day. But before that a most extraordinary incident occurred.

The next morning we had packed the car, Toby was on board and Babs at the wheel was ready for "off". I was just about to step in when a woman spoke to me. Now this in itself was not extraordinary. It seems to me sometimes that half the population is in the habit of stopping strangers and speaking to them, while others, probably the incident prone, seem to attract them like a magnet however many other people there may be around. It has happened to me so often that I once seriously considered carrying maps so that I could direct lost people. It would be quite impractical as I would need to hump a library around, for it happens in all manner of places; in crowded London streets, in open country, near home and in strange parts. If I were in darkest Africa I am sure someone would pop out from behind a tree and ask "Pleeze, ees thees the way for Istanbul?" or wherever. Something like this did happen once, only it was on Walton Heath about three miles from home. Babs and I were walking across the heath when someone *did* pop out from behind a bush and addressing me said "Have you seen Norah Rose?" Now by a strange coincidence I happened to know a Norah Rose who lived in a town about seven miles away from this quite lonely spot.

"Why, I saw her a week ago last Saturday in Sutton," I replied conversationally.

"I meant today," she exclaimed rather haughtily. "She is leading the field study group and I thought you were a member." Perhaps these strange coincidences are more common than I thought for when I related the incident to Norah Rose when I met her some months later, expecting her to be astonished, all she said was "Oh! yes, I *was* rather late."

Being picked on in a crowd is more puzzling. Once I was on a packed bus travelling to Victoria station in the rush hour. As we all clung on like flies someone leaned over the other passengers, tapped me on the shoulder and said "Will you please tell me when we get to the Army and Navy Stores?" At every stop I was asked if this were it so in the end I gave a running commentary, a sort of guided tour to the Army and Navy Stores. It was quite a relief when at last we reached it as I hadn't much breath left, squeezed as I was among all those passengers. This incident would not have been extraordinary if it were not for the fact that my persistent questioner was the conductor of the bus and this his first run on that route.

I have a theory about these encounters. Unable to follow the advice given by all those self-improvement books which promise success and a brilliant social future if only you train yourself to sally forth each day with a smile on your lips, radiating joy and confidence to all with whom you come in contact, I can only totter forth with furrowed brow and sheer misery oozing from every pore as I try to remember such things as where I put my Income Tax form or wonder what I can possibly get for the dog's dinner for a *change*. "Ah!" think these unhappy or lost strangers, "Here is someone even more miserable or worried than myself. Surely anyone with problems as big as *that* will lend an ear to mine or help me?"

Be that as it may, this person who stopped me in West Looe only wanted to have a chat. Babs, to whom this "instant friendship" was old routine, became restive and began to look rather meaningly at her wrist watch. That is until I poked my head in the window and said "This lady will clean our cottages for us." Babs was out of the car in a flash. One of our unresolved problems was that we needed someone to do just that and generally look after the cottages until we could come again for the summer holiday in two or three months' time.

As we showed her over the cottages our new found "treasure" made a remark that literally made us stop dead in our tracks.

"I shall be glad of a nice little job like this," she said. "I have a room just a couple of minutes away from here in Hannafore Lane. You see I mostly live alone because my husband is the gardener over on the island and I won't stay there any more. It takes half an hour by boat and it is a terrible journey, sometimes the sea can be so rough. I just couldn't stand it any more."

We couldn't believe our ears and bombarded her with questions. "Who lives there? Is it possible to visit the island?" An elderly couple owned it, she told us. No, it was most unlikely that we would be allowed over there. They didn't like strangers visting them. "Elderly!" we both thought, not realising how comparative this term can be. "They won't want to live there for ever. They may even want to sell it, perhaps in the near future." Aloud we said, "Perhaps your husband would ask them if they would kindly allow us to land for a short time."

"I am sure they won't," she replied, "but I will get Arthur to come and see you when he is over here when you are hack in August."

Thrilled with our lucky contact we got back in the car to leave Looe at last. Or so we thought.

This is a modern fairy story and like all good ones it would not be complete without a fairy godmother and three wishes. Only the fairy god-mother in this case was in the unlikely person of Alfy "Onions" (his sur-name was really Martin). Alfy was one of the people who had been born in our cottage. He was also porter to Mr Nancollas, the estate agent who had made the survey of the cottages. We had come to know Alfy through the fortnightly auction sales. In our absence back in Surrey Alfy had bid for us for items in which we were interested, up to a limit agreed between us based on his recommendations. He subsequently transported the purchases, including the folding bedstead, to the cottages. By reason of starting life in our No 1 cottage he took a special interest in us. As we passed the auction room on the quayside on our way home at last, Alfy appeared and stopped us to have a cheery word and wave us on our way. We chatted for a few minutes. Then as Babs put in the clutch we said "Well, Alfy, if we are going to spend a lot of time down here we shall need a boat, so you might look out for one for us, also we should like the milk store in the courtyard if that should become vacant, *and*" we added laughingly "if ever the island is for sale you might let us know." It had to be said laughingly for we had more or less gone over the top in buying the cottages and making the improvements. Nevertheless we had hopefully made our three wishes never thinking as we waved Alfy Martin goodbye that he would become our fairy godmother.

Back home we had other problems to crowd these thoughts out of our minds. The headmaster at Babs school, who twice had been seriously ill, died suddenly. Apart from the fact that they had started this new school together and he had become a personal friend, Babs had the additional worry of running the school solo again until a new headmaster was appointed. No sooner had he taken up his appointment than *he* was off sick for three months with heart trouble. Babs had little time to think of cottages in Cornwall or an island in the sun.

I had my problems, too, although they came into the nail biting category. First and foremost was how to resign from Hall's. Bab's summer holiday would be for six weeks and I simply had to be free by then to spend it with her, so that we could set up the pottery, enjoy the cottages after spending Christmas, Easter and Whitsun holidays working on them, and give Babs the break she so badly needed. Mr Samuels had been more than generous in letting me have extra leave at these holiday times so I did not want to let him down.

A minor problem that niggled me was that I had acquired a "banger" to get me down to Epsom and so relieve Babs of the chore of taxi-ing me to and fro from all the activities in which I had become involved. It was a beautifully kept car, almost vintage, and in perfect working order. Unfortunately I hadn't the courage to drive it. The husband of a colleague at Hall's came out with me two or three times a week to give me moral support. We drove over Epsom Downs where I executed three point turns, started on hills, drove in busy traffic and round the terrifying uncertainties of roundabouts. I had actually passed the test first time some years previously but having little driving experience since to my credit I insisted on having "L" plates up so that everyone would keep clear of me. My friend's husband laughed. He didn't know what I was worrying about. In fact he seemed to think that I was an accomplished driver and he certainly never appeared to mind putting his life in my hands. Nevertheless I just could not bring myself to go out in the car alone. So there it was in the drive, having to be moved every time Babs got the Wolseley out of the garage and still she had to pilot me around.

About this time too I felt despondent about my lack of progress at pottery. All the others in the class were turning out beautiful works of art, and they were so experienced. One was a teacher of pottery, another was on a diploma course and a third held her own exhibition annually. Mr O'Neill and his assistant Peter, who has since demonstrated pottery throwing on a T.V. show, were between them throwing a piece that was an impressive six feet high. It looked as though it had come straight out of *Chu Chin Chow*. I looked in despair at my own six inch efforts, higher than which I seemed unable to throw. To cheer me up Mrs O'Neill showed me how to throw multiple pots. To do this you threw maybe three pots of the same dimensions, you then knocked the bottoms out of two of them, mounted them one above the other and on the wheel somehow fused them into one tall pot. All went well until a stupid little accident held up further progress. One day at the office while rushing down the corridor to answer the phone two of my fingers got caught in the backward swing of the door. Hearing a scrunch I was not surprised when the fingers began to swell. To stop them stiffening up I used my hand as much as possible, throwing on the wheel that night until I could have fainted with fatigue. It was a wonder that I did not pass out for the next morning the hand was so swollen and painful that the chief clerk insisted on running me round to the hospital in the office car, and there it was discovered that one finger was fractured. Now with my hand in a splint and swathed in bandages I couldn't do any pottery at all.

Feeling generally rather despondent I resorted to that well tried panacea—a hair-do, with successful but totally unexpected results. Babs was to meet me outside the hairdresser's at the end of my appointment with Toby. When I came out, a very excited Babs awaited. With her was my old school friend "Tommy" whom I had not seen for a long time and the cause of the excitement was not the fact that they had run into each other.

"I've found someone to take on your job," cried Babs triumphantly. It could not have been a more fortuitous meeting. Tommy had recently given up a sweet shop she had been running to help eke out the family finances. Now that the children were educated and off their hands they had sold the shop, but Tommy soon found that she needed something to occupy her and was looking round for a job. Tommy had always, I remembered, been very good at maths at school, and with her experience of running the shop, balancing up and dealing with cash and customers would be child's play. Babs had once again come to my rescue.

The next day I went in to see Mr Samuels and told him that I wished to leave and why. "But" I added, "I have found a replacement, and, in fact, you will find that she is much better than I am." He was very charming about it. Everyone, I suppose, dreams of a cottage by the sea. Perhaps he did too. Anyway he was most sympathetic and agreeable about the arrangement, subject of course to interviewing Tommy, and he wished me well. Maybe he was just glad to see me go, but I don't think so. He was a nice man. Tommy got the job and apart from a merger and a different location she is still there to this day.

So, thanks to Babs, that problem was settled and for good measure Tommy's husband bought the banger from me.

There was an unexpected piece of good news at the Art School, too. To my great surprise and delight one of my multiple pots had been selected for the Art School exhibition. There it was among all the really gorgeous pieces by the experts. If anything was calculated to boost one's morale this was it. As soon as the bandages were off my hand I was back at the wheel and with renewed confidence, after being so long in the doldrums, my throwing began to improve at last. Another piece of news was even more unexpected and exciting. Mrs O'Neill came up to me at the wheel and said "The family and I are going to the New Forest for our holiday and Dennis has suggested that we come on to Cornwall for a couple of days to help and advise you with the setting up of your pottery—that is if you would like us to."

This was a wonderful offer especially as it would be in the nature of a busman's holiday for them. I couldn't help doing a dance of delight there and then in the pottery, and felt like throwing a lump of clay up at the ceiling. Babs was just as thrilled and, as the headmaster was now back in harness, we just could not wait for school to break up for the summer holiday and so be on our way once again to Cornwall for this momentous holiday. Just how momentous it was to be we could have no way of knowing.

Our good neighbour, Mr Oliver, advised us to leave our paint and brushes behind. "You will always find something to do if you take them, so have a real holiday for a change—you certainly deserve one." This was advice we were very willing to take, so that it was in carefree mood that we set forth sans paint, brushes, turps and rags, but loaded up instead with relaxation impedimenta of books, radios, T.V., cameras, sketch pads and the inevitable bottles of wine plus, of course, our good companion Toby.

We were settling into the cottage on a wet and windy day, which is not uncommon in early August, when Mrs Scott called to see us to report on the cottages which she had kept in excellent order. She told us that her husband Arthur was over from the island on his day off and would shortly be in to see us. Not long after this there was a knock on our "horse-box" door. The wind howled as we opened it and there, framed in the doorway, stood a figure clad in oilskins, sou'wester and sea boots. Accustomed as we were to males immaculately dressed in gents natty suiting or stylish tweeds this apparition looked to us like someone straight out of an Agatha Christie thriller. As he stood palefaced and silent in the oak-beamed room with rain dripping from his oilskins on to the stone-flagged floor we both felt, knowing that he had just sailed over from the island, that this was a most dramatic moment and he the most romantic of figures. Alas! our dreams and illusions were shattered when he spoke. He had had a wet, rough and uncomfortable journey, and sadly for us there was no hope of our visiting the island. "The Whitehouses" he said, "just do not like strangers setting foot on the island." He promised, however, to ask at a suitable moment, but he held out no hope at all. We were not too downcast. The fact that the gardener's wife worked for us and the gardener himself had been to visit us brought the island sharply into focus. Only one more step and we might indeed set foot on the island. "Our chance will come" we told each other optimistically. That chance was to come, but in a most unexpected way.

The weather soon cleared and was brilliantly sunny. Looe in season was very different from the rest of the year. We had only seen it in late October, Christmas, and Easter and the season had scarcely begun when we were last down at Whitsun. Now the streets and quaysides were teeming with summer visitors. Hired boats plied between the river and the open sea against the background of the many coloured sails of the luggers riding at anchor along the harbour walls. This, the fishing fleet, would be sailing with the tide, their owners alternating fishing in the summer months with taking private parties on sharking trips out beyond Eddystone lighthouse, twelve miles away. Holiday fishermen and small boys cast their lines hopefully over the harbour walls, sometimes entangling with passing craft. Gulls swooped overhead on the look-out for tit-bits, their wings flashing against the blue sky and the backcloth of the pink and white-washed cottages perched on the hills that rise steeply on either side of the river; their haunting cries pierced the air above the chugging of the engines and the creamy voices of the boatmen calling across the water to muster customers down the harbour steps into the boats.

One of these boatmen, to our surprise, turned out to be Alfy Martin, resplendent in fisherman's jersey, cap and sea boots, following his summer occupation of hiring out "doodle-bugs"—the local nickname for small self-drive motor boats. He appeared far too busy to be interrupted, involved as he was in dealing with the queues of eager would-be motor boaters.

We explored Looe, but could not see the island. East Looe has a narrow sea front tucked between Banjo pier—a stone jetty extending beyond the harbour walls—and the cliffs, but any view of Looe Island, as we discovered it is called locally, is obscured by Hannafore Point which juts out into the sea on the West Looe side of the river mouth. In fact many visitors to East Looe spend their entire holiday ignorant of the existence of an island "just around the corner."

We spent the first part of the holiday exploring the beaches of Cornwall. For some years, long before the popular pastime it is now, we had been avid collectors of gemstones. Cornwall is a happy hunting ground for gemmologists and on previous holidays we had spent many absorbing hours searching for semi-prescious stones on the rocky beaches. A Cornish lady, whose profession it was, had in the past given us much valuable advice and guidance, and we were now able to identify carnelians, banded, moss and fortification agate, rose quartz, amethyst quartz and topaz. Our collection now began to grow impressively. Bucketfuls of "treasure" appeared in the courtyard to be sorted out at leisure. "Perhaps," we thought wistfully, as we dropped them into pans of seawater to bring back the colour and brilliance that had attracted us to pick them up, "Perhaps one day we shall find enough valuable ones to buy 'that island' if ever it is for sale." Maybe we rubbed a magic gem as we fingered through the myriad coloured pebbles. Maybe it was just chance or destiny taking a hand once more in our affairs; whatever the reason, something decided us on one particular day and no other to have a word with Alfy. We had seen him many times dealing with the seemingly never ending queue of customers for his boats. This particular day was after we had been on holiday for about two weeks, for having the cottage meant that we could spend the whole of the school holiday in Looe. Alfy was as busy as ever, but I remember saying "We really must speak to him—he may think that we are ignoring him." Rather diffidently we edged our way up to him.

"Hallo! Alfy," we said. "We don't suppose you will remember us, but you helped us with our furniture back in the winter." Quickly he detached himself from the crowd.

"Of course I do," he said, "and I have been on the lookout for you today—*The Island is for sale!*"

As though someone had fired a gun and without saying a single word to each other we raced to the ferry, shot across the river and up the stairs to the office of Nancollas & Lampshire. We paused for breath only to find that Mr Nancollas was out. His secretary made an appointment for us for 2 o'clock that afternoon. As soon as the doors were open after the lunch hour we were there.

"I am so sorry I was out when you called," said Mr Nancollas, "but I was over on the Island taking it on our books."

"That is exactly what we have come to see you about" we said to a very surprised Mr Nancollas, marvelling to ourselves that we should have picked on this very day of all days to greet Alfy Martin.

A few minutes later we left with an order to view—there were no details available yet, of course, just a hurriedly typed slip of paper. The asking price we noted was £22,000. It might just as well have been £2,000,000 or £2,000, for all were at that time equally beyond our reach. We did think, however, that as islands go it seemed a reasonable amount. This, being 1964, was before the days of roaring inflation, but it was still a sizeable amount for anyone to find—a fortune to us.

Our main reaction was that we had this magic slip of paper, a passport to "our island". The future would take care of itself. We did not even discuss ways and means—we dare not.

It was too late to go over that day. In any case Mr Nancollas wanted to warn the owners that we were coming if he could get a message to them. Apparently he was not able to do so for the next morning, as Alfy was fixing up with a boatman to take us over, a boat came into the harbour mouth and a couple stepped ashore. A helpful boatman ran after them and introduced us, for they were the owners of the island, Mr and Mrs Whitehouse. Rather startled that they had prospective buyers before details had been circulated they nevertheless cancelled their shore trip and took us straight back to the island.

Although we were so excited at the prospect of viewing the island we were sorry to hear the reason for the sale. Mr Whitehouse had contracted a serious illness and his doctor had insisted that he should remove to the mainland where medical aid would be immediately available. They were a charming couple and obviously loved the island. They showed us the

34

main dwelling, "Island House" with its farmhouse kitchen, stoneflagged and oak-beamed; the lounge with its huge windows facing south and west with magnificent views of the sea; the two cottages and the many outhouses. We climbed the hill some 150 feet high and down through the woods to the tractor shed. We were shown the cliff walks, the beaches, the bridge to the "Little Island" and the daffodil fields were fifteen different varieties grew. These start to bloom at Christmas time and were sent to Covent Garden by the hundredweight.

But of all the fascinating things we saw the one that rivetted our attention was the generator building. The front part of this housed a diesel engine for generating A.C. electricity. A doorway led to another room at the rear. This was about forty feet by twenty feet, one wall of which was lined with a row of large glass accumulators. Concrete blocks supported heavy wooden beams which ran the entire length of the room, and, apart from gangways, filled all available floor space. Mr Whitehouse explained that the previous owner, Major General Rawlings, a "D" Day Commander in the second world war, had retired to the island, and with the assistance of two families had run it as a market garden and daffodil farm, the mild climate, which was similar to the Scillies, making it ideal for producing early crops. In his day the electrical system had been D.C. and had been stored in accumulators in this room—hence the concrete blocks and beams for supporting them. Tragically the General died suddenly while on his way to Plymouth by train. Mr Whitehouse explained that when they came here to retire they brought their gardener and wife with them. Although they continued to cultivate the daffodils as they were in situ, they had no intention of carrying on with full scale market gardening and so did not need the powerful electrical storage plant. He had therefore dismantled it and installed the small but efficient Lister Start-O-Matic A.C. Generator, merely retaining one row of batteries for the initial starting up of the engine—or so we understood. All this was very interesting but technically beyond us. What held us spellbound was that this room, full though it was with concrete blocks and wooden beams, was simply crying out to be converted into a pottery.

Entranced, we walked back down the path to the beach where the boatman was waiting to take us back to Looe. The island was idyllic, an absolute paradise. "But it is a dream, an impossible dream," we thought as we turned to shake hands with Mr Whitehouse. The next moment we really thought that we were dreaming.

"I suppose," he said hesitantly "you haven't had time to think about it. You will need to talk it over, of course."

"We certainly would like to buy it," we both exclaimed together, "indeed we *would*."

"I would like you to have it and if you are seriously interested I will drop the price by £2,000 and let you have half the purchase price on a private mortgage of 6½%."

We stared at him in amazement. Did he really say that? Suddenly the impossible seemed within the realms of possibility.

"In that case," we both said at once, without any hesitation, not even turning to each other for confirmation, "we will have it."

Dazed, we returned to the mainland to think out ways and means of raising the other half of the money. Luckily we had a house that we could sell and I had some shares acquired in more affluent earning days when I had indulged in the giddy excitement of dabbling on the stock exchange. Babs had a legacy; then we had the cottages. With sessions of "Monopoly" in mind we thought that if necessary we could mortgage those. One way or another we might be able to raise the money—we *would* do it!

The next day the O'Neills were due to come down to advise about the pottery in No 1 cottage. Whatever would they think now? Having sat them in a circle in the little sitting room of No 2 we both stood behind the counter arrangement that served as a partition between the sitting room and the slip of a kitchenette, and handed them cups of tea, dispensing them as though we were serving in a cafeteria.

"We have an announcement to make," we said. "There has been a change of plan."

They all looked up expectantly wondering perhaps if the pottery project had been ditched and their journey had been for nothing.

"We are buying an island," we announced," and the pottery is to be there instead."

They were dumbfounded and then as excited as we were.

"Nothing has been settled yet," we told them," and we haven't actually found the ways and means, because the idea is as new as yesterday."

Instantly Dennis said that they would extend their holiday so that they could come over and see the island. We managed to get a message over to the Whitehouses and the following day a boatload of us sailed out of the harbour and disembarked on the island beach. As we all trooped up the path An O'Neill turned to us and with wonder in her eyes said "I shouldn't

36

hesitate—you *must* have it."

Before Dennis, An and family departed the following day they came to see us again in the cottage. Over coffee Dennis said that he had thought up a few ideas that might be useful. He would, if we wished, lend us two of his fulltime diploma course pottery students for two or three months. They would convert the spare generator room into a pottery. This would not only be a help to us but would give them valuable experience in setting up a pottery as they were near the end of what was at that time a seven year course. They would be experienced potters and could do potting for me as well. We were delighted with this idea as quite a bit of structural alteration would have to be made before the generator room could be used as a pottery. Hefty young men would be invaluable in getting rid of the builtin concrete blocks and knocking a hole in the outside wall to make a door, and windows. Dennis also offered to come with his family the following summer to help with pioneering generally in any way that was needed. He thought that Peter Steele, his assistant—his co-thrower on the six foot pot— and his family would also be willing to come and do the same. They would all bring their own tents and be self sufficient and no burden to us. These were wonderful offers and seemed to set the seal on the venture. Getting down to practical details had the effect of dispelling the dream-like aura that surrounded the whole enterprise.

After they left we faced a few other practical details, details that were more in the nature of obstacles to be overcome. First and foremost was the question of raising the money, but this we dismissed rather casually. £10,000 is a large amount in anybody's money but in 1964, before inflation took the bit between its teeth, it was a fortune. And that would only be the beginning—there would be solicitors' fees for both selling our house and for buying the island; repayment of an existing mortgage, and removal charges, to name but a few. In fact the sum that was eventually required exceeded the basic amount by about 40%-50%. This problem we were convinced would be resolved. Surely we were meant to have the island, we said to each other, as we reflected in wonderment on the fact that every move we had made during the past year and any chance encounter had led us to what seemed this moment of destiny. Somehow or other the money would be forthcoming—nothing could diminish our buoyant optimism about this.

The one fact that did bring us up with a jolt was the question of Babs' career, for it suddenly hit us in the face like a slap of cold water that she would have to give up her job. In the fever of excitement at the enchanting prospect of owning an island we had overlooked this vital point. Nevertheless we airily brushed aside this problem, too; she would get a teaching post in Cornwall. It would mean giving up her senior position, which was considered a plum job in Surrey, and a big drop in salary, but some sacrifice had to be made, we told each other, in exchange for a passport to paradise. If we had known at the time how few teaching posts were then available in Cornwall and how rare the movement of personnel compared with the general post that went on in London and the Home Counties we would have been appalled at our optimism. However we remained completely sanguine—we were in a dream world and as each obstacle arose in our minds we just talked it out of existence.

After a time reaction set in. These big and very real problems caused us no concern at all. What did begin to worry us and nag us out of sleep was the ever growing fear that some rich person would come along and outbid us; our belief that the island was meant for us did falter at this possibility. There were certain preliminary formalities to be gone through before we could return to Surrey and wind up our affairs there, and these took time. So in theory we had time on our hands to enjoy at leisure; in practice we just did not know how to contain ourselves. We endured many agonising moments and almost gave up eating for the rest of our stay. There was the day, for instance, when we sat above the rocks at Hannafore, and just gazed across at the island. To our consternation we saw a man standing on the cliffs at the eastern tip of the island. He did not move and to our despairing minds he appeared to be surveying the scene of his future possession. "He'll outbid us!" we both exclaimed hopelessly. Another ten minutes went by and still he remained motionless. "He is absolutely gone on the place," we muttered. Despondently we fetched the binoculars from the car hoping that by magnifying his image we could will him away the more easily. To our intense relief we found that the object of our fear and despair was nothing more than a post. Later we were to discover that it was the tabernacle for seating the flagstaff.

More ominous was the day Alfy Martin detached himself from his queue of holidaymakers to speak to us.

"Mr Nancollas has taken a man out to the Island," he informed us. "I think it may be another client." His face was sympathetic and troubled, for as our sponsor, so to speak, he was as perturbed as we were. To keep our nerves from snapping we went for a run in the car along the coast to

Downderry. This was a mistake, for looking westward there was a magnificent view of the island. From this part of the coast it appeared to be much farther out to sea and in the soft light of the westering sun it looked infinitely alluring. We could not bear to look nor endure the suspense any longer, so we drove dejectedly back to Looe. Alfy's crowds had melted away by this time and he was waiting for us.

"It's all right," he said, smiling cheerily, "that was Mr Whitehouse's solicitor."

Our fears were not unfounded, however. This was before the days of gazumping and so far nothing had been signed and no deposit had been paid. Therefore when Mr Nancollas told us that some famous West End actors were after the island and offering far more than the original asking price we were in utter despair. The next day we saw Mr Whitehouse on the quayside. He came towards us. This would be it—the coup de grace; our hopes dashed to the ground and with one blow the end of a dream. After the greetings he looked intently at us.

"Some actors want the island," he said. So it was true and we knew that we couldn't compete. "I know that I cannot ask you legally, but I would like some reassurance that you will not resell to them."

"Resell!" we exclaimed, almost shouting in relief, "Resell! Of *course*, we won't resell, we are only interested in buying." There was no reason, of course why Mr Whitehouse should not sell to them himself at the higher price, but, as Mr Nancollas told us later, he really wanted us to have the island. Nor could he be certain that as soon as everything was signed and sealed we would not, without even taking possession, resell to the actors and make a handsome profit. In fact the ink was scarcely dry when we did eventually sign before we had an offer of £33,000, and could, just by the stroke of a pen, have made what would have been to us, a small fortune. In letting us have the island at a reduced price Mr Whitehouse was taking a very real chance. It was fortunate for us that loving the island as both he and his wife did that they liked our idea of setting up a pottery there, for we had discussed our project with them. On the other hand it must be said that later, when we had become well established, local opinion had it that it was also fortunate for the island that we bought it. Had it been on the open market it is certain that other offers than that made by the actors would have been made. The Scillies apart, an inhabitable island off the coast of Cornwall is a rarity. This one, said to be the largest, is outstandingly beautiful and unspoilt, and would have been ripe for exploitation and commercialism. It was considered a danger that it might fall into the hands of a developer and be turned into a holiday camp.

These conjectures and fears apart it was apparent from this conversation on the quayside that the negotiations were still taking place as arranged. So dear Mr Whitehouse who, sadly, died not many months after returning to the mainland to live, became our knight in shining armour who made it possible for us to take the chance of a lifetime and make that childhood dream come true.

Our friendly bank manager in Surrey advanced the £2,000 needed for the deposit so, the preliminaries over, there was no reason why we should not return home to work out the manifold problems of uprooting ourselves and finding the rest of the money. For some inexplicable reason we decided to stay on and finish the rest of the holiday as we originally intended. To be precise we, as usual, talked ourselves into staying, although there was nothing further we could do for the time being to expedite the negotiations. Firstly, we could not actually take possession until Christmas because Babs had to give a term's notice. Secondly, we really wanted to keep our eye on the island until the last possible moment because nothing would be absolutely certain until contracts were exchanged. We must be on hand as long as possible, we told ourselves, in case there were a hitch of any kind. Thirdly, and the most important reason, although we did not even admit it to ourselves, was that we wanted to put off the moment when we should have to face harsh reality as long as we possibly could.

So far everything had been done by mirrors; our friends, if they knew, would say that we were living in cloud cuckoo land. There was no escaping the fact that as soon as we returned home we would come down to earth with a bump. When Babs resigned she would be cutting off her career for an uncertain future. Then there was the matter of selling our home and giving up our whole way of life and friends to live on a remote island where we should be the only inhabitants. The only inhabitants? this raised a doubt which we pushed firmly down every time it raised its niggling head. The doubt was, not that we should be the only inhabitants, but that there might be only one inhabitant—me, for Babs would surely have to live on the mainland during term time. As Cornwall is some eighty miles in length the teaching post she obtained might possibly be too far away for her to use the cottage in Looe either, except at week-ends and holidays. Then there was the biggest problem of all—finding the money. This, the hardest nut of all to crack, concerned us the least. In fact we quite enjoyed thinking up ways of getting it. Many, one could almost say, happy hours were spent during the last fortnight of the holiday discussing schemes, so much so that we practically formed our own Government "Ways and means" Department. Not that we were idle in other directions. Life on the island conjured up all sorts of fascinating occupations and pastimes. One which appealed to us especially was astronomy and where better for a grandstand view of the stars? We therefore were delighted, when on a foraging expedition in the Barbican at Plymouth, to pick up a highly efficient Japanese telescope that had a magnification of twenty-five times and zoomed up to eighty times. It cost £12 and seemed a very reasonable price to pay after spending our time thinking in thousands of pounds.

Chapter 3
Exits and entrances

In early September we at last returned to Surrey to set the wheels in motion at that end, having left all the legal arrangements to do with the transaction in the hands of Mr Browning, the solicitor who had acted for us over the purchase of the cottages. Mr Nancollas was to keep an eye on our affairs in other directions. As Chairman of the Council, equivalent to Mayor, he had an official interest in the future of the island as well as the professional one of selling it to us. He took a particular interest in helping us, for selling an island is not an everyday occurrence in the life of an estate agent, and there were many details to be sorted out that were difficult for us to attend to from a distance of 240 miles.

When the news broke our friends were horrified.

"Whatever will you do, leaving all your friends?" asked Cyril and Doreen, two very good friends of ours. Cyril, a teacher by profession but an expert handyman, had always kept a kindly eye on us and helped us with painting, decorating and in the garden. He was quite concerned. How would we manage?

"Who will run our parties?" wailed Doreen, his wife. This was no idle question. These were the parties that Babs organised, ostensibly for various charities to do with the local N.U.T. They were highly successful and raised nice little sums for the funds concerned. Their popularity, however, was due to the fact that they provided social occasions for our friends in novel and enjoyable circumstances. Babs has an undeniable flair for organisation, and these parties were planned with as much overall vision plus attention to detail as would have been given to a vast military operation.

They went something like this. A theme was chosen and guests were required to come dressed accordingly; they also brought appropriate food and drink—although Babs usually provided the bulk of the "eats" as this gave her scope for artistic ability. When, for instance, the theme was "Cornish" this was loosely interpreted as anything to do with the sea. The Sunday before the party we felt it was essential to make a 100-mile journey by car to the coast and back merely to collect seaweed to use as part of the decor. Willing helpers festooned our sunlounge with cricket nets on which were hung these strands of seaweed, shells, corks and anything else that had a remotely maritime connection. An artistic friend, Joan Passingham, then erected a painted backcloth to represent a Cornish harbour, and to this she, with considerable ingenuity, had given a remarkable illusion of 3D. It appeared to reach on to the dining table which Babs had cleverly covered to give a startlingly vivid impression of the sea. Amid the waves rode all manner of craft, from sailing dinghies to ocean-going liners. They were all edible, as were the pebbles on the beach. Apart from concocting these delicacies Babs temptingly arranged prawns and shrimps in scallop shells which nestled beside the harbour walls. Seagulls and miniature lobster pots completed the scene and in the light of the storm lanterns, which were the only source of illumination, the general effect was surprisingly effective. And this was only the sun lounge, for the whole house was given over to these parties and in the garden, too, for those held in the summer. At this particular one Joan Passingham, after she had set up her harbour scene, took up residence in the attic where she invited guests to climb the loft ladder at sixpence a time to see the "water otter", this being a kettle nestling in a bed of straw. We had fortune telling, too, but it was not foretold, nor did we guess, that this particular party had a prophetic significance, for it was dreamed up before our thoughts turned westward; at least, our thoughts of removing there lock, stock and barrel.

Friends of all age groups attended these parties, and cars lined the road in both directions as far as the eye could see. Neighbours would have been startled to see pirates, gypsies, Spanish matadors and Chinese Mandarins, according to the theme, stepping out of the cars and marching up our pathway clutching bottles in one hand and all manner of musical instruments in the other—from guitars to African tom-toms—if we had not had the forethought to invite them, too. If they did not accept, at least they had been warned, for the festivities went on until the small hours of the morning and summer parties took the form of barbecues preceded by a garden fete, often attended by about seventy guests. At the barbecues held in the copse at the end of the garden the men did the cooking; in fact they did the whole thing, for they also arranged fairy lights in the trees, Chinese lanterns, and laid on a cable to play the tape recorder on which, as one of my small contributions I had prerecorded suitable background music.

Not being a party person myself I nevertheless did my bit in the name of charity and loyalty to one's flesh and blood. I usually made two other contributions. One was to hold competitions; these took the form of puzzles stuck around the walls with fiendishly difficult clues which I took great delight in compiling. They were extremely unpopular as no one could ever solve them. Nevertheless they added many sixpences to the funds and kept down the cost of prizes which rarely had to be handed out. I, also, with the help of a crony with similar tastes dispensed drinks from a bar set up in the hall. This effort was much more popular—especially with the two of us. Guests on arrival were offered a choice of punch or fruit cup. In the room behind the bar we mixed our concoctions, and, as Gibby considered himself a connoisseur, we naturally had to do much tasting to make sure that we did not offend the palates of our clientele. Around 11 p.m. without fail my party spirit evaporated rapidly. So much so, although there were some who gave a different explanation, that it became imperative for me to have a cat-nap. Like Churchill, I told myself. I also convinced myself that as parties were going on in different rooms—cards in one, music in another, parlour games in a third and chit-chat in the kitchen, hall and other odd corners—I would not be missed if I detached myself from the festivities and had a quiet nap. Unfortunately certain astute friends nosed their way to my room almost as though a trail had been laid. Although my bedroom was quite small it housed an impressive amount of possessions. One wall was lined by a huge bookcase which our elder brother, many years ago, had cleverly constructed from an old-fashioned kitchen dresser. It was crowned by rows of gallon jars of fermenting home-made wine. The room also served as a dark-room and in addition to an enlarger, a kitchen cabinet full of photographic equipment and chemicals graced the wall at the foot of my divan for which there was only just room. On this divan, a fugitive from the party, I reclined like a latter day Cleopatra holding court with friends who wanted to discuss photography, winemaking or, the more scholastic ones, books. After about an hour's relaxation in the prone position I was ready to re-join the fray until it broke up, usually about 3 a.m. Babs on the other hand was quite indefatigable; she glided from room to room, handing round her delicious concoctions, looking radiant to the end, and still having enough vitality left when all was over to calculate how much her pet charity had benefited.

Who would run the parties indeed? Last year Cyril and Doreen came to see us on the island. After affectionate kisses all round Doreen said "Do you know we haven't had a single party since you left!"

A few days after our return home school re-opened and, to give the full term's notice necessary, Babs tendered her resignation to Surrey County Council. For the first time this, more than anything else so far, brought home to us the enormity of our undertaking. In addition to having to find the money, for negotiations to buy the island were going well ahead, we had now cut off our main source of income. Whoever heard of a pensioner underwriting the costs of buying an island? and the shares I intended to sell were hardly likely to rock the Stock Exchange.

The outlook did look a trifle bleak. Mr Nancollas had asked if he could try to sell our house for us. It did not seem a good idea as he was so far away, but we nevertheless agreed to let him have a go. Weeks went by during which we did not have a single enquiry about the house and although Babs had written to both Cornwall and Devon Education Authorities and scoured the *Times Educational Supplement* every week there was apparently not a single teacher's vacancy in the West country. We were not actually downcast. The idea of living on an island was so thrilling that we were still inclined to push these major problems into the background and concentrate on the, to us, more important aspects, such as what equipment we would need to take with us. Babs for instance made a sortie up to Chelsea and acquired a magnificent stone-cutting and polishing machine from a firm who supplied the experts; archaeologists, university expeditions and the like. It cost just over £120. It would pay dividends, she said. In any case, we both agreed, it was a good capital investment. It must be admitted, however, that "capital investment" was a term we always trotted out to justify the purchase of anything which seemed essential to us at the time.

I already owned a Mamiyaflex camera with three supplementary lenses, ideal for the kind of general freelance work I had been doing. But the telephoto lens had not sufficient focal length for the bird photography which would be an obvious "must" in our future life. A Pentax camera that would take a 400-mm lens seemed to be the answer. This supplementary lens is about one foot long and had the added bonus that it could also be used as a portable telescope. Then an Olympus "Pen" EE, a miniature camera that could be slipped into one's pocket, and would take 72 half frames would be ideal for "note-taking". Eventually one would knock up oil paintings from it for which the whole art world would be clamouring—of course! Acquiring this "essential" equipment knocked me back about £150, but in fact, according to my reckoning, cost me nothing, for I had made an unwritten law that any money I earned from photography would be ploughed back into photographic equipment. This way I had something to show for all the hours spent in the darkroom until 4 a.m. and paying extra income tax for the privilege of doing so. To help fill in the time profitably I also enrolled at the Art School for Photography.

But silence continued on the housing and scholastic side, broken only by the Wailing Winnies chorus of our friends. We, too, sometimes had our moments of doubt and despair. It is difficult to ride the crest of a wave all the time.

It was during one of these sloughs of despondency, on a Friday lunch-time, that Babs rang me from school, her voice choked with emotion. My heart thudded. She never telephoned from school so it must be serious. Instantly I knew—she couldn't stand the worry and suspense any longer. "God! she's going to jump in the river" was the thought that leapt through my mind, although there wasn't a river for miles around.

"What is it?" I quavered, my throat tight with fear.

"There's an advertisement in the Times Educational Supplement," she stuttered, "for a senior mistress . . . Guess where? . . . LOOE!" She couldn't believe her eyes nor I my ears. Surely this was Fate!

In a daze she sent off for the application forms, returned them complete with references and testimonials, and awaited the outcome in a state of animated suspension. The mechanics of life went on but we might as well have been puppets on a string for all the world about us cared.

Then one day a letter plopped on to the door mat; she had been short-listed for an interview. Although this was a terrific piece of good luck the tension did not lessen; if anything it increased. The waiting time until the fateful day stretched agonisingly on. "Maybe it's a foregone conclusion job," said Babs ominously, "and I am called to make up the numbers." We went off our food again, although it did not make any difference to our weights—it never did.

At last the day for the interview drew near. We travelled down to Cornwall after school, making this unscheduled trip in a fever of excitement and fear. We swore that Toby could have driven the car, since he had made the journey so many times. He had an uncanny way of knowing when we crossed the border from Devon to Cornwall whether at Gunnislake or over the river Tamar, whether by daylight or in darkness. As soon as we approached the border he would be up on his hind legs, paws up on the front seat, waving his gorgeous tail and barking joyously. He never evinced such excitement crossing the border in the reverse direction; nevertheless he acknowledged the transition by taking up his usual stance, leaning forward with his paws on the front seat but merely peering through the window and giving a faint swish of his curly tail to signify that we were over the border. Every owner, of course, has the cleverest dog in the whole wide world. We were no exception. This time, however, we registered only a glimmer of pride as the usual shouts of delight took us over the Tamar in the darkness and into Cornwall. If people had seen our strained faces they would have thought that we were on the run from a big London bank robbery at least.

We slept restlessly in the cottage that night. Whereas the rosy glow of our early dreams of living on an island had clouded our minds to facing harsh facts, the importance of the outcome of the interview had brought them sharply into focus. The interview was in the afternoon but, as is usual, the chosen applicants are allowed to look over the school beforehand and ask any questions they wish. Babs brought me breakfast in bed preparatory to driving up to the school, about a mile out of Looe. I couldn't eat it. I was ill, feverish with headache and bad tummy pains. We tried to share the food but Babs couldn't eat anything either so we gave up. Bab was gone most of the morning while I stayed in bed dozing fitfully. At last I heard her footsteps, her high heels dragging over the cobblestones in the courtyard. "No hope, then," I muttered to myself into the pillow. She came into the bedroom and immediately burst into tears. I joined in. Between sobs she told me that she didn't stand a chance. The post was for the senior mistress, but the subject that went with it was needlework and one of the other candidates was the needlework expert for the whole of Hampshire or some such county; another candidate was the resident domestic science mistress. Although Babs was qualified in needlework, having taken it at college, the post she had just vacated did not include teaching officially, even if filling in due to illness gave her a wide variety of experience. The technical claims on the needlework score of these two candidates were greater than her own and this she felt would carry the day.

Babs repaired her face, smartened herself up again and bravely set off once more for the afternoon's ordeal, while I buried myself in the bedclothes again, trying to quell the nausea and sickness that prevented even dozing this time. Wild thoughts raced through my feverish brain. Would this astounding opportunity be dangled before her eyes only to be snatched away at the last? I couldn't bear the agony of waiting and eventually fell into a nightmarish half sleep. Suddenly the bang of the car door being slammed awakened me. I heard Babs's footsteps tapping quickly and lightly over the cobbles and I knew she had the job. She burst into the room and we hugged each other as she told me that she had been appointed, that it must have been her senior position and experience that had filled the bill and she was to take up the appointment next term after the Christmas holiday. An extraordinary coincidence was that the vacancy had been caused by the resignation of a member of staff who, after years of teaching at the school, had suddenly announced her forthcoming marriage. The engagement must have taken place just about the time when we first had the opportunity of buying the island. Jubilant beyond measure we celebrated by having a slap-up meal, the first for weeks, for, as soon as I knew that the job was hers, my symptoms disappeared miraculously and I jumped out of bed completely cured. Moneywise Babs would drop several hundreds of pounds a year by giving up her deputy headship for, although this was the senior mistress's post, the school was less than a third the size of the one she had left, but, as we had said many times, who would not do this if it meant having a stake in paradise, for so our island seemed to us? It was an incredible stroke of good fortune that Babs should have landed this job for it was an excellent one indeed and surely fate must have taken a hand in arranging that it was only a ship's hawser length from the island, in a manner of speaking. We recrossed the Tamar once more and as Toby swished his tail and peered through the window at Devon we both shouted "Good Boy! CLEVER BOY! Toby."

Back in Surrey we decided that we must do something about selling the house ourselves as so far we had not had a single enquiry and it was now October. Accordingly we dropped a note to Mr Nancollas and put the house in the hands of several local agents. It was not at that time a sellers' market and we did not get a single bite, but this did not worry us unduly, for we were great believers in property as an investment and hoped that in the course of time ours would get the fairly high price we were asking. It was a good detached property near the famous Epsom Downs racecourse and had a lovely garden, part of it landscaped by a friend, Graham Jones, with standard roses leading to an archway of ramblers; this led through from the lawn and flower borders to fruit trees, more lawn, vegetable patch and so to a copse where it was a delight to swing in a hammock, with the sun dappling one's face, listening to bird song and the murmur of insects and the breeze rippling through the leaves. We had moved here some ten years before after mother developed heart trouble and the doctor said that we should move her away from the large rambling house in which we then lived, with its many stairs and steps, to somewhere more compact and on the level. While she was still alive we had added every modern convenience we could think of, including night storage heaters, which at that time were an innovation. We had a "treasure", Mrs Penman, who came three hours every day, and a gardener of the old school who tended the garden one day a week. Although there was the beautiful Surrey countryside on our doorstep and it was possible to drive to the coast without passing through a single town there was actually a bus stop outside the front gate to take one to Banstead village or on to Sutton. No wonder our friends thought that we were mad to give up all this to live alone on an island off the wild coast of Cornwall, especially as we were not exactly youthful specimens of the weaker sex.

In other directions events began to move rather rapidly. Completion date for the purchase of the island drew near. This would mean yet another trip to Cornwall to sign the documents—whether a personal visit was strictly necessary I cannot remember—but we arranged that we should in fact travel down there to do so during Babs' October half-term holiday. It seemed incredible that it was just one year ago that we had, on the spur of the moment, during this self-same holiday gone down to Cornwall to look for a cottage. Now we not only had two cottages but were about to acquire an island as well. We had asked Mr Browning, the solicitor, to make the actual date for signing 21st October, this being Trafalgar Day. There were certain naval traditions in the family that made this date seem appropriate and desirable. Our father had served in the Merchant Navy, our younger brother had volunteered for and served in the Royal Navy and, during the war, I had been fortunate to serve in the W.R.N.S.

Meantime we had to find the rest of the money. There was still no sign of selling the house at our figure. Most of the agents wanted us to drop our price considerably in order to make a quick sale. This we refused to do. We needed our asking price and we felt sure that, if we waited, the pendulum would swing and it would become a seller's market. It was also a poor time for selling shares. My stockbroker, whose imagination was caught by this wildly romantic idea of buying an island, said that he would get the best price he could when the right moment came and he would sell only those shares that would make a profit. Babs luckily had a nest egg and this together with a bridging loan advanced by our friendly bank manager at the Westminster took care of the immediate financial problems.

"You will sell the cottages of course?" said a male acquaintance, rather pompously, not caring much for the idea of women venturing into the realms of high finance and property deals with any prospect of success.

"We had not envisaged doing so," we replied just as pompously. In fact we still had it in mind that, just as in "Monopoly", we would turn over the cards and mortgage them if absolutely necessary. But to sell, No! For one thing Babs would need one cottage as a *pied á terre*. The other cottage, which would no longer be needed as a pottery, we decided we would furnish completely, and let for summer holidays. This would provide the extra income we felt sure we would need for the maintenance of the island, for we did not see ourselves as full-time market gardeners, if at all. For another thing we were natural hoarders. We loved buying and acquiring things, but we were loathe to part with our possessions once they were ours. "Might come in useful one day," the litany of all hoarders, was ours also. It certainly applied to the cottages. Apart from anything else, we had a great affection for them and for the life we had made among the folk around, many of whom had become our friends.

So in high spirits we made this, our penultimate journey from Surrey to Cornwall, for completion date formalities. Mr Whitehouse had asked if we would be willing to make a covenant with the National Trust to protect the island from commercial development during any future ownership. To this we readily and eagerly agreed for we too were anxious that this beautiful unspoilt gem should never be exploited for commercial gain. Mr Browning did point out that, otherwise, future owners might not experience too much difficulty in obtaining planning permission for certain developments, as the geographical position of the island, its size, lack of mainland services or public transport made economic self sufficiency virtually impossible. We had heard that at earlier changes of ownership Looe Council had turned down opportunities to purchase, even when the price was fairly minimal, no doubt realising that its upkeep would be a drain on the rates. Previous owners apparently all had private means or, apart from the revenue from market gardening, some other form of income, as in our modest way we also would have.

So come Trafalgar Day, 1964, unbelievably the island would be ours.

The Whitehouses had moved to the mainland back in the summer, so the weather being fair and the sea calm we hired a boatman to take us across. First we sailed right round our future home taking photographs.

Although only 22½ acres the island, with its indented coastline, appeared much larger. The west coast, wild and rugged and remote looked like a Land's End in miniature. Here, above the forbidding cliffs of rock and caves, the island rose to a height of 150 feet. On the north and east the wooded hillside sloped steeply down to cliffs above shelving beaches of rock, sand and shingle. The south coast, like the west, was buttressed with perpendicular rocky cliffs but sloped down to a promontory on the south-eastern tip where it was joined to the little island by a stone bridge. It was here that the tabernacle for the flagstaff that we had mistaken for a rival purchaser stood, a lonely sentinel against the skyline. The trees that bordered the cliffs of the eastern shore and climbed the slopes of the hill that crowned the island were a blaze of reds, oranges and gold as the leaves gleamed in the autumn sunlight.

We landed for a short time and were amazed to find outdoor tomatoes ripening, the trusses heavy with fruit; butterflies fluttered among huge clusters of blackberries along the hedgerows and, incredibly, we had to take off our jackets and walk in short-sleeved summer dresses as we walked down the cliff path to the little island. And this was late afternoon near the end of October. We had stepped into another world. We were in time to see a most spectacular sunset from the bridge. The lichen-covered rocks below us and the dramatic cliffs of the southern coastline glowed gold, purple and wondrous shades of rose in the rays of the setting sun far out in the Atlantic. The swooping seagulls screamed above the murmur of the sea and the only sign of human life was our future home, a white house on the cliff top above us. We were relieved to note that although the house stood only a few yards from the cliff edge to the south and another cliff on the other side, the hill rose steeply behind it; this not only protected it from the west but gave the house an air of solid security, no doubt due to the psychological confidence inspired by being positioned with its "back to the wall".

Back on the mainland we had a few ends to tie up with Mr Nancollas who had undertaken to make an inventory of the lock, stock and barrel. Included were farming machinery, a caterpillar tractor being the most important, and among many other items of equipment three boats and some outboard engines. It hadn't escaped our notice that two of our three wishes had now come true in a most miraculous way.

"Milk store, here we come!" we said over a celebratory drink, as though it mattered now. Nevertheless that wish too was granted although we had no inkling at that time that one day it would be.

As Babs had a bit of holiday in hand we stayed on a day or two and set about buying some suitable clothing for our future life. First we equipped ourselves with weatherproof anoraks, oilskins and sou'westers; we then visited Mr Toms of East Looe to be fitted out with sea boots. There was a twofold reason for visiting him, for in addition to selling the kind of footgear we wanted, he also had a son, Wren Toms, whom we understood usually did the ferrying of furniture and equipment for the island and this was the only way we knew of contacting him.

"Yes! you will certainly need Wren," said Mr Toms. "I will tell him."

Hindsight would have told us that it was probable that the whole of East and West Looe, including Wren Toms, knew our intentions and requirements but, ignorant of this, we were only too happy to know that this important person would be made aware that we should like the use of his skilled services at Christmastide, even though the request was by proxy.

Rather pleased with our purchases which were in striking contrast to the fashionable wearing apparel we were in the habit of buying for our business efficiency and modern smart teacher acts respectively, we, for the last time, we hoped, returned to Surrey.

There everything worked up to a crescendo of excitement and activity. Dennis and An O'Neill had arranged that I could attend Art School all day and every day whenever possible so that I could have the maximum of tuition and practice. One day I was throwing on the wheel from 9 a.m. until 9 p.m. In a coma of exhaustion I tottered off to catch the bus as Babs was not available to collect me, to find later that the O'Neills were searching for me everywhere to run me home as they thought that I looked like passing out on the wheel, and feared that in fact I had done so in some dark corner. Heaven knows how Babs coped with the Christmas term with the move dominating our lives. There were the school and form Christmas parties, carol singing, Christmas Fayre, parents' evening and, as was usual at her school, an ambitious and highly successful Gilbert and Sullivan production. Babs I think was responsible for the costumes or make-up or both and she was in a frenzy of school activity the whole term.

Moving at any time for any family is a nightmare. We had our special problems that sent us demented. What should we take that could go over the sea in an open boat in winter time, and, being compulsive hoarders, what should we sell that would not cause us future heartbreak? Mr Nancollas had offered us the use of his store on the quayside under his office but that would be only a temporary haven as he needed it for his fortnightly auction sales. Luckily most of our big furniture had been sold on our previous move from the old house but we still had some heavy stuff. We had some dealers who instantly made a bee-line for the antiques, and if we agreed to sell them they would take anything else more or less as a favour—at knock down prices, of course. So we tried out a few pieces at auction sales but the prices offered came nowhere near their value. This exercise was a mistake anyway, as we found ourselves buying things instead, which only added to our problem. In the end we decided to keep the antiques to furnish No 1 cottage, taking the more manageable ones over to the island. The big furniture we would sell privately by advertising. To our surprise we had sold everything we advertised in next to no time. Everything went at the asking price with no quibbling at all. We supposed that would-be purchasers would not come unless they wanted to buy and, furthermore, they could see where the articles came from, unlike the anonymous pedigree of those offered in sales. Whatever the reason it solved that problem.

There were other problems in plenty. I had 40 gallons of wine fermenting and these we decided were a "must" to go sailing over the sea—likewise the many hundreds of books we possessed and were considered essential. Babs and I had so far agreed over every major issue, often without the need to consult each other, buying cottages and an island for starters. But as is often the case in families we disagreed over something quite trivial. Not that it was trivial physically. The bone of contention was the enormous bookcase in my bedroom. We did not actually argue about it— it was just that at regular intervals Babs said flatly that it was too big to go and I just as doggedly said that I was not leaving it behind. In the end we reached a compromise—we would leave it to the carriers to decide. So when the manager came to give an estimate for the removal later he said that everything would just go into two pantechnicons and the bookcase could go if there were room at the last.

"If so," said Babs philosophically, "it can always be sold at one of Mr Nancollas's auction sales—it will be in the right place."

Meantime with more buying time available than Babs, I acquired other items that I thought might come in useful in our future life. Among these was an electric drill with all the attachments, including a lathe and an electric saw, all of which frightened me to death as I had never been the slightest bit mechanical. Marjorie's brother came over and demonstrated them to me and like a conjurer made the whole operation seem like child's play (Marjorie was the friend who had been staying with us in the cottage when I first set eyes on the island on that momentous early morning walk at Whitsun). I also made a trip to London and bought an Adana printing machine, after a demonstration by a young man who did it with a flair that again made me feel that I was watching a conjuring trick to which I could never aspire. Maybe he thought so too. However, I had seen really excellent results from the efforts of children at Babs' school exhibition so I thought that perhaps its manipulation would not be quite beyond me. I also bought a hurricane lamp from Blacks, the tent people. Here I plucked up courage to ask about getting a discount as I had just read an article in a newspaper which advised one to do this when buying equipment. Why I chose the purchase of a hurricane lamp as a guinea pig it is hard to fathom as of all our purchases it was a comparatively minor item, but to my surprise it worked, in a way. The assistant asked, "Just *one* hurricane lamp?" "Well," I added hurriedly, "later I shall probably want another, or even two more." "Then I suggest you get those from our warehouse where they deal wholesale. Here is an invoice for this one. Send it with your next order to this address, where they will allow you a discount on this one too." And with this the helpful assistant wrote down the address and handed me the slip.

Emboldened by this success I put the same question at my next port of call, an electronics shop in the Edgware Road. Their impressive display of tape recorders in the window had attracted my attention many times on my way to my dentist in a Square just off Marble Arch. I already owned a fine stereo tape recorder that, if you shut your eyes when listening to it, gave the illusion that you were actually at a concert in the Festival Hall. That, in fact, would have been a better place to house it for it was so large and heavy, being a prototype and manufactured just before transistors streamlined such equipment, that it always needed a strong man to move it. What I now wanted to complement it was a small portable one for recording bird song. Transistor models of these the shop had in plenty and when I enquired about them someone was called forth from behind the scenes to deal with me. He must have thought that I intended buying the lot for no other claimants to his time got a look in. As to discount, he pointed out that as retailers they could not deal wholesale but he could let me have 5%. I was so pleased about this that I told him where I intended using it. This had repercussions for this was not the last time I was to hear from this gentleman who, it transpired, was a visiting director. The tale of how Eric Cox came to stay on the island must be told later.

I wished I had read the article about asking for discounts earlier for I had already ordered a cement mixing machine, a greenhouse heater, a soil sterilizing stove and a brick-making machine. Although we had disposed of two three-piece suites, two bedroom suites, a hall stand and other fairly large items of furniture, the place was beginning to look like a warehouse as almost daily fresh parcels and packing cases of new equipment arrived.

"We shall need three pantechnicons soon!" cried Babs in desperation. Her stone cutting and polishing machine was a really large affair with a built-in stand so this she had arranged to have delivered to the store in Looe. I did likewise with the potters' wheel I had ordered through John Shelly. This was a large traditional kick-wheel made by a Dorset wheelwright to John Shelly's own design and was similar to the one I had used on his course.

"Anyway the telescope won't take up much room," I consoled Babs. We were delighted with this. One starry night we tried it out. We were amazed to find that the very first star we pointed at was not a star at all but the planet Saturn with the rings plainly visible. It was a thrilling sight and sent us buying even more books on astronomy to add to those we already had.

We also bought a Kenwood Chef mixer with many attachments from the area rep., a charming fellow who afterwards invited us to his place at Guildford for drinks and coffee and, indeed, he too has been to visit us on the island, not to sell anything for there were no more attachments left to buy. We bought, too, a "Sunbeam" cooking pan and a mass of other kitchenware we thought would be useful in a farmhouse kitchen. In addition, we already had most of the gadgets and equipment that annually tempted us at the Ideal Home Exhibition. One would think that we were about to colonize an uninhabited country with no hope of ever seeing the motherland again. In the event nearly all these acquisitions proved invaluable and saved us much time and money. The two exceptions were the greenhouse heater which became redundant for the simple reason that due to the mild climate of the island the greenhouse, even in the depth of winter, never needed heating. The other was the cement mixer. It was not that it was incapable of doing the job. On the contrary, it was most efficient. Nor was cement mixing as a way of life in our calculations wrongly forecast. Year in and year out cement is mixed up even more often than farmhouse puddings. But I had overlooked two important points, for it must be admitted that buying the cement mixer was my abortive brain child. The first was that I would not have time to do everything. Although I loved using that mixer it did take me away from pottery and other crafts. Secondly, I could not persuade anyone else to use it. It would appear that any first class worker suspects anything that smacks of gadgetry, and especially mistrustful are country folk. All our helpers prefer to keep to the spit and shovel method, finding it perhaps more satisfying. Not so Paul Shelley, the greengrocer in the middle of Market Square in West Looe. He asked if he could buy it from me. Although I found it useful for mixing up compost I was very happy that it would be put to its rightful use and recently swopped it with him for a custom-built bookcase in parana pine, and very elegant it looks.

The manager from the carriers had said that we need not pack a thing apart from our personal belongings. His men would bring packing cases and do the lot. So the problem now was that if ever we really moved from Surrey we should need a packer just for our private belongings, for neither of us has ever been able to travel light or live neatly. Most of our friends are the type who, if they come for the day carry, apart from the regulation bunch of flowers, nothing else at all. A weekend visitor brings nothing more than an airline type handgrip inside which there is still enough room for a hostess gift of whisky or gin. If we visit their homes unexpectedly you would think that a glossy magazine staff was awaited any moment to do a feature article, or that the Queen might drop in. If ever anyone knocks on *our* door unexpectedly, redfaced we cower in a corner among a heterogeneous collection of possessions, and hiss at each other, "We're OUT! WE'RE OUT!" We cannot even go to bed without taking enough impedimenta for a fortnight's holiday and making several journeys into the bargain. My particular choice of essentials usually comprises three books, four magazines, a tape recorder, pocket radio, notebook and pencil, throat pastilles, hot drink, hand cream and nail file. By the time that little lot are organised, all of which are supposed to be conducive to sleep, one is out like a light before one's head has so much as touched the pillow. Small wonder then that we queried how we should ever move from Surrey. Luckily Doug, our niece's husband, who had spent Boxing Day with us in the cottage had offered to come up from Saltdean, where they lived, to do our private packing for us. And Doug had been in the Navy. It reminded me of the time when I was in the W.R.N.S. and had to leave Scotland, where I had spent my service so far, to go to O.T.C. at Greenwich Naval College.

I had accumulated so many belongings that I thought it would be better if I had stayed in Scotland for the duration.

"Leave everything to me," said the Chief Petty Officer who was throwing a farewell party for me. "Don't pack a thing apart from your suitcase." The next day seven naval ratings appeared with a Leading Hand in charge. In no time at all seventeen boxes all roped up in true naval fashion were stowed on to the waiting R.N. transport, the top crowned with a bicycle and portable stove. Naval parties being what they are it was as well that, as I giddily headed south the next day, I only had the responsibility of a suitcase. When I was finally due to leave the W.R.N.S. accommodation stowage space had grown with promotion, and the question of removal had grown so acute that I was greatly tempted to accept the invitation of their Lordships of the Admiralty to sign on for life so that I should not have to face the problem. However, the Navy came to the rescue again, headed by "Chippy", who made me an enormous ditty box that is with me to this day, and aided by the Supply Officer, First Lieutenant and many others who possibly thought that the Royal Navy could sail the Seven Seas without my help, I just about made Civvy Street.

It was a great relief therefore when Doug said he would do our packing for us. Our faith was justified. History repeated itself and after a few weekends the most precious of our multifarious possessions and the fruits of our many activities were neatly stowed in boxes, expertly roped and meticulously labelled. The way was now clear for the carriers to deal with the more usual Lares and Penates.

This was not the end of our worries however. One that we had not bargained for was the problem of the island cat. The Whitehouses had written previously to ask if we could take up residence earlier as the gardener's cat had refused to leave the island. Their daughter had been rowing over once a week to leave it food. Now they wrote again as the autumn gales had started and no one could get out to feed her. We, of course, could do nothing about it for Babs was committed until the end of term. We were 240 miles away and the move, which could only be compared with the evacuation of Dunkirk with the outcome just as certain, still lay ahead. Nevertheless we were sick with worry thinking about the cat as we listened to weather reports and heard that heavy seas were pounding the south west coasts continuously.

We supposed, too, that we should have worried that at this late stage we not only had not sold the house but no one had even come to view it.

The agents continued to pester us to drop the price but as we had had it valued we waited hopefully for the swing of the pendulum to make it a seller's market again. As we had a bridging loan we pushed this particular problem to the back of our minds. At least it gave Cyril plenty of time to do some more decorating so that it would be in tip-top order when we left. Not that the house really needed it. I doubt if any property had been painted more often than ours. We were always changing the colour scheme and helpful friends lightened the burden. I, personally, found painting therapeutic. When I had problems, and they were always looming up like leering fish, painting provided a nice cow-like occupation and the care, attention to detail and the rhythmic movements required, put any current problems in nice perspective.

Babs had many talented and helpful friends and faithfully they now rallied round. Mac was an educational officer in a remand home and a major in the Territorials and his particular skill was electricity. He always installed our gadgets for us and if anything ever went wrong he would be round like a shot and, pipe in mouth, would get whatever it was working again in a very careful and deliberate way. He undertook to remove chandeliers, wall brackets and other fitments we wished to take with us and leave everything in good order for the next inhabitants. Johnny was another faithful standby. A headmaster, secretary of the county N.U.T., and a former test pilot he could nevertheless always be relied on to come round and deal with anything electronic, plumbing problems and anything to do with engines and machinery. Jane, his wife, who came round to collect him one evening sometime before this, said with hardly any trace of bitterness, "I suppose you know that while Johnny has been round here mending your leaking taps I have had to decorate the back bedroom and replumb our bathroom myself!"

Now everyone started to throw farewell parties for us. The cry, in addition to "What are you going to do without your friends?" (which had become a theme song), alternated with, "What are you going to do without a man?", which was more to the point. Well, we hoped that the Lord would provide, preferably in the plural, when the need arose. In our youth, although it had been spent at different times, we were lucky enough to have two older brothers who were always on hand to do anything required. In adult life we were naive enough to expect that others would be only too willing to take on this role—a habit we had never quite shaken off. Consequently we had no fears for the future and brushed our friends' forebodings aside with lighthearted insouciance. In any case we had discovered that most men at heart are knights in shining armour who will tilt a lance on one's behalf if they are allowed, even if the dragon is only a leaking tap.

Not that we were lacking in offers. Doug was ready to chuck up everything and join us with his family. Mr Nancollas had written to say that he had several applicants who would like to work on the island for us and asked if he should arrange interviews for when we came down. The word had certainly got around, for we began to receive letters ourselves from a variety of people offering their services. One reason for this was the fact that quite unexpectedly a local Surrey paper came out with the banner headline "SURREY TEACHER BUYS ISLAND!" and there was a photograph of Babs and a long front page feature. We couldn't understand the furore that followed and thought that the sooner we moved the better. We had enough on our plate worrying about the possibly starving cat without being responsible for humans who would certainly starve if we took on the flocks that wanted to join us. One man and his wife persuaded us to let them come and see us. They seemed an ideal couple and we almost came to an arrangement with them but luckily the idea fell through. We had promised Doug that we would give him a chance later if we found that there could be any future for him. As he was a young chap with many skills who could turn his hand to anything he certainly would be a great asset to us. Meantime we felt we must fashion our own future.

Moving day drew near and the sorting out of possessions became more frantic. Jumble sales and the Christmas Fair at the nearby church did very well out of us for in the end we were tossing out valuable wares in our frenzy. Violet Jordan, a friend I had made at the Art School, came to say goodbye and left bedazzled with a dozen evening dresses and ball gowns of Babs, which we assured her would not be needed on the island. The logic of why she therefore needed them eluded Violet, especially as none of them fitted her, but at least it got one little burden off our hands. The gift of a huge five gallon glass carboy to Graham was much better received. He intended to grow an indoor garden in it and if he were as successful with this as he had been with our rose garden he would soon have a flourishing display.

Among the farewell gifts we received none was more treasured than a book on vegetable growing presented to me by Ernie, the gardener. It was very old and must have been in his family since the turn of the century.

Nevertheless it was the most comprehensive book on vegetables I have ever seen. Each variety, and there were some quite unknown to me, had a chapter to itself. The information given included planting times, distances to sow, seed germination time, life of seeds, estimated crops per ounce and per pound of seed, yield per yard and acre, sowing and planting calendar, the effects of different soils, climates, pests and diseases and how to deal with them and hints on harvesting, storing and cooking. In addition to all this each chapter started off with a potted history including the earliest known references to that particular vegetable. Quotations were given from the Bible, Pliny, Herodotus, the Elizabethan poets and others, and included such fascinating details as the fact that Herodotus had seen a reference to a sale of onions inscribed on the Great Pyramid. As he presented me with the book from his gnarled hands Ernie's face creased with pride. He also gave me a parting piece of advice, "Allus go in for early crops and anything yer can grow out of season. That way it's highest returns for least labour." He should know, for one of their specialities used to be growing strawberries exclusively for Wimbledon and Ascot week.

Farewells were made to winemaking pupils, National Savings groups clientele and colleagues, neighbours, all at the Art School, the doctor, hairdresser, local shopkeepers and the small boy who haunted the house, and helped in the darkroom, who said longingly how he was going to miss the "house of gadgets". Farewell, too, to my friends at Hall's and Babs to all her friends and colleagues from the many facets of her professional life. Most spoke as though we were leaving for outer space and were going into orbit forever. I did consider calling in at the Labour Exchange to say goodbye but in view of the proclivity I had for confusing everyone there it seemed prudent to give that particular call a miss. I might have found myself with another job and unable to leave Surrey after all.

Most of the parties were over and there only remained the grand farewell dinner our friends were giving for us. We had even disposed, one way and another, of all our goods "surplus to requirements". Among these was an electric mower which Phil Odd, the brother-in-law of my school friend Tommy, was going to buy from us. He came up to collect it the day before we were due to move. We happened to mention to him that we had received a letter that morning from the firm of Miles, an agent for flowers in Covent Garden. Mr Miles had written to say that he understood that we were taking over from Mr Whitehouse and that he hoped we would continue to deal with his firm. This had given us cold feet. Our knowledge of daffodils was restricted to the few dozen that we grew in the garden and we thought that all daffodils were the same—*yellow*. We were nonplussed when we knew that fifteen different varieties were grown on the island and that they bloomed in succession from Christmas until early April. We found the prospect of marketing them daunting especially as we understood that Miles was one of the largest agents in Covent Garden. We were confiding all this to Phil when to our immense surprise he said he knew the family well and had been friendly with the daughter since schooldays. He phoned Covent Garden straight away. Mr Miles had left the office so Phil got through to his home and introduced us over the telephone. Mr Miles was very charming indeed. He told us not to worry at all and that he would give us any help and advice we needed. This cheered us up enormously and we now felt that we had at least one anchorage in the sea of uncertainty of our future life.

Although the preparations for our removal had assumed a nightmarish quality moving day itself went incredibly smoothly. Thirty packing cases of books, forty gallon jars of wine, one full five-gallon carboy, innumerable crates and the roped and labelled boxes as well as the furniture were swallowed by the giant pantechnicon as though a ravenous monster was being expertly fed by a team of men who were specially trained to exude calm and confidence in an electrically charged atmosphere. Carriers must be a resilient race when you consider that their whole working life, when not spent in pounding along the main roads, is occupied in meeting people who are in various stages of overwrought nerves bordering on hysteria.

Garden equipment was to follow later and was stowed in the garden shed and garage. As well as the usual impedimenta of tools there were three mowers, a roller, hammock, garden seats, deck chairs, bird tables, lawn pricker, fertiliser dispenser and a recently acquired cedar wood shed. Mrs Penman, the treasure, was left in charge. She was going to give the house a thorough clean, get rid of rubbish and, most important of all, was appointed to deal with estate agents. Sadly, if there was not room for the bookcase, she was to sell it for us.

Anxiously I watched as the cavernous belly of the pantechnicon began to fill up until it seemed there was hardly room to shut the doors. At last the bookcase was the only piece left. With a cheery wink at me the foreman said "Just about room for that I think." And the gigantic beast outside gobbled down this huge tid-bit, clamped its jaws and rumbled off. It was to take two days for the journey and as the day was fairly advanced we too decided to make the trip in two stages. With final waves to friends, neighbours and Mrs Penman we set off on the first stage of our big adventure.

Chapter 4
Entr'acte—a link with the past

As we sped westward and our former life receded into the past with every mile we travelled we marvelled at the twists and turns of fate that had brought us on this exciting adventure. Most of our friends could not understand why we should want to uproot ourselves from our comfortable home and from all our friends for the uncertainties, privations and loneliness of life on an island, especially when the days of our youth, when roughing it might have had a certain allure, were left far behind. If there was one simple answer it could be said to be parentage, and farther back even than that.

In the latter part of the last century and the days of sail, William, our father, at the age of thirteen ran away to sea, aided and abetted by his grandmother, who, of the opinion that her grandson was being spoilt and brought up too soft by his mother, gave him a gold sovereign and a gold watch to speed him on his way.

He sailed to the Americas, rounded Cape Horn high up in the rigging, one moment borne dizzily aloft and the next almost touching the tremendous seas. Nothing would induce him to go home again, although his father tried to entice him back with the offer of another gold watch and other gifts. Eventually his father promised that if he would come back he would have him trained for the sea. At this the young William returned home and was duly enrolled and joined the training ship *Arethusa* in the Thames and later completed his training at Greenwich Naval College. Among the family papers is a letter written to him on board the *Arethusa* by Lord Jersey wishing him and "my other young friends on the *Arethusa* success in your careers" and inviting them to visit him and Lady Jersey in Australia. Among the papers there is also a certificate stating that Petty Officer William John Edwin Atkins—1 Good Conduct Badge—"could reef, able to furl small sails, heave the lead and give soundings, make bends, knots and splices, could pull in a boat . . ." Written in the Commanding Officer's own hand was the added comment "Conduct Very Good Indeed." Petty Officer

William John Edwin was just sixteen years old.

At sea again he landed in America and wishing to explore that country, he hoboed across the continent travelling from coast to coast slung under the couplings of trains and stopping off as the fancy took him. For a time he became a cowboy. The rich owner of the ranch offered him a good berth if he would stay but William still yearned for the sea and set sail once more.

He also yearned for his childhood sweetheart. From the days when as schoolchildren they had attended services at the lovely old church in Carshalton village in Surrey he had lost his heart to Alice and his dearest hope was that one day she would marry him. Unfortunately for him most other young males felt the same way and had the same aspirations. Young men, top-hatted in the fashion of the day, came to her home to pay court to the lovely young Alice; among them a Frenchman of noble family, and another who, much to the amusement of her sisters, stuck his head through the railings and vowed that he would not go away unless she said that she would be his wife; yet another swore that he would commit suicide if she would not marry him. Although so far, in spite of these impassioned entreaties, none had succeeded in winning her hand, William got to hear about these rivals through his mother who was always trying to come between her son and Alice. Instead of having the desired effect he threatened to leave the sea and come home again; he felt at a disadvantage trying to conduct his courtship from the high seas against what must have seemed to him overwhelming odds.

His grandmother now stepped in again. Among the family papers is an obviously much treasured letter from her to her grandson. In it she implores him not to leave the sea, nor must he listen to these tales, as the young gentleman in question were just friends of the family (which surely must have been the understatement of the century). She felt sorry for Alice who would have a very dull life indeed if she could not go accompanied for walks in the park or be partnered at the skating parties held when the streams and fields were frozen over. She understood Alice, who confided in her. He need not be troubled and therefore he must not do anything foolhardy. Even after all these years it is a very touching letter to read. It was also written in secret. No one must know that she had written to him and his reply must be sent direct to her. We never had the pleasure of meeting this doughty old lady but salute her for the part she played in bringing about our future existence. When one realises that she was alive during the time of the Prince Regent or William IV and would have heard first hand accounts of Nelson and Trafalgar it is not surprising that the sea was in her blood. It also spans the passage of the years and brings those far off distant figures of history vividly close and uncannily alive.

The letter having the desired effect William did not leave the sea and very soon after the longed for answer came at last from Alice. This he received just two weeks before his ship was due to sail for England. Determined that there should be no chance for her to change her mind or for anyone else to do it for her, he immediately applied to the Archbishop of Canterbury for a special licence. The wedding ceremony was to take place at St Anne's, the nearest church to the East India Dock, as soon as his ship berthed there. He appointed his future sister-in-law's husband, George, to be in charge of all arrangements, and then set sail with all speed for England. The wedding party awaiting the arrival of the twenty-one-year-old groom consisted of Alice, her sister and George. Unfortunately the ship was late docking and when they arrived at the church everything was locked up. William and George leapt over the gate and managed to catch the Vicar who, having given them up, had just left. He returned at once, opened up, let them in and performed the Ceremony with only minutes to spare before the prescribed time expired. The captain had arranged the wedding breakfast on board but when Alice saw that she would have to climb up the ship's rope ladder, terrified of heights as she was all her life, she absolutely refused to do so. So instead the wedding party repaired to her home to celebrate, buying a cake on the way.

So William at last won his bride and for the next sixty years, spanning six reigns, in his eyes she was always the girl of twenty he had married in those far off days. Was it the glamour of the sea and his spirit of adventure that gave him the edge over his rivals? We never knew. The most that we could elicit from mother, the most shy and reticent of people, was that in those days he was very good looking and looked very smart in his uniform.

As soon as William was back at sea the rival suitors told Alice that she had made the biggest mistake of her life and one even implored her to elope with him. Alice would listen to none of them; instead she left the parental home of her widowed mother and proceeded to take an apartment in whichever port William was due to dock, this most often being Avonmouth, and there she would sit in the window watching for his ship to come sailing over the horizon.

Apart from the sea, Dad's other great love was cricket. As a schoolboy before he ran away to sea he wrote challenging a Surrey team at their ground at Mitcham, where Hobbs used to practice. You can imagine their chagrin when a team of young schoolboys marched in, having walked all the way from Carshalton as they could not afford the fare. Nevertheless they had a good day and Dad was given £5 for him and his team. Later as a young man he played against W. G. Grace in a charity match and bowled him out for a duck. The great man was not at all pleased. One other ability that always impressed us was the facility he had, that none of us inherited, of being able to add up four columns of figures at once.

He never lost his spirit. When he was seventy he had to have a leg amputated owing to circulatory trouble. We were told to expect the worst. Instead, as he came to, he said "You can throw that away—it's no more use to me" and proceeded to make a remarkably quick recovery—to the great surprise of the doctors and nursing staff. At seventy-five after intense pain he had to have the other leg amputated and lived beyond all medical expectation for a further five years. Although he was by now frail, his face remained young and cheerful and he was convinced he spoke the truth when, sitting in his wheelchair, he used to boast to visitors "Do you know I have never had a day's illness in my life?" Mother was ostensibly a gentle, quiet person, but she too had a pioneering spirit although it was necessarily restricted by the ties of bringing up a family. The seafaring life that Dad led had appealed to her own adventurous spirit and she took us on holidays abroad in the days when only the rich did this and leaving these shores an exciting adventure not dared by any of our friends or acquaintances. Turning out some old household account books we were amazed to find how pitifully small the family income was in those early days—just 30/– a week—for we never wanted for a thing. The fact was that mother was an excellent manager and had her priorities right, for Dad looked to her to steer the family ship. Although he was friendly and kind to us and good fun, with a soft spot for Babs who looked incredibly like mother's photograph's when she too was young, mother was the centre of his world and that never changed the whole of his life.

Mother told us that when she married she could not even boil an egg, for in those solid Victorian days there were always servants for domestic chores even in middle class households. Nevertheless she was a fine needlewoman and made all our clothes, even the boys suits, when they were young. I remember one beautiful dress I had when I was a child of which I was inordinately proud; it was shantung with an exquisitely embroidered top. Each year either the top or the bottom was replaced; this went on for years and meant that not only had I something that always fitted me as I grew, and something new and pretty to feel proud of, but that I had never really lost my favourite dress. With my brothers eleven and twelve years older than myself, no older sisters and Babs not yet born there was no question of cast-offs or hand-me-downs. Mother became an excellent cook and her pastry rose just like the modern commercials on television. We always had farm eggs and "best fresh butter" as I well remember seeing slapped up between wooden pats, as they did in those days. How she managed I do not know but looking back I think that it was her pioneering spirit. Nothing would daunt her. If they could not afford the sort of house she had been brought up in and liked for us, she would make do. And this did not mean accepting things as they were. Oh no! It meant knocking down walls, adding a room here and a bathroom there. Out with that high bay window and in with a low bay and french windows. Turn that coal cellar into a play room; out with the kitchen range and in with an open coal fire; install a billiard table for the boys. Although we lived in that one house for many years it seemed that we moved many times, it changed so often. We never knew what sort of place we were going to live in from one year to the next; it was most exciting. One feature of it was an enormous cupboard under the stairs that was unusual in that it had a window. This I made my secret playroom. With its many cables, pipes and meters it became for me alternately the bridge and the engine room of a ship and from here I could steer the house to faraway places or even to school if it were a wet day. It was in this house that Tom (always Willie to me, as his real name was William) made the huge bookcase from the built-in kitchen dresser that was at this moment heading westward ahead of us, for even in those early days our collection of books always exceeded their accommodation. Willie also had a large printing press in this cupboard under the stairs. He was gifted and brilliant in so many different ways and this press produced the accompanying literature and brochures for his multifarious activities. Later he was to train in Art Publishing and eventually he established his own Company in London.

It is of some significance and worth recording that years later when we were all grown up and finances improved we moved to a house that by comparison was quite luxurious, sporting among its features french windows, a garden with three lofty walnut trees and an en-tout-cas tennis court bordered by luscious pear trees. Mother set about improving this house too. Nothing could stop her; it was in the blood, this pioneering spirit. Nevertheless, wherever we lived it was Home with a capital H for mother had that rare quality of enhancing any place wherever she happened to be. I think that if we had lived in a tent, to us it would have seemed like coming home to a palace. It was not by anything that she said, although even when in her eighties she was still very witty, for in spite of all this spirited pioneering she was always a quiet, reserved lady. She seemed somehow to radiate a light and warmth so that any room she was in the sun seemed to be shining there. You knew as soon as you turned into the drive whether she was in or not. I think those who advocate crêches, and husbands sharing the care of babies, do not realise what basic need they are denying their children. Who knows what social misdemeanours, wayout behaviour, and ultimately criminal tendencies can be traced back not only to broken homes but to ones where there is only a part-time mum, not from necessity but often from choice?

Of course mother was rather special. As a child I remember feeling sorry for all the other children because they did not have her as their mother, and I naturally thought they would feel just as sorry for themselves because of their bad luck. As a consequence I went around being very kind to these unfortunate beings and would invite them home to tea so that they could share in my good fortune. Unwittingly I made a lot of little friends this way and as an extra bonus was invited to join their various churches just before the annual Sunday School outing so that I could go along with them. This was an early introduction to comparative religions, certainly to the comparative merits of their social activities if nothing else. I was of course very welcome at the homes of these young friends, but if their mothers could only have known that my solicitude for their offspring was due to these ladies' supposed inferiority, the warmth of their welcome might have chilled to say the least.

In case it is thought that this view of mother is rather biased it is a fact that all her life people, including children and adolescents, gravitated to her as to a magnet. Even when she was in her late seventies we have seen men leave some glamorous female's company to talk to her, entranced for hours, and she was always affectionally referred to by family and friends as "The Lady". She came from an artistically gifted family who could all play the piano, sing and paint before they ever had a lesson. One sister was so talented that she was being trained by an Italian singing master until she gave up this vocation to run away and get married to one of grandfather's employees. Mother could sing, was a talented actress and was always chosen to play the leading lady at the amateur theatricals held in the Public Hall; her most remembered roles being Elizabeth I and Britannia. These stayed in the memory, we suspect, principally because she was chosen to play these parts by the general vote of her contemporaries, thus endorsing the opinion of the producer. Photographs of her at the time reminded us of the young Ellen Terry and we often thought how well mother would have graced the West End stage. One of our favourite ways of teasing her was to say, after some particularly tedious visitor had left, "What the West End stage missed when you decided to get married!" for mother had the facility of making the most boring person feel clever and important and apparently was quite unaware that she was making any particular effort.

Most of the tales we heard about her were told to us by our aunts, her sisters, or Dad, for she never lived in the past and was the most reticent of people. Apart from her father, who died very suddenly when mother was fourteen, her Aunt Eliza was the biggest influence in her life. She was a Headmistress who ran her own Academy for Young Ladies, and was a very grand person indeed, as mid-Victorian photographs show. Mother spent all her holidays with her and was over-awed by the atmosphere of erudition and the good manners that were expected of her. Mother was fond of quoting Aunt Eliza or her friend the Vicar to us and one dictum that came down to us was that tea should be the colour of pale straw. The Vicar's contribution to the good life was that it was essential that the last thing one should do before retiring for the night was to blow one's nose!

It must have been from Aunt Eliza that mother inherited her great love of books, especially history and poetry, and in many ways this was passed on to us. When we were young there was hardly a church or historic building that we were not taken into in our travels and today we would not dream of passing a spot on the map denoting a Roman Encampment or barrow without stopping to explore, and no holiday would be complete without acquiring a small library on the history of the district. Books were the currency of our childhood and were given and asked for at Christmas, birthdays, and as a convalescent treat after measles, whooping cough and the like. The first book I ever read long before I went to school was *The Red Eric* by R. M. Ballantyne, about a little girl who went with her father on whaling expeditions in his boat to all parts of the world. In all I read it seven times and when the spine became torn with use I repaired it with panels of suede leather, embossing the title on the leather with a red hot needle. Unluckily it was lost during wartime moves, but most of the classics that we were given in our childhood and all the twentieth-century poets, beautifully printed on deckle edged paper in their first editions, had fortunately survived and would, we hoped, be pounding their way westward.

There would appear to be a strong matriarchal streak on mother's side of the family for many of the women folk seemed quite go-ahead for Victorian days. Another of her aunts was not only a music teacher but played professionally and gave concerts at Masonic and other gatherings. What most impressed us was the fact that she had someone to carry her music case so that her fingers should not be ruined for the performances. Three other aunts of mother's had a stage coach inn apiece in their own right, in what in those days would have been darkest Surrey. We did a tour once to see these hostelries, for mother had sometimes been invited to stay with these aunts. Elizabethan and timbered, these inns are there to this day, and although they are now fashionable and in the stockbroker belt, they have not really become spoilt. In fact they look picturesque still, for they are genuinely old. Her visits to them seemingly had no influence on mother, for she always preferred tea as a beverage—the colour of pale straw, of course.

It was not surprising therefore that mother put education very high up in her list of priorities for us. There were no family allowances or grants in those days and with farm eggs, best fresh butter and holidays abroad I do not know how she managed it, but I was sent to a private school. The main bill of fare was French, Music, Good Manners, Play-the Game and Long Live the British Empire! Curtseying was taught and was obligatory daily, presumably in case you should by chance run into one of the Royal Family. Academic standards were not high but a term or two at a tutor's bridged the gap to a school where they were very high indeed. In time Babs went to this private school, too, but as I left there when I was thirteen we were never there at the same time. I shall never forget that school or the friends I made there. Incredibly, six of us still keep in touch one with another. Ethel was a particular crony and together we wrote and produced plays, put on conjuring shows, initiated a Secret Society and wrote and published a magazine. This last, copies of which we laboriously copied out by hand in penny exercise books, was an astounding success, not for any literary merit, but for the fact that it rated a mention at morning prayers.

69

Not so much a mention as a hullabaloo for, sad to relate, our masterpiece was banned on the grounds that Bessie Bunter was not a suitable person for young ladies to read about. Needless to say we were bombarded by the rest of the school for under the counter copies and offered twice the asking price of 2d to boot. What an early lesson in salesmanship psychology we were unwittingly given! Ethel came to the island only a few months ago and so well were those early links of friendship forged that we automatically picked up the threads, as we always do, somewhere between the ages of six and twelve years at which latter age our close collaboration ended, due to Ethel and her family moving from the district.

I was given a good foundation in music there, both in the curriculum and as an extra, for the school was fortunate in having an excellent music teacher, Miss Madden, a young and enthusiastic mistress. It was due to her and mother's encouragement that I was able to study music and the piano seriously until well after the age of twenty. Mother bought me the magazine *Music and Youth* and when that came out it was always a red letter day. Willie bound the copies for me and he and I practised together—he the violin and I the piano. This particular partnership came to an abrupt end when I told him that he had played a wrong note. He flung the violin across the room and never played it again.

The next school must be mentioned because it was while I was there that an island influenced my whole career, and strange to relate, it was an island that never existed.

It came about in this way. The Headmistress, an austere and academic lady with lofty ideals which she tried by precept to instil into us, had banned a play that a friend and I planned to put on for Speech Day. My friend was the leader of the school orchestra and we were arranging music not only as an overture and during the intervals but as background at the more dramatic moments. The music was to be mostly Beethoven, Tchaikowsky, Brahms and some old Irish folk music—the play J. M. Synge's *Playboy of the Western World*. "Parents," said the Headmistress "would not approve of the play—there are too many dead bodies in it." Or words to that effect. We were really shattered. The play was well under way and we had spent weeks rehearsing it and arranging the music. We thought that everyone would be stunned with the poetry and sheer artistry of our epic production, and now it was to be banned just like the magazine at the last school. I felt like running away.

When therefore soon after this the Headmistress sent for me again I was in rebellious mood and prepared, with adolescent bravado, to "stand my ground" whatever the interview was to be about. She smiled kindly at me from her Olympian heights. "You have a brilliant future before you in History" she said to my great astonishment. "Next term you move up to the Sixth Form and you will then take a scholarship to Oxford. It will mean a great deal of hard work of course, and," she added "you will have to drop Geography." Drop Geography—Never! I thought grimly to myself, unable to change from the tragic figure of a frustrated and misunderstood artist in which I had cast myself to that of a future academic. My mind was in a whirl. While I stood there thoughts chased through my mind like streaks of lightning. Oxford! I doubt if the family could afford it even with a scholarship. I was not capable of winning one anyway. How flattering, though, to think that anyone thought that I could, especially this august lady—even though she was still in my "hate" book. I did not want to become a bluestocking for at that period it was exceptional for girls to go to University unless, as it appeared to me, they were dull and brainy. I wanted, too, wider horizons than, as I thought, the narrow one of an academic career. I planned in fact to be a journalist. All this went through my mind as I stood there. But above all, the transcending thought was that I did not want to "drop" Geography.

The reason for my reluctance was this. We had recently been given the project of choosing a spot on the map of the world, fixing its latitude and longitude, then describing in the detail the geography—flora, fauna, climate, physical aspects etc. This had been a rivetting occupation and did not seem like work at all. I had drawn a map of an imaginary island in the Indian Ocean showing rivers, mountains, coastline and vegetation, then described in much detail every possible aspect including population, occupations, produce, diet, the exports and imports and even a bit of supposed history thrown in. It was all so real I practically lived on that island. So I was looking forward to Geography in the Sixth with, I thought, similar fascinating projects in mind.

This I tried to explain to the Headmistress and blurted out that I wanted to carry on with both History *and* Geography. There was a bit of a fuss; an icy reception to my plea to do both, and warnings that the History would suffer and jeopardize my chances of gaining the scholarship. Eventually to my surprise she reluctantly agreed and said that she would arrange a curriculum for me. Maybe I had gained her sympathy because as it happened Geography was her specialist subject.

So this island that never existed led us eventually to this one that did, for if I *had* followed that academic career planned for me it would have been strange indeed if the set of circumstances culminating in early retirement and the events that followed would have taken the course they did. For, sad to relate, this dual curriculum was destined to fail. In the first place Advanced Geography was a bitter disappointment. Instead of exploring the romance of faraway places the studies became all very technical dealing with isobars and contours, rainfall and atmospheric pressure. Relieved as I was to drop Latin in which I could only succeed, owing to a blindspot in grammar, in making Caesar lose all his battles instead of winning them, I now found I had a blindspot too in this aspect of Geography, whereby I had an unhappy knack of making rivers run uphill and isobars flow wildly in all directions. Added to which I found it all incredibly boring.

There was another thing. Willie was paying for me to have private tuition in shorthand as I had expressed a desire to learn this in readiness for my chosen career. Of course nothing as lowdown as shorthand, typing or any of the domestic sciences were allowed even to be mentioned at this school, so my shorthand was necessarily practised in secret. Fascinated by the sheer artistry of the whirls and scrolls I was learning I took all my History notes down in shorthand. Unfortunately history had become complicated as it embraced nineteenth-century European affairs, secret treaties, and all the intricate machinations of the politics of the period. I found to my horror that I had become so enamoured with producing beautiful flowing curves that I had taken in none of the content and I now found myself unable to read any of it back—and I dare not confess the reason why. Panic set in as I realised I would not be able to hand in work of the required standard. What with rivers running uphill on the one hand and European politics stirred into a seething ferment by the curves and hooks of Pitman's shorthand on the other it was a wonder that a cosmic disaster and a nineteenth-century world war of gargantuan proportions allowed anyone to enter the twentieth century at all.

Desperate measures were needed. Fortunately there was a way out. Sometimes the History and Geography lessons coincided and it was left to me to choose which one to attend. I now attended neither and played one off against the other by always supposedly producing homework on the other subject. Now and again I put in a brief appearance or produced a bit of written work to show that I was still a pupil at the school, but most times I found myself an empty classroom whenever I was due at either of these subjects and filled in the time reading and writing. Consequently my English Literature improved enormously. I won the Magazine prize and was made Editor of the School Magazine, but had very strange looks indeed from the History and Geography mistresses, the latter making me a special and public mention in her farewell speech when she left the school. I did wonder later if perhaps I drove her to go. Although I got certificates for shorthand and eventually some for speed I never made practical use of it nor ever had a job that required its use.

In due course Babs arrived on the scene and had reached the stage when I hoped that my school exercise books would help her in her scholastic career. My two brothers, who were already young men when I was a child, had helped and looked after me and, now that I had a young sister, I couldn't wait to do the same for her. Trevor, the younger of the two, had taught me to play chess at a very early age. He and I also played bezique before I was the age to go to school. He was incredibly handsome and great fun. There was a great rapport between him and Willie although they were so different. Willie was brilliant artistically and had the looks of a film star or West End actor and an alluring personality that drew everyone to him like a magnet, men women and children, especially women. They fell for him like nine-pins, yet he was completely unspoilt, had high ideals and burnt himself out in his endeavour to attain them. Trevor was the more studious one and I remember being very impressed by his library of books on differential calculus, trigonometry and the like, and the blueprints he produced as he studied engineering. He eventually qualified as an engineer and became a Chief Engineer at an extremely early age. Later we did photography together. Even after he was married we joined a Photographic Club in London and from our darkrooms in our respective homes would ring each other up sometimes at 3 a.m. to discuss a problem or compare notes on fixers and developers. Once we went on a photographic expedition to the Inner Temple on a raw spring day. Trevor caught a chill, pneumonia set in and within a week he was dead. His photographs were exhibited posthumously and one of these which I finished processing for him was awarded a prize at the Club Exhibition.

Photography had been an early love of mine. At the age of four years I had a frame with sensitized paper in it whereby by placing say a leaf or flower in it and exposing it to the sun for a few seconds you had a "photograph" of the subject. This was sheer magic and inspired me when I was ten or eleven years old to make my own camera from a cigar box. A photograph taken with it survived childhood and turned up a short time ago in a box of rather more sophisticated exhibition pictures.

Willie always took me under his wing. He organised my birthday and Christmas parties, putting on shows helped by Trevor, and distributing really handsome prizes to my young friends in some novel way such as having them fish for them over the top of a screen decorated to represent a tank while he and Trevor crouched behind hooking the presents on the lines. Willie designed and made fancy dresses from paper, card and wire for me and when he had painted designs on them they really looked quite stunning at the dancing class performances put on for parents and at other functions. He would even check my school clothes at the beginning of term and had a rubber stamp made with my name on it in italic script so that everything should be correctly marked.

He was a member of the Magic Circle, designed and constructed all his own tricks, printed beautiful brochures and gave performances at charity concerts, having me on stage as his assistant in some exotic garment, designed by him of course. As a hobby also he established an indoor cricket school in London planning everything himself from scratch. Many clubs were coached there by famous cricketers. He had me along there at the nets being bowled at by Wright the Kent bowler, coached in batting by a famous Yorkshire veteran, and for good measure by members of the Middlesex team and several other cricketers practising for the forthcoming test series. The Press got to hear about this and pictures appeared on the front pages of the Evening News and the Evening Standard. Dad of course was immensely proud of this, even more than the time a schoolfriend and I tramped the double journey of twenty-six miles on main roads to the Oval to see Jack Hobbs play in a Test match against Don Bradman.

When I left school Willie gave me a homily and warnings about the different kinds of people I would now meet and added injunctions not to be influenced by them. When he got married he even took me on his honeymoon with him and his bride—a situation that did not go down too well at first, even though I was only a schoolgirl. Nevertheless when once Molly, my sister-in-law, had got used to having a third person present on her honeymoon we became very close.

Willie always vetted my boy friends, and when Babs was born he took her under his wing, too. He wanted her to be named Roselyn and this she is, Babs being the pet name she has always been called as the baby of the family.

My school books only helped Babs for a very short time and soon she was way ahead on her own having made up her mind at an early age that she wanted to teach. This she did, training at Cambridge, and much to mother's delight eventually became a Headmistress, thereby keeping in the tradition of Aunt Eliza. Again, although we both went in for Amateur Dramatics Babs was the one who really kept on the family tradition by producing and acting in plays at Cambridge, later joining an Amateur Repertory Company and doing as many as five shows in a week-end all over the country, teaching Drama at Evening School and acting as Adjudicator at a County Festival.

This brief sketch of our early background and family history may explain to some extent why we were heading west into an unknown adventure. That we were middle-aged, single and therefore free to do so is explained by the fact that we were unwilling to break these close family ties. Both of us had broken off engagements in the past. Babs had only recently turned down persistent offers of marriage from her former Headmaster who, nevertheless, left her everything in his will stating that his dearest wish was that they should marry but as she could not see her way to agree to this, he left everything to her, his dearest friend.

Apart from our adventurous father and very special mother we had for many years these two handsome cricket loving brothers who were always at hand to do anything that we required. There was twenty years difference in age between Babs and them, and with me somewhere in the middle it was natural that they should have this protective attitude towards us both. This double bulwark against the stresses and strains of Life had not only given us an upbringing in a rarefied atmosphere, but in addition, an inbuilt predisposition to polyandry but not the moral latitude to go with it, or we might have broken with tradition and faced life with a brace of husbands apiece. Nevertheless I for one always found it necessary to have two boy friends at a time. This naturally led to complications, heart searchings and on one occasion to an almost insoluble situation when I found myself involved on a holiday on the continent with two such attachments who had only met for the first time on the boat train at Victoria Station. An emotional climax on top of a glacier in Switzerland of all places, where it was intended that I should become engaged to one, only led me helter skelter into the arms of the other in the valley below and to the conclusion that the marital state was not for me.

This attitude can best be summed up in a phrase coined at an exclusive little pre-wedding party in London, at which five of us consumed nine bottles of champagne in record time before the rest of the guests arrived. I run very well on champagne, at least I think I do, which really comes to the same thing. At about the half way mark when someone as usual was trying to marry me off, I waved my glass in the air and gave to the world the immortal couplet "The world is so full of lovely men, to choose just one is beyond my ken." It would have never have put Shakespeare out of business, but by full time we were all convinced it would.

Tragically we lost our marvellous brothers within five months of each other when they were thirty-nine. Our parents lived to a good age, Dad as has been mentioned, in spite of losing both legs, until nearly eighty, and mother still lovely and radiant to the last, surviving him until she was nearly eightyfive. It was our privilege to look after them both in their later years as they had looked after us when we were young, and now that we no longer had the fun of their companionship we were off to seek a little adventure of our own and fulfil our childish dreams.

So as we journeyed westward through the "darkening shires" our past was left behind; a past we left without regret for it had brought us to this momentous point in our lives and would be treasured always, sustaining us through any trials that we might meet.

Somewhere on the road ahead all our worldly possessions travelled too, containing our links with the past and our hopes for the future; a future which we sped through the starlit winter night to meet with mounting excitement.

Chapter 5

Entry of supporting characters

The next afternoon as we eased down into Looe we were amazed to see the pantechnicon just a couple of hundred yards ahead of us and we crossed the bridge over the river to West Looe as though we had made the journey of some 240 miles in convoy.

Babs had written to pass the message on to Wren Toms that we should arrive in the late afternoon of December 22nd and would he please have his boat at the quay ready to take us over to the island. There was no sign of Wren Toms or his boat—just Alfy Martin and in no time at all it was pitch dark. Leaving Alfy to supervise the unloading into Nancollas's store on the quayside in the strict reverse order necessary we repaired to the cottage and eventually met up with Wren Toms.

Like a douch of cold water it hit us that late December is hardly the best time to move furniture in an open boat in darkness to an island that did not have a harbour. What sent our spirits plummetting however was when Wren Toms said that several journeys would have to be made and that they would have to be at the top of the spring tides. We were in utter despair at the thought of having to stay on the mainland until the Spring. In our ignorance of things maritime we thought that spring tides meant just that. If I had concentrated on those isobars and suchlike in my youth we would have known as Wren went on to explain that spring tides are especially high and come twice every month with the new moon and again with the full moon. They are exceptionally high at the vernal and autumnal equinox. Should they coincide with gales accompanied with rain, rivers burst their banks, flooding occurs and disaster overtakes vulnerable areas. It was this combination of circumstances that had caused the flooding in Looe on our first visit on that memorable night in late October the previous year. As I write we have just experienced the highest spring tides for 300 years due to an unusual conjunction of sun, moon and earth. Accompanied by gales of storm force they caused a disaster the telling of which must be kept for the future! Since coming to live on the Island we have learned to regulate our lives by the tides but at that time it was our

77

first encounter with this natural phenomenon and we soon realised how our lives and future movements were hinged on its movements.

Relieved that we had only to wait until the next Spring tide due at the beginning of January we prepared to spend Christmas in the cottage. Once again Doug and Cecily came over from their visit to Devon to spend part of the holiday with us. They were both anxious to join us in our island life. Much as we would have liked to have them, for Doug was one of those chaps who could put his hand to anything, we felt that initially we could not take on the extra financial burden that their help would have entailed. With their three children there were five of them. The only certain income was Babs, greatly reduced with her new appointment, and my pension. No work or market gardening had been done on the island for six months, and it was uncertain what income, if any, there would be from the daffodils the first year. What was certain was that there would be quite a strain on our finances putting everything in order after six months neglect. We would without doubt have to pay for labour, specialised and boatwise, and we quite frankly quaked at the thought of having to feed the seven of us, keep three homes going, run a boat and a car in addition, not forgetting the fact conveniently overlooked by others that as single people we are taxed up to the hilt, and I have never enjoyed equal pay although most expenses naturally are equal. We felt we had enough on our plate and that was the understatement of the year. We told them regretfully that we must settle in first and if it appeared a feasible proposition they could join us later. With the promise that they could spend a holiday with us in the early summer we sped them on their way.

It seemed hardly credible that it was just fourteen months ago that we had come on that hurriedly planned and brief visit looking for a holiday cottage and now here we were poised to take off for an entirely new life on an island, and in mid winter too. Not that that worried us—our only concern was these spring tides which we awaited with much impatience. We filled in the time (only, in fact, a matter of days for they were due on January 2nd) by buying more "protective clothing" and a couple of outboard motors.

Of the three boats that belonged to the island, *The Islander*—an eighteen foot 6 h.p. diesel motor boat, a twelve foot metal sailing boat, and an eight foot fibre glass dinghy, two were in the harbour—*The Islander* and the dinghy. Miss Whitehouse who used to live with her parents on the island but later moved to the mainland to run a goose farm, had been rowing over to the island in the dinghy when the weather was suitable to put out dried food for the cat who would not leave. Wren Toms had commandeered some help and had been going out to the island to put *The Islander* in order, for owing to Mr Whitehouse's ill-health it had not been used for some time. One of these helpers was a massive man called Mac, a Chief Bosun on shore leave. He was also to help with the moves to the island and solved our immediate labour problems as he was willing to come over to the island and work on a day-to-day basis until his leave expired. Judging by his muscle, size and experience of the sea we reckoned he would be a great asset and just the kind of casual labour that would suit us.

At last it was Friday January 1st and we awaited the magic spring tides due together with Wren's week-end—for he worked for the Council during the week—on the next day, Saturday, but with them came strong winds and high seas. Mac called on Friday to say that the sea was "making up", that it was coming in from the west and back washing round the island. Landing the next day Saturday, he said, would be impossible. Seeing our obvious and bitter disappointment and to convince us that it was impossible he offered to take us out in *The Islander* to see for ourselves.

Babs decided not to come as she had a touch of bronchitis and was still rather chesty, so just Mac and I set sail. It was a wild winter's day. As soon as we left the harbour we could see high seas breaking over the Rannies, a reef of rocks extending from the furthermost south-eastern tip of the island, and there was nothing to be seen on the jagged horizon but white horses riding wildly towards us. Breakers surged all round the island and were smashing on the rocks at Hannafore. We rode giddily over mountainous rollers and as we approached what should have been the landing beach there was no beach to be seen at all; just a wall of shingle and seaweed thrown up by the surf and a foaming sea cascading over the rocks. The island looked as though it would subside under the pounding onslaught and inwardly I wondered if there would be any island left for us to live on. As we sailed westward past the island towards the wild sunset great Atlantic rollers loomed above us and our sturdy little boat bravely climbed up and up before plunging into the troughs on the other side. When Mac was satisfied that I was convinced that landing would be impossible we turned back. He need not have worried; I was certain that no one would be able to land ever again, and that we might as well have bought a planet in outer space for all the use the island would be to us as a future home.

All this time Babs was watching from Hannafore, and thinking how lonely and vulnerable our little boat looked in that stormy expanse of ocean for not another craft was to be seen. She was convinced she would never see us again.

Back on dry land in spite of her fears, we decided to console ourselves instead with a shopping expedition to Plymouth the next day. As though we had not enough books to take with us we added to our store by buying more, but mostly they were on fruit and vegetable growing and astronomy. We did not stay long. Back in West Looe an eerie sight caught my eye as we drove along the quayside. Our fibre glass dinghy was lying on the quayside and attached to its upturned side was a hand, just a hand, nothing more. Horrified, we skidded to a halt and tumbled out of the car. Our fears were soon stilled however when investigation showed Wren Toms aboard his own boat the *Orlando* below as the tide was out, and just about to give himself a heave up by grasping the dinghy.

"Come aboard!" he invited hospitably, extending the hand to us to help us down the vertical iron ladder into his boat. We stayed for at least an hour while he ground in new valves into his auxiliary engine. Lovingly he held up a valve or a gasket and proceeded to explain patiently and in great detail exactly what he was doing. It may not have seemed so strange to Babs who, after all, was a car driver and presumably knew the names at least of things that lived under the bonnet of the car, but to me it was all like black magic. This was the first time I had seen a gasket. I remember once on a drive in the country a strange knocking developed in the car and Babs said, "That's the gasket gone." I wanted to go back and look for it and could never understand why we did not and why we had to put up with the knocking until we found a garage. All the time Wren was explaining what he was doing an absurd jingle kept going through my head,
A-Tisket, A-Tasket, at last I've seen A-Gasket!"
Even so it did look to me rather like a glorified washer. Little did I know how closely bound up with gaskets and all their relations my future life would be.

To our delight it transpired that all these preparations were for making a foray over to the island with some of the furniture the next day, Sunday. Wren did say casually that Mac was not too keen. We could quite understand why.

Wren then made an idle remark that convinced us that MI5 had emigrated to Looe. "Mac told me that you had been to Plymouth," he said. We had not told anyone nor had we seen anyone en route. In fact our destination had been one of those spur of the moment decisions when once we were on our way. Furthermore we had been gone so short a time that the only way people in Looe could know was if we had been spotted in Plymouth and someone had telephoned the news through to Looe, and we didn't think that we rated that hot a line. Walking back to the cottage everyone we met asked us if we had enjoyed our trip to Plymouth and when one of them was Mac we asked how he knew. "Oh! Nancollas told me," he said. Sometime later we spoke to Mr Nancollas about this. "Yes! I did hear you were in Plymouth," he said non-commitedly. And there the matter ended—unresolved. It was the first but not to be the last of our experiences of the mysterious workings of the grape-vine.

High tide on Sunday, January 3rd was at the uninviting hour of 5.58 a.m. so we set the alarm for 5 a.m. It was an icy cold morning and more like the middle of the night. I donned two of everything, slacks over jeans, two thick fisherman's jerseys, seaman's stockings over socks, sea boots, woolly hat, anorak and string gloves. Mac called at 5.45 still very doubtful about the advisability of trying at all. It was pitch dark and bitingly cold.

He and Babs went round to Hannafore by car to inspect the state of the sea for Mac was convinced that this would show that an attempt would be out of the question and most foolhardy. While they were gone Wren Toms arrived and announced cheerfully, "All set fair to go." I must say his manner and appearance inspired confidence. Aged about 27 he was a tall, strong, handsome young man. He wore thigh sea boots topped by a red shirt and with his black curly hair and vivid blue eyes he made a striking figure. He looked like a swashbuckling but friendly pirate, ready to dare anything. He was aptly named Wren for his eyes were and are always twinkling, and bright with optimism. You somehow felt that if he said we were to set sail in a sieve you would go quite happily. The tale was that he used to play truant from school to be with the boats. As we came to know him we thought that if this were so it was time well spent, for there was apparently nothing that he did not know about the sea and boats. He has an uncanny knack of knowing exactly the right thing to do with any nautical problem. Some say he takes risks and he probably does, but they are calculated risks based on experience and one felt that he would not put his boat and his life in danger foolishly.

The others returned to say that the sea even in the darkness could be seen creaming round the island. Wren however was already back in the

Orlando preparing to sail.

The great loading up from Nancollas's store now began. The refrigerator and deep freeze were trundled along the quayside like skittles by the burly Mac who had shoulders like an armchair. Just as smartly they were trundled back at Wren's command, "I want all the tea chests first." There were, as we knew only too well, thirty of these and as they were full of books they had been stowed at the back of the store for the final trip, when the bookcases would hopefully be on the island waiting to accommodate them. To our horror the store now became a wreck as the unfortunate Mac had to clamber over furniture, clawing his way to the back and heaving and shoving as he tried to extricate the chests. We heard more than one ominous scrunch and hoped that a precious antique had not splintered under the onslaught or, worse still, that Mac had not cracked one of his bones. Much to our relief he still looked in one piece, and as happy as he could reasonably be expected to be, when he finally emerged and heaved the last of the chests onto the quayside.

These loaded up, Wren then allowed other items to follow. These were more or less hurled aboard willy-nilly as Wren was in a hurry and time was getting short with the tide dropping fast. We tried to see that a few useful items like a kettle and some pots and pans were thrown in but it was a chancy business.

During the chaos dawn broke, Venus shone brightly over the sea in the east, the tide went down rapidly and the vicar passed on his way to early morning service. He stopped to greet us and we were greatly comforted for we felt that we could do with his blessing. Babs and I then dashed back to the cottage to make fresh flasks of coffee while Wren roped up. We flung a few more things on board in passing and I hurriedly took photos of the poor *Orlando*. Weighed down and low in the water and piled high with an assortment of our belongings she had lost her beautiful lines and looked like some gigantic sea monster, distorted with pain and about to subside into a watery grave.

The tide was dropping fast. It was as though a plug had been taken out and Wren, having loaded and made fast everything to his satisfaction, was anxious to get away. Leaving the wreckage in Nancollas's store we slithered down the vertical iron ladder as best we could, tumbled into the boat, clambered over the piles of packing cases, pots and pans and the like to the only bit of shelter on the boat, the wheelhouse—a kind of half open cabin housing the steering and engine area. There was just room for the four of us to huddle together and by a judicious readjustment of elbows just enough clearance for Wren to steer.

Slowly the overburdened *Orlando* moved towards the harbour mouth. Once out of its protection a wild scene confronted us. A wracking sea raced across our bows. The *Orlando* bucked as cross waves broke over the deck and wheelhouse and spray whistled past overhead. A corkscrew motion then began to develop. Hemmed in by packing cases in the rear and unable to see through the streaming glass of the wheelhouse before us we clung to each other and anything we could lay our hands on to prevent ourselves from falling on to Wren, who was having to hold hard to keep the boat on course, and, for all we knew, afloat. The cargo began to creak and move ominously as the *Orlando* twisted and writhed and crashed down with a grinding thump. I thought we were hitting the seabed every time we plunged down through the boiling surf with a sickmaking jolting thud. We were in fact "crossing the bar". This is a bar of water that develops in silted up tidal river mouths when the sea is running, in the case of Looe any-way, in an easterly or south-easterly direction or any direction if the seas are strong enough. The outgoing tide from the river meets the incoming waves with most spectacular results. The effect is a series of criss-cross chopping and swift running waves that pile on each other so fast it is impossible to ride them. The resulting maelstrom is worsened if the outgo-ing river is swollen with rain and sea it meets is rough. It can be quite catastrophic. Add a gale and the maelstrom becomes a mountainous frenzy. With the wind in the wrong direction even with just a fair tide running a small boat can be whisked right round so that it faces the way it was com-ing. This was something that we did experience later in our adventures. Luckily for our peace of mind at this time we knew nothing of the bar and its evil possibilities; we only knew we were in rough and unmanageable seas.

Wren's eyes glittered with excitement, and such was the confidence he inspired that although this really was a nightmarish journey I cannot re-member that we were unduly worried even when, at the end of one par-ticularly unnerving crash and twisting jolt, Wren said as he clung to the wheel, "I didn't expect the bar to be as bad as this; it is the worst trip I have ever had!". Memory does not record any reaction or comment from Mac. No doubt like us he was clinging on for dear life to anything that was handy. We like to think that diplomacy restrained him from voicing any opinion. We have often wondered since what the local boatmen thought of this mad expedition, for not even the fishing fleet ventured out for days in that wild sea in midwinter, let alone a boat the size of the *Orlando*, weighed down as she was with a heavy cargo. We realise now that no one but Wren would have attempted it.

Thankfully as we approached the island, we saw that some of the landing beach was still there and in the shelter of the western rocks exposed by the outgoing tide it was relatively calm. Wren took the *Orlando* as close as he could without going aground. We were to go ashore in his dinghy which he had towed behind and had somehow survived the battering. It was not an easy operation to climb over the side and heave oneself into the bouncing dinghy with no ladder or rope to help. I had brought my precious new Pentax camera with me and had clung to it throughout the hazardous journey. I now handed this to Wren for safety and with Mac below to catch me, if need be, I managed to decant myself into the dinghy. What I had not realised was that Wren would not be coming ashore at this stage. He was to wait on board and steady the *Orlando* upright with wooden legs as the tide ran out and left her high and dry. He would then be able to unload onto dry land. When the tide came in again in the afternoon and refloated her we would return to the mainland. So when Babs descended after me into the dinghy Wren handed the camera to her. Mac now rowed the dinghy on to the beach and helped me ashore. Babs stood up to follow, but Mac, without looking back, got hold of the rope and gave the dinghy a tremendous heave to lift it out of the water on to dry land. The sudden and unexpected lurch took the boat from under Babs' feet and sent her head over heels backwards over the stern into the sea. She was completely submerged in the water, Pentax and all. She was gasping as we rushed to pull her out. She had swallowed a good bit of sea water and was a bit shocked but apart from being sopping wet appeared to be otherwise unharmed. We rushed her up to the house and lit a fire of sorts for as she had not got over the touch of bronchitis we did not think a ducking in the icy sea of a January dawn would do her much good. It was now that my wearing two of everything came in very useful. I simply peeled off one layer and soon Babs was dry clad. I dare not look at my beautiful new Pentax. I feared it would be completely ruined. There was nothing I could do about it anyway until I was back on the mainland.

The caterpillar tractor which we had acquired along with other farming equipment with the island now came into its own. This would ride over shingle whereas anything with wheels would sink in and become bogged down. The versatile Wren got this going and soon he and Mac trailed up the first load of packing cases. One of these was the "ditty box" full of photographic equipment and to our great delight we found a bottle of dry sherry among the bottles of chemicals. This fortified us all while Babs and I made drinking chocolate to have with our cheese sandwiches. We did not unpack the books as we had nowhere to put them and as the darkroom had not yet been allocated there seemed no point in unpacking that either, especially as no more sherry had come to light. Wren and Mac stowed all the cases in the farmhouse kitchen which now began to look like a smugglers' den or a pirates' hide-out. No sooner were they all up from the beach when Wren said we should have to leave at once to catch the tide. This time fortunately we climbed into the *Orlando* while she was still aground on her legs, and waited until Wren could float her off. While doing so we pondered on the fact that a collection of hundreds of books and some photographic equipment was hardly enough to set up home on an uninhabited island. Nevertheless it was a start and the expedition was a novel way to spend a Sunday to say the least.

We reached harbour without incident for the bar had subsided somewhat with the incoming tide and riding with it instead of against it we were soon safely moored up alongside the quay. Ethrelda, an old Cornish lady with whom we had become friendly and who had been Toby-sitting for us made up a cup of tea, and snug and warm we told her the tales of the day. Babs so far felt no ill effects from her ducking in the sea, but I had not enough courage yet to inspect the camera too closely except to mop it as dry as I could.

The next day I felt very tired and stiff and wondered if perhaps I was not young or fit enough for this island lark. After food, drink and a visit to the hairdresser's however the sap rose once more and everything again seemed possible and exciting. Mrs Mac, on the other hand, called round to say that Mac was full of cold and sneezes and had gone off to be X-rayed. This seemed a dramatic outcome to yesterday's events and we thought at once of the ominous scrunchings we had heard in Nancollas's store. We were more than relieved to hear that the X-ray examination had been pre-arranged and had no connection with our expedition.

The Whitehouses, who were temporarily living in Looe, had invited us round to tea and for the second time we had experience of the mysterious powers of the grapevine; not only mysterious but inventive to an incredible degree. Not only did Mr and Mrs Whitehouse know everything in

great detail of the happenings of the previous day, and this we quite understood for all the inhabitants of Hannafore would have had a grandstand
view of the voyage of the *Orlando*, but they knew of conversations behind
closed doors that had never taken place. One tale they repeated to us left us
open mouthed with astonishment. Mr Whitehouse had been told that a
member of the B.B.C. had taped a conversation with the Misses Atkins
and that it was being held for safe keeping in the offices of a West Country
newspaper. The informant of the informant (never identified), swore he
had seen it there himself. Why for safe keeping? we asked ourselves hys-
terically afterwards. Had we been bugged as suspects in the pay of the
Russians? Was it thought that we had bought the island at their expense to
set up a hidden submarine base or perhaps secretly land them at dead of
night to install a nuclear bombsite trained on the Naval base at Devonport?
At our trial the tape would be produced with a triumphant flourish and we
would be marched off to the Tower of London while the West Country
paper would make the scoop of the century! Perhaps even writing these
words will trigger off a set of explosive laden rumours and if we are not
careful we *shall* be marched off to the Tower "pending enquiries".

Once again this mystery was never resolved, and it was only the first of
many quite unfounded rumours that dog us to this day. A favourite old
annual is that the island is up for sale. Every year without fail someone
will step ashore and say "I hear the island is up for sale." What baffles us
is the amount of minute detail that accompanies these quite unfounded
rumours. Not only are we given the name of the purchaser, but the amount
he is paying, sometimes his address and, usually, where we are going to
live after the sale. I must say they are up to date in one respect; the rumours always take into account inflation and each year the amount for
which we have clinched the deal goes up. Our stock answer now is "Yes it
was up for sale—ten years ago—and we are the ones who bought it."

The next spring tides would of course be in two weeks' time but Wren
thought that if the weather were suitable we might make a short trip the
following week-end when he would again be free. The neap tides due then
would make a big unloading out of the question.

Meantime Babs made preparations for her first day at school and we
tried to plan our future. It was now quite obvious that Babs would have to
live in the cottage on the mainland and only come out to the island at
weekends and holidays, and now that we had had a taste of winter seas we
realised that even weekends would be out of the question except rarely in

winter time. There was a great deal of work to do on the island just to keep it going and if we intended to carry on with the market gardening and the daffodil farm we should need labour. The question was whether the income from the produce was worth the cost of labour and sea transport and the worry involved. Hosts of friends were all set to come and help during their holidays, but even though many had long school or university vacations the help would naturally be sporadic. Wren was willing to come and work for us at week-ends and for a time Mac would be available full-time. This latter hope was knocked on the head however when Mrs Mac came round again to say that Mac's X-rays had shown a thrombotic condition and work of any kind would be out of the question for some time. We went straightway to visit him. There was poor Mac propped up in a made-up bed downstairs to save him climbing. He was coughing and sneezing with streaming eyes and we felt rather guilty; not that we knew beforehand that he was under the doctor, for he looked so big and strong one could not have suspected that he had a heart condition.

As for our future, we decided to play it by ear. Our main ambition, apart from an overwhelming desire to live on an island, was to make crafts, for, as well as the setting up of the pottery, Babs was very keen on all kind of crafts, as indeed we both were.

Not for the first time we now experienced the great kindness of the Cornish people. We had been told before coming down here that the Cornish resented the intrusion of strangers—up country people, as all those who come from the other side of the Tamar river, the natural boundary that practically cuts Cornwall off from the rest of the country, are called. If this is true, and in some cases it may justifiably be so then it is an attitude that one quickly has sympathy for and can appreciate. A picturesque folk of great natural charm, the Cornish have over the centuries had to battle with the elements in all the fury that the Atlantic can hurl at them, to make a precarious and often dangerous living from fishing, farming, and in the past, tin-mining. With the advent of train, coach and car the tourist industry was born, but—and this is a most significant "but"—the tourist trade at its height lasts for but four months of the year and again is dependent on the elements. Given a wet season many visitors who would otherwise come to the West Country do not come or, once arrived, flock home in their thousands. How many urban and city folk would like to have an inflated income for one-third of their working life each year, and have to live and bring up their families on little or no other income for the other two-thirds of the year? Who would not resent "foreigners" who come to take the pickings of the tourist trade from a people who at last have been able to supplement their hard won earnings? Not that it is always the case. If people, for love of Cornwall, come here to earn an honest living and do not try to oust the locals or snatch their living from them, are not "uppity" nor think they can run the affairs of the Cornish for them better than they can themselves, they will find there are no finer friends than the Cornish. Many are welcomed and helped as we ourselves were. In any case we had not come to make a living. With Babs' salary and my pension we aimed only to live on the island and be self-sufficient financially, but how to do it with Babs having to work on the mainland was the rub now that Mac had been forced to opt out. Many of the folk we met in Looe were very concerned on our behalf.

At this time the Tyler family in particular took us under their wing. Although from East Looe originally, Zena and Peter lived just opposite from us in West Looe. One night during one of our previous visits to the cottages I had acquired from one of Nancollas's auction sales, through the good services of Alfy Martin, a chest of drawers for 10/–. Close examination showed that under its five or six coats of paint was a fine naval chest with brass handles; each drawer had been inscribed by the carpenter *Lieutenant (Electrical)*, and had stops so that the drawers would not fly out with the movement of the ship in heavy seas. Delighted with my bargain I had it out in the courtyard one night and, with the recently acquired Black and Decker and its sanding attachment, succeeded at long last in stripping off all the coats of paint to reveal the mahogany beneath. By the time I had finished, the night was well advanced, but I was so engrossed that I was hardly aware of the passage of time or the banshee-like wailings that shrieked around the courtyard from the power tool. Next morning as I was lovingly smoothing the chest down with fine sandpaper by hand a rich Cornish voice from behind me called "Good morning! I do not want to appear curious but *would* you mind very much telling me what you were doing last night. I should *love* to know." And that was how we first met Zena. From then on she was a constant visitor and many times we were invited over for tea or coffee. We, in fact, saw the New Year in with them on the eve of our now famous journey over to the island in the *Orlando* with the crates of books.

On one occasion Zena gave me a demonstration of how to make a traditional Cornish pasty. I took colour pictures of the process on the

Mamiyaflex and tried out my new tape recorder by recording her instructions, given in her lilting brogue. Serving pasties to some of our special visitors and revealing the secret of the Cornish way of making them has now become part of the ritual of our entertainment, accompanied, of course, by home-made island wine.

From the very beginning the Whitehouses had been concerned about how we would manage on the island. "Who will collect your driftwood and who will transport your diesel oil?" had been but two of many doubts these good folk had expressed on our behalf. Others, including Zena, joined in with their fears about how we should cope with the generator, and Zena was particularly concerned when Mac had to drop out, for he was her father-in-law and she reckoned he would never be in a fit state to help us. One day she came over with the news that her son Charles would help at weekends when he was home from school and that his friend Duncan was also very keen to help. Duncan apparently had been brought up on a farm and knew all about tractors, generators and the like. That very same evening Charles and Duncan came over and tried out our newly acquired outboard engines in the courtyard. The ensuing noise resounding round the courtyard and reverberating throughout West Looe made it sound as though something nasty was going on at a racing car circuit nearby. Later they decided to take the motors round to Hannafore to try as they were afraid that the thunderous roar echoing round the courtyard would break all the windows in the neighbourhood. Very thoughtful we thought for ones so young. It was not until many moons later that we learned that outboard engines are water cooled and should only be run if certain parts are submerged in water, their natural habitat when in use. Nevertheless they gave us very good service until they were lost in the great storms and tides of 1974.

Mr and Mrs Whitehouse were still very perturbed about our lack of labour on the island and thought that two schoolboys coming in their free time at weekends was hardly sufficient for the day to day running of the island. These problems we pushed firmly ahead into the future. Our priority, and the only problem that bothered us was actually getting ourselves and all out furniture on to the island; that hurdle overcome we would then be free to tackle these, to our minds, minor snags.

Meantime there were numerous comings and goings to the cottage, with many visitors offering us advice and telling us what we should do. One of these callers was from the Ministry of Agriculture. There was, he said, a plague of starlings on the island and we should have to do something about if we did not want everything poisoned by their pollution. Years ago, he said, the woods there were completely destroyed by the starlings. Farmers dealt with the problem by letting off at them with a shot gun. Although I was a "shot" it had been strictly target shooting, and I reckoned I would not have the time and certainly not the inclination to go shooting at wild life, however much of a pest. As an alternative he recommended rockets which are set to go off automatically at intervals, the explosions frightening them off every time they returned, as they surely would. As these rockets were quite expensive we decided to shelve this problem along with all the others and deal with it when we came face to face with this particular menace.

Another visitor was Ethrelda who not only was our Toby sitter, and tidied and polished the cottage for us, but she was a welcome visitor socially as we were close to her cottage a few steps up Hannafore Lane. She particularly enjoyed hearing some of my tape recordings. The machine fascinated her and nothing gave her greater pleasure than to give recitations or read old Cornish tales in dialect into the microphone and to hear her efforts replayed. She was an excellent natural performer and had recited at many concerts. Alas! she is no longer with us but her tapes recall those happy evenings and her spirited encouragement of our island project. Doubting Thomases there may have been but this dear old lady was not one of them. "You are walking into the lion's mouth," she said, "but you will find your way through. You two are the kind who will succeed there, and you will—I know you will." She was a member of the Darby and Joan Club and she invited us round one evening to entertain the members with some of the recordings and to meet Mrs Skuse, the organiser, who was also a member of the Field Study Group, a fact that Ethrelda thought might interest us. There were two repercussions from this visit one of which echoes to this day and the significance of which will be told in due course. The other and more pertinent one at the time was an invitation from Mrs Skuse, a charming lady, to go to the next meeting of the Field Study Group and meet Dr Turk, a distinguished ornithologist.

A few days later we did this and it was arranged that the group should come over to the island in the summer and do a survey of all the natural life. We were thrilled about this as we were most anxious to learn all we could about our new "country" and hoped that in due course we should have experts in their different spheres to visit us. This was a good beginning.

We had also become acquainted with Miss Kempster and Miss Hoyle, both retired teachers, who had invited us round to tea. They suggested that we might like to go to a meeting of the Old Cornwall Society as their guests. As the next meeting was on Saturday we were delighted to attend and took Ethrelda, who was also a member. We found the talk given that evening most interesting as it was given by a lady, a representative of the Ministry of Works as it was then still called, the subject being "Excavations in the Isles of Scilly". We were introduced to a number of people, who, experts in their own field or amateur enthusiasts, were just the kind of people who could give us the information we wanted so much about the history, natural, archaeological and otherwise of our island, which we already knew had a fascinating history from early times. We joined the society there and then and expressed the hope that sometime in the future they would care to visit us as one of their projects.

Earlier in the day we had run into Mr Nancollas who invited us into *The Harbour Moon*, the sparking off point for our adventure just over a year ago, for drinks. Mr Nancollas was most enthusiastic about our plans and had many suggestions of his own. As chairman of the council (a position since superseded by the current upheaval and reorganisation of local government by that of mayor) he was keen to help. No doubt he was relieved that developers or a holiday camp had not acquired the island. Although we only knew for a fact that the West End actors had been after the island, rumours persisted that a famous holiday camp was keenly in the running. He had, he said, a farmer and his son who would come over and plough the land. He suggested that we might keep goats to keep the grass down. This latter seemed to us an admirable idea, especially as it conjured up visions of goats' milk, cheese, butter and yoghurt and we filed it in our minds as one of the more feasible suggestions that had been hurled at us from all sides.

We had now been resident in Looe just a fortnight and it seemed incredible that in that short time there should have been such a fever of activity and meetings up with so many people. Of course our advent was highlighted by the fact that it happened in the depth of winter in a Cornish fishing village and holiday centre. If we had come in August everyone would have been too busy, no doubt, except to notice in passing that the island had changed hands.

Wren's plan for a small trip to the island on Sunday was out of the question for the day dawned wet and windy. A walk up Hannafore Lane over to Hannafore, a walk that Toby declined, revealed a rough sea running in from the west accompanied with slashing rain. A walk along the beach to Wallace Quay, a quay in name only for all that was to be seen were but parts of a broken and partly submerged sea wall of long ago, was wet and extremely unpleasant. The island receding into a pall of mist temporarily lost its bright allure, but not its fascination, and the warmth of a coal fire in Bassett Court beckoned us back to its comfort. Poor Toby who was in his fourteenth year was suffering from "the screws", so to alleviate his pain we administered some aspirin.

All our hopes were now pinned on good weather for the following week-end when the spring tides were again due. The intervening days were not without incident. The first was a letter from a girl called Ruth. Her parents ran a smallholding up at Shutta, where Babs had had to reverse on that pitch-dark night on our first stay in Looe, and Ruth, recently back from working in the U.S., offered her services to us until her parents required her help in the growing season around May. In July she was to start training to become a probation officer. She called round to see us and was very keen to live on the island to help us for the next few months and was willing to come just for the cost of her insurance stamp and her board and lodging. However we persuaded her to accept £3 a week so that she would have some pocket money and, that fixed, she went off to straighten up her affairs. This seemed a very good arrangement to us. It would keep all the good folk quiet who were worrying about how we should manage, in particular about my being on the island alone, and it would give us a bit of breathing space to find our bearings without the commitment of permanent help and the financial liability it could become.

Secondly, Babs had now taken up her new appointment and was involved during the daytime in getting *her* bearings. The third incident caused us a bit more concern. Mr Nancollas called round to say that he was disappointed that Wren had been unable to make a trip over to the island at the weekend as he needed the store for his next sale and would-be vendors had nowhere to put their articles for sale. He therefore was arranging for one of the fishermen, (who, being self-employed, was freelance and therefore free, if necessary, during the week,) to move the furniture the very next day. Well, this was fine, but we did not think that Wren would be pleased. Having taken on the assignment, hazardous though it was, he would not willingly give it up. In fact, as we came to know him better, we realised that he had accepted it as a challenge with relish and it had become the breath of life to him. Luckily or unluckily depending whether you were Wren or Mr Nancollas the problem was resolved by the weather remaining wet and windy all week.

We knew that Wren would make an all out effort at the weekend for not only was it spring tides when he could make a major embarkation but if he missed yet another week-end someone else would be moving our furniture out. Looking back we know now that fishermen would not exactly be vying with each other for the privilege of getting their boats bashed to bits on our rocks. Only recently a small fishing boat sank off the rocks and it was fortunate that I was around at break of dawn on a late winter's morning to dispense dry clothing and cups of hot coffee to some local men, who, though not fishermen by occupation, had lived in Looe all their lives and knew every inch of the coastline. We knew therefore that we might be in for an even more hazardous trip and were perhaps slightly relieved when by Friday the gales had not abated, but more than apprehensive when Wren made an assignment for 4.30 a.m. on the Saturday to size up the possibilities sea-wise.

Our resolve was further weakened by the fact that we did not get to bed until 2 a.m. due to a series of visitors, all of whom had their own ideas on how we should cope with the problems of running an island. One man in particular, and I cannot recall how we became acquainted, was full of the idea that we should install yet another generator; that the diesel oil for it should be piped over from tankers on the mainland and everything else should be transported by helicopter. "Only £25 an hour" he said lightly. Not for the first time we wondered if we were the first human begins who intended to live permanently on the island. If all these schemes that were dinned into our ears at intervals were so wonderful why had not previous owners, many of whom had been monied people, adopted them? We know the answer now. Ever ready to pick up a crumb of knowledge and by our upbringing polite by nature, we listen.

We are still surprised by the number of "experts" who march onto the island and tell us exactly how to run the island and point out the grave mistakes we are making in varying activities—even though not one of them has ever coped with life on an island or has been professionally involved in any of the spheres about which they claim an expert knowledge. The professionals are, we find, much more diffident at handing out advice. Nevertheless we always listen when we hear what is almost an Island Litany: "You know, what you ought to do is . . ." even though it is something we have tried and discarded years ago as impractical. We continue to hope that we shall pick up a pearl of wisdom. Babs is much more tolerant of unsolicited and often foolish advice than I am. If I am tired or have had to cope with a lot of stupidity and the well-worn opening phrase is aimed at me I sometimes "up and at 'em" and tell them exactly why we do not keep cows, sheep, geese, rabbits, deer, peacocks or what have you. It is almost worth the expenditure of adrenalin to see the look of stupified surprise on the faces of our amateur counsellors.

At this stage in our island saga we were avid listeners thirsting for knowledge, and, bedazzled by these grandiose schemes, rolled into bed unable to sleep for excitement even at 2 a.m. The time of high tide—4.30 a.m.—did not, therefore, seem a highly desirable time to arise in mid-January to face a sea journey in a more or less open boat. Promptly on the half hour Wren called and while I sank back thankfully into bed the luckless Babs drove Wren round to Hannafore to look at the state of the sea. Tremendous seas were running and Wren regretfully decided it was too rough to transport furniture. He suggested instead that the three of us drive into Plymouth to Clode's, the ship's chandlers on the Barbican, and buy some chain for the *Islander's* mooring buoy. He was to call for us at 9 a.m. Even before that still tender time of day, when it was scarcely daylight, our little cottage seethed with comings and goings. First Charles and Duncan arrived nautically booted and spurred, all set for a trip to the island, and they were bitterly disappointed that it was too rough. They were followed smartly by Zena, not, as one might expect, anxious about her offspring embarking on some foolhardy and dangerous expedition, but keen to join the entourage herself.

Ruth, her appetite whetted, also turned up to see what the chances were of coming over to the island. As she was a Roman Catholic and would be at church in the morning it was arranged that if we were able to get over the following morning she would come round to Hannafore after the service, climb over the rocks at low tide and yell to us, who in turn would have clambered as far as possible to the low tide on our rocks, and yell back at her. The reason for this quite unnecessary assignation eludes me, especially as we should, if we did make the island on the morrow, be more than fully occupied heaving furniture frantically against time, as the tide came in, and we should have to catch it. One can only put it down to "island fever".

Entry of Supporting Characters

Our gentleman friend of the night before—he of the generator, helicopter and pipelines-over-the-sea ideas—must also have been possessed of island fever for he too was round bright and early. In fact he was embellishing on his schemes when Wren arrived at 9 a.m. Wren, who himself was not short on ideas, his favourite being the building of a harbour wall to make landing in rough seas possible, listened goggle eyed as we all sipped coffee. The post brought us back to reality. Before the three of us, plus Toby, drove into Plymouth we learned that my camera, which I had at last sent off to my photographic suppliers, was probably a dead loss, and the estate agents had so far been unable to sell our house, and again wanted us to drop our price. The camera was insured so its loss was not the disaster it might have been. As for the house, our bank manager was still friendly, in fact *very* friendly, for Babs had received a letter asking if she would consider keeping her current account with him after she had moved from the district. "It was the first time," said Babs, "that any bank has vied for the privilege of handling my overdraft." At that time teachers' salaries were hardly large enough to set the banking world alight and she was usually slightly in the red. Spring was not far off and with it, we hoped, shoals of house hunters. In any case we were not in the mood to worry— we were off to the Barbican from which the *Mayflower* had set sail. Clode's was just a few yards from the steps where this event took place and a plaque commemorated the event.

The chandler's was a fascinating place. One climbed down steps to an underground store that dated back to Nelson's time, and it was a veritable Aladdin's cave of maritime treasure trove. Led by the colourful figure of Wren clad in his red shirt and tall sea boots we clambered over piles of chains, ropes and pulleys and threaded our way past storm lanterns and a ship's locker and ship's figurehead that looked as though they too had been there since Nelson's day. At last Wren selected some chain that was to his satisfaction. This was measured by the fathom and Wren had six fathoms cut off, but to our surprise it was sold by weight. Weighing it was a long and cumbersome operation. We were even more surprised to find that the cost was only £3, for the length of chain and its girth made it look as though it was all set to tow the *Queen Elizabeth* at least. While the weighing, rattling and clanking was going on Babs and I explored this subterranean hoard of treasure. To our delight we found a loud hailer of a bygone age, one that in our imagination could surely have voiced the commands of Sir Francis Drake, no less. Fashioned long before the days of plastic and electronics it appeared to be made of a kind of tough whale hide—or perhaps that of some strange sea monster, we thought fancifully. Over a yard in length it amplifies with a resonance unmatched by a modern powered one we have since acquired, and many times has summoned folk from the other side of the island, or sometimes attracted, when necessary, the attention of a passing boat. We thought it more than a bargain at 15/–.

By this time ropes, plugs, links and thimbles (these last having nothing remotely to do with needlework) had been added to our purchases, and by the time it was all loaded into our estate Mini there was just room for Toby to perch on top of the mountain of chain. The weight made steering difficult and we more or less floundered back to Looe, rather like manouvering a tank through bogland. We counted ourselves lucky to make our way over the hills without incident, or being arrested. Toby, a dyed-in-the-wool conservative, as most dogs are, had a habit of objecting to anything that to his mind was "different". "Different" embraced anyone from a parson in a dog collar, a kilted Scotsman, a sari-clad Indian lady, boy scouts and anyone coloured. They were all classed in his doggy world as definitely odd. He voiced their non-acceptability by barking loud and long from the back window of the car until the object of his derision had receded far into the distance. Unhesitatingly Toby now added a pile of chain to his list of offenders, especially as he was perched on top of it, and to show his displeasure he howled his head off all the way back to Looe. Added to our very real fears that we might swerve into a ditch were the worries that not only might we be arrested for drunken driving but that we should be reported to the R.S.P.C.A. for transporting a dog in chains along the Queen's highway.

Luckily we made Looe without incident by lunchtime. Wren then unexpectedly announced that we could make a short trip to the island to take any light hand baggage or parcels. We had been haunting Nancollas's store for days to see if our gardening equipment had arrived. This had now come and the removal men must have lifted everything in sight for besides piles of neatly stacked flower pots were boxes containing odd bits of raffia, broken flower pot pieces and near empty cartons of fertilisers and the like. Strings of onions now festooned the bookcases and, well to the fore, we were pleased to see boxes of our seed potatoes. These last seemed ideal to take for, with a bit of luck, we might have an opportunity to plant some. The trip would also be an opportunity to check on the daffodils. It was a constant worry to Mr and Mrs Whitehouse that the daffodils, which often started to bloom at Christmas, would be up and we should not be there to deal with them.

Armed therefore with boxes of seed potatoes, which inexplicably seemed to us the only useful things we could take by hand, we boarded the *Orlando* accompanied by Zena, her husband Peter, Charles and Duncan, trailing our ten-foot metal boat as a dinghy. Toby we left by the fire as there was no time to get Ethrelda as a Toby sitter and at his age we did not want to expose him to arduous sea journeys. After his ordeal by chain in the morning he was in any case quite thankful to rest his weary head.

Once out of the shelter of the harbour, wild seas met us and we literally bounded over the rollers which clawed at us from all sides as they broke over us in clouds of stinging spray. This time we made for the comparative shelter of the jetty beach on the eastern shore of the island. This was protected by an arm of rocks from the westerly gale which was roaring through the Island Roads—the strip of sea between the island and the mainland at Hannafore. Great seas were smashing on the main beach where he had made our previous landing and we were thankful when we at last made the lee of the island. It was tricky, nevertheless, to climb over the side of the *Orlando*, down into the bucking metal boat. Wren rowed me over to the jetty, a kind of small concrete platform built on a shelf of rocks below cliffs that slope down to the sea. The jetty was buttressed by stout upright timbers while behind, rough hewn steps wound their way to the top of the cliff where a path led to the jetty cottage and on to the Island House above and beyond. The posts were designed for tying up a boat—but on a calm day. Today the westerly gale backwashed the seas round the island and together with the ground swell from the spring tide the sea raced past the jetty like an express train. Very skilfully Wren managed to manoeuvre and juggle the metal boat into one of these runs. As we swept past the jetty on the crest of a breaking roller at breakneck speed he yelled "JUMP! Grab a post—it's slippery!" With the abandon of despair I flung myself onto the jetty clinging with both arms round the nearest post as the metal boat shot past from under me. I managed to haul myself on to the jetty which was indeed as slippery as black ice from algae built up over the winter months with rain, and the seas sweeping over it with spring tides. I managed to slither my way on to the steps to await for Babs to be decanted. Wren however had decided that it was too dangerous to land anyone else at the jetty.

I watched apprehensively as he rowed the metal boat with Babs on board between the rocks and over the breakers on to the jetty beach. Massive mounds of seaweed were being piled up on the beach by the crashing rollers. Babs, who was poised in the bows ready to land, now rolled over the side and let the surge of seaweed float her ashore. The others, plus the boxes of seed potatoes, were now landed on the beach too, but Wren, who had found the trip more hazardous than he had expected, would only allow us twenty minutes ashore.

Quickly we chitted out the potatoes, made a hurried tour of the nearest daffodil fields, none of which appeared to be in bloom, then prepared to launch ourselves back over the surging seaweed breakers. Following the custom of the Queen and Prince Philip, Babs and I elected to embark separately on the two trips necessary to transport us to the *Orlando* moored out beyond the rocks. One of us, we reasoned, should try to survive to take over the occupation of the island if ever the elements permitted that day to dawn. Once over the tricky business of negotiating the breakers crashing on the narrow rock channel and boarding the *Orlando*, heaving in the swell, the journey back to Looe harbour seemed comparatively calm and secure, although punctuated with sickening lurches to starboard and unexpected flights into mid air followed by crashes that half drowned us in sheets of spray.

As the sum result of this quite hazardous journey was the landing of a box or so of seed potatoes and a negative search for daffodils we did not feel particularly exultant as we trudged back to the cottage to change into dry clothes once more. We would have been even less elated if we had known that these potatoes, which we later planted with much care, would be stricken with a blight which that year swept the whole country. I doubt whether we harvested more than seven pounds that were edible. In time, labour, and expense no potatoes could surely have cost so much before or since. As at that time we rarely ate potatoes because we were on a diet I think if the phrase "Is your journey really necessary?" had not already been coined we should have invented it ourselves there and then.

Babs was up early the next morning, Sunday, in case Wren called for them to inspect the sea at Hannafore. This would be the last chance for a big move of stores before the next spring tides due in two weeks' time on 30th January. With Mr Nancollas on his tail we knew that Wren would have a try if it were at all possible, although we did not think that there was the remotest chance of yesterday's seas dying down for days even if the gales abated.

High tide at 5.24 a.m. passed and there was no sign of Wren. Lying in bed and listening to the 6.55 a.m. weather forecast I knew why. It forecast storms—gales everywhere—a wild day, becoming more severe. That was enough for me and thankfully I turned over and snuggled down into the pillow. It was as well Babs was up and dressed, for Duncan, his appetite whetted by yesterday's jaunt, called to say that he had walked over to Hannafore and it was quite calm there. This I could not believe. However, Babs and he went to see if perhaps Wren was on the *Orlando* getting it at the ready. As he was not they climbed high up the steep steps to Chapel Ground where his cottage was perched on the side of the Downs. Wren in fact was only just getting up as he too had heard the forecast, but taking Duncan at his word about the state of the sea at Hannafore he said he would be ready in half an hour. Never at my best in the morning I yelled through the ceiling from my warm and cosy bed that I was not going. Babs yelled back from below that she was not going to climb all the way up to "Bali-Hi", the name of Wren's cottage, to tell him so. A most inapposite name for the cottage in the circumstances, I muttered into the pillow.

Meantime Wren and Duncan both arrived for Babs to drive them round to Hannafore so that Wren could inspect the sea for himself. I now arose and dressed, not to get ready but to protest. After all, I wanted to live on the island, not be washed up there as a drowned corpse. A few minutes later they returned and Wren announced categorically that "No fisherman in Looe would go out in a sea like that." Coming from Wren that was a concession indeed; not that we had seen any other boats at sea since we had come at Christmas for the gales had scarcely abated from one spring tide to another. Nevertheless, as I had been the lily-livered one of the quartet I was relieved to hear on the 9 a.m. news, "A wild night everywhere. No one should be out, especially at sea." A comment that was tailor-made for me and confirmed my belief in telepathy.

As consolation Wren brought in the coils of rope purchased the day before and, doing deft things with spikes and thimbles, showed us how to splice rope. The outboard motors were brought out from behind the sofa and in no time at all the one downstair room of our "two up and one down cottage" began to resemble the deck of a ship. The usual stream of visitors now began to call. Zena followed by Charles, Ruth and her mother on their way to Mass, and Mr and Mrs Whitehouse relieved to know that the daffodils were not yet ready for harvesting but still anxious about how we were going to manage the generator without a man. After copious mugs of coffee followed by homemade wine Wren, Duncan, Charles, Ruth, Babs and I walked round to Hannafore at low tide to find the channel Mr Whitehouse had told us they used for rowing the daffodils across to the mainland when it was too rough to make the harbour.

It was easy to find the landmark he had given us on the mainland at low tide for it was in fact the sewerage channel. Fortunately it did not appear to be functioning, which was just as well since it was difficult to keep our feet on the slippery rocks and wet seaweed. We made out way beyond it and now had to find our way among a labyrinth of rocks, all the time keeping a bearing on a point of the island which was the landmark for that side. Unfortunately in mid-channel we were almost mown down by a storm of hailstones, and wet, cold, bruised and all but bleeding we slithered back over the seaweed festooned rocks and returned to the cottage to dry out. It would not have been everyone's idea of a Sunday morning walk and we felt that we had done enough pioneering for one day.

We were joined for lunch by Duncan, a lad of many talents and interests, one of which we had in common and appealed to me enormously—the making and flying of kites. The top of the island seemed an ideal place for kite flying and I only hoped that there would be time to indulge in this pastime. As this was one of the few interests not shared by Babs she rather thought not.

Wren had invited the three of us up to "Bali-Hi" for tea, and, while his wife provided the eats, Wren entertained us with further demonstrations of rope splicing and knot tying. I, for one, had never inherited Dad's aptitude in these skills. I had never been a girl guide and although I had mountaineered among the glaciers and ice peaks of the Alps where the correct tying of a knot was a matter of life and death, and although we had been given instruction during our training period in the W.R.N.S., the art of knot tying had always eluded me. Babs, without the benefit of life in the Navy or the experience of dangling over the edge of a crevasse or precipice on the end of a rope, made a far more apt pupil. Probably due to her penchant for needlework, by the end of the evening she had become quite adept. Nevertheless we had a most enjoyable time; our education had been considerably broadened, for Wren expounded in detail on other maritime matters, all of which we found instructive and fascinating, and it was, to say the least, a novel way of being entertained to Sunday afternoon tea.

Chapter 6

Alarms and excursions

Until the next spring tides were due we reckoned that islandwise it would be a period of marking time; tidying up in Nancollas's store and bracing ourselves for ordeals to come being the order of the day—a lull before the storm we were sanguine enough to hope. In the event there was no lull. Babs, of course, was busy at school finding her bearings and plotting her course there. Certainly a great deal of sorting went on in the store every day. I was round there every morning lugging out some essential that we needed and, ably helped by Zena, did a lot of re-stacking. This was necessitated by the fact that there was a hole in the roof of the store, through which the rain poured. It took a great deal of ingenuity to shield our more precious possessions under hardier ones and much expenditure of energy and sure footwork to achieve this without disaster to the furniture or ourselves.

It was predictable, too, that we should continue to have an increasing number of visitors to our cottage, offering their advice and expressing the usual fears on our behalf. We made sure that we had a good supply of coffee and plenty of homemade wine on tap; not that the hospitality was all one-sided for we received many invitations to visit our new friends.

What we had not anticipated was what can only be described as an adult version of the childhood "whispering" game. In this we recalled you sat in a circle: someone whispered a short sentence or phrase to the next child who in turn whispered what he or she thought had been said to the next one and so on until the last one to complete the circle called out the final version. I suppose all of us as children have had hysterics at what to one's simple childish mind seemed screamingly funny. We now had hysterics of a different kind as our succession of visitors passed on to us the versions they had heard of our supposed plans. Listening to these we felt it prudent to say as little as possible, make suitable disbelieving clicking noises with our tongues, pass the coffee and comment that our only plan was to move ourselves and our furniture over to the island as soon as possible, and that this seemed highly unlikely until the summertime—if then.

We were dumbfounded therefore when a complete stranger stopped us in the street and said that he had had pointed out to him exactly where we were having the airstrip laid down for the landing of aircraft. Next, Mr Sargent, the Harbourmaster, approached Babs and told her that we should have to consult him and get his permission, which he was highly unlikely to give, to build a harbour, as nothing must impede the fishing fleet when they took to sea.

Airstrips! Harbours! A landlocked fishing fleet—the mind boggled. And all because of a few pots that at that moment seemed to have no chance of being thrown at all except in the teeth of a gale in desperation. After all, with only a few months' potting behind me we hardly expected hordes of devotees to come on pilgrimage from all four corners of the earth to pay homage at the feet of my genius, and an airstrip *and* a harbour could be preparation for no less. Babs, of course, told Mr Sargent, a kindly and helpful gentleman, that he had been misinformed, that his fears were quite unfounded as we did not anticipate that our modest income of a teacher's salary and my pension would run to the building of a harbour in the foreseeable future.

Still reeling from these wild rumours of our supposed plans we suddenly found ourselves a subject-for discussion at the Harbour Commissioners' meeting. And we only knew about this when someone brandished a copy of a West Country Sunday paper at us. In this was a report of the meeting at which Mrs Couch, the president, said that she had been approached by Looe boatmen as they viewed with grave concern the danger to which their for-hire boats would be subjected if they were allowed to land on the rocky coast of the island. Mrs Couch herself expressed equal concern. The report did not give any further details of the discussion, but it was enough to fill us with indignation and wrath. The other rumours had us curled up with laughter as they were so ludicrous, but this was more serious; it was a report in print of an official item on the agenda of the Harbour Commissioners' meeting. This was a matter we knew we must do something about.

When I first read the account I could not wait for Babs to get home from school for I had only seen the Sunday paper on the Monday morning after our rope splicing demonstration. Meantime, to work off some of my indignation, Ruth and I went round to the quayside to make an attempt at getting one of the outboard motors started on the fibre glass dinghy. Ruth, unusually for a girl, loved engines and things mechanical, and soon succeeded. Spurred on by, her example I gingerly had a tug, but, remembering the account in the paper, pulled much more violently and the thing miraculously leapt into life. This for some inexplicable reason gave me the inspiration for what we should do—write a letter to the papers, of course! After all, wasn't this what every "Perplexed Blue-eyed", "Distraught Mother of Six", or "Indignant Ratepayer" did when they had a grievance to air or a problem to be solved? We certainly, as "Irate Islanders", qualified for the former, and for our money, the latter too. Accordingly I dashed back to the cottage and drafted a letter, with a copy and a covering letter to be sent to Mrs Couch, for courtesy's sake. After all, she could have done no less than report the grievance made to her and the boatmen had every right to lodge a complaint and express their concern if what they had heard was true. This was the rub. We had no intention of allowing boats to land on our island. Like the previous owners, we intended to guard our privacy jealously. At most we thought that we might let a few privileged private parties of people interested in crafts come to view the pottery, for, simmering at the back of our minds, was an idea—that we should do our bit to keep crafts alive; that in time we might accommodate a few retired craftsmen who would not only make crafts to sell to help support themselves and the island but teach their skills to others. These summer schools would, we hope, make the whole project economically viable. In addition these craftsmen would each contribute something to the common good according to his ability eg. till the land, keep goats, bees and poultry, or be responsible for carpentry, engines etc. All this might be possible with some chance of success if we aimed at a "floating community," we thought, whereby our craftsmen might come for a season only and longer if it worked well. We had no illusions about the difficulties of communal life and knew that its success hinged entirely on the character and personality of each individual and depended hardly at all on the trials, privations and disasters that might have to be endured.

Of one thing we were certain—the island must be kept inviolate— there must be no commercialism. Before the banners of Conservation, Ecology, and Environment were fluttered before the urban populace we were hoisting our own little flag and were determined that any income we might derive from our crafts would be used to help preserve the island as an unspoilt beauty spot. It was no wonder therefore that we were incensed that our modest and, according to our reckoning, worthwhile aims were misconstrued.

Babs on her return vetted the letter and added her comments. In essence it stated what our aims were, asked the press if they would refute these wild rumours that were circulating and suggested rather tartly that it would have been a good idea if someone had approached us about our supposed intentions before reports were officially made and broadcast based merely on hearsay. Furthermore if we did not get the backing of local bodies we would keep the island strictly private and allow no one to land at all, as indeed was and is our right as the owners of private property maintained solely by ourselves, without any financial assistance or grants, local, public or governmental—and a right furthermore that had been strictly preserved by previous owners. And why not? We have yet to meet anyone who would welcome any Tom, Dick or Harry to come and picnic in their back or front garden uninvited. Yet, as we were to find later, there are many who hold the oddest ideas about other peoples property—particularly if it consisted of an island.

Having written all this to our satisfaction we contacted Mrs Clemens, the local correspondent for *The Cornish Times*, a lady with whom we were acquainted. She came round like a shot and was indignant on our behalf. Not only would she re-write her own report intended for the weekly *Cornish Times* due out later in the week, based on our letter, but she would send a copy to the West country daily paper, *The Western Morning News*.

Suddenly it was as though we had set alight to a stick of gelignite. First *The Western Morning News* came out with banner headlines in the centre page "LOOE ISLAND—OWNERS MAKE STATEMENT." This was followed in other papers by similar reports and accounts. Everyone we met seemed to be waving copies of these papers excitedly at us. Later, private indignation meetings were held at odd street corners and outside shops—meetings to which we were invited to join—to protest because one paper had made no report at all. The anger quickly subsided however when this particular newspaper joined in and published our letter in full. This was only Tuesday but that same evening Westward Television flashed a picture of the island on the screen and quoted excerpts from our letter. This caused a great deal of excitement in Looe, for being mentioned on television was fame indeed, and we were the centre of many little group meetings in the baker's, the greengrocer's and the butcher's. At school the children were full of it and thrilled that their teacher had been quoted on T.V.

We, in fact, did not see the item for we had been invited that evening to Ruth's house to try some of her mother's home-made wine. We were also introduced to some friends, the husband of one of whom said that he gave us twelve months on the island and then we should give up—if we were not drowned beforehand! Although we were quite flattered, as we had heard that most of the fishermen only gave us three months, we replied succinctly that at the present rate of progress we doubted if we would even have taken up residence by then.

The next day we were asked if we would appear on Television that very evening. A car would call for us and take us to the studios in Plymouth. We politely declined, our main reason for refusing being that we should not have had time to have had our hair done—and this was not the last time we opted out of appearing on television for this reason. We were told what good publicity it would be, an incentive we have never appreciated for it sounded to us more like a commercial for a laxative or a breakfast cereal proclaiming how "good it was for you". Maybe it was all right for some, but we did not *want* publicity, and even if we had, the state of our hair was the over-riding factor.

Also, by return, we received a charming letter from Mrs Couch thanking us for sending her a copy of our letter to the press, wishing us well in our project and hoping that sometime she would be able to come over and visit us.

This particular furore died down as suddenly as it had arisen and was rather neatly finished off, we thought, by the receipt of a letter from the *Western Morning News* enclosing a postal order for 5/– for publication of our letter—the going rate at the time. How nice, we thought, to be paid for laying down the law. We made it, too, the first contribution to our Island Fund.

The furore did not so much die down as became superseded by another. Mr Nancollas called round to say that he had again arranged for a fisherman to take over the furniture and the expedition was all fixed up for the next day. We sympathised with him for we knew that he really needed his store for his auction sales, but we knew also that Wren would be needled to say the least. Either way we did not think that we should come out of the situation too well. If the furniture were taken out the next day would it—we dare not even ask—be left on the jetty or the beach, exposed to the elements? There would be no Wren to move it by the caterpillar tractor; Babs would be at school, as would be our schoolboy helpers, Charles and

Duncan. It seemed that either our furniture would be left high but not dry on the beach or Wren would feel impelled to have a go at the week-end whatever the weather. We knew that very little daunted him weatherwise; it was going to be a case of "Fasten your safety belts!" either way, for if the weather did foul up Wednesday it would surely worsen with the increasing spring tides due on Saturday.

Wren called in later and when we told him of the plan for tomorrow, as we expected, his generally cheery face blackened and he went off downcast and despondent. Later he returned his face beaming once more. "Good news," he announced, "Gales are forecast for tomorrow, and the wind is already getting up."

He was right, terrific snowstorms and floods hit the whole country that night. The next morning we found West Looe Quay under water and cars and boats were lined up alongside each other deep in the overflowing banks of the river just as they were on our first visit to Looe fourteen months ago. With the combination of gales, rain and winter spring tides the river could not contain the volume of water which was rising rapidly and fast approaching Nancollas's store. With some of our furniture wet from the leak in the roof above and now threatened with the overflowing river flooding in from below it did not seem to have much chance of surviving. Alfy Martin however assured us that all would be well for even if the water did reach the store they had storm barricades at the ready. What were we worrying about with only the ordeal by sea for our possessions to face? We were relieved now that the books were safely on the other side; but should we ever join them, we wondered wistfully, and would there ever be an opportunity to read them again?

The tension mounted as it always did prior to a proposed voyage over. Nevertheless there was nothing much we could do before Saturday so we were happy to accept an invitation to the home of Mrs Coon, the school secretary, to meet her husband who was a keen and knowledgeable amateur ornithologist. He had a rare collection of books, especially on his chosen subject, many first editions and beautifully leather bound priceless volumes which lined the wall of all the rooms and the hall. We had a splendid evening and looked forward to a visit from him to the island at a later date. This he subsequently made and we learned a great deal from him about the wild life of the island. It is sad to realise that we can learn no more from him.

We also paid another visit to Miss Kempster and Miss Hoyle who had invited us round for the evening. They were most interested in our project as Miss Hoyle herself did pottery and Miss Kempster, a retired headmistress, was having lessons in painting from a local artist. They have both been over to the island several times to see how we are progressing and never fail to buy a piece of pottery to help the Island Funds. Miss Hoyle, who came from a Looe family, actually had a relative who was one of those who was born in our No 1 cottage. We invited them round to tea the following week, an invitation which we gave with some misgivings for they had a very nice comfortable home perched a little way up one of the steep roads leading to the downs from the quayside, and it had a fine panoramic view of the river and harbour and the hills rising above East Looe. Our little home on the other hand, much as we loved it, currently resembled a cross between a railway station and the deck of a ship, a ship, moreover, halfway to shipwreck. The tiny cobbled courtyard, picturesque in less hectic days, could now best be described as a shunting yard; beyond our acquisitions which had overspilled there from the cottage there was no outlook at all except the side of a cottage looking down on us from its higher level—hardly, we thought, the setting for an "At Home".

On the way we made a diversion to the store to find a projector as Zena, who had by now introduced her brother George from East Looe to our little circle of "Islanders", wanted us to see some of his colour slides—close-ups of butterflies, birds and flowers. After much clambering about in the dark we found it but by the time we got back to the cottage it was too late for a film show, added to which certain parts of the projector and plugs were missing. The next morning I was despondently searching for these bits and pieces for it was cold and wet in the store when Ruth, knowing where to find me, arrived in great excitement as she had found a source of manure, an item for which I had sent out calls in readiness for our proposed mushroom growing. She knew someone who had a riding school and we could have as much as we wanted just for the fetching. Highly elated, we collected up some sacks of this rich by-product of the horse, then we carried it on to a clearing owned by her father, where there was much wood to be had for the picking-up. With great expertise she showed me how to split wood with a single blow and with the two choppers which she had thoughtfully brought along we soon had a good collection of firewood. Unfortunately it began to pour with rain and the wood got very wet. I had in mind to present some to Ethrelda who at her age felt the cold, and she enjoyed nothing better than to bask in the warmth of her open fire.

Even in Cornwall we were having flurries of snow in the rain, and the rest of the country was practically ice-bound. We called in at our cottage to dry the wood off by the fire and then, to finish our winter "harvest festival", we went by car to some nearby woods to gather some moss for Ruth's mother who wanted some for her flower baskets. Contrary to the saying about gathering moss I felt very much like a rolling stone. I had literally rolled from one minor activity to another as I waited for Babs to come home from school for the week-end so that we could prepare ourselves for the move that we anticipated Wren would call for the next morning, whatever the weather, which had shown no signs of improving.

It was fortunate that Zena postponed the film show, due to Peter having a cold, for Ethrelda called to ask if she and her daughter Muriel who was visiting her from "up country" could spend the evening with us. This of course did not prevent other visitors from popping in, including our friend of helicopter and pipe-lines-over-the-sea fame, Zena with her brother George who offered to bring private parties over in his boat the *Crilla*, and a couple of "up country" emigrants who had only just seen the reports in the press about us and thought we might be interested in reading them! Ruth also dropped in to pass on the message from Duncan's mother that if we should go to the island tomorrow we must on no account let Duncan use the caterpillar tractor as he was subject to epileptic fits. Finally Wren appeared to say, as we suspected, that he thought it might be possible to make an attempt in the morning. Mr Nancollas had been after him and as after this week-end the next spring tides would not be due until February 6th we knew, as a matter of pride, that Wren was after winning the "Nancollas Spring Handicap", fishermen aiming to pip him at the post or not. We managed to squeeze everyone into our tiny cottage and at one stage the room began to resemble an overloaded lifeboat, an illusion heightened by the howling wind and slashing wind outside and the talk of the proposed journey into the elements on the morrow.

Chapter 7
Storm noises—off stage and on

As high tide was not until 9.57 a.m. Wren called next morning at the reasonable hour of 8.30 a.m. and for the first time Babs took him round to inspect the sea at Hannafore in almost broad daylight. Although a southerly gale was forecast Wren thought that we should be able to make it. Since coming to live on the island we have come to dread a winter southerly gale perhaps more than any other for we are particularly exposed to the south, and our bedroom and lounge are both facing in this direction. It is a wind that always seems to blow at force 8, 9 or even 10; it rips off tiles, blows down trees and is accompanied invariably by a slashing rain that penetrates usually watertight windows, seeps through the roof and doors, and generally makes life unusually unbearable. In a severe storm the sea breaks over the cliff top, flinging seaweed and bits of rocks over on to the end of the garden. The wind hurls itself against the window with such violence that sleep is almost impossible, and when I have been alone on the island it can be a daunting experience wondering what havoc the dawn will reveal, or if one will survive till the dawn.

In my ignorance then I happily began to hum *Blow the Wind Southerly*. Now I can never hear that lovely song without thinking that Kathleen Ferrier or the composer could never have experienced a southerly gale—Cornish style. If I had the gift of composition I would certainly give it an *1812* tempi and ordain that none but a Wagnerian quartet should sing it with organ accompaniment that would make the *Ride of the Valkyries* sound like an afternoon jaunt in a pony and trap by comparison.

Knowing nothing of what awaited us we cheerfully went round to Nancollas's store and helped by Charles, Duncan and Ruth began the task of moving out everything that we thought we should want and Wren thought he could manage, and put it on to the quayside. Now began the task of lowering the furniture by ropes over the side and down into the *Orlando*. It was as well Wren was so competent, as his crew consisted of we three females and two schoolboys. Later we were joined by a passer-by, Den Smith, who in the season ran a speed boat. While Wren lashed everything down Babs and I went and did some shopping for food. We ran into Mr and Mrs Whitehouse who were still anxious on our behalf. In fact Mr Whitehouse offered to come over with us there and then to look at the machinery and show us how the generator worked. Knowing the state of his health and the fact that it was mid-winter we thought that this would be most unwise. Regretfully he had to agree, but we thought nevertheless how kind it was of them to take such an interest in our welfare. Of course they knew what difficulties we would be up against, and they found it hard to understand that in spite of their warnings and advice we should be insouciant about the whole affair. Knowing what we now know we would probably have been as concerned as they were. However, we would never have got to this stage or bought the island in the first place if we had weighed the pros and cons at every juncture. We had come from the wrong family to do otherwise or be put off by a few difficulties.

At last the *Orlando*, heavily laden with our precious possessions dangling precariously from furniture perched aloft the wheelhouse, nosed her way slowly towards the open sea. All went well at first although the sea was roughening as we left the shelter of the harbour. The furniture creaked ominously and there were the usual wild lurches as we crossed the bar. With each of these crashes Babs leaned over to hang on to a heavy antique chair that for some reason, probably an afterthought, was suspended over the stern and seemed in imminent danger of nose diving to the sea bed and becoming treasure trove for some deep sea diver of a future generation.

The troubles really began when Wren tried to beach the Orlando. This, we have since realised, is never attempted by a sea-going boat of that size and with that draught on an open beach even in the summer on a dead calm day. As the island had no harbour a boat with the draught of the *Orlando* would moor off in deep water and landing would be made by dinghy. This of course was impossible with furniture to land. On the previous occasions Wren had skilfully beached the *Orlando* by bringing her in so far, moored off while she was still afloat and as the fast out going spring tide receded put down "legs" to keep the *Orlando* from keeling over as she was left high and dry. The difficulty now was that the sea was already making up fast with the outgoing tide, whereas one might have expected the southerly gale to break with the incoming tide in the late afternoon. The result was that great seas, made vicious by the ground swell, came running in slewing the *Orlando* round and in danger of bringing her broadside on. In the shallow water, as the rollers receded far out leaving her high and dry, helpless she might keel over. We only knew this with hindsight as we have many times had this difficulty with our own boat the *Islander* which is only a 22 ft motor boat, but as lethal as a torpedo as she charges helplessly with the speed of an express train in the raging surf that beats on these shores long after the gales themselves have abated.

All we knew at the time, luckily for our peace of mind—comparative peace of mind that is—was that we were in some difficulty. We had no real fears, for Wren, the most competent of seamen, would not engage in any situation unless he could forsee a way of dealing with it. But he loved a challenge and would accept any that would test his skill and ability. This proved to be one of many subsequent ones in which we were to be involved.

As we were hurled to the shore by the breakers Wren ordered Charles, Duncan and Ruth to leap over the surf on to the beach. As they floundered ashore Wren threw them a rope and roared to them to pull and hang on for dear life. Babs, and Zena who had joined us at the last minute, were ordered aft on to the deck head for balance, while I was detailed to take up my station amidships, for ballast presumably, ready to be sent scuttling wherever the need for weight was greatest. Wren himself disappeared astern.

Suddenly he yelled "It's my transom!" above the roar of the sea as the *Orlando* was swept out with the tide. For one moment I thought he was referring to a part of the male anatomy about which I had not heard and which was now at risk. Then it passed through my mind that perhaps it was a Cornish expression for trousers and that they were being ripped off by the breakers. Suddenly I realised from the gesticulating going on astern that it was a very important part of the boat that was in danger.

Meantime Charles, Duncan and Ruth with heels dug into the shingle were lying flat on their backs and tugging on the rope to try to keep the bows from slewing round. Wren roared at them at intervals, "PULL! PULL! HARDER" and as their heels scrunched even deeper into the shingle and they lay even flatter on their backs they looked for all the world like the losing team in a tug of war. Babs and Zena bobbed up and down on their precarious perch while I was slung around like a sack of potatoes as I clung to the deep freeze, of all things.

Wren at long last managed to steady the boat and by much heaving by the younger generation and skill on Wren's part, with a mighty scrunch the *Orlando* was at last beached with her legs down to keep her upright.

Wren seemed quite happy, so presumably the transom had been saved. This operation of beaching the *Orlando* had taken about an hour and by now the sea was far out. As soon as we had scrambled ashore I took photos, but we were distressed to find many dead gulls on the beach, victims of the furious wind—a sight unfortunately to which we have now become somewhat inured, so common is it during the long months of winter gales.

Wren soon had the caterpillar out and he, Charles and Duncan, unloaded and began the long haul of rumbling up the steep shingle path from sea level to our house on the cliff, possibly a third of a mile trailing loads of furniture. Ruth was left on the boat as "look out", though looking out for what it was difficult to conjecture. One thing was certain: it would not be for the fishing fleet or any other craft except possibly a fugitive Russian submarine for I was willing to swear that there was nothing afloat around the coasts of Britain that day except ocean going liners or ships of the Royal Navy making hard for port.

Zena now came into her own and took charge of the kitchen, for the simple reason that she was the only one slim enough to weave her way among the packing cases, washing machine, deep freeze, refrigerator, bookcases and other large pieces of furniture all of which were festooned with smaller articles. As the boys piled more and more furniture and boxes into the kitchen and then into the hall we were in danger of being incarcerated for the rest of our natural life. With the brilliance born of despair we now evolved a system of self preservation for the claustrophobic among us. Two of us managed to fight our way out and as the boys pushed more and more furniture through the open door Zena tossed articles and books over the increasing mountain of what is quaintly called artefacts to us. We then loaded these into wheelbarrows and trundled them down to what was once a barn and has now become our craft room. So we established our first transit camp on the island. As a brickmaking machine nestled alongside wine-making equipment, a telescope and a soil sterilizing stove we did have a passing thought about what archaeologists of the future would make of this little lot as with puzzled grunts they unearthed the remains in perhaps the year 4000.

This operation was going very well and Zena had just pioneered her way across the kitchen to the stove to make a nice cup of tea all round when two things happened simultaneously. Babs and I, who had cunningly wormed our way to the scullery sink by the back door turned on the tap to fill the kettle which Zena had more or less lobbed over to us. The water that gushed out was a foaming brown liquid with a most vile stench that had us retching on the spot. We looked at it, horrified, and Wren barked over his shoulder as he roared off in the caterpillar like a latter day chari-oteer, "Everyone to the boat at once! The gale has got up and the sea is rough!"

The rain lashed at us as we clambered on board. Darkness fell. Wren clad in oilskins and sou'wester had us all lined up, as with grim face he told us exactly what we were to do.

"It is not just a question of saving the boat," he announced, "it is a matter of life and death!" He explained that we could not take off until there was sufficient water to float the *Orlando*. Tremendous seas were running in, crashing over us from the west and threatening to capsize us. The next moment they sucked back leaving the *Orlando* high and dry and, without the support of the sea, she was again in danger of keeling over.

"Do what I tell you, instantly!" he ordered. At that moment a huge sea crashed down on us. "Everyone to port!" yelled Wren. We all hurled our-selves over to the other side of the boat. "To starboard!" roared Wren. And we all scrambled back again. We could not anticipate which way we had to throw ourselves for in that broiling sea the breakers came in all direc-tions and Wren hung over the side judging to a nicety exactly where and when the next roller would break over us. We were not allowed to move except as ordered, for it would have upset the balance of the boat. We could see huge breakers creaming over the rocks even in the darkness—it was that wild. Rain poured down our necks in spite of sou'westers and oilskins, but we had much implicit faith in Wren that in the short intervals we sat as though we were in a bus and Zena and I had a long discussion about piles, of all things, inspired by the fact that we were sitting in pools of an icy mixture of rain and sea water. And so we went on hurling our-selves to port or starboard as directed. There was no confusion as to which was which for we knew it was the opposite side to where we happened to be; we just pitched ourselves bodily across from one side of the boat to the other and hoped for the best. It was fortunate that Wren did not spice his orders with "Abaft! Abeam! Hard Astern! Amidships!" or whatever, for we surely would have finished up doing a nautical version of the Lancers or the Grand Old Duke of York.

Wren did clever things with his precious transom and at last, after about an hour, and with much creaking and lurching of the gallant *Orlando* we could feel deep water under us and we were afloat! Once away from the

113

shelter of the western rocks of the island the full force of the gale hit us. Wren however looked happy and relaxed now that he had only the straightforward problem of a raging storm to cope with. In spite of a very rough passage indeed, when we were tossed about like discarded clothing, and sodden clothing at that, we finally sailed safely into Looe Harbour.

Wren, who is practically a teetotaler, came into *The Jolly Sailor* near the cottage and we all had a rum to warm us up. Wren now asked if Babs and I would come along with him to see his father to placate him, as Wren said that he would be very angry that he had been at sea on a night like this. Babs and I accordingly went along as a kind of buffer but we really could not think of anything to say that would make the expedition sound like a Saturday night pleasure trip. Mr Toms, for whom Wren had a great respect and affection, was very angry indeed. "You take risks," he said wagging his finger at Wren, "and one day you will meet an unlucky sea. No one else would think of going out in that weather. You should listen to what the old fishermen say before going out in a sea like that." We knew that it was a bit of bad luck that the southerly gale had blown up earlier than anticipated and we knew that Wren had dealt with the problems with consummate skill. To him it had merely been a challenge to his ability to cope with the situation. We did not think our opinion would carry much weight as we were the wrong sex, age and occupation to vaunt expert knowledge. So far we had not said anything helpful and in fact, apart from "Good evening", all I did venture to remark was that if Sir Francis Drake had listened to the old fishermen he would probably have finished by being just an old fisherman. Just then Wren's wife came in, presumably to see if her husband were still alive. The conversation then petered out and we all went home.

The next morning Wren turned up bright as a button to say he thought it was calm enough to make another trip. Luckily it began to pour with rain and as Wren does not like getting wet from plain ordinary rain, he called it off. It was just as well for the sake of our remaining furniture, for at least by remaining in Nancollas's store only some of it would get wet.

We might justifiably have looked forward to a Sunday day of rest after the tribulations and labours of the day before, but it was not to be. From the word go the usual constant stream of people began to call, headed by the Whitehouses, who said that the whole of Looe was talking about our exploit. Most of the day we politely handed round cups of coffee as we listened to everyone's opinion, the consensus of which appeared to be that we were quite mad, that we were hardly likely to survive long enough to take up residence on the island, and that if we did, it was reiterated that after three months we would have "had it". It appeared that half the population had been watching from Hannafore the voyage of *The African Queen*, as the indomitable *Orlando* had been universally dubbed. No one had apparently expected us to return alive. Before the coffee finally ran out Wren brought in a little light relief by hospitably inviting Babs and me on board the *Orlando*, as he had stripped down the engine and he thought we might like to see it. "Soho, here we come!" we exclaimed gaily as we poured the last dregs of coffee down the sink and made tracks for the quayside for the "stripping". "Your transom's very 'andsome," I volunteered, bringing in rather aptly, I thought, the Cornish expression to describe anything praiseworthy. Then I left Babs, as the more mechanical one, to appreciate the finer points of the intestines of the hospitalized and surely weary *Orlando*.

Chapter 8

Social and unsocial interludes

The next day we met Mr Nancollas who was a bit irate because not everything had been removed from his store. When we explained what a tricky operation it had been to move even one load he instantly mellowed and invited us into *The Jolly Sailor* for drinks. He had a lot of worries on his mind for, as Chairman of the Council, he was responsible for arranging a memorial service for Winston Churchill on the following Saturday. Nevertheless he said that he was arranging a cocktail party for us and Friday February 5th was fixed as a hopeful date for our farewell launching party.

As it was a bright sunny day, although bitterly cold with the rest of the country still under snow and ice, Ruth and I thought that we would try out the outboard motor on the fibre glass dinghy again and if it were calm enough go out to the island in it. I had been out to the island before in a small boat when a friend came to visit us in October. Babs and I had navigated keeping to the same channel between what we thought were beds of seaweed as the professional boatman had taken us. It was as well that our judgement had proved correct for what we thought was seaweed darkening the sea round the beach were in fact reefs of rock and the channel through them very narrow indeed. What we did not know until we came to live on the island was that winter gales can change the whole outline of the foreshore many times, covering some rocks with shoals of sand and seaweed and exposing others that had not been seen for many years. Channels and landing points have to be carefully assessed and can be quite different between one summer and another, depending on the ravages of the winter seas. Knowing none of this at that time I was quite optimistic at steering through the "sea-weed beds" again if the seas of the week-end had died down enough for us to get out of the harbour.

I like rowing and feel at home in a boat, but I am only used to the conventional wooden row boat. I was therefore disconcerted to find that a fibre glass boat bounces on top of the water like a cork and reacts to the slightest movement of its occupants. As Ruth and I took it in turns to pull at the starting cord of the outboard motor, with both our weights and that

of the motor in the stern, the bows pointed skywards and with each unsuc-
cessful tug it felt that we might go spiralling upwards into outer space at
any moment. When in addition the boat started to leak I decided that perhaps it would be unwise to make an island trip. With the help of Zena who
had appeared as though conjured up like a spirit from the deep I stepped
out on the quayside. Ruth decided to have another go at getting the engine
started. This she successfully did, but for some fathomless reason, as the
boat got under way it meandered slowly in semi-circles, finally fouling the
ropes of the *Orlando*. We managed to get it disentangled, I pulling from
the quay. Ruth disembarked, and we decided to call it quits for that day.
All this time we were watched by some of the fishermen on the quayside.
Not one of them made any remark but I did wonder what they thought of
our antics, especially when I listened to the weather reports and heard
that wild seas were still lashing our coasts, and in particular in the South-
west.

Zena and I had arranged to go to the Catering Exhibition at Truro on
the following day, with a view to laying up stores in bulk. The island
seemed so inaccessible that we were now planning to take up residence
there as though we were going to the Antarctic with no hope of seeing
"dry land" again for a year at least.

It therefore was not strictly necessary to have a demonstration of an ice
cream making machine, but we were fascinated by being able to get cor-
nets out of it fully charged with ice cream. Regretfully we decided that it
would not fit in with our plans—varied though they were. Also, it cost
£8000.

Next our attention was caught by the Hammond Organ display. This
seemed a "must" for the future. We tried one out that took our fancy and as
the chords swelled and echoed round the Exhibition we got quite carried
away until we found that it cost £1000. The salesman then introduced us to
one that only cost £600, but that one did not appeal to us half as much. I
then explained that what with an overdraft, a bridging loan and mortgages
I for one could not afford one at all. The salesman did not mind a bit and
offered to bring one over to the island to demonstrate. He said that it did
not matter how long we left the idea in abeyance for he found that if
people were really interested, as we obviously were, they would buy
one eventually although it might be after an interval of years. Up to a point
he was right. A few years later Zena did *buy* one and many times Babs
from the cottage has heard the mellow notes of hymns wafting across

from Zena's house on the other side of the Square. The salesman, if he should read these words, must forgive me, for although I, too, eventually bought an organ, it was (alas! for his sales), a church organ, the acquisition of which and its removal to the island almost deserves a chapter to itself when the time comes to relate it.

So far we had only looked at equipment that depended on electricity. As no one thought us capable of running the generator anyway perhaps it was just as well that we transferred our attention to food. The weather was still bitterly cold and we had negotiated icy roads to get to the Exhibition, so bulk soup figured largely in our purchases. In fact the consignment we bought that day lasted us for five years on the island and remained in good condition to the end, and a gargantuan tin of salt was only finished last year. I acquired a lot of free samples, made some good contacts and, as the Exhibition was open for the rest of the week, I told the various salesmen and demonstrators that I should be back with my sister if we did not manage to make a trip to the island.

The next day I spent quite a time in Nancollas's store looking for various articles. We had now been in the cottage since before Christmas and there was always something we were needing for our enforced stay on the mainland. On one visit I took the young assistant from the television shop as somewhere in the store were two television sets; one, which had been given us, needed overhauling and putting in working order, and our own, which was now required for Saturday. This was the day of Winston Churchill's funeral and Ethrelda had asked if she could come and watch it on television. Luckily neither set appeared to have suffered from the leaking roof, for they had been well protected by the removal men in the first place.

Wren called on Friday to say that the wind was in the East, a direction hated by all the local boatmen. In any case, he said he did not intend to try for a move the next day; he did not think that it was quite the thing to have an expedition over to the island on the day of Churchill's funeral, so he was going to move furniture for his father instead. His reasoning being, we supposed, that moving his father's furniture was a humdrum, run of the mill chore, whereas a move over to the island could be rated as an epic Saturday spectacular providing entertainment on a grand scale for the gallery of locals at Hannafore.

So on Saturday morning Babs and I prepared to make another visit to the Catering Exhibition, but we were not surprised that Ruth and her mother, whom we had invited to accompany us, did not turn up, for the roads were icier than ever and their house at Sunrising, on the hills above Looe, would be virtually icebound. We were late starting. For one thing we were held up by the usual round of visitors offering advice, help and the customary hair tearing about how we were going to manage on the island. We suspected that in some cases it was a matter of finding out if we were still alive and if so whether we had been carted off to the looney bin. After that it was difficult to get the car started and when Babs finally got it going Ruth turned up on foot and was most surprised to find that although we had not gone, we were still going! It was too late for her to negotiate the mile climb up to Sunrising and slide down again with her mother, so Babs and I set off, skating carefully round the bending 40 mile run into Truro.

We need not have bothered about being late because out of respect for Churchill the Exhibition was not opening until 2 p.m. Babs was most impressed with the Exhibition. She approved the mammoth orders, whisked me firmly past the Hammond Organ Section, and did the round of the free samples. Most of the demonstrators remembered me and were pleased to meet Babs, for the fact that you are going to live on your own island acts like a magic password. It puts one in a different class from those who merely own a Rolls Royce, a swimming pool and a villa in the South of France or the Costa What-have-you, judging by the effect it has on people. If only they knew that financially it was, in our case, done by mirrors, and living on it a cross between *The Birth of a Nation*, and *Sunday Night at the Palladium* with overtones of *Alice in Wonderland*.

Our favourite stand that bitter cold afternoon was the Cornish Mead display, the samples there not only warming up our chilled blood but inspiring us to set ourselves up with a few bottles to take back with us as an insurance against the cold.

Ethrelda asked if she could bring her daughter, Muriel, to watch the recording of the funeral that evening. We put out some refreshment plus some Cornish mead and, having installed our visitors, went over to Zena's for the postponed showing of the slides. It may seem odd to leave guests to entertain themselves, being absent hostesses so to speak, but the truth was that we did not want to watch the funeral. I think we felt that it might bring home to us what the outcome of our own little flirtation with destiny might be. Zena, who had been with us on some of our more hazardous expeditions possibly felt the same for she did not intend to watch it either—hence the film show of birds and flowers—not, we thought, a disrespectful entertainment. Around 10.30 p.m. her brother George and his wife, having shown us some very fine slides, now expected to see the late showing of the day's solemn proceedings so we excused ourselves on account of our neglected guests. On the way over we ran into Wren who, with his wife, was trundling some of his father's furniture in a truck, so even that little chore had been relegated to the hours of darkness, when the day of national mourning was finally over.

As Wren had forecast, an easterly gale blew up on the Sunday so we now had just one more week to wait for what we hoped would be the penultimate move with furniture before we took up residence and prove at first hand how we would make out on *Desert Island Discs*, a programme that never failed to fascinate us. We were keyed up with excitement, and as far as we could see the intervening week would be a social one culminating with the cocktail party on Friday.

First Miss Hoyle and Miss Kempster were coming to tea on Monday, February 1st. The date made us realise what a very-long month January had been and how much had happened since leaving Surrey just before Christmas even though we were still living on the mainland. Now, although it will have been apparent that during this time we had been involved almost non-stop in entertaining—that is, when we were not actually on the high seas or marooned on the gale lashed shores of our island—these were the first guests we had actually *invited*. Therefore we felt we must put on some sort of show. By this we did not mean that we should bring out the best linen and china that in any case was still in Nancollas's store, but we did want them to feel that they were not only welcome but expected. It was all very well to scream at droppers-in, "MIND THAT ROPE!" while you handed round coffee in mugs rinsed out under the tap and offer biscuits, if any, from a packet. Our regulars had not only come to expect this reception, but actually liked it, for it made them feel at home. If on the other hand you are an invited guest you do at least expect a chair to sit on, and not have a pile of debris tipped off on to the floor before you can do so. Ruth therefore volunteered to come and help do some housework before our guests arrived. Neither of us claimed housework as our forte, having other interests to occupy our time, but we set to with a will. We swept out the sand and seaweed, made sure the rope was stowed well away, made neat piles of Ethrelda's sticks of wood drying by the fire, and after a thorough do of dusting and polishing, the room would certainly have passed muster for a new "daily" if she was coming for the first time to clean up. The only problem was what to do with the sacks of manure. If we put it out in the courtyard it would spoil the picturesque look for, bearing in mind that Miss Hoyle's aunt had been born in our cottage next door and she might have looked on the visit partly as a sentimental journey into the past, we had stuffed everything that was in the courtyard out of sight or carted it round to Nancollas's store. So for once the courtyard did not look like a transit camp and was as picturesque and charming as the day we had first seen it framing the top half of the vendor of the cottage in the horse box door. We sniffed at the bags. There was no smell so we shoved them behind the sofa with the outboard motors and coils of rope.

Ruth had just rapidly and discreetly disappeared out of the courtyard when our guests arrived, accompanied by Babs who, just arrived from school, wore not only civilised clothes but a look of relief to find the usual shipwreck transformed into an old world fishermen's cottage again.

We had a very pleasant time and thoroughly enjoyed discussing among other things the local flora and fauna, for both our visitors were keen naturalists. Miss Hoyle lent us a book on lichen and fungi and will not have realised until she reads these words how close she was sitting to a relative of the real thing.

After they had gone Zena dropped in with some haemmorrhoid cream done up in Christmas paper in a Bisto tin, in case the need should arise, she said, after our mid-winter night ride sitting in pools of icy water! She almost did not come in for she thought she had come to the wrong cottage—it looked so tidy and respectable.

The next day should have been uneventful. We had been invited to spend the evening with Ethrelda and as there had been no drama on the high seas at the week-end, no frantic callers were expected forecasting doom and disaster. Having just acquired a book on *Cooking in Norway and Denmark* I had experimented with some quite ambitious open sandwiches, made some ice-cream with Saturday's free samples topped with banana, walnuts and cream, put it in the fridge and settled down to some wood carving with a piece of driftwood I had picked up on the island. It was an exciting shape. I decided it should be called Sun God of the Incas and had just inserted the edge of the chisel when something, I do not know what, made me look up. There in the doorway which had opened silently stood the figure of a man. Something seemed to clutch at my heart. Nevertheless I said "Good morning," but there was no answer. An eerie feeling crept over me as the man neither moved nor spoke. I put down my Sun God of the Incas and stood up. The thought flashed through my mind that perhaps as my blade incised into the wood I had conjured up a spirit from the ancient world, an angry god who objected to my tampering with their sacred relics of which this might well be one. But the figure in the doorway did not emanate sunrays nor belch forth wrathful clouds of smoke from its nostrils. It wore a raincoat, trilby hat and glasses. The face began to twitch and I gripped my carving tool just in case . . . Suddenly the man began to giggle, threw off his hat and glasses, spat out his orange peel teeth to reveal no sinister stranger—but Zena. After that we went over to her place to make some Cornish pasties and simmer down from laughter and hysterics which can be quite as exhausting as drama on the high seas.

Ethrelda was thrilled with her supply of firewood and we had a very pleasant evening by her fire as she told us tales in her rich Cornish dialect. In the middle of this a friend of hers called. She wore a red hat, a kind of tammy, and although she took her coat off and settled down she did not take the hat off. After she had gone Ethrelda volunteered the information that she never did take it off and the saying went that she kept all her money under it. I have often thought since that the same could be said about me because when the easterlies blow I have to practically live in a fisherman's woolly cap; the only difference being that mine would be stuffed with I.O.U.'s and final demands. Actually she had some nerve trouble for which later she had to go for hospital treatment. She was a very cultured lady, of good family and she had a beautiful speaking voice. It was fascinating to listen to her telling local folklore and especially so when she told us exactly where buried treasure was reputed to be on the island. Many times we had heard from local people about the buried treasure that they vowed was on the island. It was also said that there were tunnels leading to the mainland used by the smugglers in olden times. If all the tunnels that we had heard about existed the harbour master would be a sorely troubled man, for the sea would surely have drained away into this labyrinth of subterranean tunnels and the fishing fleet would be landlocked indeed and never able to put to sea again. One such was supposed to come out in the "Smugglers" restaurant in East Looe and only last year we were told that the owner had excavated it as far as the Banjo Pier. We could not wait to get on the island and look for the buried treasure and the tunnels ourselves, although often it seemed that that day would never come and I would spend the rest of my life in Nancollas's store and Babs would spend hers shuttling to and fro to Hannafore with Wren to inspect the state of the sea.

I had to make yet another visit to the store to hunt for evening shoes for the cocktail party, although I had doubts as to whether I would be able to get into them again after spending so much of my time in sea boots. Fortunately they did fit but it did seem strange to wear a cocktail dress again after practically living in jeans, a seaman's jersey, oilskins and a sou'wester.

We had an excellent evening. The guests chosen to meet us appeared to be bankers, hoteliers and financiers—people whom Mr Nancollas had thoughtfully decided might well be of assistance to us in the future.

In our former existence cocktail parties were a part of everyday life. One was inured and sipped drinks amid the rising murmur of small talk with no more effect than downing lemonade. As the drinks diminished and the noise correspondingly increased one would be stimulated into thinking that the inconsequential remarks tossed around were the quintessence of wit good enough for the West End stage. It was all, as these affairs are, rather frothy and transient and already half forgotten by the next day. Such light sophistication however was a thing of the past and I for one was out of training. At the end of the evening I suddenly felt very tired. I put it down to all the exertions of the past few weeks, the sea journeys, humping of furniture and all the acrobatics performed in Nancollas's store; it had finally caught up on me I told myself sleepily but happily. Whatever the reason, when we left all I wanted to do was to go home and fall into bed. This was not possible for we had been invited to go on to visit Mr and Mrs Bassett. Mrs Bassett was a colleague of Babs, and her husband, a geologist, was going to show us some of his collection of rocks and minerals. Naturally Babs was very keen as this expert knowledge would help her enormously with her stone cutting and polishing. We had not been there very long when suddenly right bang in the middle of a conversation I fell asleep. I was out like a light.

Waking suddenly I saw an array of sparkling chips of rock swimming before my eyes. "Ha!" I exclaimed, fishing out some dim memory of the long ago schooldays "Iron pyrites!" Incredibly they *were* iron pyrites and the remark might have saved the day but for the fact that I promptly fell asleep again. Mrs Bassett has been over to the island several times since and it may be just imagination on my part but it seems to me that she looks very thoughtfully at me when I reach for the homemade wine bottle to pour some out for my guests.

Chapter 9

Unrehearsed incidents

The next day when we hoped to move most of the remaining furniture the wind was in the north east and fresh, but although it was only the 6th of February the bitterness had gone out of the wind. It was not exactly warm, but the wind did not cut you in two.

We cleared Nancollas's store of everything but a motley collection of garden tools, some wine carboys and *the* bookcase, which Wren unfortunately thought might be too big for him to manage. The *Orlando* as usual looked overloaded and deep in the water as she moved down the river. Once out of the harbour the wind began to freshen, and going over the bar was tricky, the short high cross waves making us pitch, toss and bump. The furniture slithered to and fro across the open deck and once again we were drenched with sheets of spray. Surprisingly, when once we had crossed the bar we only took about ten minutes. The sea was relatively calm and the landing on the main beach was unbelievably without incident of any kind.

Once ashore we tried to get as much done as possible in the time. First we attempted to sort out some of the chaos of our previous visits, for on these occasions no sooner had the furniture and chattels been dumped at the house than there had been a dramatic cry from Wren of, "To the boat, there is a storm breaking!" The resulting pile-up was indescribable. It was now almost impossible to get in the front door and penetrate the jungle of bookcases, tea chests, wine jars and photographic equipment festooned with an incongruous mixture of smaller articles. So we made the decision that there was no alternative but to manhandle everything twice, if we ever hoped to sort ourselves out when at last we finally moved in. We therefore designated the ex-barn—the enormous room that led down some steps and along a passage to the jetty cottage—as a transit camp, the idea being that if we moved everything down there except furniture we knew we should need in the house, we could sort out our possessions at leisure when once we had taken up residence—not knowing, in our innocence, that leisure was the one commodity that would be forever in short supply.

While Wren, Charles and Duncan brought up the fresh intake from the beach Babs tried to organise a system to save space now and time in the future, and was dubbed Queen Bee of "Operation Wheelbarrow", while Ruth and I raced trying to sow seed potatoes. We had been told that the climate on the island is one month in advance of the Cornish mainland, which of course is well ahead of the rest of the country and traditionally the first island potatoes are sown on Boxing Day. It seemed imperative that we should try and keep as near to this tradition as possible, especially as Paul Shelley, the greengrocer, had said that he would give us 3/6d a pound for early new potatoes, a very high price indeed in 1965, and this of course was the wholesale price. The first suitable field we dug was full of last year's unlifted main crop and we tore off down the path to find somewhere else. We did this at the double expecting to hear the clarion call "To the boats!" from Wren at any moment. In doing this I fell over some disused machinery and equipment that spewed across the path in front of us. My foot caught in the handle of an old watering can and at the speed I was going I pitched headlong among the rest of the rusty debris, twisting my knee.

Falls are one of the everyday hazards of island life. Rough tracks and pitted shingle paths are the more luxurious ways of getting from one part of the island to another. More usually one has to slither over seaweed, rocks and shingle paths slippery with algae, or hack a way through undergrowth snared with bramble shoots like wire traps, or trip over hidden lumps of metal or tools carelessly cast aside by someone, not realising that grass can grow four or five feet high and entangle anything in its path. Track clearing and keeping the main paths negotiable is a perennial and never ending task, for in a climate where frost is virtually unknown nature unchecked is very bountiful, especially to her favourite subjects the weed family. Leave the weeding of a shingle path for but one season and it is back to rough grass by the following year.

The long-sighted brigade are at particular risk for they are always focusing well ahead. Perhaps that is why some of us are naturally conditioned to have eyes only for the distant goal and do not see the more immediate obstacles, and not necessarily in a purely physical sense. Whatever the reason, my knee was hurt and painful but not enough to stop us planting the potatoes which we did at breakneck speed. I even had time to stay behind and sow some broad beans and, hopefully, lettuce and chives.

As there was no dramatic call from Wren we managed between us to get quite a lot done that day and we also had a foretaste of the delights the island had to offer, for we sailed back to Looe on a warm, starry night that was just like summer. It was incredible for early February, especially as the rest of the country was still icy and in some cases snowbound.

It was so enjoyable that we asked everyone to come on a picnic the next day and decided that it was warm and calm enough to take Toby. There were only a few bits and pieces to transport and to my great joy Wren said that he would have a shot at getting the bookcase over. Zena and Peter were not free to come but Ruth's mother and father did, armed with seeds and plants and ready to give their expert advice, also Wren's wife Valerie and, of course, Duncan.

With some trepidation on my part we saw the bookcase lowered over the quayside with ropes on to the deck of the *Orlando*. Once on board it was roped and buttressed with various sacks of fertilisers and the ubiquitous bags of manure. It was the easiest journey we had had so far; nevertheless I had some bad moments when the bookcase slithered from one side of the deck to the other when we crossed the bar, in spite of being securely roped, and at one stage it looked in danger of tipping over the side. However it survived the journey safely and once on the island we went our different ways. I, for one, not having the courage to watch Wren disembark with the bookcase and engage in the delicate operation of hoisting it on to the trailer of the caterpillar and tow it up the steep and bumpy path to the house, left the beach and with some of the others went about our various activities. Ruth and her father explored the caves, and then he and Ruth's mother did a tour sizing up the planting possibilities. It was arranged that they would get sacks of peat with their next order and a supply of wooden slats for making up our own seed boxes. Some of last year's tomatoes in the unheated greenhouse were still ripening and we were looking forward to doing some cultivation in the exceptionally mild conditions that the island obviously enjoyed.

Wren spent some considerable time putting a new head on the tractor and having warned Duncan again not to attempt to use it, he managed to ease the bookcase into the "transit camp". There it stands to this day and very impressive it looks too for now it is a fine room. The one-time barn, which had also been a music room in which Myra Hess practised on the grand piano when she was a guest of a professor of music from the Royal Academy who then owned the island, had, when we came, seen better days. Some of the floorboards were rotten from the earth beneath and some of hardboard with which the walls had been panelled were growing a white fungus from the same reason. For many months it remained our transit camp. Now we have had the rotted hardboard replaced with pyrana pine panelling. It is a carpeted room and with the walls hung with original paintings, handwoven panels and antique swords, together with pottery gifts from craftsmen displayed on wooden or hessian-covered benches and tables and the room furnished with some antiques, a Regency chaise lounge, and dominated at one end by the bookcase, the general effect has a certain richness of style. On the cliff top of an island it is quite unexpected. Most visitors, having tramped up the shingle path from the beach, express delighted surprise when they enter and many are known to sit for their entire visit in the sunshine streaming through the big bay window, instead of exploring the island they have come to see. One local friend, Gwen Miles who visited us for the first time was amazed. "I expected a hut with sawdust on the floor," she said. One corner of which we are particularly proud is where Babs has a fine display of semiprecious stones which she has cut and polished and fashioned into jewellery for, buried treasure or no, the island is rich in natural treasure. To our great joy we have found, as we understand Myra Hess had before us, a wealth of semiprecious stones on the beaches, especially after the winter gales. Among these are topaz, cornelians, banded agate, rose and amethyst quartz. This is pulling aside the curtain for a peep into the future for on that day the room was completely bare but for an old kitchen sink lying carelessly in the middle of the floor and soon to be surrounded by a mass of our diverse possessions.

While the major operation of moving the bookcase in was going on I was busy in the greenhouse trying feverishly to sow as many seeds as possible. Consequently I was the only one near the house when I heard a terrific crash. I rushed round to the side of the house and found the caterpillar tractor lying on its side belching forth smoke where it had fallen from a high grassy bank, standing on which was a very shaken Duncan. He had not, it transpired, been able to resist the temptation to try out the tractor; it had veered off from the track and out of control had crashed over the high bank on to the path outside the kitchen window. Luckily Duncan had the wit to leap off in time and was unhurt. I was afraid that the engine might burst into flames or explode and set the house on fire and I got Wren on to the scene as quickly as possible. He at once turned the engine off and sent Duncan off for planks of wood. Wren then not for the last time showed his great skill at leverage. Just by the use of planks which we placed according to his instructions he was able to get the tractor upright again although it is so heavy that it cannot by brute strength be pushed even one inch. It was damaged of course and spare parts had to be bought and a great deal of Wren's time spent on it before it could be put to use again. In fact for many years it was never quite the same again and was liable to give up the ghost and stop dead in the middle of an important operation, Wren's fear was that this might happen on the beach below high water level and be impossible to move. It is only recently that Wren was able to bring someone over who was an expert on this type of machinery and was able to put it in first class working order, much to Wren's satisfaction, and it is now able to move two tons of solid fuel without the fear that it may all be swallowed up by the ever hungry sea. It must have been a major operation involving cranes and many men to deliver the tractor to the island in the first place, although presumably it would have been in working order and could be driven straight up the beach.

Some weeks after this incident Wren, wishing to try out his running repairs, in his usual confidence-inspiring way, actually got me driving the thing from the beach up the steep path with a ten foot sheer drop just a hairsbreadth away. There were these two things like joysticks; in one direction they acted as brakes, but propelled in another they actually steered the thing. With Wren standing on one foot on a bit of its anatomy somewhere behind me yelling directions in my ear in an inferno of noise that by comparison would make Concorde sound like a bumble bee, I drove it up the path and in a masochistic kind of way actually enjoyed it. No doubt this was partly due to the fact that I had *survived*. It did bring home to me vicariously why it is that most men are so engine mad, because the feeling of power it gives them.

That day Wren was very angry that Duncan had disobeyed orders but said very little, for Duncan was a nice lad—just a bit too enthusiastic. It certainly put us back a bit financially and it was a nuisance that we could never rely on the "crawler" as it was frequently called, for it was much needed for the transport of the all important diesel oil for the generator, but at the time we were only relieved that Duncan himself was uninjured for it might well have been an accident with fatal results. Duncan was only fourteen at the time and a boy keen for adventure. He helped us many times at weekends during his schooldays with great and unfailing enthusiasm. After he left school he had a full-time job and we saw little of him. A year or so ago as a young married man of twenty-one, still keen on the active life, he used to go skin diving and one day just outside Looe harbour he was tragically found drowned.

We sailed back to Looe that night in pitch dark and apart from the difficulty of climbing from the bounding metal boat on to the *Orlando* there were no difficulties of any kind. Toby had thoroughly enjoyed his day and even leapt from one boat to the other quite happily which, as his maritime experiences had been strictly limited to trips up the Thames (a mode of transport not readily acceptable to his doggy conservatism), was surprising. He obviously intended to be an islander and as such was prepared to accept the hazards this entailed.

Chapter 10

More stage props assembled for opening night

There was now just one more week to "D" day, for as the removal of our possessions was more or less complete we could see no reason why we should not take up residence. Wren, cautious for once, counselled us to stay overnight only on the Saturday, presumably so that we could find our bearings. Babs of course would have to return to the mainland for school on the Monday.

Meantime a busy week lay ahead of us. Zena and I plus Toby went into Plymouth on Monday to buy up-more provisions. First we went into Dingle's, a big store, and took Toby with us. Now Zena did not have a dog and was inclined to think that we made rather a lot of Toby; perhaps she was of the opinion, although she was too diplomatic to voice it, that we over-rated his intelligence. Whenever we left him in the car well blanketed from the cold, for he was, after all, thirteen and a half and with a heart condition, she would make such remarks as "Have you left him a book to read?" or "Look! he is waving goodbye to us." Toby decided that he had had enough of this sarcasm and intended to pull a few tricks out of the bag to show how superior he really was. First he did his usual "Goodbye Cornwall! Devon here we come!" routine as we crossed the Tamar, and for good measure turned and gave a friendly "Thank-you" bark to the car park attendant in Plymouth. His *pièce-de-résistance* he kept for Dingle's itself. Going up in the lift we said that we would go to the second floor to get some tools. "First floor—ladies' underwear!" intoned the lift attendant. Many got out but Toby did not budge. "Second floor—do-it-yourself!" and out marched Toby ahead of us and everyone else. We were as impressed as Zena and immensely proud.

I bought a lovely Japanese hatchet and hammer, an electric frypan (generator, here we come!) lots of kitchen gadgets and finished up buying a Peter Scott wildfowl record. I also browsed through language records trying to decide which new language I would study in my spare time. After all, an island on the south-western outposts of our shores was as likely a place as any for the landing of foreign spies or other aliens up to some nefarious business or other. Not being able to make up my mind which country presented the greatest danger I decided that I would make do with the French and German, and brush up my knowledge of these. We then went on to the cash-and-carry and loaded up the car with enough tinned and dried food to last us until the next Ice Age joined us to the mainland again.

The rest of the week was predictably unpredictable. We expected callers, of course. Word had got around, we supposed, that we were about to move over and so the regulars turned up with offers of help. Mr and Mrs Whitehouse, still very concerned on our behalf, volunteered to come with us on Saturday to show us how to start the generator. The rest of the country was still ice-bound and as it was early February bad weather and gales were not only possible, but, as we now know, extremely likely. The worst storms we have had on the island, with many disasters out at sea in the area, have been during February. We did not think that Mr Whitehouse in his serious state of health should commit himself, for having promised we knew that that kind gentleman would hate to back out on his word. Instead we agreed that he should explain how the generator worked. I found it to be quite beyond me but Babs seemed to follow what he was talking about to some extent. I tried to look intelligent so that he would not be too worried about us but I was banking on Babs' superior mechanical ability, to which she in fact makes little claim, to get the thing going. We told them about the foaming brown liquid that gushed malodorously out of the tap. Mr Whitehouse said that a weed must have got into the water storage tank in the wood. How right he was! When later we found the tank it looked as though "Doomwatch" had been on location there. Great leering fronds of a particularly malevolent species of weed festooned the nearby trees and draped themselves menacingly round the tank as if in the act of throttling it. I swear that baleful eyes leered at us as the tentacles embraced and penetrated into our precious water store inch by inch even as we watched.

"Sodium chlorate is what you want," said Mr Whitehouse, and sodium chlorate was added to our still growing list.

There were at least twenty-five callers that day, although some of them did not really count as they were the same ones calling again and again, like Ruth, Zena, Peter, Wren, Duncan, "Pipes-over-the-water", Ruth's mother and father and Mr Nancollas (now highly delighted that he could at last have his own store back). In addition the reps with whom we had become acquainted at the catering exhibition now began to call. One nice touch was when we were able to offer the Twinings' tea rep a cup of his own free sample. As they all called we ordered vast quantities of detergent, coffee, dried milk, Horlicks and drinking chocolate, which was a little optimistic considering the state of our water supply. Then there were the appointments with insurance agents.

If insurance had seemed complicated before, the intricacies of trying to cover our far flung little empire of house, cottages, farm buildings, boats, engines and boathouse as well as all the contents and equipment, for storm damage as well as the usual cover, almost defeated us. We were insistent that everything, but everything, should be covered for storm damage whatever the cost, for we had experienced enough of the force of the elements to realise what havoc they can wreak. Consequently our premiums were extremely high. "Never mind," we thought "come wind or high water, we are covered." How naïve can one be. We found to our cost that we had not been astute enough and we now know that money cannot buy everything. It may not buy love or health and we would add to that that it cannot buy insurance. When last year we lost the boathouse and its entire contents, three outboard engines, an inboard engine, three boats, a thirty-foot barge, farm equipment and two very good mowers we put in a very modest claim for £1000. Our claim was settled for £120 and not a penny more could we get. The inboard engine alone had cost £140, and our premiums over the last few years would have bought us a couple of fine boats with engines to spare. When a year or so ago a landslide demolished the pumphouse for our spring water supply in the cliff that was rated as an "act of God" with nil compensation and it was only due to the courtesy of the assessor, and a tree that had conveniently fallen in with the rest of the debris that it was pronounced that God was only 75 per cent to blame and we were awarded 25 per cent of our claim, which at least was enough to pay an engineer to estimate for a new one. We are of the opinion that most of the disasters of that nature here should not be blamed on God. To us that is sheer blasphemy, for they are nothing less than acts of the Devil, and that proviso not being mentioned in insurance policies, I reckon we should get our full whack, just like anyone else on the mainland, but maybe they do not get it either. Perhaps the next best thing to owning an island is to own your very own insurance firm. I must be fair, though. I had another letter from my photographic firm—the same day that the twenty-five visitors called—to say that the Pentax could be repaired after all. This was at considerable expense to the insurers, for the camera was almost a complete write-off, and six months later I received it in good working order without a penny cost to myself.

Babs and I did not see much of each other during what we hoped would be the last week we should be officially domiciled on the mainland. She of course was fully occupied during the day at school and now, as is usual with teachers, but not always acknowledged by the general public, after school activities were encroaching on her private life. Over the years I have seen this done with enthusiasm and dedication and it should be recognized by those who only remark about the long school holidays.

One of Babs' activities at that time was to sit on a brains trust at the local youth club. As usual, she was more concerned with her appearance than with her intellect. Not having much claim to either during this period I was not invited but I had a couple of problems of my own. The first was a visit to the dentist. I had had toothache the week before and Ruth had kindly let me have her appointment. Mr Leck had said that the tooth would have to come out and the next day was the day fixed for this. I was not looking forward to the visit—not that one ever does—but the reason I was less enthusiastic than usual was that the knee that had been injured on Sunday was troubling me. I could not sleep at night for the pain was like neuralgia, also the leg from the instep to above the knee was very swollen and a nasty black/blue colour. It was painful to walk on, and I felt quite sorry for myself when I turned up at the dentist's surgery. To my great relief Mr Leck said that the tooth would not have to come out after all and a stopping would do. He added however that a wisdom tooth would have to be extracted at my next appointment. This I thought I could not afford to lose as I had always been short on wisdom teeth, the full quota never arriving in the first place. I reckoned I would need all the aids to wisdom I could lay on to keep us on the paths of sanity, but Mr Leck no doubt thought that day was long past. Who in their right minds, with a full set of wisdom teeth in working order would embark on the venture we had undertaken, off the wild Cornish coast in mid-winter of all times? As the future was to prove, there was no end to the possibilities of madness that one could get up to, for there is something about island life that breeds ideas like the yeast in fermenting wine.

Back at the cottage Duncan called on his way to the doctor. He apparently had suffered no bad effects from his accident with the tractor and we hoped that the visit to the doctor had nothing to do with this. On the spur of the moment I decided to go with him and have my knee looked at.

Usually one assumes that if there is not a broken limb most minor injuries cure themselves, given time, but I was going to need my leg on that island, and not only was it not so far curing itself, but it seemed to be getting worse, and was beginning to look like an elephant's leg. Dr Harvey said that he did not think that it was phlebitis. Good God! the thought had never entered my head, and I am not often lagging behind in the imagination stakes. Apparently a deep vein had been damaged and had flooded the leg and I would have to wear an elastic bandage for at least three weeks. It would be very painful for those three weeks he said and gave me some painkillers. He also informed me that he would be unable to travel to the island to look after me. I did not know if this meant that there was no Health Service on the island or whether he himself could not come and it would have to be someone else if the necessity arose. If the former surely I would not have to pay the full amount of the National Health stamp— happy thought—until I remembered what happened the last time I had official dealings over this all-important scrap of paper, and I certainly did not want to land myself with a job in Looe or I should never get to live on the island. I dismissed the problem, to be sorted out in the future, for there was enough to occupy us in setting ourselves up on our dream island, although in attaining it was often more like a nightmare.

The two cottages presented a bit of a problem. If we did not do something about them they would soon become derelict. The Smuggler's cottage, which had not been lived in since the Whitehouse's gardener left the previous summer, was growing black fungi over the ceiling and inside walls, and the lovely enclosed walled garden in which grew peaches and figs as well as apples, pears, plums, blackcurrant and masses of roses, had become completely overgrown in those few short months; the absence of frost allowing the tangled undergrowth to burgeon all year through. The other cottage of which the one-time converted barn was part, had apparently been used partly as a packing station for the daffodils. Already floorboards were rotted and stove in as you trod on them and one's feet went through to the earth beneath. We did not relish the idea of seeing them become complete ruins. The only choice, apart from doing a Queen Elizabeth I act and doing the rounds of sleeping in each place in turn was, we thought, to put them in good order and accommodate friends when they came to help. The O'Neills and Peter Steele and his family from the art school were bringing their tents to camp that first year to help us pioneer but it would be something to aim for if we could house a future generation of helpers in the cottages. Thus were sown some more seeds of conservation. We were in fact a little ahead of this trend as far as the general population was concerned, for at that time the word "conservation", if it were bandied around in ordinary social circles, meant little more than the underlying principle of one major political party, or a constipated condition of mind attributed to it if you happened to belong to the other.

As a start in this direction we decided to acquire some bits of furniture for the cottages, and went along to Oliver Hicks' fortnightly sale which was conveniently due that week. Mr Hicks was—as the reader may remember—the estate agent in East Looe from whom we had bought our two little cottages in Bassett Court at what now seemed a lifetime ago. It was therefore with a feeling of nostalgia that Babs and I went along to the preview. These auction sales are really a part of the local social life, and Mr Hicks and Mr Nancollas take it turn and turn about to hold them in East and West Looe respectively. We both felt rather guilty as we passed Nancollas's store on West Looe Quay on our way to cross the bridge to East Looe for we knew that we had put the spanner in the works, however unintentionally, as far as Mr Nancollas and West Looe auctions were concerned. As we could not attend the sale itself we left a bid for two iron bedsteads and a wall cupboard. The next evening we called in and found that we had acquired all three items—12/6d each for the bedsteads and 10/– for the cupboard, which with the commission came to £1.18.0. Oh! happy days of pre-decimalisation and raging inflation. We loaded them on the car and for the rest of the week, which included an invitation to visit a lady potter, they went with us wherever we went, for we felt that it would have been adding insult to injury to put them in Nancollas's store. We must have looked like refugees searching for a home, which in a way was what we were.

It was becoming imperative that we make our final move soon and hoped that the following Saturday would be "D" Day for the longer we stayed on the mainland the greater the amount of our acquisitions grew. Every time I went on a foray for kitchen equipment and foodstores it became a compulsion to pick up some more seeds, fertiliser and a book or books. Wren now told us that we needed cement and Ruth said that a couple of tiler's hammers were essential. Not, as one might suspect, that we were going to take up tiling in our spare time, useful as this skill would have been, for it is almost routine that tiles fly off the roofs every winter, but because Ruth's father advised us that we should need them for cultivating on a hillside. His holding at Shutta was on a steep hillside and in this aspect the island is similar. All the daffodil fields slope down from the top of the island and there is only one spot that is a plateau of sorts and this is the lawn at the back of the house. Even this looks man-made for on two sides it finishes abruptly on high banks buttressed by dry stone walls. This is a fine flat lawn that Mr Whitehouse used as a croquet lawn; we doubted whether we would have the time for keeping it in such fine condition or for playing croquet.

It was nevertheless quite incredible what we thought we should have time for, and the more we dreamed about our future island life the more our minds tumbled with ideas. We now had enough stores and kitchen equipment to start a large scale catering establishment, although our collection was intended as a hedge against total isolation from civilisation and after our experiences in trying to set foot on the island this seemed a distinct possibility. We had amassed sufficient seeds, seed potatoes, fertilisers and sacks of sphagnum peat to run a market garden extending over the whole twenty-two-and-a-half acres, although only five were under cultivation and these given over mostly to the daffodils. The photographic equipment and impedimenta would have made a studio photographer green with envy; the stock of film was enough to take a shot every minute of every daylight hour for months to come, or so it looked. In addition I had acquired materials for colour processing to add to the other darkroom work. The collection of stones that we had made over the years went over by the sack load together with Babs' rather splendid and professional stone cutting and polishing machine for this was before lapidary became the popular hobby it is today and the many types of small polishing machines now obtainable were not yet generally on the market. The pottery equipment and sacks of clay and glazes were to be housed in a building large enough to serve as a pottery for a whole art school.

We now added tins of paint against the time when we could decorate the two cottages, plus plenty of timber and nails for repairs—the electric drill and attachments would certainly come in useful for this, always supposing we had electricity. The printing press would take care of any ambitions we had in that line, and the woodcarving tools would soon turn driftwood into masterpieces. We had stacks of canvases, oil paints, pastels, sketch books and the rest of the paraphernalia of painting to stun the art world with our creations. In fact, with my penchant of putting last things first I had brought some rather good beading to frame these masterpieces although so far we had scarcely put brush to canvas. We had of course the equipment for other crafts to fill in our spare time, metalwork, lino cuts, collage, marquetry, copper enamelling, to name but a few. Although Babs now realised that apart from school holidays she would be lucky to get to the island at week-ends except in the summer months, she was not daunted by her huge collection of semi-precious stones, but in fact surveyed it with relish.

For leisure we had our books and music. Our collection of musical instruments was quite considerable, and was to be crowned in the future with the church organ, while for listening we had the stereo tape recorder and record player. Our growing library would extend our knowledge of marine life, ornithology, geology, archaeology, small boats, astronomy, and fishing. As Wren succintly remarked, it would take two hundred years to read all the books we were taking with us. If between any of these activities we got tired at looking at stars through the telescope we could always make a few bricks with the brick-making machine. It might be a good time to say now that the future, hazardous, unpredictable and frustrating as it often became, did not and does not take the edge off our enthusiasm; on the contrary, it sparks off even more ideas. To change the metaphor we have found that after a winter of minor and sometimes major catastrophies, when our ardour seems temporarily to fade, the spring comes without fail, the sap begins to rise, and new ideas and projects flower and flourish again.

The fact that we were going to live on this lonely island had an extraordinary effect on people. An older generation than ours thought that we were completely demented; our contemporaries were divided into those who wished they had the courage to join us, and the others, the majority, who blanched with fear at the thought. Those who were solidly behind us and who yearned to come too were not only those who were half our age, but an even younger generation going down to the five—to nine-year-olds. With sparkling eyes they helped us with their might and main, and now as teenagers say that it was the most exciting time of their lives, and one they will never forget.

With all the enterprises with which we were engaged we were, I am sure the reader will agree, not exactly the doddering type. Hard physical effort was required just to land our goods on the island. Once there, one had to be extremely fit and resilient to endure the sustained arduous exertions required to live there. We both frequently have been waist deep in raging surf trying to stop the weighty *Islander* from going broadside on. We have had to hack our way through fallen trees, sawing off huge branches that have blocked our main and only path after winter storms and once when I was alone on the island twenty one hundredweight sacks of coal had perforce to be slung overboard on to the beach below high water mark as it was too dangerous to beach the *Islander*. I had no choice, if they were not to be swept out with the next tide, but to move each one up over the banking shingle and seaweed and up to the house. So many of the conditions with which we have to contend could not be coped with by anyone of advanced years nor viewed with equanimity even by those of middle age. You can imagine our utter astonishment therefore when some little time after we had gone to live on the island some visitors landed and said. "We hear that two old ladies own the island." "If so, I am one of them," I replied tartly. I must add, though, that their amazement was even greater than ours, for they could not believe that we were the ladies in question.

Apart from all these occupations we had in mind that in our spare time we would write a history of the island. The clerk to the council had kindly allowed us to sit in the council chamber and take notes from their original copy of *Bond's History of Looe*, published in 1823, which referred to even earlier histories. As a recent purchaser of *Encyclopaedia Britannica* I was the proud possessor of a sheet of tokens, each one of which entitled one to a specialised research on any chosen subject. One of these tokens I had duly sent off with a request for a detailed research into the early history of the island. We hoped that this when it came, together with our notes, would form the basis of our own book.

Tales of smuggling, buried treasure and tunnels to the mainland we had of course heard many times and we hoped that by our own research and checking facts locally, interesting details would come to light about this colourful period of the island's history.

The island is rich, too; in legend; the most fascinating being that Joseph of Arimathea was said to have landed here with the Child Christ on his way to Glastonbury. The fact that the chapel, dating back to 1139 at least, came under the see of Glastonbury when Benedictine monks were on the island had given rise to much speculation to others before us and we were surprised that there was no record of an excavation ever having been made of the chapel site. The possibility therefore of having one was well to the forefront of our future plans.

To add to the folklore of the island it is said to be haunted and there are accounts of ghosts being sighted, but like many hauntings they cannot be authenticated. When we came to live on the island we certainly felt that a very strong influence existed which others apart from ourselves claimed to have felt. This influence has a way of inspiring some artistic people so that they are able to produce of their very best. Others feel as soon as they set foot on the island that they must help in some way. It is almost a compulsion with them as they slave away for the whole of their holiday, not satisfied unless in some small way at least they are able to leave their mark. Wherever their journeyings take them later they treasure the memories, even years after, and from all parts of the world we hear from them: Life for them will never be quite the same again, for they have been touched with island magic. One visitor, Duncan Chapman, brings plants from Africa, South America, California or from whatever country he has been visiting, and plants them on the island during his few hours stay. Other dedicated enthusiasts make their annual homage and during their stay will make or do things which will be of practical use; they will build walls, extend the jetty, make seats, plumb in water, erect water tanks, clear tracks, till the land, sow, weed, cut the fields and decorate the cottages. Not only will they pay for their holiday but after they have gone away they will send presents and cheques. Among these are the young, about whom so much criticism is made, and whom we have found to be some of the island's most ardent devotees. Even casual visitors will give more than is asked for the crafts, and only the other day someone insisted on paying £2 for a cup of tea! So if you should hear an argument going on in the cafe/craft shop you can almost be sure that it is someone insisting on paying over the odds.

It must be said that all this helps us to keep the island unspoilt and uncommercialised for in aiming at this as our ideal, it is run at a loss and we have to subsidise the project from our own income. Nevertheless it is a strange phenomenon that people should have this attitude in these days of strikes, protest marches, and student and customer revolt. On the other hand the island has a way of rejecting those of whom it disapproves; in these unfortunate visitors it seems to bring out an almost evil streak. We can spot them as soon as they set foot on the island. Within a few minutes of their arrival we know that before their time is up they will be hot foot back to the mainland, with its supermarkets, bingo halls and pubs just as soon as a boat can carry them. It is not that they are necessarily city or urban conditioned, for we have many townsfolk who have become island-ers but instinctively we know that the island is going to reject them. They will shoot back faster than they came, denied the touch of island magic. We cannot wait for the moment of their going, for they have a disturbing influence on all who reside here. We cannot explain this, we can only record that it happens. Happily they are in the minority and leave us to wonder about the almost magnetic power of the island.

Chapter 11
End of dress rehearsal and first night

On Friday, 12th February at midnight we loaded up the *Orlando* with the last remnants of our possessions from Nancollas's store, plus all our recent acquisitions including the chlorate of lime to purify the water tank. This we would have to clear ourselves if we wished to have drinkable water. We were a little surprised about this, for one of the legacies we had acquired with the island was a final demand for the rates. We had paid this without giving it too much thought, but it now began to dawn on us, and currently with the tremendous increase in rates, with growing concern, that no public services are provided for the island at all, but regular as clockwork in come the demand for rates. At this particular time our only real concern was whether chlorate of lime would be any more palatable than weed-infested water, but trustingly we heaved it on board. We had had a busy evening with everyone milling round the cottage, charging in and out like Charing Cross station in the rush hour—so much so that we actually had our evening meal standing up behind the counter of the kitchen and dispensing coffee to the very last dregs of our mainland supply. We finally got to bed at 2.45 a.m. and by then the wind was already freshening from the north-west, a direction that in winter can mean sudden violent squalls accompanied by slashing rain. Luckily we were not aware of this possibility and slept soundly, for on the morrow with any luck we should be resting our heads on our desert island.

"Take off" was planned for 8.30 a.m. It was a sunny gusty morning and the weather forecast for our area was "snow, ice, gales and storms." In spite of this Wren thought that it would be all right to go. Opinion was divided about this and by the time "let's go" had won the day it was 9.30 a.m. and the tide was receding fast. Earlier Wren had taken the *Orlando* out into Looe Bay beyond the harbour. As we had loaded her up the night before all we had to do was to ferry ourselves out to her in the metal boat. The outboard refused to start up so we had to row out. Two trips and we were all aboard the *Orlando*—Wren, Babs, Ruth and myself and Peter, who was coming to see if there was any way we could run the deep freeze from the generator, always supposing we could work it at all (at present it only ran for a part of each day when required and not at all during the hours of sleep). Toby, Charles and a few last minute stores and clothes were to be towed behind the *Orlando* in the metal boat.

It was dead calm in the bay as we were sheltered from the offshore north-west winds by Hannafore and the westerly rocks exposed by the fast receding tide. Once we were out of the shelter of this arm of the shore the sea began to cut up and was very choppy indeed. Soon we ran into squalls which drenched poor Charles and Toby with sheets of spray. We were to moor in the Jetty Bay and ferry in by the metal boat. Unfortunately there was no shelter in the bay from the north-west squalls, which became even more frequent and violent. Very gingerly Babs, Ruth and I lowered ourselves into the metal boat to join Toby while Wren and Charles changed places so that Wren could row us ashore.

Though not quite as bad as the time when I had to jump for it as from an express train and clung suspended from the jetty posts, the landing was hazardous enough. Wren decided that the beach in the bay was the best bet and between squalls he rowed us through a narrow channel between the rocks, and we were more or less shot ashore on to mounds of seaweed as though we had been slung out of a catapult. While Wren rowed back to fetch Peter and Charles we slowly and carefully made our way, sinking in seaweed up to our knees and clambering over slippery rocks until at last we climbed the slope up the cliff above the jetty. It took several of these journeys to get everything up and on to the house. By then a good three quarters of an hour had elapsed and we fully expected that the other three would be ashore by the time we had made our last trip.

There was no sign of them, and looking out to the *Orlando* we could see no sign of life at all; no Wren, no Peter, no Charles. In fact we had the eerie feeling that we were gazing on another *Marie Celeste*. We waited perhaps another half an hour, and during this time our imaginations ran riot as we listened to the screaming of the wind as it tore across from the north-west whipping up the sea into a broiling mass of foam, and topped by the wailing of the gulls as they rode the wind. We had a feeling of impending doom and it was with a gasp of relief that we saw Wren clamber over the side of the *Orlando*, albeit alone, and row ashore to us. Peter, who had not been keen that we should come in the first place because of the weather, apparently liked the look of it even less when we ran into the squalls. Now that it was worsening every minute he did not fancy landing and not being able to return to the mainland, so he wanted to return at once. Wren, having told us all this, recommended that we too return immediately as he did not like the look of the weather either.

Instead, we mutinied. Hitherto we had done everything at Wren's bidding. Unquestioningly, through storms, before the break of dawn, in the pitch dark of a bitter winter's night, swamped, frozen, pitched around by the elements, all but tossed overboard, we had obeyed orders without complaint. But to be told to return tamely to the mainland now, that we would not do. With herculean efforts we had at last set foot to stay on our island; we were equipped, prepared and feverishly eager to rest our heads there for the very first time after months of waiting and many weeks of endeavour. Now, with the magic moment within our grasp, it was to be snatched away. We could not take it and suddenly we blew out tops. "Nothing", we said firmly, "would induce us to return to the mainland. We were here and here we meant to stay—and that was that." Wren very reluctantly agreed. This reluctance we realised later was not due to the weather conditions, but to the fact that he was disinclined to leave us there while he had to go back to the mainland with the others and be separated from the island project on which he was so keen. For some reason he said that we must keep the metal boat with us. Whether he thought we might change our minds and want to row back to the mainland we did not enquire, but we would have agreed to anything so long as he did not try to persuade us to return with him. Ruth, he said, was to come out to the *Orlando* so that he could get back on board, and then she was to row herself round to the main beach.

We watched the *Orlando* sail away, and I then went down the path to the main beach to help Ruth beach the metal boat. The reason it could not be brought in to the jetty beach, which was nearer to where the *Orlando* had been moored, was that the winter spring tides crashed right up on to the cliffs there at high tide, and would have smashed to bits any boat left there. The main beach was a wide sloping expanse of shingle and sand and was reckoned to be a safe haven for boats to be tied up. An enormous barge was kept there as well as a winch and the boathouse. From photographs it would appear that this last had been there for about a hundred years and we never believed for one moment that these could be swept away. For some years, summer and winter, we were able to keep two boats tied up to the trees well above high water mark. This, then, was where Ruth was to bring in the metal boat. Unfortunately with the wind being directly on-shore there, it was exposed to the full force of the squalls which had grown in intensity. I arrived to find Ruth up to her waist in surf trying to hold on to the boat which was being swept broadside on in the breakers. It looked in imminent danger of capsizing and submerging Ruth or carrying her out to sea in the long vicious runs. Luckily Babs arrived on the scene and sending Ruth up to the house to change into dry clothing, Babs and I, à la Wren, tried to lever the heavy boat ashore with the use of planks which were stacked up by the boathouse. We extended the cable of the winch to its limit and slowly, inch by inch, levered the boat up to within a rope's length of the cable end. It was a difficult operation, for all the time the surf was dragging at the boat and pulling our feet from under us. At last we managed to attach the rope to the cable but twice the rope broke and twice the boat was sucked back into the breakers. Babs hung on for dear life to the stern, and as I was the one with the rope I tried frantically to tie a knot to join the broken ends. Now it will have been apparent that the intricacies of knot tying had always defeated me. Years ago I had dismissed it into the limbo of life's failures together with sewing, making custard and learning Latin. Suddenly there was no choice, for Babs could not leave her end of the boat or it would have been swept out to sea. Desperation is a good teacher. Belaying the rope around my middle to keep the bows of the boat steady and to give myself a bit of spare rope that was not dragged taut with every surge of the sea I attempted to join the broken ends. The resulting knot will not be found in any naval, boy scout or girl guide manual, but Glory Be! it held. With spray more or less coming out of my ears I christened it a Great Granny knot and many times it has saved the day in similar desperate situations. The only difference being that it is never quite the same knot twice; on the other hand would it not be a very peculiar world indeed if all great grandmothers were identical?

A few more heaves of the planks and we were clear of the breakers. The boat was full of water and too heavy to tilt over to empty, but after much bailing out we were able to winch her up high and dry above the tide line.

After we too had changed into dry clothing we decided that as we were all quite exhausted by this time we would take it in turns to have a rest, one of us being left on watch. Memory does not provide the reasoning behind this but presumably it was so that someone would be able to give the alarm if the island should take off in the storm force winds and churning seas. Toby seemed very happy. He had settled in as though he had lived on islands all his life and was the only one who opted not to rest.

We managed to find some driftwood and got a fire going in the lounge—the kitchen still being an impenetrable forest of tea chests. We had bought a certain amount of fresh water with us but finding a tank of rainwater outside the house we boiled some of that over the fire and made ourselves one of the most welcome cups of tea we had ever had, while we reviewed the situation. By now the light was fading fast and we decided that the first priority was to get the generator going, not so much for lighting because so far we had not unearthed our supply of electric light bulbs, but because we were most anxious to use the record player and play *Bali Hi* from *South Pacific*, as we thought that this would be the most appropriate music to play on our first night aboard our island.

It was dark by the time we reached the generator room which was at the end of the path, not far from the main beach. By the light of a torch we peered at intricate diagrams on a large instruction sheet. According to this the generator was a Lister *Start-o-Matic* and would start up automatically with the flick of any electric light switch on the island. It was soon apparent that it was not going to do it this way tonight, or, as we subsequently found out, any other night for a long time. Although we did not realise it then, the batteries which provided the power for this automatic starting were completely dead through not being used for so many months, and the electrical box controlling this was out of action for the same reason and also because of the penetration of the damp sea atmosphere. It was all quite Greek to us but Babs, as the car driver, read out and interpreted the instructions, and gave us her version of what she thought they meant. One thing was obvious; the thing would have to be started manually. This meant swinging a handle and simultaneously moving little lever-like things and pushing them into specified points. Ruth was detailed for some bits of this mechanical dexterity. Babs, with torch in mouth, conducted from the "score" at the same time pulling and pushing levers that had rusted up from lack of use, a feat a contortionist would have found difficult. This left me as the swinger. Now I am no swinger, neither by inclination nor physique. I grant you I was brought up on eurhythmics, could swing a cricket bat and other weapons in the gameswomanship artillery tolerably well, but muscle hardly came into it. In fact the reverse was the case, rhythm taking the place of strength. In any case cricket bats, tennis, badminton and squash racquets and hockey sticks are inanimate objects; they have no life of their own and only generate the power you give them.

When it comes to objects that leap into life the moment you touch them I am just plain lily-livered.

An instance of this happened, I am ashamed to admit, during the war. While we were awaiting the time when we could volunteer for the W.R.N.S. or what have you, some of us filled in our spare time by joining a few auxiliary bodies such as part time Land Army, Home Guard and the Fire Brigade of the factory where our London Offices had been evacuated. The Fire Brigade consisted of teams of four, each of which took it in turns to guard the factory at night against attack by incendiary bombs. This was a distinct possibility as we were still near enough to London to see the glare of the red sky as London burned under the incessant attacks. The main piece of equipment was a trailer pump and a fire hose pipe, and our Fire Chief instructed us in the use of the pump, had us climbing up thirty-foot ladders with hose pipe over shoulder on to roofs, got us crawling under canopies of smoke so that we could instruct others, made us practise the fireman's lift and generally train us in how to deal with the various hazards with which we might have to cope. On fire duty nights we would get up our own alarm drills, screeching on the whistle and racing up the fire escape of the deserted factory building at dead of night with hose pipe over shoulder trying to beat the record each time. All this was exciting and thoroughly enjoyable, but there was one aspect of it at which I quivered with fright. This was starting up the engine of the trailer pump which meant swinging a handle, as on a car. As captain of my team responsible for calling these practices I could hardly opt out of starting up the engine on account that I was afraid. It would have been disastrous for morale and, I told myself, just the sort of loophole that Hitler would have been looking for, so I just had to grit my teeth, shut my eyes, and swing. I considered that that little operation was my major war effort and deserved an award for bravery. Along with the certificate on behalf of the King for services with "Dad's Army" and the one from My Lords of the Admiralty for the privilege of serving in the W.R.N.S. should be a medal specially inscribed to me, who "With great courage while under stress and strain, without regard to wild fears, did swing the handle of the trailer pump under her command." Maybe others feel the same way about this starting handle business; or maybe I was frightened by a clockwork toy when I was a baby; only a psychiatrist would know.

The fact remained that I was faced with this problem all over again, only this was no starting handle of a car; it was a massive affair, and looked as though it was capable of starting up the Queen Mary all by itself. According to Babs voice in the darkness you had to turn it rapidly until you got compression, "or convulsions" I thought grimly as she considerately shone the torch for me. I could not even turn it round, let alone rapidly. "You have to push it right in first," said Ruth. "Look, like this." She pushed the handle in and swung it round in no time at all, then went back to her post waiting for me to swing so that she could push in the vital bits. "It's a knack," she added. "You are right there," I thought bitterly, "you also need the arm of an all-in wrestler." Desperation again came to my aid. I swung and swung until I thought my arm would come out of its socket. Suddenly I felt resistance. Although I did not know it, I had "got compression". "Swing harder!" they both yelled pushing things in like mad. Babs shouted that I was to push in a twiddly bit too—she had just read it. Suddenly the generator roared into life and a light slowly came on, as in an Agatha Christie thriller. It was like some fiendish magic. Open-mouthed I gazed in wonder and then in horror, for in the excitement of success I had left the handle in—well no one had told me to take it out—and there it was, spinning madly round and round. "Good God! it will take off like when those Scotsmen throw the hammer" I thought frantically. I was in the direct line of fire—there was only one thing to do—hoof it-and at the double. I shot out of the door, and panic stricken, looked over my shoulder to see if it were following me; instead the light went out and the engine clanked into silence—the others had coolly turned the engine off.

We had another go. I got compression, we all pushed in our twiddly bits, the engine began to clank again, then throbbed rhythmically, the light slowly came on, and with great aplomb I pulled the handle out. Success at last! It was just as well for we had to go through this routine for another two months before the weather was fit enough for an engineer to come out and make it work automatically again.

Back at the house we found to our astonished delight that we had some electric light there too. We did not bother to find a bulb for the lounge for the driftwood fire gave a warm flickering glow, a fitting accompaniment to the roar of the sea below. We boiled up some more water for coffee and made omelettes over the fire. It seemed to us that no coffee had ever been so fragrant nor a meal more delectable. We found an electric point for the record player and happily tossed more logs on the fire as we listened to the haunting melody of "Bali Hi". Toby sat with us, very much at home and none the worse for his drenching of spray and rough crossing.

As the generator had been started manually it had to be stopped manually too, so down Babs and I went to the generator room and just by the touch of a switch stilled its mighty roar and plunged the island into darkness. This done we trudged, as we would for many nights to come, up the shingle path under the darkling woods beyond the Smugglers' cottage and so back to our house on the cliffs. Once there, with the help of a small oil lamp rather like Aladdin's lamp, we found some mattresses, cleared a space on the bare boards of the lounge floor, and just as we were, without getting undressed we all three and Toby lay side by side just like sausages in a pan. The full moon had broken through the scudding clouds sparkling on the wild sea below and bathing us in its soft light. As we lay there in front of the blazing driftwood fire a light flashed on the wall above the fireplace. It came and went at irregular intervals but in a rhythmic pattern and our contentment was complete when we realised that it was from Eddystone Lighthouse, 12½ miles away and our nearest neighbour.

So at last we had come to our heritage; the island that had dominated our thoughts for so long, and the realisation of a dream cherished since childhood.

As we rested there side by side we thought of the struggle, the uncertainties and the drama in achieving this momentous point in our lives. Now at last the months of endeavour had culminated in bringing us to this, the beginning of our new and uncharted life. For a long time feverish thoughts jostled each other, defeating sleep as we anticipated with eagerness the challenges before us. What would the future hold? The possibilities seemed limitless and infinitely enthralling.

At last sleep gently quietened our restless minds. As we drifted off towards tomorrow we felt we were on the brink of a great adventure, but if we could have forseen what lay ahead we would have been astonished to know that the hazardous events of the last few weeks were but the overture.

The curtain was about to rise on sufficient scenes of comedy, tragedy and drama to fill a book.

⇑ Jetty Cottage

A common subject on the island but which needs patience to photograph ⇒

⇑ Kim - Border Collie from Plymouth Dog's Home. Kim *knew* when Lennard was leaving Looe Harbour.

⇑ Joan - who died in 1977. Named after *Black Joan*, a smuggling inhabitant from past times.

⇑ First view of the island, from Wool Down

⇐ Smuggler's Cottage

⇑
Island House

Dick Butters, Ferryman Supreme ⇒

⇑ Approaching the island

⇐ Unloading fuel for the generators

⇐ Willing helpers!

Babs meets a visitor ⇓

⇑ Willing helper!

An unfortunate dolphin ⇒ beached itself on the island in the early seventies

⇓ "Little Island" and the bridge across.

⇑ Attie writing
"We Bought An Island"

⇑ Home-coming
after two weeks in hos-
pital

⇐ Fire Practice by the
Looe Fire Brigade

⇐ A flying visit

St George's Island ⇒
from the air

⇐ A close-up from
the air

View towards Rame Head ⇒
and Plymouth from the
garden of Island House.

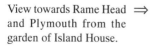

↑ Rock Swimming Pool off "Little Island", with the Grimer family, who were regular early 'helpers', enjoying themselves.

⇐ "Cheers to you all - come and see us soon"

↑ Attie - May 1995 - Babs ⇒

Book 2

"Tales From Our Cornish Island"

The PROLOGUE

'What is it like living on an island?' 'How can you possibly live alone there in the winter?' 'Whatever do you do with yourselves?' 'How do you manage for food, water, electricity and so on?' These and similar questions are shot at us *ad infinitum* by the many holiday-makers who visit us during the summer months, incredulous that two sisters, now both retired, should be able to resolve these problems and yet remain, as one gentleman gallantly put it, 'normal'.

This book attempts to answer these questions, although it must be left to the reader to decide if in fact we are 'normal', that is, assuming that normality can be defined. This book also sets out to give an account of our early pioneering days. How we came to acquire an island in the first place, as we were the wrong age, the wrong sex and in the wrong income bracket to make this seem possible, is described in *We Bought An Island*. To the many kind readers from all parts of the world, island lovers all, who have written asking for a sequel, this, in a way, is it. I say 'in a way' for a sequel suggests to my mind, not a resumption, but the end of a story, and these tales, by their very nature, are part of a continuing saga. Even as this is being written incidents crowd in thick and fast. Events are as unpredictable as the weather. The warp and weft of every-day life may have a certain pattern, varying with the seasons, but the adventures and excitements, the hazards and challenges and the ideas that are sparked off add a tumult of colour that bedazzles the onlooker and participant alike. An ordinary action such as the turning on of an electric light switch is fraught with anxiety. Will the generator start up and so give us light? Again when we retire at night will it be stilled as it should by the flick of a light switch in the bedroom? If the pilot light still glows, then, even if a gale is blowing, one must don oilskins to trudge nearly a quarter of a mile down the path to the generator to investigate.

If, on the mainland, you take a walk down the garden path to the road, would you expect to see anything out of the ordinary, except that perhaps the roses have blown down in the wind, the Joneses are painting their house again, or the workmen are digging up the road. A routine walk here down the path that ends on the beach is a daily adventure. What will be found there: a shipwrecked boat? a dead dolphin? a new model boat in full sail? a perfect china owl bobbing in over the rocks in a westerly gale? antique cannon balls? drums of lethal chemicals liable to explode at a touch? a sheep's carcase? furniture in good shape? semi-precious stones? tragically, a dead body? All these and many more have been found at the end of a saunter down our path.

Ordinary day-to-day life is highlighted dramatically. Add to this the projects undertaken that the island inspires, and life becomes crowded, leisure an elusive dream.

The difficulty then in satisfying the curiosity of those who would know how we make out on our island is finding the breathing space to sit down and write about it. Life is very much 'now', with our sights set only on the near future. Inevitably there will be unfinished tales and unresolved problems, as indeed there were in the first book not, as one reviewer thought, to whet the appetite of the reader, but because, unlike fiction, where plots must be neatly rounded off, this is about real life, and real life is not parcelled off into self-contained episodes.

Here on the island it is in fact a cross between running a ship and a farm, without crew or farm workers. It seemed an insuperable task to write the first book during the twelve winters or so when I was alone on the island. The writing of this sequel has been eased considerably since my sister, Babs, retired and now lives here all the time. Without her unfailing encouragement it would not have been written at all. She has spurred me on when my spirits flagged and has given unstintingly of her precious time and energy to help and advise me. I am indebted also to the regular voluntary helpers who, during the summer months, have relieved me of some of my share of the day-to-day work of the island. They have backed up Babs—who has been at the helm during the busy summertime—in every possible way. We are both of us grateful to our floating community of friends for their hard work and their versatility.

We have been told that it is refreshing to read a book in which there is no sex or violence. This is not strictly true. There is sex in abundance but it is that of the proliferating wild life, and violence we have in plenty but it is that of the raging seas that pound upon our shores and the storms of up to hurricane force that beat about our heads.

THE PROLOGUE

It is impossible to relate all the events and exciting happenings of the past twenty years in one book. This one therefore has been written in the form of tales, each dealing with a different aspect of island life and showing how it has evolved over the years. There are many more such tales to be told and others related here to be continued, for life is changing all the time.

Do you have to be a particular type of person to take to, or more to the point, endure island life? All we can say is that when we first came here we were considered to be the most unlikely would-be islanders and there were some who thought that we should only stick it out for three months. That we have just celebrated our twentieth anniversary here in a raging storm in February 1985 proves that if you have been touched by 'island fever' it matters not at all, for you have been inoculated for life against the hazards which will surely beset you, or so we ourselves hope, as each day dawns.

The *PIONEERS' Tale*

The metallic sound of clip-clopping awakened me from a deep sleep. Bewildered, I sat up surprised to see that, apart from shoes, I was fully dressed. More surprising still I was not in bed but flat on the floor, and I was not alone. The dying embers of a driftwood fire stared at me from a huge stone fireplace, the glow drained of colour by the sunlight streaming through the windows.

Where was I? Who was with me? Why was I sleeping fully clothed on the floor boards of an empty room?

With an exciting thud of my heart memory came flooding back. My sister, Babs, and I had spent the first night on our very own island. How had this come about?

Babs and I had dreamed the impossible dream of owning an island, and by an incredible series of unforeseen events it had come about. For me it was fortuitous that I had retired early so was still active enough to take on what, to all our friends, seemed a daunting challenge. The island, St George's, locally known as Looe island, although only one mile off the south Cornish coast, is pounded by wild seas for many parts of the year so at those times one might as well be 100 miles out in the Atlantic. Although not a desert island—it possesses three dwellings, Island House, two cottages, a generator and many outhouses—it has no inhabitants other than the owners, now miraculously our two selves. Babs, eight years younger than myself, had resigned from a plum job as Deputy Head and Headmistress of a large school in Surrey so that we could come to live here. Luck played a part in that the post of Senior Mistress at Looe County Secondary School became vacant and Babs obtained the appointment. Even so it meant a drop of several hundreds of pounds a year in her salary. Income-wise I only had my pension from I.C.I. at whose Head Office I had worked in London, but we reckoned that the chance of acquiring our very own island was worth any financial sacrifice, any risks. Indeed when we burned our boats for this once-in-a-lifetime opportunity, Babs had resigned her post with no other job in view, and through early retirement my pension was quite modest.

No wonder our friends thought that not only were we foolhardy but stark staring ravers, to roar off westward in mid-winter to live on an uninhabited island off the wild Cornish coast with only the certainty of my pension to sustain us. Dame Fortune, however, decided that we needed some encouragement for, by the wave of her wand, this senior teaching post became vacant and magically it became Babs's.

We had previously, following my retirement, bought two tiny fisherman's cottages in West Looe, one of which was to be a pottery, my designated second career. With the acquisition of the island we decided to move the venue of the pottery there, retain the two cottages—one for holiday lettings to help subsidize the upkeep of the island, the other for Babs to have as a *pied-à-terre*.

The latter was essential, for it soon became apparent that any commuting between the island and school would be out of the question. The weather and tides dictate the times when ferrying is possible. Winter storms and gales in autumn and spring can cut one off from the mainland for days or even weeks at a time. Since moving down to Cornwall at Christmas 1964, we had made several perilous journeys to get our furniture over. This had been possible only because of the seamanship and daring of Wren Toms, a young local Cornishman, who had cheerfully and eagerly taken on the job of transporting us over in the *Orlando*, a thirty-foot open boat whose only protection from the elements was a wheelhouse. Nevertheless five journeys in January and February 1965, had brought all our belongings over, including a massive eight feet high bookcase, thousands of books and forty gallons of home-made wine. The consensus of opinion locally was that we would last three months if we were not drowned before then.

Wren Toms had a reputation locally of being a daredevil who took risks, but it appeared to us that he met problems as challenges to tax his skill, which rightly, he did not underestimate. The fact is that it was entirely due to his ability that here we were, in mid-February in raging seas, at last resident on our island. He had brought us and the last of our possessions the previous day in fierce north-west squalls. Conditions were so bad that, once we had landed, he had advised us to return to the mainland and to come back another time to stay. We could not see the logic of this and, frustrated as we were by the abortive attempts to move since Christmas, this we flatly refused to do. Here we were on our island and here we meant to stay. There was the small matter that Babs would have to go back the next day anyway as she was due in school on Monday; but this

Saturday, 13 February 1965, we decided, history was to be made. It was compulsion to us that that night our heads should rest on the island. The other heads, being Toby our faithful, smooth-haired, curly tailed fox-terrier-brand friend, and Ruth, a girl who was going to help for a few months.

Many had wanted to join us in our project, the main contenders being Cecily, our niece, her husband Doug and their family of three children. It was obvious that our own modest income, without any family allowances or tax relief, would not run to supporting another family. Therefore any family who joined us would have to work the land sufficiently to earn the extra income necessary for their maintenance. We very much doubted the feasibility of this.

It seemed to us that we needed breathing-space. We would settle in, we decided, and view the possibilities from first-hand experience. In any case in those first early days our only desire was to live on the island, cope with the daffodils, cultivate the land and, in our leisure time, practise our crafts. We certainly did not want to take on any extra financial obligations, and we had no far-reaching plans. For the moment we were content to enjoy the heady delights of savouring island life. We were still in dreamland and did not want to come down to earth just yet.

When, therefore, Ruth, recently returned home from a stay in the US, her imagination caught by the chance of living on an island, offered to come and help us just for her keep and Insurance Stamp for a few months, we were delighted. No commitments for the future, no financial strain of supporting a family; as a short-term plan it seemed ideal. She could stay until May, when her parents would need her help on their smallholding in Shutta, by Looe. The arrangement had the added bonus that Ruth would have first-hand knowledge of market-gardening. With the island's early spring and the daffodils about to blaze into colour we could do with, if not a man, at least a lady of the soil. Wren, who had a full-time job working for the Council, had offered to help at weekends, as had two schoolboy volunteers. This, then, was our labour force.

This was how it came about that Ruth was the fourth member sleeping on the bare boards of Island House on that wild February Saturday night. It was also the reason for the metallic clip-clopping that had awakened me on the Sunday morning after our first exciting night on the island, for, on investigation, we found that the mysterious sounds that we had heard above the roar of the sea and the haunting cries of the seagulls, were caused by Wren who had left so reluctantly the previous afternoon. He had in fact returned soon after dawn and was chipping a channel through the rocks to the jetty with a pickaxe. It seemed an extraordinary occupation for dawn on a Sunday morning in winter, but Wren was no ordinary person. He loved the island and, as we now realized, because of this, identified himself with our problems and helped us so willingly with our projects.

To those who enjoy the amenities of urban or suburban life the prospect before us would have seemed incredibly primitive. We had come from Epsom Downs on the outer fringes of the Green Belt, with one foot in the country. We had enjoyed a comfortable life in a detached property, all electric, and full of labour-saving devices. To help us also in our full-time busy lives we had a daily help and a weekly gardener. Now we could only have electricity if we could get the generator going ourselves. A six months' period of non-habitation of the island had cancelled out its supposed automatic abilities. This entailed a quarter-mile trek down a muddy track to the generator to swing an enormous handle to get it started. Last thing at night we had to tramp down again to stop it so that the lights would go out, returning and going to bed by the light of an oil lantern.

Our freshwater storage tank had a weed growing in it. Consequently when we turned on the tap in the kitchen for a nice 'cuppa', out gushed a foaming brown liquid with a smell so putrid it had one retching on the spot. The Aga, the only visible form of cooker, was rusted from lack of use and the damp sea-air. An atmosphere of slow decay and death pervaded the whole house with the gloom that descends like a mantle on an old building that has had no human life breathed in it for many moons. In addition to this was the inescapable fact that the only food we had was what we had brought with us, and with the raging seas between us and the mainland, shopping trips seemed remote, to say the least.

This then was the situation that faced us on that first morning on our island of dreams. In retrospect I am sure that most normal people, housewives certainly, would have felt like jumping off the nearest cliff in despair. As only island lovers the world over and through the ages would understand, we did not appreciate the paucity of our situation, for unbelievably it seemed to us that we had attained paradise. Heady with island fever, we saw everything bathed in a rosy glow of achievement. Babs and I looked at each other across the bare boards, the inert and rusting machinery, our toppling piles of furniture strewn like wreckage in the general air of dankness, with unspoken exultation beaming between us. We were on our island at last. Nothing else mattered.

Presently Wren came in from pickaxing the rocks. He had recovered from his disappointment of the day before now that he was in on our adventure again, and was as chirpy as his name. Emotional like all Celts, he admitted to sinking into a slough of gloom on his return to the mainland the previous day. Now that he was back on the island he was full of enthusiasm again and, over coffee brewed from rain-water over the driftwood fire, he expounded in detail schemes for making a harbour. 'Mind you, it would cost many thousands, and there would be the problem of labour,' he added casually, but immediately brushed aside these two major obstacles and went into great technical details of how it could be achieved. We listened bemused. What a way of spending one's retirement! Builders of harbours indeed! Nevertheless, in our exalted mood, anything seemed possible. Encouraged by our interest and with his contagious enthusiasm and confidence-inspiring manner he took me down to the rocks and showed me how to wield the pickaxe so that I could go on enlarging the channel he was making to the jetty and so, presumably, start the foundations of the harbour. As the resident sister I, apparently, was the one most likely to benefit from his expert tuition and put it into practice.

Of all the activities I had hoped to indulge in in my retirement I had never envisaged pickaxing rocks. However, always willing to learn a new skill, I had a go. I found to my surprise and delight that the cunning use of rhythm, based on early training in eurythmics, gave a certain amount of ease in wielding this fearsome implement, without exerting too much energy, and I was able to chip away to Wren's approval. Nevertheless it was not one of my ambitions to become a lady champion pickaxer. Privately I earmarked this activity for delegation to some future 'friend' more naturally endowed physically than myself. I intended to 'channel' my energies in other directions. Although at the time of writing we have not so far built a harbour, a series of muscular young men, and older ones too, have chipped away and we now have a sizeable channel and, with the tide in, quite big boats can moor up by the jetty.

After Wren had inspected the generator and declared that the lack of automation was beyond his skill and knowledge, and a job for the Lister engineer, he prepared to return to the mainland to bring his wife over for a picnic lunch. That the sea was lopping all over the place worried him not in the least. He rowed out to the *Orlando*, went ashore in that and around midday returned with Valerie and a picnic. We thought it very brave and loyal of her to come, for charging across the wild seas in mid-winter for a picnic on an island was not exactly an ideal way of spending a Sunday afternoon. She was dressed rather nicely with a fur tippet to keep out the cold—she also wore high-heeled shoes. Suddenly we felt rather sordid in our jeans which we had slept in all night, and our seaweed encrusted gumboots made us feel like something that the sea had washed up. Valerie produced a delectable picnic lunch and we fell on her delicious salmon sandwiches with fervour. We sat on cushions on the floor but managed to find an odd chair for our visitor from the furniture which was amassed higgledy-piggledy in the hall and kitchen. For the first, but not for the last, time since living on the island we felt that we had lost any hostess image that we may have had in our previous existence.

After coffee, to the accompaniment of more big talk of future plans, mostly about harbours and the like, we came down to earth to the more mundane task of settling in. Valerie helped move some of our books down to the dwelling above the jetty—this we later named Jetty Cottage. From here we could see a door built into the cliffs above the jetty beach. To reach it one had to climb up some stone steps built on to the rocks below. This, incredibly, was the entrance to the source of our freshwater supply. We subsequently discovered that the island is abundant in fresh water; the difficulty is the vast expense involved in locating its best source, channelling it and storing it against the times of summer droughts. This problem was to dominate our lives and still does. That it has always been a problem was obvious from the signs on the island of several disused and presumably dried up wells. As people of wealth had owned the island in the past it was apparent that it was not an easy problem to solve. The system we had inherited was novel to say the least. The door led to a tunnel which has been bored some thirty or forty feet into the cliff; this acted as a channel for the spring water which flowed into a well which had been excavated eight feet or so below the entrance. A petrol pump had been installed on a concrete platform above the well; the water was pumped up to storage tanks in the woods high above the daffodil fields, and gravity fed to the three dwellings, where, in theory, one turned on a tap and out gushed spring water. Our first job then was to drain the tanks of the putrid water, sterilize them with the sodium chlorate we had brought with us and flush them out. We scarcely had time to start on what was later to prove a mammoth task and to note in passing that the first daffodils were peeping through, when it was time for the shore party to embark. Sadly we saw Babs, Wren and Valerie off. They rowed over the bucking seas to the *Orlando* and we waved to them as they disappeared into the darkness.

Warmed if not cheered by baked beans and eggs cooked over the roaring driftwood fire, we filled our flasks with hot rain-water for a late night drink and coffee in the morning. We then made our pilgrimage down to the generator to turn it off, and so up the track again, the lamplight flickering eerily in the overhanging trees.

Unbeknown to us we were watched by a pair of eyes.

Back in the autumn, the Whitehouses, from whom we had bought the island, wrote to us in Surrey, from Looe, where they had already moved so that Mr Whitehouse could have the medical attention he needed, to ask if we could take up residence straight away as a cat had refused to leave the island with them. Their daughter Toni had been rowing over each week to leave dried food for her in the scullery of the house where a window had been left open, but autumn gales had made it impossible for her to continue to do this and they feared for the cat. We, of course, 240 miles away, could do nothing to help, as Babs's resignation did not take effect until the end of the Christmas term. It seemed impossible that the cat could survive, although rumour had it that she had been seen fishing off the rocks. If this were so, she must have been a very remarkable cat. Remarkable she was, for survive she did. The Whitehouses left in August and we did not take up residence until February. On each of our forays with furniture during January and early February we had left several plates of dried food, water and milk for her as Toni Whitehouse had done. Always on our return all the dishes were empty but one. However long the intervals between our visits there was always one dish left in reserve. Surely even non-cat lovers must realize that only a superior intelligence would leave an iron ration in reserve for emergency. Not once, however, had she revealed herself and so it was now. Each night we left food and drink for her in the scullery and by morning it had gone. For many weeks there was no sign of her in person; silently and mysteriously she came and went. But that she was watching our every move was later revealed in a most uncanny fashion. Meantime we continued to provide for our invisible guest.

Having done so that night, Ruth, Toby and I retired to bed, this time, more conventionally, in a bedroom, because before daylight faded we had dragged some mattresses upstairs. The house is situated on a promontory and on one side the front door is not more than ten yards from the cliff edge. The house appears to be built on rock; and one hopes that this is so, for the Whitehouses said that during their stay they had lost eight feet of pathway from this very edge, due to a landslide. Another eight feet would be periliously near to the front door. One of my early fears was that one morning I would step straight out of the door, over the cliff edge to the sea below. One soon learns to be philosophical however; more pertinent hazards jostle out the fanciful ones and one tries to harness a fervid imagination to a practical use. In any case the joys of living on an island far outweigh the dangers and disadvantages, the discomfort and sometimes sheer physical misery. This is difficult to explain to those who have never succumbed to the lure of islands (or mountains, with which they are akin); but it is true that once an island casts its spell one is held in thrall. Willingly, challenges are met head-on; pitting one's wits against the difficulties thrown at one by nature and machinery becomes a way of life, and the physical discomforts are endured for the ineffable joy of living in an enchanted, magical world.

So it seemed that night as I looked out of the window of the bare bedroom, across the moonlit sea to Eddystone lighthouse flashing its friendly light twelve and a half miles away. I drifted off to sleep to the roar of the surf on the rocks below, and I exulted in my good fortune, only sad that Babs would be resting her head in the cottage on the mainland and would be regretting, too, that we were not together to share these rare and exciting experiences.

As the sun streamed through the windows next morning, our first Monday on the island, we lit the fire to make coffee and discussed plans for the day. Ruth had been detailed by Wren to rub down the buoy ready for mooring our boat the *Islander*. The buoy, a massive lump of rusting metal, looked more like a wartime mine washed up by the sea, and Ruth was welcome to this task. I opted to take another look at the generator. It seemed important to the smooth running of our lives to overcome the burdensome chore of making the twice nightly pilgrimage, first to swing it into action, then later to silence it so that we could retire to bed. As those who have followed our earlier adventures will know, I am not enamoured of machinery. On the contrary I have an almost pathological fear of it and of engines that leap into apparently uncontrollable life at the touch of a switch or lever. I have never had the least desire to subdue them to my bidding and have always been more than happy to leave even the driving of a car to others more eager than myself. Nevertheless it seemed desirable to come to terms with some of these monsters if we were to survive with a modicum of comfort.

If I had known then how much our lives were to be dominated by machinery in all its fiendish forms, and subject to its most malevolent moods, I might never have set foot on this particular island, but made hotfoot for a desert island where fire would have to be conjured up by rubbing two sticks together, and a light obtained, if I remember rightly from childhood reading, by igniting a brazil nut—of all things! I knew for certain that I should have to live with the generator, for Babs—a car driver—who, one assumed, would have at least a working knowledge of the mysteries lying under the bonnet, and should not therefore be daunted by wheels and cogs and things that whirred and spluttered, would be living on the mainland for the greater part of the time, and Ruth, who revelled in things mechanical would be leaving in two or three months time. Resolutely, therefore, I entered the generator-room and read the instruction book. 'If engine fails to start, locate N and M. Press reset in case K has tripped. 'It read like a piece of spy fiction. Who were the sinister N and M? and had K really fallen for their wiles? Or perhaps MI5 was responsible but was too secret to be mentioned!

Hastily I retreated. Wren was right, it was a job for the Lister engineer. So off I went to the beach to collect driftwood and seaweed. We had been told that potatoes grow particularly well on seaweed and it seemed a matter of some urgency to plant some as soon as possible. The island has an exceptionally mild climate, similar, we had been told, to that of the Isles of Scilly; also, that produce was a month ahead of Hannafore, only one mile opposite on the mainland. The general saying, too, was that one layer of clothing less was needed on the island than in Looe. Being surrounded by sea the island rarely has frost, and snow is so uncommon we have only seen it three times in the twenty years we have been here. On each occasion it was a mere sprinkling and disappeared before the day was out. This is astonishing, for in Looe, every winter, frost and ice make the roads dangerous, and it is a regular feature for the steep hills rising out of Looe to be gritted to make them passable, and Babs has frequently had to deal with an iced-up car. This was a common occurrence at Epsom Downs, our former home, and an accepted hazard of our long winters there.

So it has never ceased to be a wonder to us that our new home enjoys a sub-tropical climate. Honeysuckle blooms around the porch at Christmastide and it has become an established tradition with us to gather as many garden and wild flowers as we can to make a Christmas garland. Usually we can reckon on picking at least thirty varieties, including sweet-smelling violets which bloom in the woods from November to March. In the warmth of our short winters growth is rapid too. Whereas we were accustomed to sowing biennials in the autumn to flower the following spring, we found that by following this practice on the island, plants would come up in a matter of weeks and be in full flower the whole of the winter right through to summer. On a January day it is a glorious sight to look out of the window and see the borders a blaze of colour from the many-hued wallflowers and stock, soon to be followed by fields of daffodils. Before winter is scarce departed the woods become a sea of primroses and bluebells and we feel that St George's is indeed one of the 'Fortunate Isles'. All this we were yet to find out.

We had been told that it was tradition to plant early potatoes on Boxing Day. As it was now February it seemed a matter of urgency to sow them as soon as possible and I was determined to get started at once. That second morning, therefore, with the house in utter chaos, I spent carting wheelbarrow-loads of seaweed up from the shore-line to a field near the house. I then dug a long trench, lined it with seaweed, covered this with a layer of beautiful friable soil, which we knew from having tested it previously to be almost 100 per cent loam and slightly alkaline, then planted Arran Pilot seed potatoes in the prepared trench. On one of our brief trips over Wren had announced, because of the stormy seas, 'Hand luggage only!' For some obscure reason potatoes seemed to fill the bill and subsequently we staggered through the surf with a sackful apiece of seed potatoes, and frantically chitted them out in the twenty minutes we were allowed ashore. On another trip in January we had spent our precious time digging a field at breakneck speed as though our lives depended on it, planting as many as we could in the time. I do not recall why potato planting was such an obsession with us. We had never bothered to grow them previously; tomatoes, runner beans and lettuce being the extent of our culinary ambitions. Always flirting with diets, our own intake of potatoes had been a modest seven-pound pack to last the whole winter, potatoes being unfashionable with the diet-conscious at that time. This near-mania for sowing them, then, can only be attributed to the seductive appeal of producing a crop way ahead of ordinary mainland mortals. A local greengrocer had offered us 3s. 6d. a pound for any earlies we could produce, so we knew the island seaweed-grown potatoes were a highly desirable crop, for 3s. 6d. was a very high price indeed in 1965, especially as this was the wholesale price.

Alas! for these grandiose schemes. That year a blight ruined the nation's crop and the field we planted suffered the same fate, but for some reason this particular brave little row escaped and by May produced the largest and most delectable potatoes we had ever tasted. This was the general consensus of opinion, too, as we handed them out like a rare and exotic fruit, and with the overweening pride of inordinately proud parents. We sowed more than potatoes that day for we planted with them an interest that has flourished and multiplied over the years. Nowadays I dig hundreds of feet of trenches; we drag up truck-loads of seaweed and line the trenches with this and comfrey plus our own compost from the many heaps which we build. Over the years we have grown dozens of different varieties. These seed potatoes we obtain from Donald Maclean of Crieff, Perthshire, the acknowledged doyen of the potato world. He cultivates some 359 different varieties (the figure given for 1985) and he will sell them in small quantities, even as few as two or four tubers of the rarer ones, to those who wish to experiment. We so desire and I keep charts and analyse the data to find the best kinds for our soil and climate, and we hold potato tastings to judge the flavour and texture. Two of our voluntary helpers, Jim and Barbara Chanter, in addition to chopping logs for our winter fires and helping our conservation project in many useful ways, lift our main-crop potatoes. They plump for 'Vanessa'. Clarrie, who, with her friend Betty—both retired agricultural college lecturers—comes to help every year, favours 'Estima'. She takes a penknife from her pocket and with a deft flick of her wrist will delicately shave the merest wisp of skin from her chosen 'Estima' to reveal with some triumph the golden flesh beneath. Mesmerized I watch, as before my eyes, she transforms the humble spud to a gleaming jewel, waving her penknife much as a conjuror waves his wand. We give the gold award to 'Bintje', The 'Duke of York' ties for silver with 'Estima'. 'Romano' gets the bronze. However, there are many more for us to try, and experiments to make.

This operation took the whole of that first Monday morning, for in addition to the lengthy task of digging the trench and lugging up seaweed I had to locate the trays of seed potatoes. It may seem incredible that two large trays of potatoes could go missing but the truth was that our early days were bedevilled by a complete inability to find *anything*. The nature of our moves over, in rough seas in mid-winter, meant that all our belongings had been piled indiscriminately in the hall and kitchen of the house. Imminent storms forced hurried retreats to the boat to make the safety of

Looe harbour, and each succeeding trip only added to the chaos. On one unexpected calm crossing in early February—a summer-like day—we had attempted to make a slight clearance by removing some of our goods and chattels down to the large room leading off from Jetty Cottage. This room which was a converted barn, and had at one time been a music room, we designated as a transit camp and hoped to mount it as our operations room and restore some sort of order out of the chaos. It was a mammoth task, however, and we only had time even on this less frantic of our visits to move a few of the more cumbersome of our possessions, as a wheelbarrow was our only means of transport. At least we could just get into the house and make a passage through the hall to the lounge where we had slept on that first memorable night and where we now cooked our meals over the driftwood fire.

You would think that coming from a compact modern house, we would have plenty of room on an island for all our worldly goods. Although from the outside Island House looks large, a mansion dominating the cliffs above Jetty Bay—some visitors wonder why we do not use it as an hotel—it is in fact just two up and two down: two bedrooms above and, below, a large lounge and a farmhouse kitchen, flanked by a wide hall. All three are oak-beamed and the hall and kitchen as well as the adjoining scullery are stone-flagged. Half-way up the stairs is a large bathroom supported by outhouses below and crowned with a flat roof nestling below the gables of the house. This flat roof would make an ideal observatory, for with no town or city lights to dim the stars and no air pollution it would be a perfect location for the study of astronomy. With this in mind, but at present only a dream, we have acquired quite an extensive library on this subject.

In searching for the elusive trays of seed potatoes I pounced with triumph among the mountains of artefacts on a log saw. On our many moves from Epsom Downs we usually stayed overnight with friends of ours, Jack and Betty MacAllister, who at that time lived in Newton Poppleford in Devon. Jack had presented us with this brand new saw as he reckoned that our need would be greater than his. A thoughtful gift, for although I had no intention of taking up pickaxing as a retirement activity, I conjectured, and rightly, that sawing would be a most useful skill to acquire in our new life. And so it was and still is. Never a hatchet or chopper lady, a saw seems to lend itself to my particular style. It is the rhythmic movement that appeals more than the clashing cymbal-like action required to chop and hack. Whatever the reason we have, over the years, acquired an impressive array of saws. The names alone have often persuaded us to buy them. A coping saw, surely, is one to give confidence whatever the challenge; and a rip saw, what better one to use if one were feeling in a fine carefree mood! Often have I wondered how we could ever live without the support of, for instance, a tenon saw—the euphony of the word alone opens up whole new vistas of gracious living.

This log saw was the first and one of the most valued of our collection, and many has been the time when I have silently thanked Jack, who, unfortunately, is no longer with us, for his contribution to our island life. It seemed a good idea, now that I had this newly found treasure, to saw up some wood ready for the evening fire.

Driftwood fires sound romantic to those who depend on central heating or gas or electric fires, and so they are. There is nothing to compare with sitting snugly in front of one on a stormy winter's night, the blazing logs sending out a rich warmth and assailing one's nostrils with aromatic delight. As with all pleasures, however, especially those of an island, there is a price to pay. Of all open fires a driftwood fire has a voracious appetite. It is all too easy to fall into the trap of spending the greater part of each day collecting wood and sawing it in order to have enough to burn at night.

There was no danger of this happening today, for having found the saw I promptly lost it again. Re-losing found objects seems to be an occupational hazard here. Short of slinging everything for the day around one's neck there is no answer except to lead a tidier life or cut down one's activities to single figures. How many hobbies have the houseproud? If they have any they would definitely not be the messy types where impedimenta is strewn all over the place. Perhaps the answer is to live in a confined space, like a sailor in his cabin, for how true it is, like Parkinson's Law, that the more space there is the more one will find to fill it.

On that first working day it hit me between the eyes that to achieve anything at all without spending valuable time searching for and losing everything again, some sort of order must be made out of the chaos in the kitchen. Over lunch of toasted cheese sandwich, made over the driftwood fire and helped enormously by quaffs of peach wine Tokay 1962, I persuaded Ruth, who was hell bent on scraping rust off the buoy, that we really must sort things out a bit. Supposedly it would have been the first thing a housewife would have set about, but neither of us was a housewife by training, inclination or choice. On the other hand I doubt if a dedicated housewife would have allowed herself to get into this situation in the first place. However, one has to do chores, even in paradise; so reluctantly, that afternoon, we began to push some of the furniture out into the hall. If we had known that we could not run the deep freeze from the generator we had then and had for many years to come, we might even have pushed it over the cliff, but by moving it into the hall we had some walking space in the kitchen.

Soon it was time to go down to the main beach for an assignation to wave to Babs over on the mainland. While awaiting her we collected more driftwood that had been tossed up by the afternoon tide. At last I espied her through the binoculars, a lonely figure on the rocks at Hannafore. Somehow she looked pathetic and it was with a great sense of loneliness that I watched her wave, turn and climb back over the rocks.

Ruth and I had managed to drag a couple of bedsteads upstairs by moonlight, so that night we slept in great luxury, Toby thankfully sharing my bed. So far he had not accompanied me on any of my expeditions and when I did lure him outside he had hurriedly retreated. Even the calls of nature were dealt with quickly and quietly. Although I accompanied him, these sorties were no farther than was strictly necessary, then back we had to come to the comfort of his new home. He was, after all, thirteen and a half years old with a heart condition, and, like all pets, he was very conservative. These habits persisted for a considerable time. We were perplexed, and worried that he would not get enough exercise and that being an islander did not suit him after all. We need not have been concerned. Having established his roots he gradually extended his territory and eventually the whole island became his domain.

That night I revelled in the luxury of a comfortable bed and as again I drifted off to sleep by moonlight the world seemed a good place.

The next day it dawned on me that although we were civilized to the extent that we had actually undressed and slept in nighties in proper beds, this was Tuesday; we had not had a wash since Saturday morning on the mainland, and we had been completely unaware of the fact. Frantically I looked for my toothbrush. Having at last located it I performed my ablutions with water from the hot-water bottle, as water from the tap was giving off most unpleasant effluvia. A change of clothing seemed desirable but here again it was difficult to locate any. Incredible as it may seem I spent the rest of the day half-clothed in the few items I could find, secure in the knowledge that there was no one to see me except Ruth, Toby and the gulls. When we at last ventured out for our perpetual search for driftwood my anorak enveloped me in its comforting warmth and gave me an illusion of respectability—so far! In retrospect it seemed a far cry from the days so recently relinquished when I commuted daily to London, rising to the personal challenge that I must face each day in a different outfit and bedecked with earrings, matching lapel brooch, discreetly elegant ring and an immaculate hair style crowned with a hat—a 'must' in those days for anyone with any self-respect. Casual clothes were for weekends only but chosen equally carefully with an eye to colour and suitability. Perhaps suitability is the key to the metamorphosis that this short taste of island life had brought about. Hand-tailored suits and stylish outfits may have been mandatory in my former life, but the island demanded jeans, oilskins, sea boots and anoraks and happily I bowed to its dictates. The anorak that only partially covered my half-clad figure that day has passed into history, for patched and mended many times by Babs—for I have no skill with a needle—I still don it thankfully each winter for the worst of the outside jobs.

Thus clad, Ruth and I, accompanied by Toby, who was persuaded to come if I put his lead on, made our pilgrimage to the generator room. To our consternation the generator would not start. Reference to all the important charts suggested that the air-filter might need cleaning. While Ruth was trying to locate this I found that Toby had disappeared, lead and all. Worried beyond belief I dashed up to the house to find that the heavy door has been pushed open, but of Toby there was no sign. Frantically I called him. I called again. After a long pause there was a faint and distant 'Woof! Woof.' from above. He had taken himself to bed. I took some peach wine down to Ruth for it seemed to me that a bit of stimulus would help fathom the mysteries of filthy filters and the like. And so it was. The filter suitably cleaned according to the instructions, the generator was away and once more we had electricity.

Close by the generator room is the tractor shed. This is a large brick building which houses a tractor, a plough, an assortment of farm machinery and all manner of garden equipment and unidentifiable ironmongery—some of this last seemingly dating back to the last century. This highlights another problem of island life. How do you dispose of articles that have outlived their usefulness, if they are not burnable, for the dustmen never call? This we have never satisfactorily solved. Neither apparently, had the previous owners, judging by the bric-á-brac, obsolete machinery and kitchen equipment that cluttered the many outhouses. One blackened metal jug caught my eye. It was almost certainly a Victorian hot-water-jug. In spite of its neglected condition it had a nice line and sense of balance. Over the years I grew fond of it, blackened as it was, and took it up to the house several times meaning to clean it, but somehow never got around to doing so. A few years later one of our helpers, a young graduate, knowing of my interest, bought himself some cleaning pads, and secretly spent every evening cleaning and polishing it. One morning there appeared on our doorstep a gleaming brass hot-water jug, burnished with loving care, by Julian, and transformed into an article of real beauty. The following year we saw a similar one in an antique shop. It was smaller and rather battered. It was priced at £28. At today's prices it would probably be worth considerably more.

This day, however, I seized on a treasure that made me shout with delight—a tin bath. Triumphantly I dragged it up to the house, filled it with rain-water and heated it over the log fire. Fortunately the fireplace, made from island rock, is very large and in olden days would have been used for spit-roasting. We now had a field day. First we washed all our cooking utensils, then our clothes, and finally ourselves, with, I hasten to add, a change of rain-water between each operation. It is surprising how luxurious and comforting it is to have a bath in front of a roaring log fire and I was reminded, as I so often am, after returning from some bruising and sometimes bloody expedition, of Rupert Brooke's 'benediction of hot water'.

Greatly refreshed, I decided to explore the island. There had been little time to do so since our arrival for we had been fully occupied with our battle for survival. The extent of our exploration had been to penetrate the jungle of our possessions in search of some vital object, and our forages no farther than to the generator room or down the path to the main beach in the inevitable search for driftwood. Not that the island is big, but its topography makes it appear larger than it is. Only twenty-two and a half acres in extent and about a mile in circumference it is possible nevertheless for the island to hide anyone's whereabouts for hours, even when just a stroll is involved. Many islands are barren and treeless. St George's, unlike most small islands, is wooded. It is 150 feet high and hilly in every direction. In fact there is only one piece of land which is level, a lawn at the back of the house, and it is man-made, having being levelled and shored up by dry-stone walls. This, in its former glory, was a croquet lawn—a delightful game we had both enjoyed in our youth—but alas! we have so far found no time for it in our busy lives here.

The island's illusion of size is enhanced by the indented coastline, a labyrinth of caves, rocky coves and steeply rising cliffs. The western seaboard is like a Land's End in miniature; exposed to the full fury of the westerly gales that roar in from the Atlantic, its rocky cliffs jut out into the broiling sea below, which never seems calm on that side of the island. From the summit one looks westward past Hoare Stone to Gribben Head with Mevagissey and Dodman Point beyond. On a very clear day it is possible to see the Lizard Peninsula, and it gives one a feeling of immensity and a sense of being part of the universe to realize that beyond the horizon the first landfall would be South America with perchance a glance at the Azores on the way. It is a very steep and often dangerous climb down to the caves below, in one of which, we were told, a silver sword was found before the war.

It was up to the top that I climbed today. Behind me just below the summit nestled a field protected on three sides by woods and bramble. It is here that the first daffodils, 'Magnificence', appear. Usually they begin to bloom in January, but they were late this year and today I had my first sight of them, and I knew that one of our first island activities was about to begin. We had been told that fifteen varieties of daffodils were grown on the island, five acres being under cultivation. This is not instantly apparent for, except when the daffodils are in bloom from January to March, the fields are verdant, the grass apparently giving some protection against the gales. Visitors who come in the summer when the daffodil bulbs are dormant see only what they think is lush meadowland divided by luxuriant hedges of mauve veronica and pink 'escallonia. 'Why', they demand, to our constant irritation, 'do you not keep sheep and cows?' Some remain unconvinced even when we explain that if we had the expertise, time and inclination we should have to give up the daffodil farm, for not only would the blooms be trampled upon but they would be poisonous to livestock. Farmers, of course, never ask us. It is usually those from urban areas, who when motoring through the countryside see the apparently idyllic sight of sheep and cows grazing on farmland. In the past I had a friend who was a farmer, and seeing at first hand the ills and disasters that can beset livestock, I was convinced that this was not the kind of life that I could happily share or one of which I could make a success. I knew, too, that however much of a strain teaching was at times, Babs's thoughts had never turned to sheep and cows as an antidote. Neither of us had, of course, ever during our careers yearned for a daffodil farm, but this was a *fait accompli*, and although we were well aware of our ignorance, and had moments of trepidation, in our more optimistic moods we told ourselves that it was nothing more than a glorified garden on a grand scale. That there was much more to it than that we were about to find out.

Excited that soon we should be harvesting our first daffodils I quickly skirted the woods and descended by the steep track to the south-eastern tip of the island and across the narrow footbridge to the 'Little Island'. From the peninsula the 'Little Island' points like a finger south-east past Rame Head to Prawle Point in Devon. In all directions gulls wheeled and screamed. In a full gale they will ride the wind; one after another they will rise on the eddies and gusts and gracefully dip down again. This will go on for hours and it is quite hypnotic to watch them. Was, perhaps, the inventor of the Yo-Yo inspired by gulls?

I did not stay to explore the 'Little Island' for I had another assignation with Babs to wave to her on the mainland, but although I looked carefully through the binoculars from the main beach, there was no sign of her at all. Despondently I began to pick up driftwood when, to my astonishment, I saw our boat the *Islander* leaving the harbour—a lone craft in that expanse of sea. Soon there was great excitement for in addition to Babs and Wren, Ruth's mother Mrs Jennings, Mrs Whitehouse, her son Desmond and our two schoolboy helpers, Charles and Duncan, stepped out of the boat.

Babs brought with her a wonderful assortment of food—chicken, pork chops, vegetables, apples, chocolate, bread and most important of all—fresh water. Soon our lounge was alive with the buzz of conversation. To show the measure of their concern for us everyone spent the whole time telling us what to do until my head was spinning. That night I went to sleep to the relentless rhythm of 'what you should do is . . . What you should do is . . .' pounding through my head. It is a litany that has gone on over the years. Hardly a visitor sets foot here without telling us what we ought to do. If we did all the things suggested we should certainly not have any time for visitors! Imagine a farmer waiting at the farmhouse door to welcome visitors and entertaining them to tea during the sowing or harvesting season, or breaking off milking the cows or shearing the sheep to answer questions about farming life and and what it is like in the winter!

The next morning, our first Wednesday on the island, we again filled our new-found treasure, the tin bath, with rain-water, heated it on the open fire, and luxuriated in the bliss of a bath—island style. It seems extraordinary in retrospect but I remember deciding that this operation, necessary and enjoyable as it was, took up too much time, and any further ablutions, I said, must wait until the weekend!

Around lunch-time we noticed that suddenly the sea had almost disappeared between us and Hannafore. Unbeknown to us this was one of the biggest spring tides of the year when high and low water are at their highest and lowest. Traditionally on Good Friday it is possible to walk across from the mainland dry-shod. Over the years, however, we have noticed that this exceptional spring tide is variable and may occur either in February or March. It is only possible to walk across if it is calm, which it rarely is at this time of year. Even then one has only minutes to spare to make the return trip. It is quite frightening to be slithering on the seaweed-strewn rocks, in the middle of the channel, with the sea rapidly encroaching on either side. It takes little imagination to realize that if one should slip the future could be very bleak indeed, and that within a very short space of time the sea would be many feet above one, and increasing to a fathomless amount with the racing tide. No wonder many locals say that they have never attempted the trip across. Today there was no question of walking across; the sea was running swiftly and deeply through the only possible channel; The rapidly receding tide revealed a mass of menacing rocks between us and Hannafore and gave the extraordinary effect that the island was rising out of the sea. It seemed an excellent opportunity to do a survey of the rocks and sea-bed, and so chart a passage for our boat. In my ignorance I did not realize that the winter seas have a tremendous effect on the state of the beaches and sea-bed. Cliffs of shingle thrown up by a storm from one direction will be obliterated and replaced by a vast expanse of sand from an onshore gale. A north-west squall will drive sand in one's face, stinging it raw, so that it's like floundering in the Sahara in a sand-storm, albeit a frozen one. A south-east gale will sweep away the sand, revealing rocks that have not been seen for years.

Happily unaware of these dramatic changes in the topography, I had a quick glass of peach wine, pulled on my seaboots and, with a notebook and camera, waded as far into the middle of the channel as I could. Even as I stood there sketching, the wind changed with the turn of the tide and freshened from the east, a direction hated by the local fishermen. With the sea now rolling rapidly in on either side it seemed prudent to return to the shore. It was as exciting as my mountaineering days when one stood on a peak in danger of being enveloped by swirling mists which had risen from nowhere, making it hazardous and sometimes impossible to find the path down to the valley, and one was in danger of being benighted unless the mist lifted. Now, though, the path was quite clear—back to the beach as soon as possible. From high up on the beach I took photos of the now fast-disappearing rocks. Soon the mainland receded, almost as though the island had set sail and soon one would be in mid-Atlantic. This is an illusion that persists to this day and is further heightened by the fact that the island, except for its two beaches, rises perpendicular from the sea. The house, which stands on the cliff top, has a bathroom with magnificent views in three directions and is like the bridge of a ship. When the seas sweep past below one can almost feel the movement as though the island were riding the waves. This impression is so vivid that we keep a compass in the bathroom to check the direction of the wind, although it is patently obvious that the points of the compass do not change.

After my charting expedition I reluctantly returned to the mundane task of clearing out the kitchen. In a few hours it became quite habitable but there was no way we could get the Aga to start. As it was all rusted up from lying idle for six months in the damp sea atmosphere and the wet days of autumn and winter, there was only one solution that we could see; dismantle it as much as possible and scrape off the rust. This we did, taking any parts we could detach on to the lawn outside the front door. We scrubbed industriously with wire brushes in the most incongruous setting imaginable. There we were on a cliff top, a couple of veritable Cinderellas, up to our elbows in rust and dirt, our faces smudged with soot. We scraped away at these assorted bits of ironmongery, in clouds of rust, to the accompaniment of the roar of the sea below and the haunting cries of the seagulls, their wings flashing in the sunlight. Around us golden daffodils were appearing everywhere, belying the fact that it was mid-February. Beyond, the green seas raced past the island from the east, white horses riding the crest of the waves and sparkling in the sunlight. Encouraged, no doubt, by the setting, not to mention the ubiquitous peach wine, we worked with a will. I blessed the greengrocer, back in Banstead in Surrey, who had let me have crates of over-ripe peaches at 2s. 6d. a crate, for I was able to bring several demijohns of this golden nectar to the island. In no time at all the Aga bits and pieces were polished bright, and reassembled. We would, however, need some charcoal to ignite the fuel, and I hoped that Babs would bring some on her next trip.

Her half-term holiday was due the coming weekend, so the next priority now that the kitchen was more or less habitable was to get the flagstaff in working order in readiness for her arrival. For some reason it seemed essential—although we had more pressing problems, such as the putrid water that still gushed out of the taps—that we get the St George's flag flying so that we could greet Babs in style. Babs and I are very proud of this flag. We inherited it with other island accoutrements, together with another flag which we were told you used if you required a doctor. Mr Whitehouse told us that the idea was that you lay it out on the boathouse roof. One of the stories that Mrs Whitehouse told us was that they had arranged a signal with a friend of theirs who lived over at Hannafore whereby they would put a white sheet on the boathouse roof as an invitation to tea. The coastguard mistook this for the medical SOS and sent the lifeboat out! We have sometimes wondered during the time I was alone on the island how it would be possible to stagger down to the beach, climb up to the roof of the boathouse, and put the flag there if one were so ill that medical aid was required—and who would see it supposing these acrobatics *were* performed if it were dead of night or there was a thick sea mist?

But as usual there were more pertinent problems to be dealt with without worrying about hypothetical ones. We were told that we were allowed officially to fly the St George's flag, a privilege, we understood, accorded to Admirals of the Fleet and Church of England churches. In some guide books the tale goes that in a sea battle of long ago, Looe, then a port, sent twenty-one ships of the line, second only to the number from London. The battleship St George did so well that St Michael's Island, as it was then called, was renamed St George's Island. We have copies of old maps dated 1588, the year of the Armada, giving the title St Michael's. Present-day large-scale maps give it as St George's or Looe Island. Naturally we favour St George's. The Vatican may say St George is no longer a saint but he still represents England, and with great ceremony each year on 23 April we celebrate St George's Day and Shakespeare's birthday by hoisting the flag and drinking a toast in island wine. In wine-making circles, traditionally, dandelion wine is made on 23 April. Weather permitting, as part of the celebrations, we do so too, and drink of this delectable nectar, if there is any left from the previous year. It is a fancy of mine that one year we will have actors performing parts of *Henry V* on top of the island, with visitors en masse contributing to the crowd scenes. How appropriate on 23 April it would be to hear the rousing words from Act III, Scene 1:

> Follow your spirit, and upon this charge
> Cry '*God for Harry, England, and Saint George!*'

Unfortunately on this day although we had a flag there was no flagpole. On the cliffs on the south-east promontory of the island, above the bridge leading to Little Island, stood a tabernacle; this is a kind of socket made of three pieces of timber sunk in the ground, bound with iron bands and standing some four feet high. This made a receptable for the flagpole. There were, in fact, two tabernacles, one quite rotten from years of weathering. In course of time we were to discover why there was no flagpole—it is impossible for any to survive the winter storms for long. Over the years we have lost several and a year or so ago, during a particularly violent storm, the tremendous seas broke right over the cliff top. The tabernacle itself was uprooted and swept by the sea to the cliff edge on the other side of the promontory. Inexplicably it was the sound one that went and the semi-rotten one has come into its own again, serving us in good stead right up to the present time. As I write the current flagpole has a slightly drunken list to starboard, the result of an early autumn gale, auguring ill for its survival this coming winter. On this day we were lucky enough to find a very tall post in the sweet pea area of the Smugglers' Garden, which we thought might do, and a hunt among the treasures in the tractor shed produced a pulley. Eventually after many abortive attempts we managed to hoist the flag. Satisfied that we could greet Babs in appropriate style when the time came, we hauled it down, dismantled the precious pole, and returned to the house to clear a space in the bedroom for her.

On Saturday, just one week after our historic landing, about the time when Babs was due, Ruth and I marched out to the cliff top in a biting blizzard, with the pole perched on our shoulders, for all the world looking like a clip from a Laurel and Hardy film. We managed to slot the pole into the tabernacle and attached the flag to the rope. Expectantly I stood by ready to hoist it as soon as we spotted the *Islander*. Earlier we had noted a great swell coming in from the east. Now it was racing in, crested with white horses. This meant that there would be a 'bar' in the river mouth, making it difficult or perhaps impossible for any vessel to leave the harbour.

I trained the binoculars on the harbour mouth. There was not a boat in sight; indeed there was not a sign of craft anywhere at sea. Anxiously I scanned the road above the rocks at Hannafore in case Babs should be there to give a signal. Suddenly I espied her blue anorak and the unexpected sight of our Mini with the fibre-glass dinghy aloft. So they were going to row across the 'Island Roads'—the channel between the island

and Hannafore. This would be some expedition; not only was Babs coming with stores, but friends of ours from Surrey, Brian and Anne Rainforth and their two young children, were to stay with us, for it was Brian's half-term holiday also, for he, too, was a teacher. Hastily I hoisted the flag, which stuck at half-mast at the first attempt. An evil omen, I thought grimly, but after a few furious tugs from us both it made it to the top. We then raced down to the beach leaving the flag flying defiantly and bravely in the now blustering wind. At last we could see Wren rowing Anne and the children across in the little white craft. Meantime Babs and Brian were climbing down over the treacherous rocks on the other side, loaded with stores and luggage. The plan was, Wren told us, that having landed Anne and the children, he would row back in our larger metal boat, to bring over the other two and all the gear. We all lent a hand to get the heavy metal boat down to the shore to launch it. Eventually everything and everyone were safely across the racing tide, high but not dry, for they were all soaked to the skin from spray and lopping waves. No one appeared to be worried about this and our little party, loaded with stores and luggage, made its way up to the house. Excitement was so great no one gave a thought to changing into dry clothes. Proudly, on the way up to the house, we showed Brian the generator. Oozing sea water, he nevertheless was greatly impressed, although he had very little chance to appear otherwise. It must be said, for the record, that even after all these years, the generator is still our own little bit of magic. We never cease to marvel that (when once it became fully functional) at the flick of an ordinary light-switch anywhere on the island, it will leap into life and the whole island will, in the immortal words, be 'lit up'. Sad to say the magic does not always work, but then, does any magic? Or, come to that, does any machinery?

Babs and I went out to the flagpole and ceremoniously hauled down the flag. As dusk was fast approaching Wren and Ruth took their leave, for Ruth was to spend a few days with her parents while Babs was with me. They rowed back to the mainland in the fibre-glass dinghy, with the trolley for hauling it over the rocks at Hannafore perched aloft, and a weird craft it made it look. We then entertained our guests to a slap-up meal—island style—of eggs, bacon and baked beans; the driftwood fire adding its own subtle aroma. Eventually, after much talk and laughter, we retired. Babs, bless her heart, was very impressed with the bedroom. The fact that she had a proper bed to lie on and sheets to sleep between would seem to her, no doubt, the height of luxury after her first night on bare boards.

There was certainly nothing else in the bedroom for her to admire, for it was otherwise quite bare. The others bedded down in Jetty Cottage in some fashion or other.

The following day we set about trying to get some of the more important things in order. Babs had brought some charcoal with her, and our de-rusting efforts must have been effective for she had the Aga going in no time at all. Since that day it has become the heart of the island. The constant heat transforms the kitchen from the lifeless shell we found to a place of warmth and friendliness that seems to envelop all who enter. It appears to exert a magnetism, for young and old alike are drawn to it and bask in its warmth even in the height of summer. Appreciatively they sniff the tantalizing smells, and they say that there is just something about it that makes them want to loiter awhile. Maybe it is the fragrance of newly-baked bread, mingling with the headiness of fermenting wine. The sight of gallons of brilliantly clear wine in the demijohns stacked in racks from the stone-flagged floor to the oak-beamed ceiling has an irresistible appeal, with perhaps the hope of island hospitality to come. It is not only that, for the kitchen has the same attraction for little ones of four years' old and non-drinkers alike. We, too, feel the same and are never happier than when we are pottering about there immersed in our many activities. This is strange, for it is the only room on the island that has no view. One door leads to the scullery, the other into the hall; a third wall houses the enormous Aga, cupboards, shelving and the like. Only the fourth wall has windows. These certainly are large, and pierce the side of the house whose walls are three to four feet thick, but they look out to a high bank, beyond which hedges and fields slope steeply up to the woods, masking any views, for the house is actually cut into the hillside. It is cosy in the depth of winter, when the wind is howling and the island is lashed by storms, to sit at the kitchen table making our various crafts, or to have a bake-up. There would be no view anyway, for the windows everywhere are generally thick with sea-spray which flies over the top of the house, falling in scuds of foam, covering the lawn beyond like a carpet of snow. This is peeping into the future, for at that time we had been on the island just a week, with many daunting tasks to tackle before we could indulge in the making of crafts, enjoy and have the satisfaction of baking, or bask in the ineffable luxury of just sitting. Suffice it was that we had the Aga going and one could say that the heart of the island was beginning to beat again.

The next imperative task was to tackle the problem of the water supply. We had previously inspected the two water-storage tanks in the woods
and had made an abortive attempt to clear out the stinking weeds growing
in them. Now on lifting the lid and looking more closely we found that a
tree was actually growing in the outlet pipe. First we emptied out all the
stagnating water. Brian then cleaned it out while we drained all the water
from the tanks and pipes in the house and cottages. After a good 'do' with
the sodium chlorate in the offending tanks we went down to the jetty beach
and climbed the steps up to the door in the cliff face. Within was the petrol
pump. This we managed to start, which was remarkable considering that it
had not been used since last summer and would be damp from its close
proximity to the sea which had been pounding at the steps a few feet below all winter long. During that day and the next we continued to pump
water into the tanks and run it out of the taps in the dwellings to flush out
the system. By the end of the second day, although there was still a faint
smell, we decided that the water was good enough for washing, so daily
ablutions were now added to our curriculum. If any of the smell clung to
our skin, we were of the opinion that we were all in the same boat, so to
speak, and would not notice each other—we hoped.

After a day or two more of pumping and emptying we held a committee meeting, and issued the 'Flushing Report'. For, greatly daring, we had
been sipping it at intervals, and when the taste of the sodium chlorate had
disappeared, and nobody had actually collapsed, we decided that it was
now good enough to drink. Presumably we boiled the water as an added
precaution, but after this lapse of time I do not remember. I rather doubt it,
for one of the effects of island life is that one begins to live dangerously in
some ways, at least by mainland standards. A casual insouciance creeps
into one's attitude towards matters that would be quite unacceptable in a
more sophisticated society. This does not mean that our standards are necessarily lower, but they are different. When you live close to nature you
have to get your priorities right, and fussiness over food and drink gives
way to thankfulness that you have any at all. Only gradually were we able
to substitute our own island standards of good wholesome food, grown
without poisonous chemicals, for our previous brand of fastidiousness.
Some whims were discarded instantly.

Coffee was a case in point. In my previous civilized existence coffee
was of supreme importance. For me there were only two acceptable beans:
one was a Kenya coffee bean from the Army and Navy Stores; the other,

freshly roasted beans from the Algerian shop in Soho. After a long day in the office I would dash up to Soho and arrive home late in the evening clutching my precious parcel, the delicious aroma of the beans—still warm from roasting—assailing one's nostrils and full of 'Eastern Promise' of the delights to come. I would then hand-grind the beans and serve coffee *á la filtre* to everyone. Both jug and cups had to be thick brown earthenware: the delectable flavour and the fragrance that arose seemed well worth the effort and added a subtle patina to one's daily life—or so I thought. Instant coffee, of course, was despised and none was allowed in the house. You cannot get freshly roasted beans on an island in winter time, short of growing them yourself—and this may yet be attempted in the foreseeable future—so what do you do when you are faced with the certainty of being cut off from the mainland? You do a volte-face and get in a good stock of instant granules by the one and- a half pound tin. It is served in thick brown earthenware mugs and, made with island spring water, it really is quite delicious.

Bread is another case in point. Nowadays we bake our own as a matter of course, but in those first early days stores and baking were out of the question and the only food we had was what Babs managed to bring with her. A loaf of bread, therefore, was something to be prized and cosseted. It may not make the Guinness Book of Records but, when alone on the island, I did stretch out one loaf to last three and a half weeks. Certainly it grew a mould at intervals, but the answer to this was simple; you scraped the mould off and put the loaf in the Aga to freshen it. I had one rough rule of thumb: mould on meat, fish or fowl was a 'BAD THING' and out went the offending items to the ever-eager gulls. Mould on grain subjects such as bread came into the category, according to my reckoning, of penicillin, and therefore, in moderation, should have no deleterious effect. Question? How can gulls survive on putrefying flesh that would poison humans and pets? Answer: I do not know. Question? How did I survive this crude distinction? Answer: I do not know, but some nineteen years later I am writing this!

The foregoing will, I hope, answer in part, those who ask 'How did you make out in those primitive conditions after the ease and comfort of civilized suburban life?' The simple fact is that you have to adapt. Not everyone can do so and only those who can should try island life. Babs and I are of the vintage that is supposedly set in its ways. If we were we would have taken the first boat back to the mainland. On the other hand we have had day visitors, half our age, who ask rather fussily 'where is the separate "Ladies" and "Gents"?' As this is our home and not a railway station, I say as pleasantly as I can: 'Where yours is in your home'. If they only realized how lucky they were that we could offer them any such facilities at all! Having a lavatory that worked and having enough water to flush it was one of the major luxuries of life that we aspired to but did not always attain, in those early days. 'Water, water everywhere, nor any drop to drink,' was not only our theme song but, as a variation on a theme, we could have added 'nor any drop to flush'. Nowadays we have, we think, reached the height of sophistication in pumping sea-water to perform this vital service. How this came about must wait to be told later in our island saga.

However, at this time we felt that things were beginning to look up. The generator started after a fashion, the Aga was going merrily, we had a water supply, and we had beds to sleep in. What more could we ask? Well we could ask how we were to cope with the daffodils that were peeping up in all directions. Before doing anything about them we were delighted to find a boiler in the outhouse under the bathroom. To our great joy we managed to get this going and were able to luxuriate in hot baths; wrapped in hot towels from the tank in the airing cupboard we felt that we had reached the very pinnacle of gracious living.

Now that our creature comforts were taken care of, we concentrated on our more immediate plans. Anne volunteered to help sort out the books and first there was much shuntings of bookcases. The biggest was one that our brother, Tom, had made from an enormous kitchen dresser, when he was a young man. This was about 8 feet tall and 8 feet wide, and after a perilous journey across the sea in an open boat, was now housed in our ex-barn/transit camp adjoining Jetty Cottage. This became the home for many of the classics. Also in this huge room were some built-in bookshelves and these stored a miscellany of our guide books, maps, foreign dictionaries, primers and the like. Up in the house Anne tried valiantly to sort according to categories and size, an almost impossible task as they ranged from huge bound copies of *The Illustrated London News*, *circa* 1879, to small pocket editions. Our tastes were catholic to say the least, and over the years we had amassed a sizeable collection on varying subjects covering history, poetry, music, art, archaeology, biography, philosophy, belles lettres, mountaineering, wildlife, the theatre, travel, astronomy, cricket, cookery, pottery, photography, gardening, assorted crafts, to name a few, as well as several sets of encyclopaedia. Some subjects needed several shelves apiece. Anne burst out laughing when she came to the section on 'Retirement and How to Enjoy It'. She wondered if we ourselves had written them. She was not alone in this opinion. Our mother, who had a wonderful facility for summing up a situation or expressing an opinion in a succinct phrase, had once said, when I proudly showed her my latest book acquisition: 'All the books you buy, dear, you could write yourself.' I would agree with her over the books on retirement, and now that Babs has joined me we could certainly tell the world 'How to Enjoy Retirement', although I must admit our way would not be to everyone's taste.

Brian elected to carry on with chipping the channel through the rocks to the jetty—the first of my 'friends' to whom I thankfully relinquished this task. Our major concern was to sow as much as possible in the marvellously fertile soil and harvest the daffodils which were now appearing in different parts of the island. With great excitement we picked our very first bunches and as we gathered them we remembered how expensive they were in the towns and cities at this time of the year, and what a breath of spring they brought in our cold winters high up on Epsom Downs in Surrey. We wanted as many as possible, for Babs only had two days' holiday for her half-term and it would not be very long before Wren would be coming to fetch her. Suddenly we espied him rowing across from Hannafore, for the sea was coming in fast from the east and it was not possible for any boats to leave the harbour. Valerie was with him, and we admired her for this, for it was no weather, sea-wise, just for an outing. In spite of what must have been a bumpy trip for Valerie, with great patience she showed us how to bunch daffodils the professional way, for her parents had a large farm and she had grown up with dealing with the early daffodils for which Cornwall is famous; so we were very glad of her expertise.

While this was in progress Wren joined Brian at chipping away at the channel to the jetty. Then to celebrate our very first daffodils we had a lunch of wine, ham salad and chips followed by fruit salad and cream, served with a flourish in the pottery soup bowls I had thrown on the wheel at Epsom School of Art. These were glazed oatmeal and white; they had ear-like lugs but they were not quite uniform in size. However, they were my very first set of thrown pieces and An O'Neill, my pottery teacher, kindly said that this distinguished them from mass-produced factory ware. She fostered them by firing them especially so that we could take them to the island as a memento of my time at the Art School. Later, a sculptor who stayed with us for a while on the island and helped me with pottery, instructed me in the making of moulds and produced a master-mould of one of the soup bowls so that these works of art should not be lost to posterity.

Some have remarked on the clarity with which these meals of so long ago are recalled in fine detail. The truth is that it was a miracle that we ate at all, as we had no stores, no produce and no deep freeze. Each meal, then, was a triumph to be remembered and lovingly recalled. To be self-sufficient in food is essential if one is to survive on an island. Now that Babs is here all the time it is even more important. It is one of our more enjoyable projects to produce gourmet meals from very simple ingredients, and we have become expert in the use of left-overs. Nothing is ever wasted and if any food exceeds its life expectancy one of the cats is summoned to act as 'taster'. When I wintered here alone I reckoned that I could go for three months without duplicating the menu and only cooking from scratch once a week. Although we now have a deep freeze that can be run from our electrical supply (always supposing that the generator does not go on strike), we still employ these prudent techniques, ones that could be used just as well on the mainland, with much saving in time and money, with the added bonus of eating tasty, unadulterated food.

Alas! it was soon time for Wren to take Babs back from her short break. It was almost dark when the three of them, plus the precious daffodils, rowed off in the fibreglass dinghy. Babs, for some reason was sitting aloft the trolley which would be needed to haul the boat up over the rocks at Hannafore. Soon they were swallowed up in the darkness, and nothing could be heard but the roar of the sea. I had given Babs a lamp to signal when they were safely across for there was a strong tide running from the east and I was concerned for their safety in that tiny craft—a mere eight feet in length. I was greatly relieved, therefore, after some twenty minutes, to see a tiny light winking at us from the mainland. Later Babs told me that the journey had been very bouncy as the freshening sea smacked the dinghy broadside on. Perched aloft on the trolley she found herself bounced up and down, sometimes riding high in the air, and the next moment coming hard down on the iron bars. It must have been frightening to be tossed high above a tiny dinghy in pitch darkness, but seemingly she was quite unperturbed by the danger. The after effects were all that concerned her, for she was bruised black and blue, and she found it extremely painful to sit down for several days.

Brian and Anne were to be with me for a few more days so we carried on with what seemed the more important tasks, sowing vegetables seeds and onion sets, sorting out the books and getting the furniture in some sort of order. Books and their housing, although they seemed to dominate my thoughts, were only one of many problems. For almost the first time in my life I began to sleep badly. Sleep had never been a problem, except when we were enduring the anguish of wondering if the island would ever be ours. Although lacking in other skills I was lucky enough to possess the ability to sleep at will. A flick of the finger and I could be out like a light, anywhere, anytime, and could awaken to order in as little as two minutes if necessary. These catnaps would recharge the batteries until the small hours, so that five hours per night were sufficient to give long periods out of the twenty-four hours for the highly interesting and compulsive activities that life has to offer. This ability to be on nodding terms with another world, so to speak, sometimes has its disadvantages. Once when I was young I was cycling along country lanes with my schoolgirl friend, Tommy. She turned to speak to me and was horrified to see that I was fast asleep and was heading straight for a hedge. Sadly this facility for instant deep and refreshing sleep had now forsaken me. Every hour or so I would awaken, my mind buzzing with all the things to do, and new schemes chasing each other around my head. While I slept intermittently I dreamed whole films, in colour, with complicated plots and exciting and dramatic endings, and complete symphonies played by a full orchestra, in stereo. They were all completely imaginary—just figments of a fevered brain. The only thing that got me off to sleep again, when I did awaken, was the compulsion to see the end of the film with its denouement, or to make sure that I was there for the grande finale of the last movement of the symphony.

This would never do. The precious energy essential for these early pioneering days was being drained away. For pioneering it certainly was. We had taken on a whole island complete with daffodil farm and market garden, a house and outhouses, two cottages in a sad state of disrepair, farm buildings and machinery, an orchard, a generator, a water-pump in the cliff, three boats, a boathouse, three outboard engines, and we knew precious little about running any of them. On top of this we planned to superimpose our own activities. High on the list was a pottery. A building abutting the generator room had been earmarked for this. The Jetty Cottage outhouse was to be converted into a darkroom for the all-important photography. Somewhere had to be found for Babs's stone-cutting and polishing equipment. Then we planned to keep hens, goats, start a vineyard and practise other crafts for which we never had the time; on the list were wood carving, copper enamelling, marquetry, woodwork, leatherwork and painting. What we had not foreseen was that the heady excitement of actually living on an island and seeing the vast potential would spark off fresh ideas daily. It was an though an invisible electrical current galvanized our brains. Neither had we the wit to realize that what we planned would require an army of technicians, farm labourers, builders and the like, when our entire labour force totalled one resident lady pensioner, and weekends only—wind, weather and tide permitting—Babs, Wren and two schoolboys. The most important factor that we seemed incapable of facing up to was, that under these primitive conditions, or at least conditions lacking in the modern amenities to which we were accustomed, actual day-to-day living would consume so much time and energy. We have often wondered how, on that radio programme *Desert Island Discs*, the castaways had the strength left to put on or listen to their eight records, let alone the time to browse through Shakespeare, the Bible and the tome of their choice. For us, in those early days, surviving was a full-time occupation—and often still is.

No wonder then, sleep was fitful and feverish. Inexplicably, with our usual proclivity for brushing aside major problems, trivialities were the most troublesome. So often it was the worry of items forgotten or mislaid that jolted one into wakefulness. One instance of this forgetfulness was a chicken that Babs had kept in the fridge in the cottage on the mainland, intending to bring it over to the island at the first opportunity, knowing how short of food of any kind we were. This she did. We put it in the lounge in the sunshine to make sure that it would be thoroughly thawed—then promptly forgot about it. About a week after she returned to the mainland I came across it, looking rather sad. However, I popped it into the Aga, which was now burning beautifully. It seemed to recover in this new environment. Greatly daring we ate it. It tasted delicious. Once again we lived to tell the tale that our friends of our more fastidious days would have found hard to believe.

This sleeplessness, however, left me exhausted and quite unfit for our strenuous physical life, until I hit on the idea, like others before me, of having a pencil, paper and torch by my bedside. This did the trick for although I still awakened frequently, when once I had jotted down the brilliant idea or location of lost articles, sleep came again instantly.

All too soon it was time for the Rainforths to leave. I picked bunches of daffodils for them to distribute among our many friends back in Surrey, including the O'Neills from the Art School and of course themselves. Wren brought Babs back for the weekend, loaded up the *Islander* with all the luggage, then made the startling suggestion that I might like to accompany them to the mainland and he would bring me back. This I had no wish to do at all. As far as I was concerned the island was my life from now on, and the mainland held no attractions for me whatever. It is a feeling that persists to this day, and I only go when absolutely necessary for visits to the hairdresser, dentist, etc. and an annual foray for stores. A visit for pleasure just does not enter into the scheme of things. We have everything we want here: books, music, TV, innumerable hobbies, the market garden and daffodils, and above all the ever-changing sea and the beauty of the island itself, *and* we have no traffic, no clanging of the telephone, no supermarkets and no neighbour trouble. I was, therefore, horrified at Wren's suggestion and was adamant that I would make my farewells here. Wren, however, was very persuasive and cajoled me into going by promising that he would show me how to run the *Islander* on the way over, and I could bring it back. So after a pleasant instructional trip it was goodbye to the Rainforths and hello to Zena who came over to the cottage and made us all a cup of tea. Zena was one of the first of the Cornish friends we had made during our enforced six weeks' stay on the mainland until we made our final move over to the island. She had identified herself so much with our island project that it was a joy to see her again.

I then had the great thrill of steering the *Islander* all the way back. 'A perfect landing!' announced Wren as I beached her with a satisfying scrunch. Now, as a bonus, I was allowed to take part in a more horrendous operation of working the caterpillar tractor. 'Allowed' was hardly the word for I had no desire whatever to be a tractor driver. But Wren is not only very persuasive, he enjoys passing on his skills to others who may benefit from their use. As I have found, often to my cost, that 'Yes' slips more easily off the tongue than 'No', I now found myself gingerly mounting this fearsome monster.

The reason for using it was exciting enough. A few days previously we had espied on the east side of the main beach one round and two hexagonal hand-hewn pieces of granite or stone, each about a yard in diameter and several inches thick. They had been exposed by an exceptionally big spring tide. As far as Wren knew—and he had known the island all his life—they had never been seen before. How long they had been buried in the sand and what exactly they were we still do not know. It was a most exciting find, however, for the extraordinary thing was that one of them was similar to those on the chapel site on top of the hill. According to the records the chapel, which no longer exists except for a few remaining stones, was built in 1139. The two hexagonal stones were of granite and matched those of a granite structure sited by the house. This is of unknown origin. We were told by the Whitehouses that it was the font from the chapel; although there is no proof of this there is obviously some connection between this, the remains on the chapel site and now these stones found, inexplicably, high up on the beach. If they were not to be buried again by another spring tide, perhaps for centuries, it was essential to move them soon.

That this important, and to my mind, dangerous operation was to be performed there and then by just Wren and me seemed utterly preposterous, for it was seemingly impossible to budge them one inch. Wren now proceeded to demonstrate his skill at levering. First he managed to prise one up an inch or two with a plank. My job was to push another plank into the gap thus made. Wren then raised the stone a few more inches and I pushed another plank in. So this prising, levering and pushing went on until these three most unwieldy and heavy objects were slowly and carefully lifted and manoeuvred on to the truck. This was now harnessed to the tractor where I reigned in unmitigated terror. Scarcely recovered from my menial but nevertheless nerve-racking task of plank pushing, I was now commanded to pull various levers, and 'have a go'. The monster jolted into life beneath me and amid much screeching from below, and yells from Wren, above the roar of the engine, we were away, a ten-foot perpendicular drop to the beach below, an unpleasantly close few inches to my left, luckily avoided. As we reached the top of the path Babs came running out of the house to see what all the racket was about, and I do not suppose my terror-stricken face allayed her fears. At last, to my intense relief, our precious burden was deposited by the bank at the side of the house, and there these relics remain awaiting some expert to identify them.

Thus, in the space of an hour or so, I had not only made an unexpected trip to the mainland, but had learned how to handle an eighteen-foot diesel motor-boat, driven a tractor, learned a little about the art of levering and had helped rescue these important finds and bring them to a place of safety. With hindsight I realized, of course, that Wren had planned all of these happenings from the beginning.

The DAFFODIL FARMERS' Tale

Now that the Rainforths had departed, Babs and I planned our time until Sunday when Wren would bring Ruth over to the island and take Babs back to the mainland. First we decided that we must have a 'sort out. Not all is glamour or even sheer hard work on an island, although there is always plenty of the latter. Some of it is merely fretful, just as it is on the mainland. Precious hours of her stay were spent in 'sorting out'. This seems endemic to our island life, for even to this day this occupation dominates our lives as much as the weather does. The Queen may be dogged by red despatch boxes, but we are dogged by looking for lost items. We look at each other through clenched teeth and mutter, 'We will have to have a "sort out"', but how time-consuming it is! Seemingly possessions are like weeds—many of them are the right things in the wrong places, at least they are for us. We have a house, a couple of cottages, sheds, outhouses and a generator room to confuse us. We wonder what it must be like to live in a castle or palace with dozens of rooms to search through for lost items. I am also puzzled by the fact that an inert object like a ball-point pen seems to have a life of its own. Although we buy them by the dozen they will all elude us and find some secret hiding place known only to themselves. I am sure that if this island is excavated in a thousand years time some archaeologist will mark on his map: 'Possible site of early ball-point pen factory?'

With spring upon us, however, sowing and planting seemed more important than dealing with inanimate objects. With much enthusiasm we sowed sweet peas, tomatoes, sweet corn, runner beans and melons, and made cuttings of carnations. All of these were started in an unheated greenhouse, so convinced were we that spring came very early indeed to the island, judging by the daffodils that were now coming up almost everywhere.

The main daffodil fields are between the house and the main beach. They slope down from the woods almost to the cliff edge, separated from this only by the path to the beach. They are divided by colourful hedges of

37

pink escallonia and purple veronica and are fenced off from the path by ash palings. These fences were obviously intended to act as wind-breaks, for these fields are exposed to the full force of gales from a northerly or an easterly direction. Some of the fences hung around in a drunken fashion and gave us some idea of the strength of the winds.

When we explored the top of the island we found more daffodil fields exposed to the south and south-west, and the fences here, although protected by impenetrable brambles, were in an even worse state of repair. It looked as though they had been laid waste by a hurricane. This, in fact, is exactly what had happened, and we found, in the course of time, that winds of storm force ten and even hurricane force twelve have ravaged them from time to time.

Fencing then would be a major problem, and we began to realize that there was more to cultivating daffodils than picking pretty bunches when the rest of the country was under snow and ice. In view of the havoc that the winds could cause we were puzzled that along the path from the house to the beach some of the fencing had been replaced by embryo privet hedges. As these were spindly little cuttings of some twelve inches high we wondered what protection they would give to the daffodils and what advantages they had over fences. Although we did not appreciate it then, the planting of the privet was a wise alternative to fencing. In less than seven years we had a row of fine thick hedges and now they are so high that it takes a tall person on a step-ladder to trim them. In fact they look as though they have been there since the days of Elizabeth I. This has given rise to a fancy of mine that we might construct a maze, although it is a matter of doubt if we would ever have the time to plant and tend it. Many were the times, over the next few winters, when I wished that the previous owners had planted those cuttings earlier in the life of the island as a daffodil farm, for every time there was a gale, down would come some fences. From the very beginning of our life here people have said: 'How I envy you living on an island!' Perched on a step-ladder dragged up to the top of the island in the teeth of a gale, banging in posts with a sledge-hammer, the rain streaming down the neck of my oilskins and the ladder swaying precariously in the wind, I have often wondered if they know what island life is really like. It is a continual battle with the elements, and charging around with a step-ladder and a sledge-hammer in a full gale with icy rain slashing against your face is only one of the many hazards met with in this 'idyllic' life, as we were to find out. Nevertheless, the sense of achievement in overcoming the problems and challenges far outweighs the feelings of despair that threaten to engulf us as some new crisis rears its head.

Although not physically demanding, the next problem we faced was a knotty one. Of the fifteen varieties, which were which? Although in our ignorance we thought that all daffodils were the same—yellow—we could now see that each field was quite different. Some were indeed yellow with large trumpets, others were smaller and had red centres; others again were white with yellow centres. Anyway, we decided, it did not really matter for there were not enough in bloom in any one field to fill a box. At Epsom Downs we had been introduced by phone to Mr Myers, the wholesaler at Covent Garden to whom the Whitehouses sent their daffodils. A friend of ours happened to be a family friend of the Myers and so a useful contact was made. Mr Myers had offered to give us any advice that we might need. We did not think that we needed it just yet. The Whitehouses had left behind an assortment of boxes, tissue paper, brown paper, string and other impedimenta to do with the marketing of daffodils. We now knew from Valerie how to bunch them professionally, so on the Sunday, before Babs returned to the mainland, with loving care we bunched up the choicest blooms of all the different varieties that were then in flower, and packed them artistically and with much care in one of the boxes. They looked really beautiful and we closed the lid, sealed and addressed it with a certain amount of reluctance and a great deal of pride. There were some bunches over, so Babs took some back with her to distribute to our friends in Looe and to take to school. At the cottage Babs made out the invoice and securely tied the box for its journey by train to Covent Garden; took it by car to the station, and, much as a fond mother might wave her young son off to his first prep school, saw it safely ensconced in solitary state among the thousands of boxes already on their journey from the Isles of Scilly via Penzance to London in the 'Flower Special'.

Zena and Charles took the remainder and sold them locally at the current rate of 1s. 8d. per bunch, much to Babs's surprise but delight. We had marketed our very first daffodils—we were now established daffodil farmers! We came down to earth with a bump when we received a letter from Mr Myers. It was very friendly and polite but he would like to point out that each box should contain one variety of daffodil only—a mixed box would not do for marketing wholesale.

This posed quite a problem. We knew each field grew a different variety and we had inherited a load of impressive looking labels printed with the name 'ST GEORGE'S ISLAND' in large capitals followed by VARIETY: QUANTITY: with appropriate spaces left for entering the details, and addressed to MYERS & CO., COVENT GARDEN, LONDON. We now had to resolve the problem as to which label applied to which variety. How does one distinguish 'Magnificence', 'Scilly White', 'Unsurpassable', 'Fortune', 'Mount Hood', 'Aranjuez', 'Cragford', 'Yellow Cheerfulness', 'Beersheba', 'St Agnes', 'Scarlet Gem', 'Sempre Avanti' (so evocative of musical evenings) and 'King Alfred'? The following weekend Babs and I went down to Jetty Cottage, which at that time was a more or less derelict building; we picked our way over joists that exposed the bare earth beneath, to a room floored by concrete. This had obviously been used as a packing station and an adjoining room as the office. Here among the papers we found a list of daffodils with the prices fetched against each kind. We decided to name the daffodils, as each field in turn became ready for picking, in the order in which the list was written, and we would label them accordingly. Surprisingly enough this worked, for during the whole time we sent them to Covent Garden we never had our labelling queried, although we ourselves were never sure of the difference between 'St Agnes' and 'Cragford'—they were so alike—one being a bigger version of the other; probably, we thought, an older sister. We hoped that soon we should have enough of each variety to fill the appropriate box.

During the following week I inspected the fields. I had heard somewhere that it was the present-day method to pick and pack the daffodils when in tight bud, and it seemed to me that one field was at this stage. Ruth had resumed her de-rusting of the buoy, and she was rubbing down her 'land-mine' as if it was meant to be the most gleaming bit of metal in a war museum of torpedoes and the like. I persuaded her to leave this operation for a short time to inspect the daffodils. 'Too tight!' said Ruth, 'the necks have to bend over.' Nevertheless, thrilled that we should have enough to fill several boxes, and afraid that by the weekend they would be in full flower and past their peak for the tight bud condition required, I said: 'Let's get them over to Babs anyway. They will probably bend over later,' I added hopefully. In the end we decided to pick those that looked as though they were thinking about performing the required gymnastics; get them over to Babs, and if there were not enough to send to Covent Garden they could be sold locally.

THE DAFFODIL FARMERS' TALE

We proceeded to launch the fibreglass dinghy with a fair amount of argument as to the best method to stop it going in circles and drifting back, high and dry, on the beach again, without getting wet ourselves. The difficulty was that it required a certain depth of water to float the dinghy in the first place. By the time we managed to clamber into the bobbing craft the combined weight of our two selves and the daffodils, and the fact that the tide was going out, set us back on dry land again. There we were—in spite of all our pushing, shoving and heaving of ourselves, pulling on the oars or trying to punt off with them—sitting in the dinghy on the beach for all the world as though we were about to have a picnic. There was obviously much more to launching a boat than we realized—Wren had made it look so easy. However, after more argument and a great deal of laughter we managed to flounder into the boat and at last got away with our precious boxes of daffodils.

The sea was calm for a change so there was no difficulty in rowing across to Hannafore. The problem was in finding the right channel through the rocks. Mr Whitehouse had told us how to line up various landmarks to find the way in; the best apparently being the sewerage channel, as this would take us right up to Hannafore beach. This involved negotiating a vast area of rocks. Soon they were looming above us in all directions, and we were lost in a labyrinth of pinnacles. In and out and around, we pushed and prodded with the oars, but as the tide receded we soon found ourselves almost high and dry and marooned. We scrambled out and tried to pull the boat higher up the gully in which we found ourselves. We pulled her as far up as we could and did our best to tie the rope round one of the rocks. Then we lifted out our precious boxes of daffodils and somehow managed to slither our way over the rocks to the shore.

Up at the cottage we waited for Babs to come home from school. She was delighted to see us and thrilled to have the daffodils. She came round to Hannafore to see us off but to our consternation the boat was not there; the tide had turned and taken it away. Panic now ensued. A kindly gentleman, Mr Curtis, came to the rescue and not only gave us a lift back to West Looe but arranged for Jack Dingle, a local boat owner, to collect the drifting boat and take us back to the island. The sea had strengthened with the incoming tide and Jack Dingle said that it was too dangerous to land us on the main beach. He therefore landed us and the dinghy safely on the eastern side of the beach and we were very grateful to him and Mr Curtis for saving the day. It was not quite the end of our disasters however. We found that the sea had taken away the wheelbarrow in which we had transported the daffodils down to the shore and the trolley for the dinghy. However, all was not lost, as the saying goes. The next day the outgoing tide gave us back both the wheelbarrow and the trolley; we were able to rescue both and by washing them with rain-water to counteract the effect of the salt sea-water, and by the diligent application of grease to the vital metal parts we were able to put them to good use again. As a further consolation Babs got the top prices for the daffodils she sent to Covent Garden and Zena the excellent price of 1s. 9d. a bunch for those she sold locally for us. We began to think that we really *were* daffodil farmers.

We were soon to realize how true this was. Daffodils began to spring up everywhere—the fields were a sea of gold. We blacked-out every conceivable room and outhouse on the island and filled them with bucket after bucket of daffodils, for the darkness necessary to keep them in bud as long as possible. Babs came at the weekend and we all three bunched and boxed, bunched and boxed. Babs took them back to the cottage on the mainland and was up until the early hours, labelling, invoicing and tying up the boxes. Then before going to school in the morning she loaded the car and delivered the boxes to the station to catch the Flower Special.

The following weekend Barry, a relative by marriage, his wife Margaret, and Dave Tank, their brother-in-law, came to help. Margaret was almost lost to sight as she staggered under the huge loads of daffodils larger than herself. Incredibly we managed to bunch and box them all and with some loss of sleep by Babs they caught the Flower Special. Relentlessly, however, the daffodils continued to spring up everywhere—the whole island seemed to be covered with them. My ribs began to ache with so much stooping and the soreness was so severe that I could not sleep, it was like a nagging toothache and the pain pierced my side every time I breathed; but I could not stop—the daffodils *had* to be gathered. I picked about 800 to 1,000 each session with little time between for a snack. We then had to load them into buckets and lug these around the island so that we could find some protection of darkness for them, for the hot March sun would bring the buds out in full flower if we did not hurry. Soon the white 'Beersheba' reached their peak. This was the largest and most prolific field of all; a large and elegant white daffodil, it resembled a lily and always fetched tip-top prices at Covent Garden. Even in a glut year 'Beershebas' always held their price for they were in great demand for weddings and funerals; locally they were not so popular, as they were considered to be too funereal. As they were destined for Covent Garden and would be in transit for a long time, they had to be in the very peak of condition, that is, in tight bud, so we were under great pressure to lift them and store them in darkness. There seemed to be millions of these white daffodils in that field—it was like trying to eliminate the Milky Way. We were absolutely loaded with daffodils everywhere, for it was the very height of the season. We knew that Wren was due in two days time so we changed from picking to bunching. This was a relief for my painful side but there was still a great deal of physical lugging about of buckets, heavy with water as well as the flowers, for now the difficulty was in finding dark rooms, for the bunches took up more room than the gathered armfuls.

The day Wren was due it was brilliantly sunny, with the sea a Mediterranean blue—even in London the temperature was seventy-five degrees, very high for March. The sea, however, was making up and white horses began to appear. The wind was freshening all the time from the dreaded easterly direction. Nevertheless we had to start the long job of boxing the bunches to be ready should Wren come. In the early evening Babs and Wren appeared on the beach at Hannafore. They signalled across—it was too rough. Despondently we unpacked the boxes and hastily made wire frames to fit the baths in the cottages to support the precious bunches, for already some of the buds were beginning to open and must not be crushed. We also had another problem. All the seeds which Babs and I had sown so enthusiastically had now germinated and should be pricked out, and, in the hot greenhouse temperature, needed watering and constant attention. No wonder a book on horticulture had said that it was not possible to grow daffodils commercially and run a smallholding efficiently, for both required undivided attention at the same time.

The next day it was still sunny and warm but with an easterly gale lashing in. If Wren were to come that night it would have to be about 11 p.m., at low tide, when there would be the chance of a temporary lull. At our regular time for signalling Babs appeared at Hannafore—apparently he was going to try. That would mean using his own dinghy from Hannafore as no boat could leave the harbour. Ruth and I then raced from cottage to cottage and the outhouses, gathering up buckets of daffodils, and we then proceeded to box them again. We had to hurry, so there was no time to drain the bunches thoroughly and they had to be packed with care. In all there were twenty-two large boxes and four smaller ones and each was so heavy it was difficult to manhandle them. We were still desperately tying up the boxes when we espied lights wavering down over the rocks at Hannafore. The lights congregated on the rocks and for a long time there was no visible movement and utter silence except for the howling of the wind. We were frantically tying up the last of the boxes when we heard the sound of the tractor coming up the path. As we helped load the boxes on to the truck, Wren told us that Babs, his wife Valerie, and Zena and her son Charles were all over at Hannafore. It had been a treacherous climb down over the slippery rocks. He had informed the coastguard in case he found himself in difficulties because it was a hazardous expedition, even for Wren; there was an easterly gale blowing, the low tide had exposed a mass of dangerous rocks and all this had to be negotiated in pitch darkness. We flashed a signal with our Tilley lamp that he had arrived safely, then made our way back down the path. It was no easy matter for Wren to drive the tractor for the trees overhead intensified the darkness and our lamp did little to help. We managed to move our heavy metal boat to the water's edge for this was needed to take the bulk of the boxes. We flashed again that Wren was about to start on this quite perilous journey. He then set off standing up in the boat, piled high with boxes and, pushing from the shore with an oar, he glided off into the night looking for all the world like a gondolier.

Fraught with anxiety we sheltered in the boathouse. Suddenly the Tilley lamp gave out and the intense blackness of the night that now enveloped us only added to the nervous tension. After a long interval we at last heard the welcome scrunch of the boat on the shingle as Wren emerged once more out of the gloom. We now had to manhandle the metal boat up the beach and this was no easy matter, even for the three of us, on the upward slope from dead low tide. Wren now had to row back in his own boat.

As far as Ruth and I were concerned this was the end of the operation, but for the others it was just beginning. All the heavy boxes and Wren's boat had to be hauled up the seaweed-strewn rocks. Added to this Valerie had a bad back, and Zena was not allowed to lift anything, so she was the very necessary lamplighter-in-chief and cheer-leader. One box fell in a pool and the precious contents of Beersheba were drenched with sea-water. In spite of this, we were relieved to find later that they had come to no harm and, with the rest of the consignment, fetched the top price. Finally all the boxes were hauled up, but the boat was another matter, and in the end Wren carried it up on his back. About 1.45 a.m. they signalled that the car was loaded with the first consignment and, the perils over, we broke off all communication.

With all the weaving of lamps up and down the rocks and the shore on either side of the channel it must have appeared to any onlookers who were around in the small hours of the morning that a big smuggling operation was taking place, or that villains were up to some nefarious deeds. For what right-minded citizens would choose dead of night around 2 a.m. in an easterly gale for an innocent expedition? We were thankful Wren had taken the precaution of informing the coastguard. Transport was not only one-way. Babs had sent over a parcel of a daily paper, bread and some biscuits. Back at the house about 2. 30 a.m. we made hot chocolate and fell on the biscuits, for we were frozen stiff and had scarcely eaten anything but snacks for days.

We knew that Babs would not be quite so fortunate for she now had the task of invoicing and tying up the boxes in pairs, ready for transporting by car in the morning to take them to the station to catch the Flower Special. As a consequence she did not get to bed until nearly 4 a.m. and was up at 6.30 a.m. as she would have to make at least two journeys to ferry them before going to school. Aware that something like that would be happening I felt I was in honour bound to get up early too, so I forced myself out of bed and climbed to the fields at the top of the island to pick the St Agnes—or were they Cragford? Toby always accompanied me on all these expeditions and sat at the end of each row as I picked. It was surprising what a comfort and encouragement this was, but I do not think it was any surprise to Toby—he knew—that was why he was there. Ruth and I, both very much under the weather, did not meet up for some time, leaving notes for each other to log our movements, but we did get together for a late lunch of boiled eggs. This cheered us up enormously, especially as I was able to report finding a patch of cultivated violets beyond the carnations, both of which we were to discover grow exceptionally well here. That afternoon we were able to put out several boxes of runner beans, lettuce and sweet corn in the capacious Dutch lights which we had found at the back of the tractor shed. The beautiful Scarlet Gem daffodils were coming into bloom—it was a lovely sunny day and, although the east wind was cold, all seemed right with the world.

The daffodils would soon be coming to an end. The difficulty now was to have some for the lucrative Easter market. With our early season this is not always possible. In fact the economics of daffodil growing is a chancy business, as is all farming. If it were a sparse year the prices would be high but there were not enough to send to market to get a good income. On the other hand in a glut year prices slumped and one slaved away night and day to harvest and market them for very little income. In fact we heard on the radio, in one glut year, when the Scillies sent huge quantities, they were burning them at Covent Garden. Unlike other goods where the manufacturer fixes his prices based on cost, with flowers Covent Garden fixes the price, based presumably on the demand. It is essential therefore to catch the market at its peak, for the overheads of labour, packaging, transport and handling fees are constant whatever the return. With the added cost and difficulties of transport over the sea, daffodil harvesting and marketing is a time of much hard work and anxiety. We had yet to face the actual cultivation of daffodils and the techniques involved. Our life as daffodil farmers had only just begun.

Before this there were other major matters to be considered. The most important was what to do about the derelict cottages. Soon, too, Ruth would be leaving and two potter boys from Epsom School of Art, as arranged by Dennis O'Neill, Head of the Department of Pottery, would be coming to help with my pottery.

The NEWCOMERS' Tale

However, before we had formulated any precise plans about restoring the cottages there were several unexpected happenings. Two of them took me very much by surprise.

One evening I went down the path to the main beach to await a signal from Babs. I was alone and as I peered into the darkness to look for a winking light I suddenly felt something press against my leg. Although easily frightened, for some unknown reason I felt no fear. I put my hand down and felt a warm furry body and, when I switched on the torch, looking up at me was the appealing face of a beautiful tabby cat; our island cat had revealed herself at last! She stayed for a while nestling in my arms—then as suddenly as she had appeared she was gone.

Thereafter, whenever I walked alone she would appear for a while and then disappear, just like the Cheshire cat. Toby, who must have sensed what was going on, was now always on the look-out. One day he found her and chased her to her cliff-top home, and I was afraid that one day he would go headlong to the rocks below. But he never chased her again, and I think it was just to find out and show me where she lived, for having made his mark he seemed satisfied. They must have come to some understanding for as I worked in the fields Toby stood guard at one end of the row while she sat at the other, both ostensibly ignoring each other. One day she appeared at the kitchen window appealing to come in. As she diffidently did so I wondered how Toby would take it. Apart from their both wanting a great deal of affection from me, this historic moment passed well enough. Toby, however, would not eat his meals for several days, and would only accept the choicest hand-fed tit-bits. I felt torn between divided loyalties, but I need not have worried. Gradually Cleo, as Babs and I decided to call her, won Toby round. She took up residence in the kitchen, and in her gentle almost timid way made up to Toby. He, as always, the perfect gentleman, responded by letting her through doors first (as he always did for us), and eventually allowed her to share his meals. She would rub up against him affectionately, and it was a relationship that was to last

47

for the rest of his life. We felt we were fortunate to have him with us still, for he had been affected by a heart condition long before we came to the island, and soon he would be fourteen years old.

The second surprise was sprung on me by Babs. She bought a goat! Although we had considered keeping goats at some time in the future, it was a subject about which we knew nothing and we reckoned it needed some study before we embarked on becoming goatherds.

It was not, however, a premeditated purchase—more an impulse buy. It happened that Babs was staying for the weekend with a friend of hers, Ann Coon. The house overlooked the backyard of a pet shop that existed in Looe at the time, but is no longer there. In this yard was a small white kid and the whole weekend it cried and cried. This was too much for Babs. First thing on Monday morning she went in and bought it. 'It' was a 'she', a white pedigree Saanen kid and she cost £4. The problem was how to get her over to the island. The pet shop agreed to keep her until the following weekend when Fred Woodley, who was doing some ferrying for us at the time, could bring her over in the *Islander*. The first I saw of her was when she gracefully leapt ashore through the *Islander's* lifebelt. She was very pretty and had friendly, smiling hazel eyes. We immediately named her Frederica, after Fred. As she had not been polled she had budding horns which later were to cause us problems, which in time because insuperable, as she became adult. Meantime she happily took up residence with us and sleeping quarters were made up for her in the back of the tractor shed, with a bountiful supply of hay. Later we moved her to the outhouses of Smugglers' Cottage where she could have the freedom of the lawns there. Cleo did not know what to make of this new arrival, and she really looked as though she was surveying her with arms akimbo. Toby, having spent all his life until recently on the mainland, seemed to accept her quite readily, as did Cleo when once she had got over the initial shock of coming face to face with this (to her) strange-looking four-footed creature.

Meantime our population was increasing, albeit temporarily in the case of the two-legged variety. With the advent of our first summer of 1965 many friends came to help us, and we were not only a hive of industry but we actually acquired a hive of bees. We had long decided that we must have bees ever since a 'Leisure Exhibition' that Babs had organized at her school in Surrey, at which the local Bee Society had exhibited. We had since read books on the subject and could not wait to populate our island with its own self-contained civilization and factory for producing honey.

Barry, who was the brother-in-law of our nephew Doug, was a bee-keeper who had at that time some forty hives, although he possesses many more now. He volunteered to set us up with a hive of bees. This he very generously did, and ever since, give or take the odd disaster that can overtake even experienced bee-keepers, we have kept bees. Some experts have told us categorically that there is not enough nectar on the island to support a hive, but every year, if the bees have not been ousted by wasps or suffered some other set-back, we have at least twenty-five to thirty-five pounds of honey and twice that amount when we have had two hives. This, our first hive, was set up in the orchard as here it would be protected by surrounding trees and hedges from the onslaught of gales.

All was not honey however, as the saying goes. As the resident sister it was decided that I should be in charge, so I was duly kitted out with veil and protective clothing. Barry visited us several times that summer to look after the bees' welfare and to give me instructions. I found it all completely fascinating and managed into the bargain to take some close-up photographs of the bees, including the Queen Bee. All went well until the time Barry came without his veil; he could not very well bring it for he swam over from Hannafore in his wet suit, catching some fish for us on the way. I lent him my veil and waited on the path outside the orchard. Barry inspected the bees, then came towards me with a section of the hive to show me something, and as he did so the bees, who must have been in an angry mood, for some reason decided to come too—in force. They then made a bee-line for me. It was like being attacked by a Lilliputian tribe of Red Indians with poisoned arrows. Barry yelled that he could not come to help or the rest would come with him. I yelled too, but somehow managed to get most of them out of my hair and made off as best I could. In all there were some thirteen stings on my face and around my eyes and it was of course very painful and swollen. That night I had palpitations. Luckily, due to my swollen eyes, I could not read the bee book to find out how to deal with the stings. It was as well, for the next day I learned that they can cause heart attacks, comas and even prove fatal.

There is no knowing what the outcome would have been if my imagination had got to work as well. However, I was so thankful that I had survived that I faced the prospect of having two teeth out that day with slightly more equanimity than might otherwise have been the case. Nevertheless, for some days I did feel that living our island life was proving more perilous perhaps than the dangers of the Second World War.

Next the bees swarmed and took up their abode in the chimney of Smugglers' Cottage. An and Dennis O'Neill, who were in charge of the Pottery Department at Epsom Art School, where I had been learning prior to our move here, were camping on the island, together with Peter Steele, another expert potter, and his family. They had all offered to come and help us with our pioneering. An and Dennis had kept bees at one time so An gallantly offered to shin up the Smugglers' roof and chimney and try to dislodge them. It was very brave of her for she, too, had been badly stung during their bee-keeping days. With An aloft and smoke from the fireplace below, eventually the chimney was cleared.

However, we came to realize that bee-keeping is not the serene occupation it may seem to those with an urban background, for we have met many other hazards on the way. Our delectable pots of honey are, we feel, hard won, but bee-keeping is a craft that goes back to times immemorial, and it seemed a natural one to pursue in the way of life we had chosen here. We are prejudiced of course, but we do think that the flavour and quality of our honey is special, for the blossoms from which the bees draw their nectar are uncontaminated by any poisonous sprays or fumes. Even the syrup with which we feed them is made from our delicious spring water. As well as supplying us with honey the bees, of course, pollinate our fruit, flowers and vegetables, so they are of inestimable value to us and well worth the hazards. Nevertheless, when Babs retired I was happy to hand over to her the reins of Queen Bee, and when I do stand on the sidelines I make sure that I am wearing protective clothing, and then I can listen to Tennyson's 'murmuring of innumerable bees' with pleasure.

Not long after Frederica's arrival it was Toby's fourteenth birthday and, as it was during the school summer holidays, we had many friends staying with us. There were about twenty altogether including a number of children. It was decided to have a party for him on the lawn and many were the secret preparations that went on among the children. A friend of Zena's, Shirley Butlin-Jones, daughter of Billy Butlin, was holidaying on the island with her young son, William, and he had certainly inherited the family flair for showmanship. With great enthusiasm and talent he spent days beforehand organizing various forms of entertainment, including a play; this latter, unfortunately had to be abandoned as *all* the children wanted to play the leading part. Nevertheless the day promised to be a gala occasion, as indeed it was.

Cleo was the first with her greetings; first thing in the morning she rolled on the mat in front of Toby and then kissed him on the nose. Next the St George's flag was hoisted as it always is, whenever the weather makes it possible, for anniversaries, including, of course, St George's Day. Later came the tea party; tables were placed end to end on the lawn and covered with tablecloths. Janet Ayrton, who was training for Domestic Science, as it was then called, baked a gorgeous cake and the table was loaded with other goodies. Carrots and ginger-nuts, being Toby's favourites, were among the fare offered as well as cakes and jellies as they perhaps might be more generally acceptable. The children now began to arrive: all were dressed in their best party clothes, hair neatly brushed and faces and eyes shining as they presented their gifts to Toby—tins of dog meat, a ball and more carrots and ginger-nuts. How is it, one wonders, that pets can make their preferences known? Every dog we have ever had goes mad over ginger-nuts, Toby being the first to show this preference when he was very young. As far as I can remember we had never kept any in the house, so how he got the message over I cannot say, but ever since we have had to stock up with these doggy delights. Frederica came too; a pile of her favourite pellets were set in a dish before her on the table. Cleo looked in but did not stay. Cats, at least ours, do not care for parties. They will lurk in the background, heads only appearing in the bushes at barbecues, in case there are any tit-bits going. They are, however, not naturally gregarious or convivial—although Tilly, one of our present incumbents, is an exception.

Balloons were produced, games played, entertainment performed and a good time was had by all, Toby munching away happily at his carrots and ginger-nuts and Frederica scoffing her pellets. It was a lovely sunny day and a great success. A day to be remembered with gladness, but with a certain sadness, too, for it was the last birthday Toby was to have.

Soon after the birthday party our furred and feathered population began to increase. Miss Whitehouse, who had a farm outside Looe, used to row over every week when her parents left the island, to leave food for the island cat, now our gorgeous Cleo. She had asked Babs some little time ago if we would like a kitten, as a litter was due in a few weeks time. The thought of giving a new little kitten an island home appealed to us and it was arranged that Miss Whitehouse would let us know when one would be ready to leave its mother, some eight weeks after its arrival into the world.

Now came a classic example of the bush telegraph, for which surely Looe must be renowned and another instance of my penchant for being incident prone. One day during this same school summer holiday of our first year, when Babs was at last resident on her island for something longer than a brief weekend, I went ashore with the potter boys. They were two diploma course students whom Dennis and An O'Neill had arranged should stay on the island to help me set up my pottery and to assist generally. This day they were going ashore in the *Islander* to collect a load of coal and, as a last-minute decision, I hurriedly jumped into the boat with them to do some shopping.

As I stepped ashore, to my amazement, a perfect stranger came up to me and said 'Miss Whitehouse heard you were visiting the mainland; she wants to see you and is driving down into Looe shortly.' How could anyone know I was coming—I did not know myself until the last minute—and how could Miss Whitehouse, who lived several miles outside Looe, know except by precognition? Someone must have a powerful pair of binoculars and a handy telephone, I thought. But why the set-up? There seemed no reason for the island to be under constant surveillance—we were hardly the calibre to be suspected of smuggling—and with so many craft about in the bay on a summer's day, the island boat would scarcely be noticeable, let alone the identity of its occupants. And why the hot-line to Miss Whitehouse? I was soon to find out 'why' if not 'how'.

In no time at all I met up with Miss Whitehouse in the square just outside the courtyard of our cottages in West Looe. In her hand she carried a cat basket—the kitten, of course! She raised the lid and inside were three of the sweetest kittens I had ever seen. 'You can choose,' she said. There was one smaller and darker than the other two—it was minute and had a tiny appealing face. Instantly I said: 'I would like that one.' 'Wouldn't you like all three?' asked Miss Whitehouse. 'Good Heavens, No!' I almost shouted. We could not possibly feed four cats, a dog, and a goat. All those tins to transport and the worry of running short in winter gales, and other unimaginable problems—the island might become peppered with pets! 'Definitely no!' I reiterated firmly as she offered them to me again. 'Oh well!' said Miss Whitehouse, I shall just have to find a home for them.' She looked so worried and dejected. Suddenly she addressed passers-by in general. 'Would you like a kitten? I've *got* to find a home for these two.' This caused quite a stir but no one came forward. It was not surprising. It was not an offer to be taken up lightly, especially if your intention in being abroad was just to buy a loaf of bread, or whatever. 'They are two lovely kittens and they have nowhere to go.' She pleaded to the world at large. I suddenly felt an awful heel. How could I break up this little family group—snatch one from their midst and leave the luckless two there, and homeless to boot? 'O.K. I will have them,' I quavered. Miss Whitehouse's face lit up instantly. We repaired to *The Jolly Sailor*, handily a few yards across the square, to celebrate. *I hoped* it was a celebration, but what would Babs think? As far as she was concerned I had merely gone ashore at the last minute to do some shopping. She would not be expecting the arrival of even one kitten.

Babs came down to the beach to meet us, I stepped ashore and gingerly put the basket down. She looked questioningly at me. 'Look inside!' I said, lifting the lid gently and holding my breath. I expected a shriek at least, followed perhaps by recriminations and a lecture on taking on more responsibilities. 'How lovely!' she cried, to my intense relief, and took them to her heart instantly.

And that was how HamRam, Bessie and Joan came into our lives.

Joan was the tiny black and white tabby and was so named after Black Joan, the sister of an island smuggler of long ago. According to legends about the island, a brother and sister at one time lived here and indulged in smuggling. When the Excise Officers arrived unexpectedly, Black Joan would row out to them and divert their attention with her charms while her brother hastily hid the smuggled goods. Our kitten was well named after her; she always remained small and dainty with beautiful black and white markings. She had immense charm—a charismatic cat if ever there was one—but she bestowed her favours sparingly. It was quite something to see a six-foot muscular man dissolve into gentleness at sight of her. 'Look!' he would cry triumphantly, 'She has *let me* pick her up.' I must confess that she was my special one, for had I not chosen her in the first place? Or maybe she had chosen me. She seemed so small and helpless, yet para-doxically, although the most feline and unattainable of the three, she had a tender heart. She made me her especial responsibility and when I was in bed with a chill or whatever, she never left me—a short necessary sortie out, a quick meal and she was back on my bed. At other times she was remote but kept a weather eye on me and honoured me sometimes by sitting on my lap. Bessie was so named because she was chubby and cud-dly; she looked just like a Bessie and she was very fond of eating.

We had not had the kittens very long and were walking down the path one day when Toby, the gentleman, for some inexplicable reason started to chase Bessie. This was quite out of character, for he had been most solicitous towards them all. Whether he had a sudden twinge of jealousy, or if some inner voice said 'You are supposed to chase cats!' we had no way of knowing. Anyway chase her he did, all the way down to the beach and the sea. It was dark and we could not see so we called and called but there was no sign of her. Eventually we returned to the house hoping that, with Toby out of the way, she might re-appear. She did not. Supper-time was long past and still there was no sign of Bessie. We tried to console ourselves that she was merely frightened and hiding for a time, but we had actually heard her in the sea. Could kittens swim? We did not know. Sick at heart we busied ourselves washing-up in the scullery. Suddenly a face appeared at the window—Bessie! Toby made a great fuss of her and I think that he had been as worried as we were, especially as he would feel that it was not gentlemanly to chase a lady into the sea. Not that she looked wet at all. It was probably Toby who had splashed into the sea and Bessie had veered off into the rocks. In any case pets have a marvellous way of looking after themselves, but this we have never learned to accept. Many are the times we have organized search parties for missing pets, only to find them serenely awaiting our return to be let in, or in the case of cats, casually strolling up the path, having been missing for two or even three days on some secret mission.

HamRam, the third of our triplets—although it would be hard to find triplets more dissimilar in looks, size and character—was named after the most famous island smuggler of them all. In fact his name, so his descendants told us when they came on a visit, was Amram, but our HamRam had already been named so HamRam he remained. Our HamRam was no smuggler but he was a very big cat and cuddly. As he was the only boy cat he was neutered in due course. He was spoiled from the very beginning, not only by us but by Bessie, who mothered him. Later when all three became rat-catchers, he would catch only the tiddley ones and leave them for Bessie to dispose of for him.

Cleo came to inspect the kittens but, as is the enigmatic way of cats, there was no way of knowing what she thought of them. We thought we had an inkling later, because when we provided boxes in the warm kitchen for all four, the kittens chose instead to huddle together on the window-seat with Cleo in their midst. We hoped this meant that she would mother them, but this was not to be. Her ears were flattened down, a sure sign, although we did not realize it at the time as we were new to having a colony of cats, that this registered not only anti-sociability but might even be an open declaration of war, rather like a knight of old with his head and lance tilting forward to the fray. Indeed we learned later that if any of our dear, lovable cats flattened their ears thus, we would be advised to hurl ourselves out of the room to the safety of the other side of the door, collecting one of them under our arm if possible, otherwise we might find ourselves in a melee of flying fur and claws, and get badly scratched into the bargain. The cats meantime would suddenly resume 'normal service' of docility and sisterly and brotherly affection, while we were still staunching blood from our lacerated skins. Cleo never went beyond flattening her ears; she showed no dramatic hostility—she just did not become their surrogate mother. They, on the other hand, accepted her but were quite happy with each other. Toby was still her favourite and the one whose company she sought.

Alas! it was a friendship that was destined not to last very long. The winter following his fourteenth birthday party Toby began to weaken somewhat and became rather frail. He took to going out at night and not coming in again. He was only on the lawn—just sitting—and he would let me carry him back into the house; each time he felt lighter in weight and it became obvious that quite painlessly he was fading away. One of his specialities was singing. We did not teach him, he taught himself and he loved listening to music on the radio, joining in spontaneously when he heard any of his favourites. Two in particular he liked were 'Bless This House' and Elisabeth Schwarzkopf singing the solo in 'The Nuns' Chorus' from *Casanova* and he would always join in when these were broadcast. He would perform for visitors too, if we hummed either of these and asked him to sing. He could sing no more but he still enjoyed listening to music. One day he did not have the strength to go out nor indeed lift himself up. He lay quietly in my arms while I gave him what warmth and comfort I could. I turned the radio on very softly for him and quite astonishingly it was 'The Nuns' Chorus' from Casanova. These were the last sounds that Toby heard.

Some say that they will never have another dog; others that it is best to have another as soon as possible. We agree with the latter, especially if it is possible to get one who needs a home. Babs and I therefore went to the Dogs' Home in Plymouth and were lucky enough to be able to have a black-and-white border collie, just four months old. His nose was still pink and so were his paws. He could as yet only squeak, which he did frequently. Since losing her friend, Cleo had been giving me a great deal of affection, but when Kim arrived on the island her reaction was to leave home. We made up a bed for her in different rooms of the house but she would not settle; for a time she stayed in some comfortable quarters we set up for her in the warm boiler-house under the bathroom, but this did not last for long.

Eventually she worked it out for herself to her own satisfaction; she set up home in the tractor shed. This was about a quarter of a mile away from the house, by the path to the main beach. It was really astute of her, for it had all the conveniences that a cat could desire. It was divided into two by a brick wall, with an entrance through to the back section. On the dividing wall enormous shelves had been built on either side for storing daffodil boxes, fruit baskets, potato sacks and trays, etc. They were about five feet in depth and ran the width of the dividing wall. Her chosen home was not only weatherproof, warm and dry, but from a cat's point of view it was a complete house—a ground floor and, above, two stories and an attic. A ladder was conveniently propped against both sets of shelving so that there was easy access to the upstairs accommodation and the rafters aloft, where planks, tarpaulins and more boxes were stored. Cleo now used the ladder to reach the upper compartment where she made herself a comfortable bed among the potato sacks. We put her meals on the lower shelf which we could reach easily. Cleo would descend the ladder to what had now become her dining-room. This half of the tractor shed faced east and when there was an easterly gale the wind tore through the little opening we had made for her in the barn-like doors, making it draughty. Cleo would then move to the back room of the tractor shed and climb the ladder to the two 'floors' there, which she now used as her temporary bedroom and dining-room, until the gale had subsided, preferring the front section, presumably because she could see all the comings and goings along the path.

In some inexplicable way she now made it known that HamRam, neutered or not, was welcome to her abode. He and he alone was allowed up in her apartments, and visit her he did. Although a big dollopy cat he would climb lightly up the ladder with a swagger and there the two of them would sit for hours. As their two faces peered down at us with the unfathomable way of cats we wondered what attraction they had for each other and we decided, as far as these things can be known by mere humans, that it was a mother and son relationship. HamRam just loved to be pampered and spoiled, and Cleo, as we were to find out later, had a very strong protective instinct. This did not extend to Kim, and for all their lives there was a state of armed neutrality between them that on one unforgettable occasion led to open warfare.

In addition to having bees and a goat we now decided to keep hens. Not only did it seem to fit in with our new life style but we had a ready-made home for them. A short way beyond the tractor shed, in a fenced-in clearing in the woods, was a hen-house in very good condition; lined with straw it would make a very comfortable home indeed—warm, dry and sheltered from gales. We read books on the subject and felt that we, or rather I, should be able to cope. Mrs Alger, a friend and colleague of Babs, heard about this and offered to give us some hens, twelve Rhode Island Reds. As she said that they were getting on in years we imported another twelve of the same breed, but younger. We stocked up with loads of straw and hen food, settled our two broods in and were now, we thought, poultry farmers!

However, as with everything we undertake, we are inclined to see only the advantages. Even with the comparatively straightforward occupation of keeping hens, there are unforeseen snags, especially if they are kept on an island. What if they fall ill or even die on you, for instance? All this and more we were to find out in the future. For the moment we felt we were establishing our roots. We had survived our first daffodil season, the greenhouse was thriving, some of the land was under cultivation, we had a goat, bees and hens, and for recreation we had music, books, a pottery, an embryo darkroom and stone-cutting and polishing equipment—and pets for company.

The leisure activities were still an elusive dream, for ahead of us was a great deal of pioneering before we could even begin to look shipshape.

The EARLY HELPERS' Tale

One of the first decisions to be made when once we had settled in was what to do about the two cottages. Although not exactly derelict they soon would be if we did not do something about them. Not wishing to live with property that would disintegrate and fall down we decided that one of the tasks ahead of us was to put them in order. We would house our friends in them, we said, for holidays and perhaps let them for summer holidays to keep them lived in and cared for. The income from the lettings would pay for their maintenance we hoped—a hope that has, unfortunately, not been fulfilled. Not only is old property notoriously expensive to restore, maintain and service, but the cost of importing labour from the mainland, and the transport of materials over the sea puts the costs up astronomically.

Smugglers' Cottage, the oldest dwelling on the island, and said to date back to the eighteenth century, is a single-storey building and situated in an ideal position. It is protected from the winds by a walled garden in which grow peaches, plums, figs, apples, pears and climbing roses and honeysuckle in great profusion. Inside, however, a black mould clung to the walls and ceilings, the floors were unsafe and one felt in danger of plunging to unknown depths below. We subsequently discovered that they were, like most of those in Jetty Cottage, built directly over the earth. The exception was the hall, which, like part of Jetty Cottage, was floored with concrete. The thought did occur to us that perhaps the treasure was incarcerated under there, but more immediate problems soon chased this fancy away. It was going to be a costly business to restore, decorate and furnish both cottages. Adapting to island life, settling in our own furniture, books and equipment, coping with the generator, the daffodils and trying to develop the market-garden was occupying all our time, so although dealing with the cottages was vital it was not part of our immediate plans.

Now an incident from the past raised itself like a spectre to haunt us. It happened in the previous autumn of 1964, when Babs was working out her term's notice prior to coming down to Cornwall finally at Christmas. I had filled in the time happily, acquiring equipment that I thought would be

58

essential for our island life. High on the list was a portable tape-recorder for the recording of bird song. I finally bought one in the Edgware Road; in a shop bursting at the seams with radios, tape-recorders and all manner of delectable electronic equipment. I say delectable because, although I had no rapport with engines and machinery, the gleaming results of space-age wizardry have a seductive appeal for me, but in truth I did not understand their workings at all, and I was bemused by the dazzling array of equipment set before me. A visiting director of the company was called from the inner office to advise me. The thought did occur to me that perhaps my enthusiasm and maybe the slightly fanatical gleam in my eye had given the assistants the idea that I was going to buy the lot, and the sale deserved to be executed by someone at boardroom level. A very charming and helpful gentleman emerged from behind the scenes, shook hands and described various models to me. Eventually I selected one that he recommended and I reckoned would not be too complicated for my non-electronic brain, nor too expensive for my rapidly diminishing stock of cash. When, during the course of our conversation he heard for what purpose the tape-recorder was to be used and where, he said that he would dearly love to visit us with his family. As he had kindly allowed me 5 per cent discount for paying cash, I felt I could not do otherwise than say that we would be delighted.

So when, in the midst of gathering daffodils, clearing up debris, shingling paths, digging and planting and trying to make some sort of order out of our possessions that were still piled around the place, a letter came from Eric Cox reminding me of our conversation and asking if he and his family could rent one of the cottages, we were non-plussed, to say the least. Never ones to say 'No' when 'Yes', often to our regret, slips more easily off the tongue—or in this case the pen—we wrote and said we were thinking of letting Smugglers' Cottage at some time and we hoped that it would be ready for early June, the time when they wanted to come.

We knew what had to be done and we thought that it was within our capabilities, that is, given the help of a few friends adept at carpentry and plumbing. What we did not realize, and it is a lesson that we still find hard to learn, is the length of time jobs actually take, taking into account all the other demands on our time. We visualize nice blank days for the job in hand, uninterrupted by meals, unexpected happenings and other people's constant needs; we do not reckon either with flagging strength and diminishing enthusiasm as day merges into evening and evening into night.

During the Easter holiday Babs and I started on Smugglers' Cottage. The floor in the sitting-room really needed re-flooring. Where there was an actual hole we stuffed it as best we could, covered it with carpet and put a large piece of furniture on top to prevent anyone from falling through. We could not spend all the time necessary as the daffodil season was late this year and we were still overwhelmed with them and coping with the Easter market. We were also toiling on the land from dawn to dusk whenever possible, that is, when we were not attending to broken-down engines, stopped-up drains, or doling out coffee to chance friends who had come to help. When Babs returned to the mainland after the holiday I continued as much as possible with the cottage. Armed with a basket of sandwiches, wine, baby transistor radio and binoculars for bird-watching and to spy marauders, and equipped with decorating materials, I would set forth for the cottage which was just off the path to the beach and between the orchard and the generator room. I scrubbed, I scraped, I put on undercoat and yet more undercoat, but with other chores accumulating and the hoeing, planting and the greenhouse work it was an uphill battle.

I was glad therefore when Hugh and Kath Gosling came to stay and help. Hugh was the brother of Marjorie Buck who, with her husband Bill, had helped us in settling into our home in No 1 cottage on the mainland in the spring of the previous year, 1964. Hugh was selling his place in Bristol and intended buying an hotel in Cornwall. They had to make several forays before they finally settled on a sixty-bedroomed hotel in Newquay. Each time they spent a few days with us and this was the first of many visits. Their help was invaluable as both could turn their hand to anything. Our rememberance of the indomitable Kath was that she spent the whole of her frequent visits clad in an apron, her head tied up in a scarf and, armed with a paintbrush in one hand and a broom in the other, she always, unbelieveably, had a radiant smile on her face.

Hugh, as well as having expertise in many handyman skills, had practical suggestions to make which helped us enormously, and were a welcome change from some of the far-fetched ones that had assailed our ears from the moment we started on our adventure. He will be remembered especially for three of his many contributions. One was the construction of a rack in the kitchen to store my demijohns of wine. This was built on to the wall and consisted of several shelves some four feet wide and three feet in depth, supported by stout posts on all four corners. It reached from the stone-flagged floor to the oak-beamed ceiling, and when he had stained and finished it, it looked very handsome indeed. Hugh demonstrated that each rack was strong enough to hold at least eight full demijohns by sitting on each shelf as he constructed it; and a funny sight it was to see his sturdy figure when he reached the top shelf, waving his arms, legs a-dangling, bouncing up and down and saying: 'You see! if it will hold my weight it will hold your wine.' Indeed it did, and still does.

Secondly, he mounted two cupboards on the same wall adjoining this edifice. One was a kitchen cupboard we had brought with us, and the other we found on the beach where it had been brought in by the sea. It was almost identical in size with ours, that is about four feet high and wide. It was in perfect condition structurally but in poor shape aesthetically. Mounting them on the wall at eye level was no problem to him; the touch of genius—and why we always think of Hugh when we use the cupboards—was the finish that he gave to them. He found some battening some three inches wide and he covered the outside of the doors with strips of these. By the time he had fined them down several times, stained and polished them they gave the appearance of rich panelling. The final touch, though, showed his real artistry. On the beach he found parts of our metal boat which had broken up in a storm. From these he cut decorative shapes to form 'wrought-iron hinges'; he then stamped and embossed them all over with a six-inch nail, painted them black and fixed them to the panelled doors, over the existing hinges. This wall was now lined with Hugh's woodwork wizardry. The whole effect was fine indeed, and fitted in with the style of the farmhouse kitchen, giving it an old-world richness and warmth. When the jars were put in place row upon row, one above the other, the scene was one which we were sure the monks of old would have approved of in theory and no doubt appreciated in practice. They gleamed and sparkled in the lamplight from a delicate gold to a brilliant ruby-red, according to their content, and enhanced our kitchen with a patina of jewel-like richness, so that on a dark winter's night it was like entering an Aladdin's cave.

Hugh's third attribute, although vividly recalled, can only be held in our memory. In addition to his many skills he had a hidden talent, that is, hidden from us until he came here; he was able to imitate the cry of the seagull to perfection. He used to roam the island giving his impersonations, much to our confusion, and no doubt, to that of the seagulls too, for wherever he went he was followed by their haunting cries, often rising to frenzied screams. We often wondered what particular significance some of his calls had to evoke these murderous shrieks.

On this, their first visit, they both worked in Smugglers' Cottage, but even with their help it was not nearly ready as busy week followed busy week. Everywhere, too, grass was growing apace. With the two mowers we brought with us we had five altogether. However, with the rough terrain, the neglect since last summer while the island was uninhabited, and the lack of frost, the island had run wild, and each of the mowers broke down in turn, or more usually lost one of its vital parts in the long grass. Hugh would mend them if possible and then be called away to unstop a drain. Brian and Anne Rainforth, with their two young sons, now returned to help us, so the work-force was growing. In addition, Mr Bray, who owned a carpet shop in Looe, and had come over previously to fix us up with some carpets and lino, said that he and his family would love to help.

On the day the Coxes were due to arrive there were then ten of us working on the cottage: Mr Bray and family were cutting the lawns, the rest of us were frantically putting finishing touches to the paintwork, sweeping out bits and pieces and moving furniture in. In the midst of this, and much to our consternation, Mr Cox and family turned up early. They stood at the gate, no doubt bewildered to see us all beavering away like the seven dwarfs—except that there were ten of us. Doubtless tired from their journey from London and the added chore of heaving themselves and their luggage in and out of a motor-boat, the sea trip, and having to haul everything up from the beach, for of course there was no one there to meet them, the unfortunate Cox family now had brooms and other equipment thrust into their hands, and they had to help push furniture into place before they could take up residence. It says something for their resilience that they have been here many times since and never fail to keep in touch. Such can be the effect of island fever.

So we had our first cottage let and our first cottage income of ten guineas, which I suppose was the going rate at the time. As we had spent a considerable sum in restoring and furnishing the cottage it did seem rather a drop in the ocean, but it was a start, Babs and I told ourselves. We would not have been so sanguine if we could have foreseen that the future maintenance of the cottage would include having the whole flooring, except for the concreted hall, replaced twice, the materials used the first time not having withstood the dampness of the earth foundations.

Putting the Jetty Cottage in order was an even more daunting task. No dwelling likes to be abandoned; when human life no longer breathes therein, the pulse stops and decay slowly sets in. Jetty Cottage had been used as a packing station for daffodils and had not been used as a home for some years, unlike Smugglers' Cottage which had housed the Whitehouse's gardener. Consequently floor-boards, if there were any left, were rotten, and all the earth beneath showed. There was dry rot and wet rot, too; it really was a colossal task ahead of us, but we could not face the prospect of living with mouldering property. It was now that the indefatigable Zena stepped in with the suggestion that her brother, George Marshall, would take on the carpentry, at which he was skilled. The cost would be far less than if we employed a firm, even if there were one willing to send its employees across the sea to work the irregular hours dictated by tides and weather. George did a fine job replacing and making good all the flooring. Perhaps most invaluable of all he ripped off all the wall-panelling, reeking with the deathly smell of wet rot, in the ex-barn/music room that was now our transit camp, and after putting everything in good order refaced the walls with some handsome parana pine panelling. This is a lasting memorial to his skill, for tragically he collapsed and died suddenly while mooring his boat in the harbour at Mevagissey just a few years ago.

Hugh and Kath now added their own special touches to make it habitable once more. Hugh did some of his clever carpentry and panelled round the bath to make a quite elegant splashboard, probably from something dredged up from the sea. Between them they decorated the walls and woodwork of the cottage, which, like Smugglers' Cottage, is all on one floor. They were putting the finishing touches and sweeping out when the boat arrived for their departure from the jetty. Kath stepped on to the boat, still wearing her apron, mob-cap and her engaging smile and as the boat pulled away she threw us a broom which she found she was still clutching.

We had some furniture of our own which we put into both cottages, including some antique chairs and tables, but much more was needed: beds, mattresses, pillows, blankets, carpets, kitchen equipment, crockery, cutlery, lino and much more. Several forays were made to Nancollas's and Hicks's fortnightly sales and to Dingle's, the large store in Plymouth and, with Zena's ever willing help, at last both cottages were fully furnished. Although it had cost us a large sum of money for what was, after all, only one of our projects, we did feel that it was the right thing to do. Not only had we preserved the properties but we had somewhere to accommodate friends and relatives who had hitherto bedded down in odd corners when they came to help us. Among these who now came were Gwen, my friend from the Camera Club days, and Jim Cutts. He had recently returned from abroad and was delighted to try his hand at some quite ambitious carpentry. Thanks to him we have some fine built-in storage cupboards which effectively sealed off the sleeping quarters of Jetty Cottage from the hurly-burly that was continually going on in our transit camp, as furniture was dragged out and other pieces acquired from the mainland were added.

Our niece Cecily, her husband Doug, with their three children Jane, Richard and Manda, now came on holiday to help us. They were still anxious to join us permanently. Doug, a natural craftsman, could turn his hand to anything and, as he could handle boats, would be a great asset. There was much discussion about this for it would be a big step for everyone. Nevertheless they decided that they would like to have a go. So a few months later they joined us.

We started out with high hopes but sadly it did not work out. The main factor was the one we feared when the idea was first mooted—that of economics. As the months went by it became obvious that there was no living and therefore no future for Doug. Mr Whitehouse had told us that the income from the daffodils just about paid the wages of his gardener—around £8 per week. Although we intended to develop the market-garden side there was no way we could see, and neither could Doug, that would provide a living for him and his growing family. The climate was wonderful, the soil fertile and the crops early but with the added cost of sea transport and the uncertainty of getting produce to the mainland for the marketing of the early crops, it was a chancy business, as we had found to our cost with our first forays with the daffodils. It would take years of letting the cottages to repay even the initial cost of making them habitable, without taking into consideration the expensive and continual maintenance that old properties require, and of course, with Doug and family resident in one of them, there would be no income from that one.

So many dream of getting away from it all, and living off the land, or the sea, and being self-sufficient. Many fail and mostly it is a question of economics, which is why, even with their inborn husbandry, the crofters have abandoned so many of the Scottish Isles to make their future on the mainland. St George's is a tiny island, just twenty-two and a half acres. Even if a large amount of capital were injected into it, we doubt it would ever become a viable proposition horticulturally, and any form of commercialism would be quite unacceptable to us. In recent years all the owners have been self-sufficient financially. We too, could sustain ourselves money-wise and we had come here to enjoy island life and develop the island's natural resources; we had no need or wish to make a living from it. But with our commitments: Island House, two cottages, three boats and a generator, together with two cottages and a car on the mainland and our two selves to clothe and feed, there was no way we could also support a family of five, especially as we were both taxed to the hilt as single people without the benefit of family allowances.

Although Doug's help was invaluable it could not add to the island's income in the foreseeable future, and it did not obviate the expense of employing specialist help such as the electrician, the Lister engineer, the plumber and the boat-builder. So although our expenses had increased by providing for five extra people and the heating and lighting of the cottage, our income had not. Financially the future was bleak for Doug, too, as all must find out who opt out of the rat-race for a life of self-sufficiency, especially if they have a growing family. The question of the children's education raised another problem. The Education Authorities paid the ferryman, Leonard Pengelly, for their daily transport to the mainland. The journeys were often rough and, with Manda not yet six, the children were often exhausted after a day's schoolwork followed by a bumpy and sometimes wet journey in an open boat at the end of it. When the weather was too rough in the summer and for most of the winter months, Babs was paid five shillings per head per week to feed and care for them on the mainland. After coming home from a day's teaching with the added responsibilities of her Deputy-Headship it tested her endurance to the limit to have to prepare food for and control someone else's children. It also curtailed her social activities to nil.

Christmas was fun for we had cleared our 'transit camp' enough to use it as a communal room for parties and craft evenings. Cecily did basketry and both she and Doug were keen wood-carvers. The children especially enjoyed the parties.

One party I remember in particular, although it was not held there but in our back bedroom in the house. Manda had decided that I was 'magic'. I had indeed, in my youth, helped our brother, Tom, Cecily's father, with conjuring tricks at children's charity shows. I remembered enough of these to mystify a six-year-old—but not anyone much older—by producing surprise items out of thin air or a nearby bush. Henceforth I was introduced by Manda as 'my aunt—she's magic'. She decided to invite me to a party—the other guests being the Rainforth's children, Mark and Matthew, aged about five and three years. Manda chose our back bedroom for the venue as it would be the most inaccessible to would-be gate-crashers. We all sat in a circle on the floor. Manda had everything set out very nicely, the crockery being a doll's tea-set. Ju-jubes were produced and counted out carefully on to the tiny plates. Orangeade was served in equally miniature cups and saucers with an adult air that would have graced a ladies' tea-party. I did feel a bit like Alice in Wonderland after she had partaken of 'EAT ME' and grown bigger and bigger, especially when I produced my contribution, which was a dish of chips that I had just cooked, for they looked so large beside the ju-jubes. However they were seized on avidly and we were all having a merry time when there was a knock on the door. Cecily poked her head in. 'Have you everything you want?' she asked. Manda dropped her ladylike air and with tea-pot poised in hand screamed: 'GO *AWAY*! NO grown-ups allowed!' That cut me down to size!

When they returned to Sussex (for luckily Doug was able to get his job back), Manda came to say good-bye to me. 'You will miss me more than I shall miss you,' she said nodding her head, 'for you will be without me, but I shall have all my friends, so it will be easy for me to forget, but it won't be for you.' I think she was right.

The WINKLE-PICKER'S Tale

With the departure of Ruth to help her parents on their smallholding in Looe, in May of our first year, at last came the day when I should be alone on the island.

It is difficult to describe my complex feelings about this. I would, of course, have preferred, more than anything, for Babs to be with me. From the very beginning it had been a joint dream, and in achieving it we had shared the same problems, adventures and dangers. As we experienced the hazards of the sea crossings in mid-winter regretfully we realized that while Babs was teaching it would not be possible for her to live on the island, except for the school holidays and calm weekends; we had come to accept that we should have to live apart for quite long periods.

Babs, of course, could have given up teaching, but this had never come into our calculations. Not only was her income necessary but there was the question of her pension to be considered. Although at that time it was thirteen years away it seemed a very desirable carrot. When we are young a job with a pension seems unutterably dull; something for the old and weary, not for us, the young ones who, of course, will live in our golden adventurous youth for ever. When in mid-stream it is quite a different matter; the idea of being paid for doing absolutely nothing has a compulsive allure, and one is thankful that a pensionable job will bring about this happy state in the foreseeable future. How soon? Without wishing one's life away one yearns for this enticing freedom. How to bring it nearer without advancing towards it?

A badly broken leg from a cliff path fall, combined with increasing responsibilities, pressure of work and the consequent late hours, filled the bill in my case and I retired for health reasons eight years earlier than normal. Although this entailed a reduced pension and the burden of buying National Insurance stamps for that number of years in order to be eligible for the Government Retirement Pension, the fact of having one's day free, and an income however small, gives one a feeling of immense wealth. This is entirely illusory of course—one has to eat, pay the bills and the

67

mortgage. However, a certain amount of illusion is necessary to see one through life if the journey is to be an enjoyable and exciting adventure— a certain amount of illusion and a certain amount of money.

We have often been astonished, not to say appalled, at the number of people who have written to us to say that, as a result of reading about our adventures, they too, have given up everything to start a new life and fulfil long-cherished dreams. I say appalled, for the feeling of responsibility is tremendous. Often we wonder how these folk have made out (and there may be others too, who have not actually written to us). They are the brave ones. Many admire us for our supposed courage. This we do not under- stand for we consider we have been most circumspect. To have been re- ally courageous Babs would have given up her career to enable her to live on the island entirely and we would have tried to live off the land, and be self-sufficient like the pioneers of old, or members of communes fashion- able in the last decade or so. As it was, we felt we had been most prudent to decide that an income was necessary. True, Babs had given up her plum job without another in sight, but not even the giddiness of island fever had lured her into giving up her career. Although we had our heads in the clouds we had our feet firmly on the ground too. Admittedly the ground is often slippery, and at times has an uncomfortable habit of giving way under us.

So tacitly we had agreed that until Babs could retire we must accept that she should operate from the mainland. I knew that she was worried about my being alone on the island, and I in turn was concerned that she would not be able to share the full island life for some years to come. But as we had no intention of depending on our own physical efforts and hack out what could only be a meagre existence (for we knew from previous owners that the daffodil farm and market-garden-cum-smallholding needed private means of some sort to keep it going), we felt that we had no choice in the matter.

Thus on this day in mid-May I faced the prospect that in a few hours I should have my first taste of being entirely on my own except for the faithful Toby and the elusive cat.

I must admit to having doubts.

I had never lived alone; had never been too keen even on entering an empty house if the family were out. I was prone to fling doors open sud- denly, as in a movie thriller, but without the comfort of the obligatory revolver at the ready. As for venturing to the copse at the end of the garden at dead of night in search of a forgotten book or garden tool, I never went without having Toby by my side held firmly on a lead.

Suddenly I felt nervous and afraid; not of being alone on the island so much, but afraid of being afraid. On the one hand I relished the challenge; on the other I doubted my ability to rise to it.

To add to the ordeal it was raining and a high sea running when at 7 p.m. Peter, Zena and Charles came in the *Islander* to fetch Babs. The jetty was awash and the seagulls screamed in anger at being disturbed in their nests. They take over the rocks on which the jetty is built during the breeding and nesting season, and to avoid being attacked by them at these times we use the landing beach, except when it is too rough to land there as it was this evening. The rain, the high seas sweeping over the jetty and the seagulls dive-bombing with murderous screams did not make our parting easy nor the start of my new life encouraging. Babs looked dejected and forlorn as she clambered into the bucking boat. Zena for once, over-come with the drama of the situation no doubt, was unsmiling beneath her sou'wester and said not a word. As the *Islander* ploughed its way towards the mainland both Babs and Zena looked as though they had just left me condemned to a life of solitary confinement on Devil's Island. Peter and Charles were too busy navigating the boat to register any such fanciful thoughts.

As the boat headed away from me I had a moment of panic; a wave of claustrophobia overwhelmed me. Subject to this in confined spaces, I never expected to experience it on this our dream island with all that space around me. However it was only momentary. Firmly I turned round and marched back to the house.

I would busy myself making some elderflower wine. Soon it was time for the news on the BBC, for running a TV from our generator is one of the luxuries denied to anyone living on a desert island. It was incredibly comforting to have a friendly face telling me the news, and I remember with great affection the kindly Robert Dougall—although I cannot recall a single item of news, if indeed I took it in at the time. To have someone talking to *me*, for such is the intimacy of television, was a terrific boost to my quailing spirit and an anchorage for my floundering thoughts.

I awakened once during the night with a wave of claustrophobia but, when I realized that it was due to nothing more sinister than blocked-up sinuses due to being buffeted by the high winds, I soon fell asleep again.

The next day the weather was still poor with heavy showers so it was not suitable for planting tomatoes as I intended. Keen to occupy myself I put down the elderflower wine I had started, and brewed some beer in readiness for future males who would surely come to help us with the generator, farm machinery and other fearsome mechanical equipment.

Suddenly I realized that I was not afraid at all; it had just been a matter of stage-fright. How could I feel lonely with the faithful Toby by my side, the intriguing cat who was diffidently trying to take up residence now that our visitors had departed, and the island hummed with life—the sea, the gulls, the wind in the trees, the woodland bird song?

My spirits began to soar; it was a great life. As I began to set about all the activities that awaited me—digging, planting, sowing, decorating, pottery, wine-making and the many schemes that we were always thinking up—I began to relish my freedom, freedom from my former life of responsibility for other people, from their demands, the temperamental clashes, the frustrations of their sometimes quite inexplicable behaviour, the irritations and the hurts. No traffic either, and—great joy—no telephones to torment me.

Not even finding a rattish-looking corpse by the gate quelled my buoyant spirits. With an easy rhythm born of optimism I tossed it nonchantly over the cliff with a long-handled Cornish shovel. With luck Babs would be here at the weekend. All was well with the world.

So began a new era in our island saga. Little did I know that during the ensuing years we should have more to do with people of all nationalities, ages, backgrounds, occupations and temperaments than we had ever done in our whole lives—a kaleidoscopic life surely not experienced by the vast majority of people and certainly not to be expected by lone islanders.

In the winter, with storms from the Atlantic sweeping in, Cornwall changes from its summer garb of picturesque fishing villages nestling between green-clad cliffs. Wild seas beat upon the rocky shores from autumn round to spring; the fishing fleet is often harbour-bound for days at a time or even for a week or two. As the island has no harbour it can be isolated for even longer periods. In a south-west gale spray flies over the top of the tall gabled house and lands in great scuds of foam on the lawn. A westerly gale roars through the woods above the house like an express train, deafening one's ear-drums. Forty-feet high trees will be mown down as a hurricane cuts through the woods like a giant scythe; mounds of seaweed pile ten feet high on the beach, so that to reach the *Islander* when the gales have subsided enough for the mail to be brought over it is necessary to slide down these cliffs of seaweed on one's backside. But often gales will assault us again before the sea has died down and the island is virtually like a ship at sea, a little kingdom of its own, dependent on its own resources. On one memorable occasion Babs was unable to land between Christmas and Easter and I just had fleeting glimpses of her as the all-important mail was tossed to me over the raging surf.

In summer it is quite a different matter. For three months when the holiday season is in full swing, although gales and rough seas can be and are a possibility, the sea is most often friendly and full of small craft. The island, as it is only a mile from Looe harbour, is easily accessible when the sea is calm. Mr Whitehouse had warned us about this. 'People will try to land and trespass,' he said. 'To keep your privacy you will have to bring out a shotgun.' Apparently trespassing had been a hazard during the summer months for a very long time. After the war Major General Rawlings, who owned the island then, would let local people picnic on the main beach. The tale we were told was that someone had come up and damaged his greenhouse, so he withdrew the facility and to stop 'uninvited guests' brought out a shotgun to shoot over the heads of would-be intruders. 'This,' said Mr Whitehouse, 'I have had to do too, and so will you.'

I was appalled. For one thing, having spent our first few months on the island in mid-winter and a blustery spring, we did not think that we should have to contend with trespassers. For another I was a 'Master Shot'; I had shot at Bisley for Surrey, and had acquired a goodly number of gold medals, silver cups and other trophies. In fact it was my conceit, still, to go to a handy fair in perhaps Plymouth and relieve the rifle ranges of as much bric-à-brac as I could carry away, for the satisfaction of seeing the astonished faces of the attendants, who had deemed it necessary to show me which end of the rifle to hold, so unlikely a participant did I appear.

'Good Heavens!' I thought, remembering the unerring training on the bull's-eye over the years, 'I won't be able to miss—the beaches will be strewn with dead bodies!'

'Perhaps he is exaggerating,' we said; 'people will respect our privacy' (indicated by the 'Private' and 'NO Landing' notices that were there when we arrived). How naive we were. As the summer came so did the small boats and land on the island they did.

Before we had to contend with this problem, however, the early part of the season, before holiday-makers abounded, had produced its own special problems. Alone on the island I would espy a beached boat and a figure on the rocks. Down I would saunter to find a 'local'. This presented difficulties. Apparently some people assumed (wrongly) that, being local, they had a right to land, unless of course, as we suspected, they were trying it on with new owners. I, on the other hand, felt that the island was our home, and guests should be by invitation. Confusion arises because it is generally thought that all beaches around the coastline of Great Britain are a free-for-all, and even with beaches that are privately owned the shore below high water is owned by the Crown and therefore the public has free access to it. That may be so generally, but our island is unusual—perhaps unique—in that in 1873 the then Prince of Wales, who later became Edward VII, sold the foreshore rights of the island to settle a gambling debt. This Mr Whitehouse told us. Not only that, he said, but he had had the facts verified legally and had paid a large sum of money to have the rights incorporated in the deeds. 'You must ensure that you keep those rights,' he explained to us, 'for you, too, have paid for their inclusion in the deeds in the purchase price. I went to a great deal of trouble and spent a large sum of money to have the facts verified and legalized.'

So I knew I had right on my side. The difficulty arose with these early intruders in that they were all 'locals'. I did not wish to offend them, for Looe folk had been very kind and hospitable to us as well as helpful in overcoming our pioneering problems. If only I knew who they *were*, but of course I did not. Not being naturally belligerent I decided I would adopt the hostess approach. 'Have we met?' I would inquire pleasantly. Then I would invite him up for a cup of tea, for it was always a 'he' who was the intruder—never a 'she'—and I would dearly like some professor of psychology to explain why. I would then mention the foreshore rights and the difficulties previous owners had had in maintaining them against summer trippers. I hoped to make the point that as far as I knew strangers on our shore might all be summer holiday-makers, and no locals would want, I thought, to be confused with trippers. 'Naturally, as it is our home', I added, 'we like to know who is on our property, and locals like yourself are welcome to visit us and have a cup of tea.'

Mostly this resolved the problem. Once, however, I could not reach the interloper easily as there was a mass of seaweed-strewn rocks between us. 'Have we met?' I yelled at the top of my voice, not sounding a bit like the gracious hostess I meant to portray. A long string of something that sounded uncommonly like oaths were hurled at me across the rocks, but either due to the distance, the dialect or both, it was all quite unintelligible to me. 'Come and have a cup of tea!' I bellowed. Another string of oaths or whatever. 'We do have foreshore rights and how do I know that you are not just a summer tripper unless you come up and meet me?' I bawled hoarsely. At this he shook his fist at me and made off. Many years later he made himself known to me at some social event. He was a charming man. He recalled the incident; his version being quite different from my interpretation of it at the time. There was no bellicose intent at all, which just goes to show how lack of communication can lead to misunderstandings not only between individuals but between nations.

I was hoist with my own petard on one occasion, however. One morning I noticed on the main beach a rather big and impressive figure, prawning among the rocks. Strolling towards him I used my standard ploy: 'Have we met?' He turned and to my astonishment he said 'We certainly have. I am Mr Wheldon. We met at Mr Nancollas's cocktail party. 'I was nonplussed. Mr Nancollas, our agent, had thrown a cocktail party to launch us to the island. The guests were mainly people he thought would be of interest and helpful to us, hoteliers, financiers and the like. Mr Wheldon was one of the latter. I did not recall him, due to the fact, as those who followed our first adventures may remember, that having lived through storms and hazardous crossings during our first few weeks in Looe I was out of training for such sophistication as cocktail parties. The recollection of the party and guests was lost in a rosy haze. 'I was getting some prawns to bring up to you,' he added. This was the first of many visits and he became a regular and welcome guest. We would drink not tea, but coffee and home-made wine. Always he collected prawns, instructing me in the technique of both catching and cooking them. He brought bottles of home-made wine, too, and we drank each other's health and swopped recipes. I really enjoyed his visits.

Much more sinister was an incident that occurred a year or so later. The danger of being invaded out of season is infinitesimal; the seas that pound round the island provide a natural moat. I was astonished, therefore, on a day in early spring, before the locals usually put their boats in the water for the season, to see a lone figure on the rocks below the jetty. I went to investigate. As I came closer I saw a huge fellow crowned with a thatch of yellow hair. I accosted him politely, my heart quaking nevertheless, for it was a giant of a man who looked down at me and he had a Frankensteinish appearance to my heated imagination. I felt no happier when he replied in a thick and almost unintelligible dialect (from outer space perhaps?) that he was winkle-picking and was there any harm in that? Well, there could be. We had heard that a gang of men from 'up country', i.e., beyond the Cornish border, was working its way up from the far west, gathering winkles by the sackful and selling them at inflated prices in London. This was not pleasing to the Cornish and neither, in this particular instance, was it pleasing to me. For one thing the modern and hygienic sewerage system that now services Looe had not then been installed, and the sewage was ejected into the sea at Hannafore. The winkles might well be contaminated. 'Yes, there is harm,' I said, 'people will be poisoned and you will be arrested.' 'Don't you worry about that m'dear. We do this all the time,' he growled in his deep bass voice, and he went on winkle-picking. 'Anyway it is private here,' I retorted. That provoked a lot of 'Ho! Hos!' and some meaningless growlings that ended in a sinister sounding 'm'dear'. But to my intense relief he made off.

The next day, to my consternation, he was there again. My friend and companion at that time was a magnificent border collie, Kim. Kim was most impressive, his fine black-and-white head looking as though he could snaffle a couple of intruders with no trouble at all, and I am sure he would deal with anyone who set about me. The problem was that he was a friendly dog, by nature and by training. He always helped me greet visitors and gave them a warm and doggy welcome. Unless proved otherwise all human visitors were his friends. Why should they be otherwise? I always made everyone welcome. Nevertheless he was an excellent guard dog and he undertook to police the whole island. He would sit on the cliff top outside the house for hours at the 'Red Alert'. He looked right across the bay to the harbour, and quite incredibly would know if it were Leonard's boat, our ferryman at the time, that was leaving the harbour, although there were other similar boats with the same type of petrol-driven engine around, refuting the belief that dogs are short-sighted. Down to the beach he would bound, ready to greet visitors and accompany them up the path to where I was waiting to welcome them. But if any other similar boats came too near into the Jetty bay he would set up such a barking, hurl himself down to the shore and whisk back and forth, still barking ferociously that none dare land.

Indeed it was because of his insistent barking in the house yesterday that I had gone outside to investigate, for some reason leaving him in the house, as I really thought that it must be a false alarm. The problem, now that I intended to take Kim with me, was how to instil into him that I was not greeting a welcome visitor, but without provoking a fracas. Somehow or other I had to assert my authority, with Kim as the implied threat. But there was the rub—I have no authority, unlike Babs, who can summons it up when necessary due to her teaching experience. For instance, if I use a nasty, deep and menacing voice to deter a pet from doing something undesirable, all it does is to come over and lick me or rub against my leg and purr according to its breed, to make me feel better.

So what now? With Kim's proclivity for being friendly to strangers of the 'Have we met?' type, and not wishing to start what might turn into a punch-up or have a knife brandished at me, I decided I would draw on my histrionic powers from amateur acting days. So I put a lead on Kim, which rather puzzled him, then we both marched across the Jetty beach and over the rocks to our winkle-picker. He seemed to look even bigger than he did yesterday. As we drew near I shortened the lead and growled in the deepest voice I could muster, 'DOWN! KIM! DOWN!' I then pulled hard back as though I was restraining him from leaping at the winkle-picker's throat. I grabbed Kim's collar tight, not only to stop myself from falling backwards over the rocks but to stop him turning round and licking me to make me feel better. I smiled apologetically at the winkle-picker. 'He is a very good guard dog,' I said 'but I will try to keep him under control,' and I gave another hard pull at Kim who, hearing my friendly tone, was doing his best to leap up and say 'Hullo!' I also tried to tuck his wagging tail under my other arm. 'Down Kim! DOWN! GOOD BOY!', I barked. Well it wasn't really a bark, but it came from somewhere low in my throat. 'There, I think he will be OK now,' I said, relaxing my grip a bit, but still pressing hard against his tail with my left elbow. 'By the way,' I added 'I am afraid that you cannot do any more winkle-picking here. We have given the franchise to a local firm. They saw you yesterday and they didn't like it a bit. I think they are coming out presently to have a word with you.' He never queried why we had given the franchise for winkle-picking in a sewerage channel; he never queried why anyone in their right mind would want it; he never queried why I had not told him this yesterday. He never queried anything at all. With hasty glances at Kim he growled, 'Well, I'll be off m'dear,' and with that he loped with great strides over the rocks to his boat and rowed hard for the mainland never to be seen again on our shores.

It was because of this incident and the fact that I would be alone on the island for about nine months of each year that Babs applied for, and obtained, a licence from the GPO for the use of a radio telephone with our own wavelength. This not only gave Babs peace of mind but it was a facility that was to prove invaluable to us and to others over the years.

The COOK'S Tale

The onset of the holiday season of our first year presented us with a problem that was to affect the whole of our future island life.

In the summer visitors come to Looe in their masses and the bay teems with craft. Small motor-boats, locally called 'doodle-bugs', are hired out and officially are not allowed to land anywhere. The attraction of the island, however, had often proved too great and they, and other privately owned boats, landed as Mr Whitehouse had warned us they would. To have strangers roam around our garden, for that is what the island is to us, and perhaps peer through our windows was too much to contemplate. One might as well live in a goldfish bowl.

To quote an immortal phrase: 'Something must be done'.

I hit on the idea of giving the impression that the island was populated with vast numbers of residents hostile to strangers, for I was sensitive to the fact that there was only one human in residence—myself—to cope with what might well become a population explosion of trespassers. To this end I picked up a couple of anoraks, an oilskin, two sou'westers and an assortment of woolly hats. At the first sign of small boats approaching I peered over the hedge on the cliff top by the house, glaring as fearsomely as I could. I then ducked down, donned a hooded anorak, glared again, ducked, changed to a sou'wester and so on, ducking, changing and glaring until my supply of headgear was exhausted. Then, gathering up all my props, I raced down the path until I found a suitable gap in the hedge on the cliff edge there, and repeated the performance. I hoped that I had given the impression that at least twenty angry people were awaiting any intruders. It must have been successful for all the little boats, without exception, turned back and made for the harbour.

The next day, at the first sign of approaching boats I gave a repeat performance, adding an assortment of garden tools and the odd fishing net to my props and throwing in some extra grimaces as an encore. For the second day there were no intruders and the boats all made back for the harbour. I was, however, exhausted and decided that there were too many other things to do than use my time and energy giving one-woman stands on the cliff top, successful though they had been.

Babs and I discussed the matter at the weekend. Of all the problems we had expected to face in coming to the island—hunger, hardships, privations, storms—yes, but invasion—never. Back and forth we tossed ideas. Suddenly I had an inspiration. 'I've got it!' I shouted. 'We will put up a big notice "Landing fee" that will stop them.' Simple. Brilliant. Babs thought it a splendid solution. How much? At that time the going rate for stately homes was 2s. 6d. entrance fee. We would do the same and become a stately island. The only difference being that we were trying to keep people away not inducing them to come.

Triumphantly we nailed a large piece of wood beneath the STRICTLY PRIVATE' notice and painted in bold letters 'LANDING FEE 2s. 6d.'— a challenge to any would-be trespassers.

How wrong can you be? Obviously I had never studied psychology nor did I have any inkling about human nature, or I should have realized that the very fact that there was a charge made it appear that to land was attractive and desirable. It is also common knowledge that anything that is free is thought of as having little worth; that the more you pay the more value the object appears to have. Unfortunately I did not have this common knowledge, nor did common sense tell us that we were in fact issuing an invitation to any passing craft if the passengers were prepared to pay.

And care to pay they did. Back in Looe Babs heard that the word had gone around. Looe folk were saying: 'How wonderful! at last we can visit that lovely island officially, *and* we can send our visitors there.' For like all guest-house owners, they liked to have local attractions to suggest to visitors, who invariably ask on arrival in a district new to them; 'What is there to do? Where to go?'

Alone in my splendid isolation, bringing up shingle for the main path— a wearisome task, but essential if we were not to be bogged down in a morass of mud—I so far knew none of this. A day or so later, dressed in old jeans and a fisherman's smock, I was astonished to see four people marching up the path each brandishing a half-crown a-piece. 'You must be the owner,' they said, thrusting the half-crowns into my hand. 'May we have a cup of tea?' 'Certainly,' I stuttered, not knowing what to say or do. I could not very well say 'Get off my island!', for there was the landing fee notice and here in my unwilling hand was a fistful of coins. To gain time to think I put on my best hostess voice. 'Perhaps you would care to walk round the island while I put the kettle on,' I invited. And to my relief off they went.

Presently there was a knock on the door. 'Oh! do come in,' I said. I ushered them along to the sitting-room, chock-a-block with books, overspilling the bookcases. 'Make yourselves at home.' I shut myself in the kitchen. While they had been walking around the island I had quickly knocked up some scones and baked them to a golden brown in our now ever-ready Aga. Did they actually *want* scones? Should I be a waitress and don an overall? Did they expect to *pay*, if so how much should I charge and would I get a tip? What should I do with it if I did get one, or what? especially or what? In the end I loaded up the tray with the tea, scones, butter and jam, donned a pretty apron which could pass muster as that worn either by a waitress or the owner of an island, and sailed into the sitting-room. As I stood there with the tray held in front of me like a batter-ing ram, so confused was I in my mind that I remember asking myself, for no reason at all, 'Is this a sitting-room? If so what does one do in all the other rooms in a house—stand?' We had migrated from a drawing-room at Epsom Downs, but it had not bothered us that we had never practised the graphic arts there, nor withdrawn to it; this suggesting an elegance of movement reminiscent of Jane Austen, and hardly applicable to our whirl-wind life there. This room here had been handed on to us as a lounge, but to anyone who knows their Mitford, this is a quite dreadful word unless you happen to be residing in an hotel or loitering in an airport—or is it?—and if so do we really care? All we knew was that we never had the time to sit or lounge here—our longest sojourn having been the night we arrived when we had slept on its bare boards.

This however was no time to consider socially acceptable or apt no-menclature. As these stupid and irrelevant thoughts buzzed through my head, the more pertinent question arose as to what attitude I should adopt. Should it be deferential? autocratic? nonchalant? welcoming? Suddenly the incongruity of the situation overcame me. Putting the tray down on the nearest table I burst out laughing. Between gales of mirth I told them my nail-biting problems. Bless their hearts—they all joined in the merriment! I flung off my apron, sat down with them and we all had tea together. They were two charming couples. One worked in a West Country brewery and promised to send me some hops for my beer brewing. He was as good as his word. In fact a week or two later gifts and appreciative letters arrived from both couples.

Delightful as this episode was it was obvious that we had another problem on our hands—two problems in fact. The first, apparently insoluble one, was the fact that people could land if they paid, and there was nothing we could do about it all the time our notice was displayed. We could, of course, do a volte-face; I could emulate the General and Mr Whitehouse by making a trio of owners who manned the guns to guard their privacy; revert to performing antics on the cliff top, or we could accept the intrusions gracefully. The second problem was that, if we did allow people to land, there would arise the question of providing tea. We were now realistic enough to face the fact that most folk, after making the boat trip and climbing around the island, would want a cup of tea. It had never been an ambition of ours to run a café. Babs was possibly better conditioned temperamentally than I was to do so. She was used to organizing fêtes, Leisure and Career Exhibitions and charity functions. Refreshments were endemic to all of these. To provide the same facilities on the island, even if she were here to do so, would be a busman's holiday. She saw her island-life interludes of the school holidays as a kind of ex-curriculum of school activities. For myself I knew how I felt and I had every reason to fear catering for other people.

During my career in the WRNS, although it was not my wish, it was entirely my own fault that I became involved in catering. Also against my wishes, I had been detailed to train for 'Admin', and to this end was posted to Scotland prior to being sent to Greenwich Naval College to be commissioned. A visiting Superintendent WRNS decreed that I should have 'port' experience before attaining the giddy heights of becoming an officer in the WRNS. Consequently I was packed off to Dover. Here, to my chagrin, I found that I was doing exactly the same sort of work in the same sort of office as I had in Scotland. Except for the shells whizzing overhead from France and the bombs being dropped from enemy aircraft above, it was just a replica of the Regulating Office at Balloch on the shores of Loch Lomond.

I asked for an interview with the Chief Officer-in-Charge. I explained to her that if I were going to be in charge of Wrens I reckoned that I ought to have some experience of their jobs at first hand. Could I please be assigned to each of the different categories to gain the necessary experience. The Chief Officer was non-plussed. Highly irregular. Not quite the thing. Some jobs too menial for a Petty Officer. She would have to think about it. Think about it she did, for within a short time I was sent for; it had been agreed and a curriculum would be made out for my entire stay in Dover, embracing all the Wrens' categories. Where they were too technical, like radar for example, I would just 'sit in'; at the rest I could have a go.

It proved to be most educational. As an officer's steward I cleaned out cabins, changed linen and pressed suits all day long and saw not a soul, for the occupants of the cabins were all out waging their bit of the war. A lonely job and, as I later discovered from some of my colleagues, rather looked down upon by a few of the 'Writer' class, albeit at one time titled ladies had taken on some of these lowly jobs in their keen desire to serve their country in the Navy.

When I did my stint in 'Supply' I was welcomed with open arms by the male Chief Petty Officer. 'They *will* send me Wrens who are good at Maths and they are all small girls,' he moaned. 'What I need are strapping lasses who can reach the top shelves and are strong enough to heave boxes of boots and heavy equipment around. I can do the sums.' I looked at his smart but undeniably petite Wrens and duly made a note of his complaint. I have often wondered if this aspect of the war has changed and perhaps even to this day the Supply Department or its modern equivalent is staffed by giant six-footers capable of heaving heavy boxes from the top shelves, or whether it is still manned by the dainty type of Wren Einsteins of yesteryear.

Next I drove round the harbour with the M/T drivers. This was hair-raising as, with great expertise, they reversed to the edge of the quayside to disgorge their goods. I learned from this that Wren M/T drivers certainly have to keep their cool! It also got me an invitation on board an MTB. Here I was entertained by the Officer I/C in his minuscule Wardroom, and I was allowed to drive the craft round and round Dover harbour at great speed. This was very exciting; the only disappointment was that it was forbidden to go outside the harbour. This was probably due to the danger of marauding enemy submarines or perhaps our own minefields. I never knew.

I was allowed to sit in on highly top secret technical operations where Wrens worked, incarcerated in the bowels of the earth. I was sworn to secrecy and warned that, to my dying day, I was never to reveal *anything* that I had seen. Whether it was fear of bringing this day nearer by so doing or the effect of the naval tradition of 'sealed lips' inculcated in one I do not know. I do know that as a result I must have given myself a mental blackout, for, though I can remember minute trivia of those Dover days, that visit is a complete blank and to this day I cannot recall a single thing that I saw nor the secret destination to which I had been taken.

Cooking was another matter entirely. Here I was in my element. No matter that I had to be on duty at 5 a.m. and chop frozen meat, pound after pound after pound, until my fingers were frozen too. Cooking fulfils a basic urge; it is creative, artistic—a craft. One is Mother Earth bestowing the largesse of nature to feed the hungry and succour the weak. Or so I thought.

'Forty omelettes for dinner tonight!' ordered the Chief Petty Officer Wren Cook. Dutifully I beat up gallons of reconstituted dried eggs. I beat with a will for hours until I had pitchers overflowing with bubbling froth. They were left to settle until the evening then beaten again. I did my very best—that I should never see the recipients mattered not at all. When the time came for cooking I had the frothiest mixture you ever did see. The golden liquid slid into the pan and a few moments later—behold a perfect omelette! But I had to do this forty times. 'Hurry!' commanded the Cook, 'the first ones have finished and want more and the others have not had any yet.' I hurried. The heat became intense as I toiled away. Frozen fingers at 5 a.m. and now on the verge of a heat stroke. The more I made the more they wanted. By the time I had cooked sixty strength and the dried egg mixture had given out. Elated with congratulatory messages that came back from the Wardroom I staggered from the galley eventually, exhausted but triumphant.

The next day the Chief PO Cook sent for me. 'You are wasted in "Admin",' she announced, 'I am going to recommend that you change your category to Cook.' I looked at her aghast. Reaction had set in. I never wanted to see another omelette again in my life. I was fed up with chopping frozen meat at crack of, or before, dawn, for I had been at it again that morning and I no longer had any desire whatever of being Mother Earth. In any event I only wanted to find out what it was like to be a cook. I now knew it was unremitting hard work in conditions ranging from Antarctica to the Equator.

Somehow or other I left Dover without changing to cook, but it was this skirmish with cooking that later involved me in catering, again carried away by my own enthusiasm.

Soon after this I was posted to Greenwich Naval College, obtained my commission in 'Admin' and, after three months up North as assistant to a Chief Officer WRNS, was sent as a matter of urgency to take up the post of Officer I/C WRNS at Cookham Camp Signal Station near Chatham. Due to the fact that it was only a small unit of 150 Wrens I was the sole WRNS Officer. On the face of it I had been selected to fill this sudden vacancy, although so newly commissioned, because of my experience of having a go at everything. Hoist with my own petard I now found that I was in charge of everything and that included catering. I soon discovered, as everyone does who has anything to do with feeding people, that they will *complain*—even in wartime. Heroically they will put up with bombing, black-outs, shortages, parting with loved ones, but food not to their fancy they will *not*. The Wrens did not complain about their food—not exactly. The daily allowance was 1s. 5d. per head. Food could be drawn entirely from Naval Stores if one wished, but I preferred to do some prudent shopping around by telephone. Soon I had quite a circle of shopkeepers in Chatham who would ring up if they had anything that was in short supply or was going cheap.

On one occasion it was highly embarrassing. The CO, in his splendid gold braid, accompanied by the First Lieutenant and the Supply Officer, paid me an official visit in my office. Somewhere in the camp a typewriter had gone missing. There was to be an official inquiry. Would I please organize a search of the Wrens' Quarters. All three towered over me. You would think that a flotilla of HM Navy had disappeared at sea without trace. At that moment the phone rang. It was the fishmonger. 'I have some bloaters in. Would you like some?' he asked excitedly. 'Certainly,' I replied crisply, trying to sound as if I were talking to the Chief Officer WRNS, Chatham. 'How many would you like?' he continued, 'I don't often get them offered to me.' 'As many as you can manage,' I replied; '*Thanks* most *awfully*,' dropping the usual conspiratory tones in which we usually spoke to each other. I put the phone down. The CO paused in mid-stream. Was I perhaps increasing my quota of Wrens without his knowledge or permission? I was always demanding more. Luckily he did not take me up on this, as he was too worried about the missing typewriter, for which I was thankful as I was not sure whether he would approve of my shopping locally instead of drawing from naval stores. As a matter of interest the typewriter was eventually found in separate parts, distributed in various drawers throughout the camp. So the quaking culprit was never found nor had to face a court-martial. As for the bloaters, the Wrens were able to feast royally on them in various guises for days on end, although it is hard to disguise a bloater indefinitely. No, the Wrens did not complain about a surfeit of bloaters.

This prudent shopping around enabled me to save money on the 1s. 5d. per head allowance. With the willing co-operation of the Chief PO Wren Cook I was able to provide three cooked meals a day plus a mid-morning snack, tea and cake in the afternoon and hot cocoa and another snack at bedtime. And I had money over. This provided luxuries like strawberries when in season and other delicacies and a reserve fund for providing refreshments at parties and dances to which naval ratings were invited.

You would think that I would be the heroine of the war—Cookham Camp. Not on your life. First a Wren requested an interview, representing, she said, several other Wrens, for she knew that a deputation would, according to King's Regulations, be classed as a mutiny. Instead of spending it on food, please could there be a share-out among the Wrens, of the money saved. Also they didn't see why the naval ratings should benefit. 'Perhaps you would like the dances cancelled,' I offered. 'No, the Navy should provide those, we just want a share-out.' 'That is quite impossible—it is Navy money intended for food and must be spent on food.' She had to accept this decision but was not a bit happy about it. The Chief P.O. Cook assured me that it was only a small number of Wrens who wanted a share-out; the majority were highly satisfied. Nevertheless I was quite chastened, for this budgeting took a considerable amount of my spare time.

Next I had another visit from the CO. The naval ratings, he told me, had started to complain. 'Why', they asked, 'were the Wrens being better fed than we are?' 'I think I should send the Supply Officer to see you,' said the CO; 'the men are complaining so I shall have to do something about it.' 'I don't think that is necessary,' I said in alarm. I did not want any gate-crashing into my coterie of shopkeepers and I did not think that a naval Supply Officer would be too pleased at having to seek my advice. 'The reason is that it is so much easier to cater for 150 than a 1,000 or so. Apart from that, men eat far more than girls. It must be very difficult.' Hoping to divert him I threw in my own complaint: 'According to the Naval quota I am only allowed one and a half cooks for the number of Wrens in my Unit and I need three—one for each watch.' He looked aghast. 'Whatever do you do?' 'Use half an officer's steward,' I replied, 'and work two watches- instead of three, but it is not very popular and overworks the cooks.' 'Well write to the Admiralty and I will endorse it,' the poor man said and left. In due course I got my three cooks, so some good came out of the visit.

A day or so later a naval rating messenger appeared at the door. 'The Commander sends his compliments and would you be so good as to come and see him at your early convenience.' Although politely couched, as in true naval fashion, this meant: 'This is urgent. Come at once!' 'It is the Wardroom now,' he said. 'They want you to do the catering for them.' Would I please therefore be the Honorary Catering Officer for the Wardroom. The steward in charge did not think very much of this idea. And neither did I. I ate in the Wardroom myself. As the only woman among so many naval officers I received special treatment—the CO for instance, a highly moral gentleman, would not allow swearing in my presence. If an officer let drop so much as one 'bloody' he was made to apologise, and of course I was never wanting for an escort to dances, concerts and parties down in Chatham. Their ages ranged from veterans of the Battle of Jutland to young midshipmen, and we all lived in happy accord. Until now. At every mealtime I became the butt of all their complaints and suggestions. 'Made-up dishes again! Why can't we have roast meat?' Very soon I discovered that all men want for lunch and dinner is a cut off the joint and two veg., or fish and chips, day after day, after day. It did not matter that there was rationing, they knew what they wanted; the rest was my affair. The only mealtimes I could enjoy, with happy faces around me, was when I could supply their beloved roast, steak and kidney pie or pudding or fish and chips. It was a wonder the war went on at all with all this preoccupation with food. I often wondered if the Nazis were at it, too, on their side of the Channel, and if they spent all *their* time arguing about their wurst and sauerkraut or whatever, and, if so, how they ever had time to come and fling their bombs at us. No wonder Hitler had to invent pilotless planes.

So the last thing I wanted in our island paradise was to be involved in catering.

All these recollections went through my head as I toiled away at lugging shingle up the path and hacked away at overgrown verges until Babs should come again to discuss these pressing problems. 'Perhaps', we said, 'a local firm or family would come over and run a tea-shop or café during the summer.' 'Not a hope,' said Mr Nancollas. 'With the tides, the wind and the weather to contend with and the short season there would be no hope of making it pay, far less make a profit. In fact they would lose money in no time at all. Nobody would take it on.'

Meantime, with the problem still unresolved, more and more people were marching up the path clutching their half-crowns. Not many. Only small groups but to me it seemed like an army on the move. I managed to contain the situation, until one day twenty-two visitors arrived at once and they all wanted coffee. I did not have twenty-two coffee cups but managed with an assortment of mugs and teacups. Then they all wanted lunch—at the same time—1 o'clock. 'OK', I quavered. Hastily I pulled some lettuce from the garden. Opened a tin of ham. Tomatoes? Yes. Fruit? I could make a fruit salad if I opened some tins as well. There was some cream Babs had brought for me at the weekend. But what about plates? I only had six. No one would understand. Earlier, when we had twenty friends staying on the island to help us, they were parked out in the cottages and we provided them with eggs to have boiled for breakfast. We dished out egg boxes. 'Just cut them up, they make very good egg cups,' we said. Well they would wouldn't they? That is what they had been stored in. 'Good gracious!' they cried: 'Didn't you have any egg cups before you came here?' 'Of course,' we replied tartly. 'Six was quite enough for the two of us. We hadn't twenty—have you?'

So I knew that no one would understand that you do not start off life on an uninhabited island complete with a dinner service including twenty-two dinner plates. Around 1 o'clock they started to stream in. I served the first six. I then engaged the next party in conversation while, out of the corner of my eye, I kept watch on the progress of Party No. 1. This was not too difficult. Visitors love to ask questions. All I had to do was stand there. 'What is it like in the winter?' 'How did you come to own an island in the first place?' 'What about electricity? fresh water? stores? Suppose you are ill?—are you ever *frightened*?' It was like holding a press conference. This questioning goes on to this day and it has convinced me, too, that I am useless at café work. Babs is much more adept than I am. As she is a teacher it comes naturally to her to do at least two things at once. I admire the way she can load a tray, make tea, take money, give change, and converse charmingly, all seemingly at the same time. If I am in the same situation, if anyone asks me for instance 'What is it like in the winter?' I tell them, giving them my undivided attention. This may be rewarding to the questioner but it does mean that the tea gets cold or is not in the pot at all, or some baffled customer finds a blob of jam but no scone on his or her plate. I cannot give change either, for the same reason. In any case I have never become used to the new money. I rarely go ashore and have never been accustomed to handling cash. I have always been a cheque person, as this leaves one's financial state comfortably in the dark. To me a 10p piece will always be 2s. As this means that everyone will get short change I ask people to count it out for themselves, and that leaves me free to answer questions. In fact, in the café I am reduced to a gibbering fool.

Today, however, my ineptitude served me in good stead. As soon as the munching ceased I detached myself from Group No. 2, raced back to the house with the dishes, washed and wiped them at great speed, set out the salad as artistically as I could, then, at the disjointed speed of the old silent films I pelted back at breakneck speed, pulling myself up short, like a Keystone Kop, at the last moment so that I could saunter in with some semblance of efficient calm. Party No. 3 was kept at bay by the same technique, but knowing that I could not bring off the ploy a third time I just did not appear at all, but lurked behind the scenes until the second lot of munching ceased. Luckily Party No. 1, who were awaiting their fruit salad and cream, got into conversation with Party No. 3. Party No. 4 was late anyway. Incredibly everyone was fed, and I persuaded myself that, with the talking going on, no one realized that they were all eating at different times and from the same plates. Not having any idea of what to charge I said the first thing that came into my head, which was 1s. 6d. per head. They all seemed very pleased and asked if they could have tea later. After this was served, which was a simple operation compared with the lunch-time marathon, they all thanked me profusely and went home. They had had a lovely day—the highlight of their holiday—they all said. Well, my highlight was that although I had served twenty-two people on three occasions, at the end of the day I only had six of anything to wash up.

As I crawled into bed that night 'had we', I asked myself 'attained the almost impossible in acquiring our very own island merely to give strangers a lovely day; our crowning success to be left with a minimum of washing-up?' As I dozed off, sleepily I murmured; 'who is the Potter, pray, and who the Pot?'

Babs and I would have to hold another emergency meeting.

The VOLUNTEERS' Tale

We decided to seek the help of the National Trust.

The area representative came to see us, made a tour of the island and said that in his opinion if the National Trust owned the island they would have to commercialize it to make it pay. That is, he said, they would have to build a number of holiday chalets and other facilities and probably convert the tractor shed into a cottage, in order to bring in enough income to pay a warden, his wife and staff. Unlike their mainland properties, the season when the island could be open to visitors would be very short and then would be restricted by tides and weather. He could not see it as a viable project. Nevertheless he wished us luck and said that, of course, the National Trust would encourage us in our endeavours.

Impasse! Back to the drawing-board. So far crowds of friends and relatives had come to stay at intervals during the holiday period helping us in every possible way. This was fine as far as maintaining the island was concerned, but if we were to allow people to land and to provide refreshments for them we should need more continuity of help. Soon after this visit from the National Trust, but whether as a result or not we did not know, we had a letter from the then Conservation Corps (now The British Trust for Conservation Volunteers). It said in effect that they would help by writing about us in their magazine and encourage voluntary help, as we were doing a splendid thing in opening the island to visitors. Our spirits rose; mentally I packed away my mythical shot gun and performances on the cliff top.

Did we want to do this? Babs had no doubts. 'With this encouragement we *should* share this lovely place with others,' she exclaimed enthusiastically. 'I am sure it is the right thing to do.' Inwardly I groaned, for Babs is far more public-spirited than I am. I saw my splendid solitude slipping away from me—this balm to my spirit evaporate before it had time to work its healing powers.

Longingly I began to dream of an island far away—in the Pacific perhaps—where no one could get at us. But I knew what would happen. Natives would land from neighbouring islands, for as soon as we took up residence, our island would appear to them to be much more desirable than their own. Should we be foolish enough to try to guard our privacy by putting up a notice saying, for instance, LANDING FEE—10 COCONUTS, it would be the signal for an air-shuttle service from places as far away as China and Japan to disgorge posses of people, demanding chow or sake or whatever. No! there was no escape. It was meant to be. Just as by an extraordinary chain of coincidences we had been brought to this enchanting island, so now it seemed we were destined to open it and share it with others. Destiny did not indicate anything about sharing the bills; probably that aspect was not within its province, but it saw to it that we would be helped in other ways.

Over the years we have been greatly encouraged by the enormous amount of goodwill and help that we have received, so often from complete strangers. Some will give donations, some gifts and others will toil unceasingly to help us. Many have become our friends. One lady regularly sent us a cheque for £100, when this was worth much more than it is today. As a business woman, she said (we heard later that she owned a five-star hotel) she knew how worthwhile projects such as ours foundered and had to be abandoned for lack of financial support.

Day visitors write us letters of thanks and send us photographs and presents. Professional artists have given us paintings of the island, sometimes beautifully framed. One couple, whose interest is folk singing, composed a song about us and the island, included it in their repertoire and made a recording for us. We are encouraged not only by our own countrymen in our endeavours. Even this very day as I write, in a temporary lull in the autumn gales, over the empty sea came two people, ferried by our present charming and indomitable ferryman—Dick Butters in his *Summer Star*. In fact there were three passengers—a German with his wife and one-year-old baby. Nineteen years ago, he told us, he had as a youth rowed here all the way from Polperro. We had made him welcome and tended his blisters. He had never forgotten the island or us. Now, a married man of forty, he had flown over from Baden-Baden for a five-day visit to Looe especially so that he could come to see us. He came laden with gift-wrapped presents for us all the way from Germany—liqueur chocolates in a handmade basket and another with chocolate-covered marzipans enclosing more liqueurs surrounding a beautifully decorated china dish.

In face of such touching tributes what can one do? To be honest, as we never wanted to open the island in the first place, we are often tempted to close it again. We came here to enjoy island life, not on the one hand to make a living nor on the other to be a public service by providing an oasis of tranquility and beauty for others. Inexorably we found ourselves becoming a public service in spite of our insular ambitions. That nothing would tempt us to spoil or commercialize the island by so doing put us on a suicide course.

The Conservation Corps, however, were as good as their word and soon we had applicants for our working holidays. As so far little was known about us we asked the Students' Union to mention our working holidays in their magazine too. We probably cast our net too wide, for not only did we get applications from dedicated conservationists and students genuinely desirous to help and practise their skills, but it also encouraged those who merely wanted to fill a gap between digs and others who saw only the glamour of life on an island and were not prepared for any hard grind.

The first mistake we made was to provide accommodation, gas, electricity and food which we cooked, all without any charge, in exchange for their work. It seemed a reasonable arrangement in theory. In practice it was quite a different matter. Most of the volunteers at that time were students. No one coming our way showed any signs of anorexia—they all had enormous appetites. Catering for up to eight helpers was like being the mother of a large family of teenagers who were at home all day long. With no maternal instinct and not very much in the way of emergency stores, I found that once again catering was raising its head like a leering ogre.

I remember one helper in particular. He fancied himself as an artist and assumed the so-called artistic temperament. He was the only volunteer at the time, as it was early in the season when no other students were free to come, and his help would have been invaluable. It did seem to me however that he just passed the time between one meal and the next, although in a very charming manner. One day I was beavering away shifting coal and digging trenches for potatoes, when he strolled up to me. I forget what particular job he had been allocated, but whatever it was he was obviously not doing it. 'I feel rather guilty', he said 'seeing you working so hard. I haven't done anything this morning as I didn't feel like it. I have been sketching instead. I do hope you don't mind.' I rested on my spade for a moment. 'That is perfectly all right,' I said. 'You will understand, of course, that I may not feel like cooking the meal tonight as I have a poem I want to finish.' He was a decent chap though and after that he did buckle to—and his sketches were really quite good.

Some students were fussy beyond belief. 'Would you please make a meat pie with onion at one end only!' asked one. 'I do not eat peaches, oranges, apples, rice, fish, poultry, cream, green vegetables, butter or bread,' said another, 'and I do not care for potatoes,' he added, 'unless they are chips.' 'What do you like?' I asked, trying to keep the menace out of my voice. 'Practically anything else. My mother knows exactly what I want,' he replied. I bet she did, but why didn't she give it to him? I very nearly did! 'Please do not serve anything wrapped in pastry,' said one. 'Meat pies only,' requested another. 'No meat of any kind,' insisted a third, 'only ham, fish or poultry.' 'I'm a vegan,' announced another.

I was getting quite demented, for one of the things that some of them did not care for either was work. I was having to fit in this frustrating catering for helpers with attending to visitors, working on the land and in the greenhouse and trying to supervise any work that was being done. Of course some were very good, worked hard and have kept in touch with us over the years, but there was no way of knowing beforehand what the intake of helpers was going to be like and what kind of food to get in.

At one of our many weekend board meetings Babs and I decided that the only answer was for the helpers to do their own cooking. We would supply the food and make a rota for 'Cook of the Day'. But this did not work for the simple reason that some of them could not cook, or even worse, jumped at the chance of having a go. One young girl said that her mother would never allow her to cook at home, although she loved it and she could do a very good soufflé. Could she have a go? I was intrigued. I would love to know the secret of a good soufflé. She asked for nine eggs. I quailed, for that would leave me with only three for their breakfast, and the dish was to provide a lunch, not an evening meal. However I produced the nine eggs and waited, for I was to share in this gourmet delicacy. Presently we were served with a perfectly respectable omelette apiece. Everyone was delighted and congratulated the proud cook. 'Now,' they said 'what are we having for lunch?' I now know why her mother would not let her cook at home. She couldn't afford it.

It was during this period that I came face to face with Women's Lib, which was then enjoying its great upsurge. To make our position 'absolutely clear', as the politicians say (I have often wondered what is clearer than clear?), Babs and I reckoned that we had liberated ourselves decades ago, long before it became fashionable. We had thrown off the shackles of domesticity without depriving men of their rightful role in life, which was looking after us. This was not part of a movement as far as we were concerned, for we believed in the right person for the right job.

Not so one of our helpers; she was a wisp of a girl, a young student, and an ardent Women's Libber. Now if the 'Cook of the Day' happened to be a fellow and he could cook—and some of them were very good cooks indeed—all was well, but if he was not, there was always some girl willing to volunteer in his place. When it came to Basil's turn, who had never cooked in his life before, our Women's Libber insisted that he do his stint and she would do his job of chopping up some enormous logs. Basil, a tall gangling youth, dutifully turned up in the kitchen for provisions and instructions. 'Is there anything you *can* cook?' I asked. 'Well, I can make a blancmange,' he replied. 'OK', I said, 'I will cook the main dish, steak pie and vegetables. You can serve it up and then produce your blancmange and fruit. That way it will appear that you have done the lot.' In a short time he had made the blancmange and put it in the fridge to set. When the pie was cooked and everything was ready to be dished up I took the blancmange out of the fridge ready for Basil to turn it out. To my horror it had not set at all—it was as runny as milk. 'How did you make it?' I asked. 'Just as the instructions said,' he replied, 'I mixed the powder with the milk.' 'Didn't you bring the milk up to the boil?' I asked. 'Oh no! I mixed it with the cold milk and put it in the fridge.' In desperation I heated up vast quantities of gelatine, stirred it into the liquid blancmange and thrust it back into the fridge; Basil went off in triumph with the steaming pie, its golden crust topping the succulent mixture beneath, and by the time the helpers had eaten their way through that, by some incredible luck, the blancmange had set. The little Woman's Libber, all hot and flustered, was almost too tired to eat hers. 'I couldn't manage the chopping,' she gulped—'it was just too much for me.'

The next day Basil was on duty in the café. I happend to be there and was the witness to a scene that I shall never forget. There stood Basil, his gangling figure towering above a table of ladies he had just served with tea, scones and jam. 'And do you know,' one of the ladies called over to an adjoining table, 'he does all the cooking here as well!' There stood Basil with a look of ineffable pride on his face, for I am quite sure he felt as if indeed he had done so.

All in all this catering became a huge burden. I seemed always to be involved one way or another with the cooking of the evening meal. Each 'Cook of the Day' had one day of the week on duty. When the day visitors left all other helpers were off duty for the evening and would then go swimming or whatever, while I perforce was on duty every evening. When the meal was finally finished and I had made sure that I was not left with greasy pans hidden in odd corners, the next day's 'Cook of the Day' came up for provisions for breakfast, lunch and so on. After doing the day's accounts and answering knocks from helpers and cottagers, 'now that you are free', I would be lucky to snatch a sandwich around 10 p.m. before crawling into bed by 'lights out' at 11 p.m. Often I would have to tumble out of bed again as someone had forgotten to switch off the light or fallen asleep reading in bed. This meant that the generator was thundering away for just one electric light bulb—a frequent occurrence that later was to land us with the huge expense of buying another generator. Babs was with me to share the burden most summer weekends and for the school holidays but the rest of the long summers I soldiered on alone. Babs, too, was not getting the breaks she needed and had the added burden at the end of her busy term-time day of buying supplies not just for me but for our large family of helpers and the day visitors. About this time inflation began to take the bit between its teeth and the cost of food rose astronomically.

'Why are we doing this?' we asked ourselves, for we were now having to use our own income to keep the island open to visitors and to feed the helpers. We had no time to enjoy the island in the lovely summer months and were getting exhausted into the bargain. However it seemed such a worthwhile project and appreciated by so many. 'The highlight of our holiday' was, and is, a constant refrain. We were, too, able to show young people a way of life that was fast disappearing and introduce them to old crafts that were new to them, for at that time there had not been the resurgence of interest in crafts that there is today.

It was not all one-sided either. Many did fine work and we remember them over the years. Such a one was Julian. A shy graduate, he was a most willing worker and when there was a wearisome job to be done he would volunteer. With so many people living on the island during the summer, water was a precious commodity. To conserve it for drinking and cooking, sea-water had to be hauled up to flush the lavatories. Every morning, or when the tide was high enough, the helpers had to bring up buckets of sea-water from below the jetty to fill a tank for the outside lavatory used by themselves and day visitors. This was an irksome and a tiring and unpopular task. Some helpers would be missing at the vital time; not so Julian—he was always there and toiled unceasingly with buckets full to the brim in either hand.

Always after they left the island helpers wrote us letters of appreciation and thanks for the time they had spent here and the experiences and pleasure they had enjoyed. When Julian wrote he enclosed a cheque for £100 to help us with our project. This, of course, was worth much more than it is today, but it would be a sizeable sum at any time, especially when you consider that it was from a young man just starting out on his career. We decided that its most fitting use was to put it towards a system for pumping up sea-water. This we did, and now, during the summer months it is pumped, at high tide, to a tank by the outside lavatory and to another tank in the Jetty Cottage attic, thus enabling the low-flush lavatory to function without using the spring water. Of course the plumbing had to be adapted to take sea-water, and the initial cost was well in excess of £1000, but apart from cutting out the time- and energy-consuming chore of hauling it up by hand, it made life easier for summer visitors to Jetty Cottage. The pump is sited on rocks above the jetty and is dismantled for the winter; otherwise it is in danger of being swept away by storms. Once an unseasonally fierce autumn gale did just that. The tremendous seas swept over the rocks and wrenched the heavy pump from its housing, to which it was bolted, and hurled it into the surf below. As I was on the island alone I had to go down at low tide and had the back-aching task of dragging it inch by inch over the sea-bed and rocks to the bottom of the steps leading up the slope to the path above. It was a difficult job to manhandle it up these concrete steps for they were open and almost perpendicular. This was followed by a long and slow drag up the steep slope to safety. So now, at the end of the summer when the last visitor or helper has departed, we make sure that it is dismantled and stored away until the following season, for there is plenty of spring water for our own needs. However, as far as we are concerned it will always be 'Julian's pump', and he certainly has done his bit for the island.

In spite of help and encouragement such as this the strain was becoming unendurable. With hindsight it seems incredible that we carried on like this for so many years. One solution, of course, was to close the island to visitors.

There was one aspect however that held us back. It was the question of Leonard Pengelly. Although several boatmen brought visitors to the island he was the chief ferryman. A fine character, he was Father of the Council, for he had served on it for thirty-five years, and a picture graced his sitting-room showing him resplendent with the chain of office when he was Chairman of the Council. He had given up fishing and other trips to bring visitors to the island. He had taken us under his wing, too, giving us fatherly advice, for he reckoned that we were a bit green where people were concerned. 'People will always please themselves, so you must look after your own interests,' was something he was always preaching to us, wagging his finger, and looking at us with his keen blue eyes. Over the years he became a very good friend to us, looked after our interests, and helped us in many ways without thought of reward. Once in mid-winter, when I had an abscess on a tooth, he came over in a near gale to take me to the dentist, waited for me and brought me back, carefully wrapping a scarf round my face. He would accept no payment. 'I was glad to be of help,' he said. Although getting on for seventy he was still a fine-looking man and a great favourite with the visitors who loved listening to his salty tales. We often think of his advice for eventually, due to increasing age and ill health, he had to give up and sadly he is with us no more. Highly thought of in the community, a memorial seat was installed in his honour and memory by the entrance to the harbour.

While he was still active, however, we felt impelled to carry on; we did not feel that we should do anything that might endanger his livelihood. Then two events happened that brought things to a head. In 1973 I was commissioned to write a book and Leonard announced that at the end of the summer season he would retire, for he was already finding the handling of his boat a physical strain. Meantime the effort of writing a book, in addition to dealing with the vagaries of students' appetites, meeting visitors, catering, coping with cottagers, working in the greenhouse and cultivating the land as well as looking after myself and the pets, began to take its toll. But with Leonard retiring the solution was simple. We wrote to the Town Clerk to say that we should not be opening the following season, because, as the *Looe Guide* mentioned that the island was open to visitors, we thought that our decision should be made known officially.

For a time we revelled in the thoughts of our idyllic life to come. We should have leisure to enjoy the delights of an island summer and I would have lunch-times free from interruptions. I can truthfully say that for the whole twelve years before Babs retired from teaching I only ever had stand-up lunches during all those summers and an evening meal was a luxury to look forward to in the winter months. No wonder, in spite of a hectically active and strenuous life, I put on weight, existing as I did on an almost unvarying sustenance of sandwiches!

It was not to be. Another dream faded into never-never land. First we had a letter from the Council asking if we would reconsider our decision, as our opening the island to visitors was an added amenity for Looe. We knew this to be so, for every year visitors told us, as they do to this day, that they were spending their holiday in Looe especially so that they could visit the island. They come from far and wide, not only from all parts of the British Isles but from all over the world. They write to us from Australia, Vancouver, the United States, South Africa, the Middle East and many other places to say that they are including Looe in their itinerary so that they can visit us. When we received the Council's letter we were glad to know that our project was appreciated and were happy to help Looe in this way, for it is a charming, picturesque fishing port and many of its inhabitants have been very good friends to us indeed.

One of these, of course, was Leonard Pengelly. He somehow got to hear about our decision to close the island and informed us that he had changed his mind about retiring; his grandson, Tony Pengelly, was going to help him. Eventually he passed on the reins to the good-looking Tony, who, with his attractive personality, was also a great favourite with visitors. When finally he took over he carried on in the tradition of his grandfather and became a good friend to us and the island. His tale will come later, for this is basically about our early days and how our life here has evolved.

We felt in view of these factors that we should carry on, at least until Leonard retired, for at that time we did not know that Tony would eventually take over from him. We are sure that Leonard, like so many locals who were born and bred in Looe, loved the island and wanted us to carry on, as, so we were touched to hear, it was thought that 'we were good for the island'. But how to carry on? We had been told that we were eligible for grants for projects such as ours, but we did not favour this on two counts. Firstly, there would possibly be strings attached and we should no longer be free agents; secondly we did not believe in grants. We felt, and still do, that it is up to us to make a success of our projects. Physical help, gifts and donations freely given was one matter, a spur to our endeavours and the greatest encouragement we could have; but expecting grants as of right was another and not in our reckoning.

At last after much pondering we emerged through this labyrinth of thorny problems with a change of direction that we hoped would prove a solution, albeit a compromise. We would offer self-catering working holi days, and make a nominal charge for accommodation. Secretly I hoped that this would discourage volunteers from applying. Without helpers there could be no visitors and, *ipso facto*, freedom and solvency would be ours again.

To this end we advertised our working holidays in *The Lady* and elsewhere, as well as sending notices to *The Conserver* and the National Union of Students. The response amazed us, for not only did the applications increase but they came from people of all ages and backgrounds— professional couples with young families, others with teenage offspring. They were glad, they told us, to escape from the rat race for a while, help in a worthwhile project and give their children a holiday in natural surroundings that would encourage them to join in communal projects. Surprisngly we had applications from OAPs too, and these have proved to be among our most enduring helpers, returning year after year. These veterans were young or in their prime during the war and as such have thrown off the image of grannies in shawls or bent old gentlemen. Leading active and often dangerous lives in those historic times they are forever forward-looking and have a resilience and a 'Give us the tools and we will get on with the job' outlook that puts many younger people to shame. Sally Roberts is one of these. She skis and partakes in many active pursuits, yet finds the time and energy to come here, often twice a year, from near Liverpool, with her friend Clare Donnelly, to help us at our busiest times on the land; and Margery Roberts (but no relation), who comes especially to help us with jam-making. A book could be written about our helpers—and probably will—for they are part of the fabric of our lives here, in the spring and summer. Young and old become a good 'mix' and everyone seems to enjoy living and working with others from differing backgrounds, and many friendships have been formed.

At the time this new *modus operandi* eased the burden to some extent and enabled me to carry on while Babs lived for the most part on the mainland, especially as cottagers joined in and helped also. But I longed for the day when Babs could retire and join me. TV programmes and articles in the National Press about our activities brought us to the public notice and more and more people came to see us. There were now up to five boatmen ferrying visitors to the island. One occasion I remember in particular, early in the season, when there were no helpers. Simultaneously five boats arrived, two disgorging visitors at the jetty and three on the beach. I had to race up the path and along the cliff top and back like a demented being to meet them. Sometimes the numbers involved were few but the mechanics of helping them off the boats, catering to their needs and helping them on the boats again were the same. Sometimes in fine weather there would be a great influx and with more good weather predicted, I would, after a hectic day, stay up half the night baking scones. Unexpectedly a gale would blow up or the wind turn easterly and prevent boats leaving the harbour for days on end. With no deep-freeze facilities, trays and trays of scones and a stock of bread bought in anticipation would all go mouldy and the expensive clotted cream go off.

Sometimes, without warning, the weather broke in early September and, with the visitor season coming to an abrupt and unexpected end, we were left with large quantities of foodstuff that would not over-winter in our damp sea atmosphere. Coffee congealed, sugar and flour hardened, tea turned mouldy, butter went rancid and tins rusted. It was no wonder that the National Trust official said that opening the island to visitors was not a viable proposition.

It never has been. With rising costs Babs and I have had to dig deeper and deeper into our own pockets to provide and maintain accommodation and facilities for visitors and helpers, with, of course, the added and increasing cost of transport of goods and labour from the mainland. Often we are still tempted to close the island and revert to the help of friends and the offers of voluntary organizations for the conservation and cultivation of the island which is our primary aim. We dream often of a more leisurely life, when in summer we could go on cliff walks, have picnics on the beach, swim in the heat of a summer afternoon, have lunch-times *sitting down*, free from interruptions, and we could at last be able to achieve the simple but impossible delight of sitting on top of the island in summertime to enjoy the view and the peace—just like our visitors.

There are moments when we do not think our efforts are worth the strain on our energy and finances; then along will come someone whose encouragement will put us on course again. One such is Kath Barker who regularly, sometimes twice a year, makes the long journey from Darlington via Dover, where she leaves her dog with her father, so that she can help us. She not only works with a will at everything, but brings some of her delicious home-baking and entertains us to delightful meals. Another such is Philla. Starting as a day visitor, she was fired by the island and our projects. She then rented a cottage, and stayed here many times with her friend, Jane, and her husband, the Rector of Botley, and their children, all of whom helped. Philla also came by herself from her busy job as a Supervisor in the Foreign Telephone Exchange in London, to stay for awhile to work on the land or do any other jobs that came to hand. Always she came with a gift, usually a bottle of malt whisky, so that, she said, we could have a 'wee dram' to cheer us along. She entertained us to many meals in the cottage and over the years has proved to be a most generous friend. Eventually she retired and moved from London to Liskeard so that she could be within easy reach of the island.

A recent ploy of hers was to arrange an official birthday for me. Babs's birthday is in June, a time of year when there is an island population. Consequently she has cards or presents from all who are here; the St George's flag is flown and a birthday party arranged. Mine is in late October, a time of gales, no visitors, and too rough for the flag to be hoisted anyway. Indeed until Babs retired I often spent it alone, celebrating at a weekend when it was calm enough for her to come over for a few hours. Philla always sends me a present, but that is not good enough for her—she likes to give it in person.

Independence Day, 4 July, was fixed, as it was already the date designated for the birthday of Lucky, the terrier-cum-labrador successor to Kim, and that of Tilly and Samantha, two of the cats who had eventually replaced Cleo, HamRam and Bessie. Their exact birthdays were not known but they were within a week or two of this date. Sue, the youngest cat, who now looks after me in place of Joan, has a known birthday, as does Emma our other dog—a Christmas present to Lucky from Sue, the vet, who until she left the district, undertook the welfare of all our pets, and in the process became an island addict. All the pets were invited to a party and the flag was hoisted. Pam Burdass, who was helping indefatigably in many ways, baked a cake as a surprise. A good time was had by all except that the cats decided not to show up—they were not party minded, they said. The dogs had a wonderful time and I basked in the glory of an official birthday—just like the Queen. Typically Philla sent me another present on my real birthday, so now I have two birthdays, but without, I hope, a corresponding increase in age. Others got to hear about this and sent me 'royal' birthday card greetings and Paul and Sandra Hughes sent me a beautiful book on wild flowers, illustrated by Marjorie Blamey, the artist, who lives in Liskeard.

We first met Paul when he came as a day visitor when he was a schoolboy of fourteen. He was remembered in particular because he dashed back to the mainland by the return boat to fetch a scientific journal dealing with the habits of seagulls we had been discussing with him. He was keenly interested in zoology and this became his specialist subject. Later he came here on working holidays and we learned from him many fascinating facts about the numerous seaweeds that grow around our shores. He kept in touch during his university days, once paying us a flying visit to give us a beautifully illustrated book on insects which has proved invaluable in our study of the wealth of wildlife to be found on the island. His sister, Clare, came on working holidays, too, and has now completed her training as an actress. Paul, now qualified and launched on his career in a hospital, brought his girl-friend, Sandra, on a working holiday, in the hope that the island would mean as much to her as it did to him. Fortunately she fell under the spell of the island too, and we were very happy to welcome them back here for their honeymoon.

Jane Cochrane, now a radiographer, was another who started as a schoolgirl helper. She met Andrew Giles here who had recently left school. Their friendship blossomed and each year they came on a working holiday together and last March (1984) they married, spending a day of their honeymoon with us.

Many of our student helpers whose careers have taken them far afield have never forgotten their time here; they keep in touch and bring us up to date with their progress. Sarah Kelly, who started as a schoolgirl helper, now a doctor and training to become a surgeon, writes to us regularly and still comes to help when she can find time in her busy life, with her brother Adam, originally a schoolboy helper and now a falconer. There is one who went to Alaska and after nine years, on a visit to this country, came to see us and asked if she could stay overnight so that she could show us her photographs and dig a patch for us. This she did and, forever, this area is dubbed the 'Alaska Patch'. Another was Pat Nevin, who after she had qualified took a medical research job in Hawaii. She sends us a colourful calendar from there every year and, when she came on a flying visit to this country for the Royal Wedding, came to see us and brought us a coral necklace apiece from her adopted island. Carol Alvin, who was on a sponsored cycle ride for the National Trust of Scotland round the coast of Britain, gave up a week of her time to help us and now lives on an island herself—the Isle of Coll. She writes interestingly to us of her life and has had several articles published about her island activities.

These and many more are interwoven in the pattern of our lives here: the families, the OAPs, the young men and women—the older ones too, who come year after year to help, bearing gifts for the island or for us personally. Many have thrown parties for us or invited us to meals. This year two young students, who were here at the end of the season, Debbie and Jacque, invited us to a candle-lit three-course gourmet meal.

We feel that all these special people deserve that we respond to their encouragement and friendship. In our darker moments, when we are tempted to close and lead a more leisurely life in the tranquil days of summer, we remember them and others who have inspired us. Such a one was Michael Trinick, the Regional Director of the National Trust, who visited us in 1982 before his retirement and said that the National Trust depended on private owners such as ourselves, who are willing to open their property to the public and preserve it on National Trust lines, an uneconomic undertaking beyond the resources of the Trust. After his visit Michael Trinick wrote us a letter in which he said; 'I was very taken with the relaxed atmosphere you had created there, and felt you must give much pleasure to many people.'

Such sentiments sustain us and enable us to carry on, and so we shall— as long as the money lasts.

The COTTAGERS' Tale

During the early period when I was alone on the island, out of the blue came a letter from the Bahamas. It was from a First Secretary who had read an article of mine in a magazine in his Embassy. He said that he was coming on home leave and would like to rent the Smugglers' Cottage if that were possible. This did not appeal to me at all. We were not established ourselves and were still having many problems, especially with the pumping of the fresh water, and, as it was term time, I should be here alone. I did not think that I would be up to coping with a First Secretary. 'He will be too high-powered for me,' I wailed to Babs. 'From an Embassy! He will be used to cocktail parties—formal dinners—just like the Navy, all gold braid and protocol. He won't be able to stand it here.' I tried to put him off. 'Primitive compared with the mainland,' I said. 'Water problems.' Nothing would deter him. The correspondence went on for some time. 'I am coming,' he said, 'if you will have me.'

So he and his wife came; his daughter could not as it was term-time and she would still be at school—Roedean. All my fears were groundless. 'You mentioned the water situation,' he said, 'I have spent all my life abroad and we have always had to *buy* our water. I shall be happy to help you in any way,' he added. And help he did. Stripped to the waist he toiled on the land; he carted stores in the caterpillar tractor, and he heaved coal up from the beach. In particular he took over tending the freshwater pump in the cliff. At this stage in its life it had an unpleasant habit of coming apart at the seams when the engine was started, drenching whoever was there with cascades of icy spring-water. As this was usually Babs or me we were delighted that our diplomat added this to the chores that he undertook. Not only did he enjoy his holiday, possibly as a refreshing change from the diplomatic rounds, but we certainly enjoyed having him and we were sorry when his leave was up and he left for Romania.

Later on when we were established and let the cottages occasionally during the summer months, there was one booking Babs made that for a similar reason caused me much nail-biting. It was for a Colonel, whose home was a Manor House. 'Not the Army!' I wailed to Babs. I always seemed to moan if any bookings were made although I knew these were necessary to keep the cottages 'alive'. 'He will be snooty, elitist. Not for us!' Now that we were settled into island life we lived in jeans, gumboots, fisherman's smocks, anoraks and woolly hats; they had become *de rigueur*. We had cast off the clothes and trimmings of civilization like a chrysalis— not to emerge as butterflies, but more like your bucolic peasant. I really enjoyed being a peasant, and the prospect of coming face to face with a senior officer in the Army appalled me. We couldn't be so lucky as with the First Secretary. 'Well,' said Babs, 'it's too late. I have booked him,' and hoofed it back to the mainland, before I could start chanting my 'Close the Island' theme.

Worse was to follow. Babs broke the news to me the following weekend, fortifying me first with a strong drink. 'He has sent his deposit,' she said, 'and he is now a Brigadier.' I spilt the drink. 'It is term-time too,' I gulped, 'I shall have to cope alone.' 'I shall be there the weekend he and his wife arrive, so keep going until I come,' said Babs.

The day he was due I was in a turmoil anyway as the electricity had become faulty and we were to have some re-wiring done. I did not have time to don my best fisherman's smock and had on my old gardening one which would not have passed any inspection nor have been fit for a collection for Oxfam.

Then I saw him. A tall distinguished man with grey hair. He stood languidly at the top of the path, hand on hip, watching a short, stocky man beavering up the path. Glistening with perspiration he was pushing with all his might and main the truck piled high with baggage. 'Good God!' I cried, 'he has even brought his batman with him.' The Brigadier did not attempt to help—well, he wouldn't, would he? At last the stocky man and his caravan of luggage made the top of the path, turned and disappeared into the Jetty Cottage entrance. Shortly after this Babs arrived. 'He's brought his batman with him,' I hissed. 'I didn't see any batman. I met him on the quayside—he is an awfully nice man,' said Babs cheerfully. 'Come and be introduced.' Down we went to the cottage and I found myself shaking hands with the stocky one, only he was not stocky any more now that he was no longer bent double from labouring up the path with the truckload of luggage.

'Who, then', I asked Babs back at the house, 'was that tall distinguished man watching at the top of the path?' 'Oh! him', said Babs. 'That would be Mike the electrician. I am so glad that he could get over today.'

During their stay the Brigadier's wife asked me about a piece of kitchen equipment that was new to her. 'That is a steamer,' I replied. 'Babs bought it in France. I am not sure how to use it myself—it's a bit different from ours. I will ask her on the radio telephone.' That night I told Babs that the Brigadier's wife was having trouble with the French steamer, and could she help? The line was crackling a bit and I had to repeat what I had said. Babs sounded really concerned. 'I will ring up the coastguard,' she said. 'I shouldn't have thought that was necessary,' I said. Babs knew him quite well but I had never heard that he was a great one in the culinary arts. 'And why should he know anyway?' I asked. 'Well,' shouted Babs above the crackling 'if it's a French steamer of course he should. What makes you so sure it is French?' 'You bought it in France, so you should know,' I yelled back. By the time we had reconciled Babs buying up part of the French Merchant Navy in trouble on the high seas with a piece of kitchen equipment that was perplexing a Brigadier's wife we did not know which sounded louder, the crackling of the atmospherics or our hysterics.

He was not the only one we suspected would be too grand for us and our simple existence but who slipped into island life like a glove. Another was a director of a prestigious firm of Saville Row tailors who had booked the Jetty Cottage for himself and his family for a month. During his holiday nothing gave him greater pleasure than to scrape down and paint boats for us. He did this year after year, asking us to make sure there would be a boat for him to paint the following year. He travelled world-wide in the course of his business and he said that painting boats and living the simple life in beautiful, tranquil surroundings was wonderful therapy after the pressures of his life. He added that it was a privilege to help and thanked us for allowing him and his family to share our island with them.

We have found surprisingly that the highly successful, hard-working business men who come here seem to find their greatest relaxation, not in sitting on a beach soaking up the sun, but by channelling their energies into some useful physical pursuit that does not tax their brains unduly. It gives them a feeling of achievement with a tangible end-result without the harassment of schedules, responsibilities, the demands of people, telephones and so on. We have found so often that these well-heeled city gents enjoy the contrast to their highly pressurized lives. We are not quite sure about their wives, who cannot shed the burden of cooking and housekeeping, but dutifully they adapt so that their husbands may for a while relax, the peace of the island acting as a balm to soothe their overwrought nerves.

One cannot, however, make hard and fast rules; we could not expect that all business men, like this director, would find their Elysium here. We therefore viewed with some apprehension one applicant for the Jetty Cottage. Roger Mitchell apparently owned his own firm in London, and the correspondence was conducted by his private secretary. Our concern deepened when the secretary wrote saying that having dealt with all the correspondence she would love to come herself on holiday and could she book the Smugglers' Cottage for herself and her boy friend? As this was for a date prior to her boss's booking we could not help but suspect that she had been sent to 'case the joint' and find out if it were up to his standards.

The secretary and the boy friend duly arrived and were installed in the cottage. It was early in the season, not too early for day visitors but we had not so far established a regular supply of voluntary helpers, and student helpers were not yet free. I was, therefore, having to do everything alone. As it was an exceptionally low spring tide I had to trundle two heavy trolleys and several planks far out into the Island Roads to take the visitors off the boats. I then accompanied them up the path where I gave them a welcoming chat by the house, and so on to serving teas and refreshments. In between I had to wash up as we had not yet acquired enough crockery to run through more than one or two sets of visitors without doing so. On departure the visitors had to be helped on to the boats again. With everyone coming and going at intervals and as the trolleys and planks had to be dragged up as the tide came in I was hard put to keep everything going smoothly. Most cottage people love to help as we had already found and usually they would happily see visitors on and off the boats and take charge of the trolleys. Not so our secretary and her friend, and for three days I did not even see them. I could only assume that they were indeed reconnoitring for the boss, or that perhaps they did not know what was going on and, like others, it was taking time for them to adjust.

On the third day, exhausted as I was from the constant racing up and down the path, numbering some twenty times, the trundling of the heavy trolleys, all the café work, but, most of all, the talking to visitors, I just flopped down in the kitchen at the end of the day, too tired even to think about a meal. There was a knock on the door. I opened it. There stood the boy friend, with a bucket in his hand and there beside him was the secretary with a bottle of whisky in hers. 'We think you need some help,' they said. 'We have come to clean your windows, and would you like a drink?'

Bless their hearts! they set to and cleaned all the spray-driven windows which I had not even noticed, I was so used to the house being constantly buffeted by storms. We all had drinks. Then they invited me down to the cottage for a meal. We had a rollicking time. From then on they helped me in every way and I was constantly invited to meals. We had musical evenings too. I put on for them a particularly fine recording of Beethoven's Violin Concerto. Not only that, we had live performances, too, for the boy friend was a musician and had brought his violin with him. The secretary seemed to have an unlimited supply of whisky and I soon found no difficulty at all in wagging my finger at her and saying: 'Do you know, Babs and I thought that you had been sent here as a spy!' She looked nonplussed, as well she might, for dealing with the correspondence had merely whetted her appetite for a holiday on the island herself.

One day she went ashore for reinforcements and came back full of excitement. 'There is a harmonium for sale in a little antique shop in West Looe,' she said. 'Let's go and buy it,' I cried instantly, for Babs was with us now and some helpers had arrived. We were off on the next boat—on to the quayside and into the shop before someone else snapped it up. 'How much is the harmonium?' I asked. 'It's not a harmonium, it's an organ and it is twenty,' the antique dealer replied. 'Twenty what?' I quavered. Did he mean twenty grand—an organ could surely command a princely sum. 'Twenty pounds,' he said. 'I'll have it!' I snapped. If Babs and I could buy an island in ten seconds flat, an organ was a mere tit-bit, and who would not buy an organ at £20? Certainly not the two of us, for I knew that Babs would be in complete agreement. Usually we only disagreed over something unimportant such as whether we needed a fresh 'J' cloth or if it would do for one more day, or some such triviality; never about anything so important as an island or an organ. 'What is more,' added the dealer, 'I will help get it over to the island.' He told us about its history. It was in fact an American organ some 100 years old and one of a type popular at the time in village churches throughout Cornwall. This particular one was from Talland church a few miles down the coast, and was being replaced by an electric one. This excited Babs and me beyond measure. According to the sketchy history we had been able to trace about the island it had been established that the church at Talland was the parent church for the island chapel, whose earliest recorded date was 1139—although it was thought that it may have dated back to even earlier times. Both the island chapel and the church at Talland came under the See of Glastonbury. That the

Talland church organ was now to come to the island seemed just part of this mysterious power that we felt had guided us here too.

Getting the organ over to the island—that was the problem. In the end about six men volunteered to take part in the operation. There was the antique dealer; Bob Whitewood, a big muscular friend of ours; Jack Tambling, a stalwart Cornishman; the violinist and a couple of extras picked up from the quayside. Without the use of a crane or even a hoist, but with much ingenuity and a great deal of brawn, they managed to manhandle it from the quayside into the open motor-boat. With the six men and Babs, the organ now made its historic journey over to the island. On arrival it was even more difficult to heave it upwards out of the bucking boat and on to the jetty. Having negotiated the steps and the paths to the house, further problems faced them. They managed to manoeuvre it along the hall although this presented difficulties, for, wide as the hall is, there was little enough room for the organ and six men around it. It was when they reached the end and had to turn into the non-U lounge that it seemed impossible; that was, until they ripped off a cabinet that was fixed to the wall at the end of the hall. At last the perspiring men, after removing a large bookcase, managed to position it in place and in no time at all the organ was installed, the bookcase shunted up the stairs to a bedroom and the cabinet refixed to the wall. Over drinks all round everyone felt that the day had been crowned with success, and in addition we had started to extend our library upstairs.

This is not the end of the organ saga, but for the time being it must be left to settle itself into its new environment for soon it would be time for Roger Mitchell and his family to arrive.

On his first day he came up to me in the courtyard by the tractor shed where I was sorting out the latest boatload of stores. 'Is there anything I can do to help?' he asked. 'You could help move some of these up to the house,' I answered, trying not to sound too eager. 'Of course,' he replied, 'but I meant generally—I understand it is usual to help.' 'What do you like doing?' I asked speculatively, ('Admin' pricking up its ears—get the right man for the right job and you are made). 'Well,' he said, 'I wondered about a bit of track clearing, perhaps.'

So to this very day we have a track called 'Roger's Way', for he spent the whole of his fortnight's holiday cutting, chopping and hacking swathes through the bramble to form a new track where perhaps no man had trod for centuries. It went round the outer perimeter of the southern cliffs down to High Cove on the rocky western seaboard. By the end of his holiday a car could have been driven there, it was so wide and clear. Unfortunately it becomes overgrown every year, for with the mild climate we enjoy, unhindered by frost, everything burgeons into lush growth from early spring. However, Roger led the way and each year helpers find traces of his track and clear it once again.

The first evening he invited me down to the cottage for drinks. There, to my unaccustomed eyes, was a vast array of gin, vodka, whisky and sherry—just like the cocktail parties of old. 'What would you like?' he asked. 'Gin and tonic, please.' This was the pinnacle of sophistication indeed after my homely if delectable fare of home-made wine. He looked disappointed. 'Haven't you any?' I inquired politely. 'It is not that,' he said, 'but I understood from my secretary that your taste is for whisky.' How was he to know that I go along with the adage 'When in Rome . . . .' His secretary's tipple was whisky and so, during her stay, it was mine. Similarly, when I was in the WRNS I joined my naval friends in a diet of pink gin or rum according to their rank. I am sure that if a Russian were to turn up here with a firkin of vodka I would soon give the impression that vodka was the only drink for me. Babs arrived for the summer holidays and all the time during their stay we were both invited to evening drinks with Roger and Averil, and a very welcome break it made for us.

Living on the job we are never away from its endless demands, summer or winter. In the summer season the pressure is tremendous—to have lunch without interruptions, constant knocks on the door, calls from the field telephone on the beach and visitors needing to be met, is a luxury never to be enjoyed for months at a time. To prepare an evening meal and eat it before 10 o'clock at night is an almost impossible dream and so often it has to be the inevitable sandwich, for cottagers, helpers and pets with their unavoidable requirements, plus making up the day's accounts, the baking and the washing-up, eat into the evening. The greenhouse and the land wait for no man, so digging, composting, hoeing, sowing, harvesting and making the produce thereof goes on relentlessly. Unlike people on the mainland, we can never visit friends for tea or a meal, or have an evening out with them, although we can and do entertain them here. We cannot take holidays, and a meal ashore in a restaurant—our only 'holiday' to be enjoyed once or perhaps twice in a year—needs a great deal of planning and organization to ensure that there are experienced helpers on the island to look after it, and tide and weather have to be taken into account too.

It would ease the burden for ourselves if we were to employ staff; we would need to commercialize the island to do so, but ours is a labour of love. To keep the island unspoilt and uncommercialized—a rarity these days—*and* let others share it means a great deal of sacrifice on our part and a drain on our resources and energy. We sometimes long for the early days when we lived here privately and were therefore financially self-sufficient, but so many would be the losers. Perhaps we are taking on too colossal a task in trying in our small way to stem the tide of commercialism. Nevertheless we have always been acutely aware that money is only a substitute for barter and what we have to offer is a way of life that money itself cannot buy. To keep going on these lines takes its toll and, by the end of the season, one can become exhausted mentally, physically, emotionally—and financially.

Many realize this and others, as well as Roger and Averil, invite us to drinks or a meal. Bea and John Harrington and their daughter Ann and, later, her husband especially appreciated our efforts and the strains we felt. Although a busy housewife and mother with a job in a library Bea, who surely needed a break herself, regularly invited us down to the cottage for delicious meals accompanied with wine. Bea probably never knew just how much good this did for our flagging spirits and how much enjoyment we derived from the entertaining company and good food. The whole family helped, too, in many ways, and John with his special expertise was one of the founder-members of our communications network, as is related later.

It always seems to be the busiest folk who help us the most. The Rector of Botley, Colin Wheatley, his wife Jane, accompanied by various members of their family of seven children rented the Jetty Cottage for many years. They all worked with a will to help us in many ways—on the land, in the greenhouse, and with all forms of maintenance and decorating. Jane without fail invited us down for delectable meals, and surely there can be nobody busier than a parson's wife who is also the mother of seven youngsters. Self-catering could be no real holiday for her. Philla, who appears in many of these tales, introduced the Wheatleys to the island in the first place, and always accompanied them on their holidays here. She always brought her own contributions to the feasts, often entertained us herself and never failed to present us with a bottle of whisky or some other goodie on her arrival on the island.

It is good folk like these who sustain us in our endeavours.

One of our most helpful and enduring families were the Grimers. A colleague of Babs at school, John Grimer, had a brother Peter in London, who, with his family, spent a month's holiday every summer with John at East Cliff above Looe. One day during the school holidays they all came over to see us on a day visit. Peter immediately booked a week of his month's holiday of the following year to stay with us in Jetty Cottage. He was by profession a dentist, but had, probably as an antidote, a quite fanatical interest in other pursuits, chief of which appeared to be electronics. The island was immediately added to his enthusiasms. One could say that it almost became a way of life with him. Later he had a poster about the island mounted in his sitting-room and, as a treat, every Sunday tea-time was devoted exclusively to Island talk. The highlight of their year, Peter said, was when holiday-time came round and they could once again set foot on the island of their dreams.

During the year Peter thought up all manner of ways in which he could contribute to our projects and life here. He would come armed with some item of his invention which would ease our lives or advance our projects. The first year he brought with him, among other things, some black compound used in the process of making moulds for false teeth; he thought we might find a use for it in our crafts. He also presented us with a telescope which he proceeded to mount for us at a strategic point so that one could see a wide sweep of the mainland coastline from Looe to Prawle Point in Devon in one direction, and past Eddystone Lighthouse in the other, westward towards the Lizard. Points of interest were inscribed on its stone mount and beside this we have a large RNLI lifeboat collecting-box on davits and a goodly sum is donated each year.

In discussing our plans we happened to mention that we needed some kind of communication with the beach so that helpers could tell us if any visitors had landed. Peter's eyes lighted up as he said: 'Could you possibly wait until next year? I would love to fix something for you.' It was better than waiting for ever, for at that time it was one of those fanciful pipe dreams as far as we were concerned.

Peter booked in for a fortnight for the following year. They travelled overnight by train from London and were out here by 9 a.m. As Peter stepped up out of the boat on to the jetty he called 'Have you a drill and a hammer?' Before the boat had pulled away, Peter, festooned with a coil of wire, was off down the path. By the end of the day we had 'Lift Off', for incredibly we were able to talk from the house to the beach. What Peter had installed was a field-telephone; he had hunted around for months and had at last located two ex-army instruments, which, though probably of First World War vintage, actually worked. To those brought up in the space age and used to the sophistication of electronic devices these would have been museum pieces, and our system antiquated; but to the monks of old who lived here it would have been an innovation inspired by higher powers, and thus it seemed to us. To call the beach or vice versa one cranked a handle and, powered by a bicycle lamp battery, the set at the other end would ring.

It took Peter most of his holiday to perfect the system to his satisfaction and run some of the telephone wire through spare bits of garden hose and attach it to trees and the wall of the Smugglers' Cottage garden to protect the wire from abrasion from the onslaught of winter storms. He also proposed to have an extension to the pottery where he intended to have a switchboard so that when a third instrument could be acquired we could communicate between house, pottery and beach. But time ran out on him. 'I will leave a diagram,' he said, 'with all the bits and pieces and instructions, so that if anyone turns up who knows anything about wiring he can fix it for you, which will be better than waiting a whole year until I return.' A far-away look came into his eyes and he promptly booked three weeks for the following year.

The very next visitors to the Jetty Cottage were the Harringtons. Incredibly John could not only do the wiring for the switchboard but he did not need to read the instructions. It was no trouble to him at all for he had actually been involved in installing Radar on the Pyramids during the war. Our three-way lines of communication were working in no time at all, for the resourceful Jack Tambling (who had helped with the organ) produced, like a conjuror out of a hat, a third instrument. As these instruments were so hard to come by, the whole operation, from the wish to the finished project, seemed like a miracle to us. We have been convinced over the years that if something is desirable, the wish is strong enough and the island 'genie' agrees that it is a good thing, then something or someone will turn up to bring it about. An easy philosophy perhaps, because if we do not get what we want we can always say 'the island does not want it,' and turn our thoughts to other matters. It saves a lot of useless effort too.

Peter brought other gifts—copper tubes sealed at one end to make specimen vases and suitably engraved with the St George's emblem; the inscription being made with a dentist's drill. He also presented us with some drills which were no longer good enough for drilling his patients' teeth but he thought might be useful in our crafts. One invaluable gift he made for us was a portable lamp which is still in use to this day, or rather night. It consists of a beautifully crafted wooden framework which houses a motor-bike battery; mounted on the front of the structure is a vertical fluorescent tube some twelve inches high. By some intricate wiring and gadgetry the battery is rechargeable and so will give us constant light when required. This was a great advance on the oil lamps with which we had formerly gone to bed after we had stopped the generator by turning off the last electric light switch in the house. Good as the oil lamps were they gave off fumes and this curtailed our bedtime reading; otherwise we ran the risk of being asphyxiated or, if we had the windows open, being pestered by moths. A shiny metal handle added to its good looks and made it easily transportable and, a unique touch, a dentist's syringe had been attached by a clip, in readiness for topping up the batteries. Neatly printed on the side of the frame and on the separate dial for registering the charge, which Peter had also provided, were detailed instructions for its maintenance and names of spare parts if required. Two batteries and several solderings later it is still as effective as ever, and we always give Peter a good-night blessing for his wonderfully useful and lasting gift, which is not only an example of his thoughtfulness and inventiveness but shows a nice combination of his dental and electronic skills.

The next year he booked for four weeks and thereafter he spent his month's holiday on the island and spent perhaps a day with his brother on the mainland. 'I find it cheaper too,' he explained; 'although I pay nothing to stay with John, the incidental spending of money for fish and chips, ice-creams, etc. for the children on the mainland costs more than renting the Jetty Cottage, and', he added, 'it is a better life for them.'

He could turn his hand to many things, among which were carpentry and cement mixing—the latter probably being an antidote to the mixing of minute quantities of fillings for his patients' teeth. Whatever the reason, we had the jetty kept in a state of good repair after the winter storms had battered it, and he expertly filled other cavities in walls and steps. Peter had a knack, too, of being able to knock up benches from driftwood in no time at all and most are still in use today; one in particular graces the patio where visitors have tea and has since been carved on decoratively by a series of helpers skilled in this craft; another commands a fine view across to Rame Head and beyond to Prawle Point in Devon, from a strategic point high up the hill at the entrance to 'Roger's Way'. The whole family offered to look after the island so that we could go ashore and thus, during their visits, we were able to spend a night or two in Plymouth or Falmouth foraging for stores and enjoying our one indulgence, a meal out.

What makes Peter so special is the imagination and thoughtfulness of his contributions to the island and the fact that so many of them were for us personally to ease our lives here. He is one of those who identify us with the island, knowing that without our financial support the island would have to be commercialized to enable visitors to come here, if at all, for—as he and others are perceptive enough to realize—not all island-dwellers in a paradise such as this would forego their privacy unless it were for financial gain. He and others like him will do all in their power to help us with our endeavours, and this encourages us beyond measure.

The Grimer children enjoyed the island life, too. The youngest one, Tim, arrived for the first time in a rucksack on his father's back. Later he graduated to riding on the back of Kim, our border collie, while his elder brothers John, Paul and his sister Zaz joined in all the island activities. Margaret, Peter's wife, was a champion swimmer and so was Zaz; the two of them managed to swim right round the island each time they came here; no mean feat, for the currents can be very strong and the distance is quite daunting.

Margaret and Zaz were not the only swimmers we have had here. One who stayed here caused quite a sensation. She was an attractive blonde, who with her small child was staying in the Smugglers' Cottage with a friend. The friend, who had children of her own, agreed to look after her child so that she could continue to study for her degree.

Probably as a relief from all the mental effort involved she decided to take a swim to the mainland. It happened to be a choppy sea; it was also spring tides when the sea-can be fast with an undertow. We warned her about the currents and that it was too rough for Leonard to bring his boat out with visitors. 'Have no fear,' she said, 'I am a very strong swimmer, and I must go as I have run out of cigarettes.' So off she went cleaving her way through the surf with a plastic bag containing her clothes slung round her neck, and watched bemused by all the island residents. Half-way across we saw her resting on some rocks exposed by the outgoing tide, for all the world looking like Copenhagen's Little Mermaid. That was the last we saw of her for a very long time. We were very concerned, especially the friend with all the young brood at her feet.

Later that day a lone boat emerged from the harbour and bucked over the breaking seas towards the island. Leonard, with the most enigmatical look we had ever seen on his face, gave a lop-sided grin as he disgorged his lone passenger, now fully clothed. 'What happened? asked the whole island population, who, all agog, had gathered on the beach. 'Well, my clothes got wet in spite of being in a plastic bag, so I went to the laundrette and dried them.' The mind boggled at the changing operation in the gold-fish bowl of the laundrette! 'It was too rough to swim back so I persuaded Leonard to bring me.' Leonard, still with the lop-sided grin on his face, gave us one of his roguish winks as he turned into the rolling sea and headed for the harbour. Unperturbed, our swimmer went back to her studies; everyone else returned to their normal occupations in wonderment that anyone would have gone through all that for a packet of cigarettes.

The MECHANICS' Tale

The best advice one can give to anyone thinking of living on an island is to take a course in DIY and to take with you a whole range of tools—and the knowledge of how to use them—or a handyman. Preferably all three.

We were not so equipped either practically or mentally. In our previous life there was always some expert friend or a professional at the end of a phone who would come at the drop of a hat to repair, maintain or put into effect some scheme of ours. The former would certainly come at the drop of a hat—the professionals took a little longer. Nevertheless we did not have to worry our pretty little heads about things that went wrong. I, in particular, was abysmally ignorant.

When we first came to live on the island I thought a plug was something one used to stop water running out of the bath, or an item by the media to promote a pop record or a book. Proudly I now know that it is a vital part of an engine and the like, which has a nasty habit of getting oiled up or dirty, thus preventing the machinery from starting up. Seemingly there is hardly a bit of mechanism that does not depend on it. Many has been the time when, over the years, I have watched strong men, stripped to the waist, sweat dripping from the end of their noses, pulling away at a piece of cord attached to some sullen bit of machinery that obstinately remained as dead as a drunk. Always there is a fringe of experts giving free advice from the sidelines. Diffident at first I lurked in the background behind this cream of the engineering world. Now I boldly step forward and in a throw-away voice nonchantly mutter! 'Perhaps it is the plug.' And—do you know?—it usually is. I then, like the Cheshire cat, dissolve rapidly into nothingness.

Luckily during the summer months the island attracts friends and visitors, who between them apparently have enough expert knowledge to sail the QE2 singlehanded, run the National Grid, to say nothing at being dab hands at plumbing, building and electronics, and have enough know-how to run up something like the Empire State Building or take the odd whirl into outer space. At least that is how it seems to non-technical, non-every

115

thing me. Mention that something does not work and unerringly someone steps forward and with a magic touch it purrs into action. Casually we would say 'A courtyard would fit in here very nicely,' or 'We would like a vineyard there,' and suddenly there is a courtyard, with exotic plants in full bloom, and there is an embryo vineyard, brave young plants in serried ranks blissfully basking southward to the sun.

My role, apart from that of producing exalted ideas, seems to be that of general run-around who supplies coffee, tea, home-made wine and tools. But how my education has improved! In those early days I did not even know the names of all those people, some of whom were friends of friends, who appeared miraculously out of thin air, and I certainly did not know my tools. So when Dave called out to me rather urgently, 'Alan Keyes!' I ran round the island yelling for him. 'It's OK,' said Dave some time later, looking at me rather strangely, as a last desperate 'ALAN! ALAN!' wafted hoarsely on the air, 'I've found them,' and he waved some bent pieces of metal under my eyes; keys which I now know, in my more mature island life, are indispensable for unlocking bits of metal which would otherwise be wedded until death did them part.

There was a friend of a friend who stepped off the boat one day who seemed to be an expert on everything. In no time at all everyone was treating this chap with great deference—as a kind of technical Guru. When, therefore, Peter with ashen face screamed from the boiler-house 'the boiler has sprung a leak, fetch Boss White—QUICKLY!' I panted to where I knew he was holding court by a defiant lawn-mower. 'Boss White!' I gasped, 'the boiler is leaking.' 'That's OK,' he said kindly, 'there's a tin on the shelf in the tool-shed.' Mesmerized I watched as he and Peter got to work with a tin of something that looked like white paste. For some reason I got the kudos for having found it so quickly. It seemed judicious therefore to say nothing and I merely smirked with quiet pride.

I was really on my mettle though when someone asked for a Stillson. Even I knew that it could not be a person. It sounded more like a cross between a cowboy's hat and a cheese. When we found that it was indispensable (how on earth had we lived for all those years without one?), and a superior kind of wrench, we bought one. We knew it was superior—it was so expensive. It has certainly proved indispensable for the generator and various pumps and pipes around the island, so when we were told we needed a smaller one as well, we gritted our teeth, financially speaking, and brought that one too. One day, no doubt, we shall have Father Bear, Mother Bear and Baby Bear.

During the summer months we have all these knowledgeable people to help us but during the winter we are on our own, and for twelve memorable winters, before Babs retired, the population of St George's Island, as one guide book put it, was 'One'; the 'One' being ignorant me. And it is during the winter months that machines fall sick, much as humans do. So I learned the hard way . . . .

One day I went down to the generator room to do the daily check and found the floor awash with oil. I slopped gingerly through it in my Wellington boots—for 'wellies' are not in my vocabulary. Mine are of sterner stuff, from the prototype that the grand old Duke himself might have charged around in at Waterloo. There, in the copper tubing that automatically fed the generator with fuel, was a hole out of which the diesel oil was bubbling merrily. I rushed outside to the 600-gallon storage tank and turned off the tap. This of course stopped the pipe from leaking but it also stopped the diesel oil from coming through, without which there could be no electricity. I remembered Boss White but he would not do; neither would Plastic Padding, nor any of the assortment of metal fillers which we had acquired. Frantically I read the small print—they all said the same: the object to be repaired must be clean and free of grease. This immaculate state was impossible to achieve. There was no way that I could penetrate the inside of the copper tubing to clean it; as well try to clean the inside of a piece of spaghetti.

Impasse! Concede defeat? Never! After all, I was wearing 'Wellington' boots; to surrender would be inconceivable. I would call Babs on the radio telephone and ask her to put my problem to Ken Newton, our engineer at the time. 'That's simple,' he said, 'tell her to cut out the piece of tubing either side of the hole, with a hack-saw. Join the two parts together with a piece of plastic tubing and fix them with a couple of Jubilee clips.' 'Jubilee clips!' I muttered. A picture of Queen Victoria flashed across my mind. 'Jubilee clips'—they sounded like excerpts from an old Anna Neagle film. Babs, who is knowledgeable about these things, carefully explained what a Jubilee clip looked like, and to my immense surprise, on rooting around the generator room, I found a couple of these metal clips. The plastic tubing was no problem. I had a length of this among my wine-making equipment. Armed with a hack-saw, which I now knew had nothing whatever to do with horses, I set about the operation. Surely this would not cut through metal. However to my surprise and delight the hack-saw went through the metal like butter and in a few minutes the offending piece of tubing with the hole in it was extracted. I felt like a surgeon. 'Harley Street, here I come!' I quipped to myself. Then my courage faltered. There, staring at me, were these two loose ends of copper tubing—dismembered—useless. If I could not join them together there would be no fuel supply, so no electricity, and there was a full gale blowing with no sign of a let-up. It was mid-winter, and no one would be able to get out for days, perhaps weeks.

Whenever there is a generator failure Babs and I say 'Queen Elizabeth I did not have electricity, nor did the smugglers on the island last century, and they managed quite happily.' However, going on the theory that what you do not have you do not miss, the reverse is also true. You *do* miss something that you have always had, especially if it runs your fridge and pumps from the bowels of the earth your one source of drinking water.

No Head of State, with his finger on the trigger could have felt more fraught than I, as desperately I tried to push the precious piece of plastic tubing on to the copper tube ends. It would not budge. Then I remembered tales of little boys with heads stuck in railings, and how butter or some such helped ease them free. I could do better than that. I had all this oil swilling round my feet—gallons of it. With some diligent massage, much heaving and shoving, not to mention a few oaths, at last the two vital bits of copper were encapsulated. Triumphantly I put my two new friends, the Jubilee clips, into place and screwed them tight. I went outside, turned on the fuel-tap, came in again, flicked on a light switch and *Lo! There was Light.* To this day several years later this, my frantic attempt at mechanical first-aid, still holds. As part of the tour of the island I proudly display this to those kind enough to take an interest and maybe admire it, for I do feel that it is perhaps the finest technical achievement of my career, if not of the age. Not that this success went to my head after the first giddy euphoria. I suspect that the only people who are impressed, apart from myself, are those who are even more ignorant than I am. The fact of the matter is that I do not have a rapport with mechanical objects, so it gives me great satisfaction when I strike up a working relationship with one of them, or in this case, it may have appealed to a latent nursing instinct to come to the rescue with some timely first-aid.

'What?' I ask, 'do *Dirty Contacts* mean to you?' When on one occasion the generator refused to start, the engineer when he examined it grunted 'Dirty Contacts!' Immediately there flashed into my mind a picture of seedy men in sleazy raincoats congregated in groups on a street corner in

Soho. Not so. Like their first cousins 'Dirty Plugs' they hang about, not in Soho, but in electrical boxes and can cause the entire generator system to grind to a halt and plunge us into darkness. Mary Whitehouse may campaign, hold meetings and make speeches to do her cleaning up. I go armed with nothing more than a piece of emery paper and a quaking heart, for I am terrified of electricity—and with good reason. As a child I climbed a pillar outside a sea-front hotel, next to ours, the better to see a fancy dress dance being held inside. Unbeknown to me the pillar should have been surmounted by a large ornamental light bulb. This unfortunately was missing and, as I put my hand inside the top of the pillar to haul myself up, something 'live' gripped my fingers and it took a crowd of bystanders to pull me away. Although it was a lucky escape, at that tender age I did not know what danger I had been in. Nevertheless, since then I have always been suspicious of electricity. Well, you cannot see it, can you? It is not only fear of the unseen and the unknown, but the greater terror of grappling with this invisible enemy that assails one, at least this one.

I really do think that life on a desert island would be easier to cope with in some respects, than with one like ours, which is equipped for a more civilized existence and where the solitary inhabitant is expected to be capable of running a mini-power-station solo. We are fortunate that currently we have a goodly knight who will come charging over the sea to succour us, when our machinery falters or passes out, in the shape of Roy, an engineer, who, with his magic touch will make it leap into life again. During the winter months, however, storms hold up these rescue attempts, but now that Babs has joined me permanently the problem, although not resolved, is at least shared. With her superior knowledge of things mechanical she does not appear to be so daunted by these crises, unless of course, as I suspect, she is much braver than I am. There is the fact, too, that she did once go on a car maintenance course. When I reminded her of this she said: 'Why do you think I left half-way through the course?' 'Perhaps you learnt twice as fast as anyone else,' I replied, hoping that flattery would get me somewhere or at least somewhere away from machinery. In a way it has, for I have now appointed myself into the spectator role with the right to interfere. Standing on the sidelines I toss out some gem of knowledge culled from past experience, even the hoary old one of 'Could it be the plug?'

The TREASURE-HUNTERS' Tale

One of Peter Grimer's gifts was a metal detector that he had made for us. This was before they were generally popular and readily available, and we spent many a delightful hour under his direction looking for buried treasure. Mostly we were too busy and he would hunt for us. He never found the treasure which is supposed to be buried here but he did find many pieces of the land-mine which had been dropped on the island during the war. Lord Haw-Haw, the traitor who was later executed, broadcast on the radio from Germany that the battleship *St George* had been sunk. The 'battleship', in fact, was the island and the bomb crater is still there. Apparently all the damage that was done was to the conservatory, all the glass of which was blown out by the blast. I always hoped that one day Peter would unearth a Roman coin. Alas! all he found, apart from a number of modern coins, was a Victorian penny dated 1897. The special feature about this was that, not only was it Victoria's Jubilee year, but it had the appearance of having been freshly minted, for everything was in sharp relief and not worn flat as most Victorian pennies were when they were in circulation, prior to decimalization.

More interesting were two cannon balls which Peter found buried on the main beach. They were encrusted with rust and so misshapen that they looked almost square. When the rust was removed, however, two complete cannon balls were revealed. How they came to be on the landing-beach which faces the mainland, just a short distance across, is a mystery so far unsolved. The first confrontation with the Spanish Armada in 1588 took place a few miles due south of the island, as copies of maps of the period show. Skirmishes with the French would have taken place in this area too. Did the fleet practise off the island in the days of cannon ball, or did a shore battery shoot short of its target at sea? There is an old gun emplacement on the island facing due south, so this suggests that during an exchange of firing with the enemy there may have been an overshot from the sea. We do not know, but they are now part of our collection of flotsam and jetsam and other finds, for we hope one day to have a small maritime museum of articles found or washed up here.

Peter, in fact, was not the first to present us with a metal detector, although it was not an electronic job, more your basic dowsing outfit. One of our earliest visitors to Jetty Cottage was a technician who worked for the Gas Board. He was a friendly chap who often visited us in our kitchen to have a glass of home brew and a chat. Over one or two glasses of my best elderflower wine he revealed what to us was a startling fact. The Gas Board, he said, employed someone to go dowsing for hidden pipes. The equipment used, he added, was nothing more than two stout copper wires, bent at one end at right angles to form handles. Held by the dowser, he said, the wires crossed when they were passed over metal, and presumably water. As it so happened I had a stock of stout copper wires in my Wirecraft kit. In no time at all we were all outside to try our hand at dowsing. Although the wires would not react to everyone, they did for Babs and me. First we tested them by throwing down pieces of metal, then in case autosuggestion played a part they were buried out of sight. To our great surprise and gratification the wires crossed every time over the buried metal. We explored untried ground and whenever the wires crossed there was always something metallic under the surface—they even reacted to silver paper hidden from view. They always worked over water, too, but as we could see this we did not think it was a reliable test.

We were not the first to try dowsing on the island, for we had been told that some years previously a professional lady dowser had been asked to locate sources of fresh water. According to our informant she had found it in abundance in various parts of the island, although whether this was before or after the tunnel had been bored into the cliff was not known.

As we had more immediate chores than looking for buried treasure we put the wires aside. Then one day a letter arrived, out of the blue, from a stranger. It was from a clergyman in Cumbria. A relative, he said, had visited our island the previous year and was most impressed with our efforts on the island. He himself was of Cornish descent. He enclosed something carefully wrapped in tissue paper, which he said had been in his family for generations. He would like us to have it. Inside the tissue paper was a yellowing piece of paper, brittle and fragile to the touch with age. It was a rough hand-made map in faded brown ink showing where treasure was buried on St Michael's Island—the former name of St George's Island. The writing and spelling were of a bygone age. We looked at it boggle-eyed. Was it a hoax? How could it be? The letter heading was that of a Priory; the writer was obviously who he said he was. Was the map genuine? Why, if it were some schoolboy prank of an earlier century, would it have been treasured for so long, and find its way to a branch of the family so remote from Cornwall as Cumbria? The clergyman went on to say that he doubted that the treasure still existed, but if we did find anything perhaps we would be good enough to let him know. He was very happy for us to have the map and he wished us well in our projects on the island.

When we first came here local folk had told us many tales of smugglers' tunnels to the mainland and buried treasure. 'The last smuggler left without revealing where the treasure was buried,' was an oft-repeated saying. Smugglers, we knew, had lived on the island. The descendants of one of the most famous, Amram Hooper, had actually been to visit us. And we do know for a fact the existence of one tunnel. Soon after our arrival one of Looe's most respected older inhabitants came to see us. He was Mr Pearn, of the well-known boat-builders of Looe of that name. At the time he was eighty-five and we felt honoured that he should make the journey to see us. The purpose of his visit, he said, was to show us where a tunnel had actually existed. He took us out to the cliff face. It had been buttressed with stonework to form a bulwark against the storms and the constant danger of erosion and landslides. In the centre of the stonework he traced with his finger the outline of a door in cement. This, he said, was the entrance to the tunnel before it was filled in with concrete. He then took us back to the room we used as a transit camp. 'This', he said, 'used to be a barn. When I was a boy of ten I used to come here picnicking with some other lads. One day we fell through the floor into a tunnel, and there are some who say that the tunnel continues up to your kitchen.' We subsequently tapped all the flagstones in the kitchen and found one that indeed sounded hollow. We have not, however, so far tried to prise it up.

The most extraordinary thing about the map now in our possession was that a tunnel was shown leading to the treasure; the entrance to it was marked with a cross, and the cross was the exact spot that Mr Pearn had pointed out to us on the cliff face. This suggested that there were two tunnels leading from the same entrance in the cliff—the one leading to the barn and the other to the treasure.

We suppose that most people on receiving such a map would have been tempted to go out immediately and start digging. We did not. Apart from having little spare time from the tasks that threatened to engulf us, we felt that it was preferable to believe that buried treasure was lying there waiting to be discovered, than to dig and perhaps find nothing and so have a romantic dream shattered. Many people would not have understood this but we did not tell them—we did not tell anybody. Partly because we were afraid that we would be invaded by an army of visitors armed with pick-axes and shovels and we would perforce have to put up a notice 'NO DIG-GING FOR BURIED TREASURE'. More recently, with the advent of sometimes indiscriminate use of metal detectors, we have had to put up a notice forbidding their use. In particular we do not want the chapel site despoiled against the time when we hope to have it expertly dug by ar-chaeologists. Another reason was that we did not think that the last smug-gler would have cared for hordes of strangers poking around—or the monks either. For it is our fancy that the monks might have buried some of *their* treasure here, too, at the dissolution of the monasteries. As the chapel came under the See of Glastonbury what more likely a place could they find to hide their precious possessions, we reasoned, than on this remote island. Neither the Holy Grail nor the Golden Gate have ever been traced, so it is not too fanciful a supposition.

We did not tell anyone about the map until five years later.

By that time we had regular voluntary helpers, one of whom, by dint of his enthusiasm and predilection for hard work will always be remembered. Phil Deem was a Devon boy of nineteen. His looks belied his age for he had about him an air of maturity and seriousness of purpose that augured well for his future; he had already been accepted as a trainee manager with W.H. Smith, and during the five years he came here on working holiday he progressed up the scale until he was promoted to the Managership of one of their large branches. As his responsibilities grew so we saw corre-spondingly less of him, but he still kept in touch as much as his busy life allowed.

One of Phil's major contributions was the digging of an embryo reser-voir. With the advent of visitors to the island the storage of sufficient spring water against the times of summer drought became a major prob-lem. Abundant for our own purposes, it had to be eked out when we had as many as twenty people staying on the island, as well as day visitors wanting cups of tea or coffee.

So we tossed the idea in the air that what we needed was a reservoir; this was in case someone who knew about these matters picked up our signal. The first one to do so was Jim, the husband of Ivy, a friend from Epsom Art School. Jim and Ivy Denner came to stay so that Ivy could help me with pottery, for she was an experienced potter, who held her own exhibitions, so her help would be invaluable to me. Jim was Managing Director of a large industrial firm and by profession was a quantity surveyor. We learned somewhat to our chagrin that a reservoir is not just a hole in the ground. There were certain aspects to be considered, such as water pressure, and this and the size of the hole were interrelated—or so we understood. There was an answer to it all however; it was just a matter of calculation, Jim said, and set about doing clever things with slides rules and the like. He produced a diagram giving the exact depth, length and breadth that would hold 'X' cubic feet of water or it may have been tons, I really cannot remember. I only know that this diagram became a treasured document to be carefully stored until such time as someone picked up our next 'radar' signals, as we were pleased to call them. Phil, in his indomitable way, was on to the idea like flash. 'I will dig your reservoir,' he said, and with great enthusiasm and vigour he laid about with pickaxe and shovel, just below the storage tanks in the woods—the designated site. He spent the whole of his fortnight's holiday, hacking, digging and heaving earth. By the end of his holiday the hole was finished—an impressive twenty feet square and some six feet deep, the exact measurements required being checked and re-checked.

And there alas! it remains to this day—just a hole. To finish the job was not just a matter of expense but of expertise. However well it was lined, with concrete or other suitable material, there was the important question of the lid or covering. As the reservoir was to be an integral part of our spring-water storage system, the cover was of paramount importance. The danger of branches, twigs, emmets or even more objectionable objects floating on the surface of our drinking-water meant that it had to have a thoroughly everything-proof roof, and the solution to this has so far eluded us. Our spring water is delicious and we do not want to run the risk of even the merest touch of pollution, by the danger of invasion or infiltration by foreign bodies. No doubt at the right time some Merlin will arrive on the scene with the solution, unless of course the island, knowing that there is ample water for the two of us and our pets, does not want to run the risk of increasing the resident population.

The following year Phil arrived, no doubt expecting to find the reservoir fully operational. To mollify him and because we felt inordinately guilty about all his efforts coming to naught, we decided to tell him about the buried treasure and that he, and he alone, should be the one to dig for it. His eyes lighted up, all thoughts of his lovely but unused pit forgotten. We swore him to secrecy, then at dead of night, some five years after receiving the map, and armed with pickaxe, shovel, map and copper wires we marched out to the spot marked 'Treasure' on the map. We held the wires out in front of us and walked slowly around the area. Suddenly the wires began to cross. There was no mistaking their reaction. Time and time again they almost bent back double for both Babs and me, and always at the same spot, marked 'X' on the map. Phil started digging. The next night after 'Lights Out' at 11 p.m. we crept out again and Phil went on digging.

By now there was a sizeable hole. During the day, so as not to excite too much curiosity, it was covered with a tarpaulin. We *think* Phil told everyone, including curious day visitors, that he was trying to locate a water pipe. However, as is the way with these affairs, the secret leaked out among those staying on the island, and every evening thereafter, when the day visitors had departed, our little island population gathered round while Phil swung and shovelled. By the end of his fortnight's holiday he was up to his neck and still the wires crossed beneath his feet. Regretfully he roughly filled in the hole, which was some six feet square, and covered it over to await his return the following year. This time his head disappeared completely from view, and he was a tall fellow. The area he now covered was extensive, too, and would have made a reservoir itself if we could have channelled water there. By the end of his holiday all we could see was a flaying axe-head, and great clods of earth hurled up to the sky. And still the wires crossed at the bottom.

But time had run out. Phil was now off into the realms of higher management which precluded any more holidays digging for buried treasure. Sorrowfully he had to fill in the enormous pit he had dug. To avoid subsidence this was done in the first place with old tins and bottles, the disposal of which is always a problem as ne'er a dustman passes our way. The topsoil was removed to the greenhouse and finally the turves were relaid. When later we re-examined the walled-up entrance to the tunnel that Mr Pearn had shown us we realized that the tunnel would have extended to well below the level Phil had reached, so if we do not initiate any more attempts to explore deeper perhaps these clues will help some future islander, who will not be so engulfed in the multifarious activities that seem to be our lot, or who may not think, as we do, that the island itself is treasure enough.

In fact this was not our very first hunt for buried treasure, and it was before we had a map to guide us. As I was not exactly there I cannot give much information about it. I say 'I was not exactly there' because it happened in a curious way. A friend of mine of long-standing, Di Sorby, and her friend Winifred Hatherly, had come from London to spend a week or so with us. This was during our very early days when we were not only putting down our roots but also branching out in several directions. This entailed a great deal of correspondence, and as Di and Winifred were experienced secretaries they offered to type our letters for us. One evening after a particularly busy session we had a get-together with one or two others who were staying to help in various ways, as a relaxation and little light relief. There was much hilarity as, over glasses of home-made wine, Babs and I regaled them with tales of our experiences in moving over to the island—the wine, of course, adding to the merriment. We also related the tales we had been told by locals of tunnels and the smugglers' buried treasure. Someone suggested that we hold a seance to find out if the spirit world would give us a message as to its whereabouts. As none of us had any claims to being a medium this idea was thankfully brushed aside.

It was then suggested that we try the wine-glass device. Cards were quickly made for each letter of the alphabet and formed in a circle on the table and a wine-glass produced and set in the centre. Then, as is usual with these affairs, there was much giggling and banter as everyone sat round the table each with a finger lightly touching the edge of the glass. Order was soon restored and the question was put: 'Would you please tell us where the treasure is buried?' There was complete silence as the glass slowly began to move. This is when 'I was no longer there' for at that precise moment I fell asleep. I did not even know that I had fallen asleep; all I do remember was waking up and finding myself sitting there completely alone—all the chairs were empty. There was just me, the wine-glass and the scattered letters of the alphabet. It was a most eerie feeling and I was greatly relieved to hear the laughter of the others returning.

Apparently the wine-glass had spelt the word 'Flagstaff', so they had all gone out with shovels and spades to the promontory where stood the flagpole near the cliff edge. But after a time their enthusiasm had waned; it was pitch dark and cold, but most of all they did not know exactly where to dig. Without an 'X' to mark the spot there was quite a large area to cover. Then there was the question of how deep? So they soon gave up trying. Also I think they all suspected each other of either consciously or unconsciously pushing the glass. Maybe, I thought, they suspected me as I was not there. But there was a strange aspect about the whole happening. The realization came to me that in the dark they had not noticed that I was not with them, or that possibly I had returned ahead of them, for when I said rather sheepishly 'I fell asleep,' someone replied, 'Yes! it was very tiring digging—I am off to bed.' It is for you to put what interpretation you like on the incident. I can only add that there was no more talk of digging round the flagstaff and no more sessions with the wine-glass. So far the treasure has not been found, nor indeed has it been looked for apart from these two attempts.

Is it really necessary to find it? If you live here the island is treasure trove in itself and yields riches of a material kind too. The woods and the sea provide a plentiful supply of logs and driftwood, not only for fires but for carpentry and wood carving; elderberries and blackberries, some the size of grapes, grow in profusion to give us fruit, wine, jam and other preserves; in the rock pools there are prawns, shrimps and crabs—and winkles, too, if you like them. The sea will yield a rich harvest of mullet and bass if you have time and skill enough to fish from the rocks. Nearest to the conventional concept of treasure are the semi-precious stones to be found on the shore: banded and moss agate, rose quartz and cornelian, to name a few. There is a wealth of shells, too, and sometimes even mother-of-pearl, and the many-hued pebbles, enhanced by polishing to gleam like jewels—these can all be used in our craftwork.

Perhaps the most valuable treasure is the soil. This is so fertile and the climate so unusually mild that there is seemingly no limit to the variety of crops which can be cultivated here. Grapes grow in abundance, as do figs, nectarines and peaches. Gales permitting, blackberries ripen until December, violets scent the woods all winter through and daffodils start blooming at Christmas or soon after. Nature here is at her most bountiful and this is indeed one of the most 'Fortunate of Isles'.

It may not be necessary to search for further treasure but truth to tell the island demands so much attention to garner her riches that there is just no time to dig for buried treasure. And there it must remain, unless, of course, we get a sign, then out will come the shovels and pickaxes again, no doubt.

The MARINERS' Tale

The session with the wine-glass was not the only eerie experience I had.

One of the best UFO stories I read about was in a *Reader's Digest*. It was reported that a party of some twelve WI ladies, or their American counterparts, had sighted a UFO overhead. Everyone of the twelve vouched to having seen it and all swore that they knew it to be genuine because there, painted under the body, in huge letters was the inscription 'UFO'.

I say one of the best UFO stories because the best one happened to me. The memory is so vivid that although it happened a few years ago I can recall it in every detail to this day.

Our friend Philla was staying with me, and although she was sleeping down in Jetty Cottage she will confirm that every word of what I am about to relate is true. We had spent the evening together talking, among other things, about UFOs as they were very much in the news just then and several sightings had been reported. Alone in the house but for Lucky, who was lying at the bottom of my bed, I was in a deep sleep when suddenly I was awakened by a brilliant white light flooding the room. It travelled across the window then was followed by a sudden inky blackness. I jumped out of bed and looked out of the window. Was it a vivid dream? No! there it was again—an intense bluey-white beam that swept across the house then out to the cliff edge beyond the lawn, again followed by intense blackness. Heart thumping, I peered through the window. Suddenly a broad beam of light enveloped me and the house, hovered over the lawn and border, lighting up the flowers with a deathly pallor. The target was obviously the house and the lawn. Transfixed I waited for several minutes, trying to collect my thoughts and give some reasonable explanation for this phenonomen. I could not think of one. That it was a searchlight was apparent, but a shaft of light of that breadth could only mean that its source, if not actually on the island, must be very close by. It came neither from the seaward side nor from the land but from the eastern or left-hand side of the island, the cliffs of which were only about 100 yards from the house.

The bathroom would provide an excellent look-out as the windows

128

were large, one facing due east, the source of the light. Holding Lucky very closely to me I crept to the bathroom. I had no sooner reached the window than the light came straight at me blinding me with its intensity. Quickly I ducked down, my face felt ashen and drained of blood, its pallor due not only to the light but, I must confess, to craven fear that I had now been seen by whoever or whatever was 'out there'. In the short periods between the probing beams I peered out into the darkness, the warmth of Lucky's body giving me comfort as well as the courage I so sorely needed. What with the constant ducking to avoid being spotted and my eyes trying to adjust from the dazzling beam that lighted up the whole bathroom to the almost tangible blackness that followed, it was some time before I saw 'IT'. 'IT' was a flashing blue lamp; not only was it flashing continuously and giving off an eerie glow but it was actually swaying to and fro and up and down *over* the sea, a few yards beyond the cliff top.

I stumbled downstairs to fetch my binoculars. Back again still clutching Lucky, I focused on this apparition. It certainly was a blue flashing lamp and now just beneath it I could make out the dark outline of something on which it was mounted. This appeared to be shaped like the old-fashioned traditional beehive, a kind of rounded turret, and it was from this, below the lamp, that the searchlight pierced the night, unmistakably focusing on the house and lawn, for having travelled slowly between these two points the light would suddenly be extinguished. The blue lamp rode aloft; it appeared to be rising and hovering over the sea. 'My God!' I cried aloud, 'it's a UFO and it is about to take off and land on the lawn!' For the blue lamp was now swaying from side to side and rose in the air as though about to ascend. My heart seemed to freeze. 'We are about to be invaded, not just by trippers from the mainland, but by aliens from outer space,' I thought in my confused state of mind. I clutched Lucky tighter to me. It was then in the ensuing temporary black-out that, raking the cliff with my binoculars, I noticed something else almost on the cliff top itself. It was the mast of a ship. 'Good Heavens! they are landing in force—a whole planet load of them!' I panicked; I shook so much I could scarcely hold the binoculars. Then I pulled myself together.

'Would spacemen come in conventional ships with masts?' I asked myself. 'Surely they usually travel in saucers?' The searchlight picked out the dark outline of the mast again, then through the window which I had now opened I heard voices. They sounded low, guttural, urgent. With a gulping sigh of relief I realized at once that they were not beings from outer space. Would they have human voices? Of course not. Surely telepathy, radio beams or sign language were their means of communication. Although not a science fiction fan I knew that creatures from outer space are always more advanced than we are; they would be more sophisticated than to use ordinary human-like speech. If they were not spacemen who were they? Who would man such a strange looking craft and search for a suitable landing-place, for it happened that the lawn was the only level piece of land on the whole island.

Why! The Russians of course, who else? Brainwashed by the media and spy fiction I knew that the Russians were never up to any good. The island was very handy for Devonport dockyard and obviously of strategic military value to any foreign power with evil intent. I had not read my press for nothing and I was well up with current affairs. 'Right!' I said, 'We will fight them on the beaches! We will fight them on the cliffs!' and with these Churchillian phrases ringing in my ears I hurriedly dressed. 'You stay quietly here,' I admonished Lucky, shutting him in the kitchen with a Bonio. I wasn't going to have him shot at by the Russians—not our Lucky. Then trembling from head to foot I ventured outside. I would not disturb Philla—there was no point in two of us being frightened. I do not recall exactly what I intended to do. Certainly not a polite 'Have we met?' for I knew for certain that I had never met a Russian here. Again the historic phrase 'Something must be done,' went through my mind.

So out I went to do it, though *what* I still did not know. The blue light was still flashing as I approached the cliff top. The searchlight beamed out again showing up the ship's mast which appeared to be almost on the island itself. I neared the edge of the cliff and was armed with nothing more than a torch when out of the darkness I heard a voice shout in unmistakable Cockney accents 'Can't you get us orf yet then, mate?' to which the reply came in rich Cornish brogue: 'Tide's coming in fast. Hold on a bit and we will make it.' I almost collapsed with relief when I realized that the mast must be that of a holiday-maker's fishing boat or yacht marooned on the treacherous island rocks. The bobbing blue light belonged not to a flying saucer nor a Russian submarine, but to a lifeboat and was the equivalent of the flashing blue lamp mounted aloft police cars, a maritime innovation unknown to me.

The next day I heard that while I was trembling in my boots half Looe had a grandstand view from Hannafore of this nocturnal rescue, which was safely accomplished, shortly after my arrival on the scene.

In the morning I asked Philla if she had seen anything, for Jetty Cottage, although much nearer to all the activity, was out of direct range of the searchlight. 'Oh! yes,' said Philla, 'I saw lights flashing and wondered what all the racket was about. It kept me awake until nearly 3 o'clock.' All of which goes to show that some of us have more equable temperaments than others, and a little imagination can go a very long way; in this case as far as outer space and Russia and back in a very short time. Faster than light one could say.

This was not the only maritime incident in which the island was involved; we have had boats stranded on the dangerous rocks a number of times, especially in the summer when inexperienced holiday-makers in hired boats, drawn to the island like a magnet, venture too close and get wedged or caught on the rocks. We will then hail a passing fishing boat to get a message to the boatman in Looe harbour who, irate at losing valuable plying time, will come out to tow them back, while we meantime have taken them in our charge, for quite often they are city youngsters who find the experience quite frightening, as indeed it can be.

Although in winter there are rarely any small craft about, there have been incidents even then. One winter's morning about 6 a.m. I was having coffee by the Aga when there was a thump on the door. As it was pitch dark I wondered who on earth would be calling at that hour. 'We've been shipwrecked!' cried voices loudly as I opened the door. There stood two men. They had been out fishing and in the darkness their boat had caught on submerged rocks off the main beach. Luckily they had been able to wade ashore and make their way up to the house, where they were thankful to see a light. I entertained them to coffee until it was light, having meantime contacted Babs on the radio telephone to get someone to come and pick them up. Their boat, which was about the size of the *Islander*, some eighteen feet and broad-beamed, was stuck on the rocks for some time. Later the two fishermen came out and made temporary repairs so that it would not sink and, when the tides were high enough, they returned to tow her away. So all ended without disaster.

Not so lucky was the speedboat that tried to land here. The father of a journalist who had interviewed us was so keen to see the island for himself that he came out at the first opportunity when neither the sea nor the season was really suitable. Again it was early morning but it was light. The first I knew about the visit was again a thump on the door. Only this time a voice cried 'A man is drowning!' We both rushed down to the beach.

There, in a strong-running sea, was a man clinging to the buoyancy seat which had come adrift from their sinking speedboat. We dragged our dinghy down the beach and I rowed out towards him. He was not many yards off the shore but the water was deep and rough and he was distressed, as well he might be. We got him ashore without too much difficulty and, when he had recovered from the initial shock and the swallowing of seawater, helped him up to the house. Throwing all maidenly modesty aside I stripped off his wet clothes, rubbed him down, covered him with blankets and plied him with hot tea. I found him some jeans and a fisherman's top which luckily fitted, and both of which were Unisex, although that epithet had not then come into the language. I was able to call Babs before she left for school and Leonard came out to fetch the two men. The speedboat, when it was raised, was in a sorry state. It had skimmed over submerged rocks which had torn seven holes in its keel. Eventually it was towed to the mainland followed later by a parcel of dried clothing. So once again tragedy had been averted.

Once I was nearly shipwrecked myself.

During the time that Cecily and Doug were staying with us I spent a few days ashore with Babs in the cottage to do my Christmas shopping. Cecily, too, came over one day to go into Plymouth with us to do her Christmas shopping. The next day Leonard was to take her back to the island and bring Doug over to pick up some fuel for the boiler. I decided to take advantage of the double trip to go over to the island with Cecily, bottle home-made wine ready for the coming festivities and attend to various pottery pieces I was making. I would then go back to the mainland on Leonard's return trip from ferrying Doug and the fuel.

It was blowing a bit from the north-west, so Cecily and I donned waterproof clothing and Babs and I loaded the open boat with stores and Christmas presents and covered these up as best we could. It was quite rough when once we were out in the open sea; it was mid-December and there were no other boats to be seen, but with Leonard at the helm we had no fear. He took us into the lee of the island and all was landed safely at the jetty. There was some discussion about whether Doug should go over for the fuel as the wind was freshening, but as the direction of the wind was north-west and the weather forecast had given no change, it was decided to make the trip, so I landed and Cecily and I moved up the stores. All went well, Leonard and Doug returned with the anthracite and landed it on the beach and stored it in the boathouse meantime. As there would not be enough tide to get him back up the river for another half-hour or so, Leonard came up to the house for a cup of tea. When we returned to the beach, in that short time, with the incoming tide the wind had turned westerly and strengthened. Waves were crashing over the rocks and the boat (which, for some reason I do not recall, was not Leonard's) was full of water. Doug pumped it out but when I got into the boat it was still leaking.

Now the troubles started. Leonard managed to launch the boat, which was quite a feat, as the surf was breaking over us. She kept going broadside on and drifting towards the rocks. Leonard pushed with the boat-hook while Cecily and Doug heaved and shoved. Although it was only a ferry-boat and not as heavy as the *Islander* it took all their strength in that surging sea, and at one stage Cecily was up to her armpits in the surf. Then the rudder dropped off. After a struggle this was rescued and put back in position and we did at last get beyond the breaking rollers into the open sea. But now Leonard had another problem. As the sea was running strongly from the west the waves were catching us broadside on and steering was difficult. One felt in danger of being pitched overboard for, in an open boat of that size, the seats were only a few inches below the gunwales. There was no time to think about this danger however—there was too much to do, for the boat was now leaking badly.

'Pump as hard as you can!' called Leonard, busy navigating with great skill in the turbulent sea. I pumped like mad for our feet were slopping in water and it took all my time and strength to stop the level rising. On a calm day in summer it takes about a quarter of an hour to twenty minutes depending on the tide, from the island to the harbour; when it is rough it can take considerably longer. It certainly was going to take considerably longer today for suddenly the engine stopped. 'Can you row,' asked Leonard, 'while I try to get the engine going?' I rather fancied myself at being able to feather a pretty oar. There would be no feathering today, however—I was much more likely to catch a crab in those wild waves—or something worse, for I was dismayed to find on picking up the oars that one of them was only half an oar. Luckily the blade was intact and somehow or other, by pulling on this one with the naturally weaker left arm, I was able to keep a straight course. In between trying to get the engine started Leonard was having to pump, for the boat began to fill if there was any lull in the pumping.

At last he said 'It's no good! the engine is flooded.' We now took it in turns to row and pump so that Leonard could keep having a go at the engine. 'Are you all right?' he asked, for we still had a long way to go. I was uncomfortably wet. I was sitting in pools of icy water, for my water-proofs were proving no protection from the waves that broke over us from time to time, drenching us with spray, and the water was slopping over my feet from the leaking boat.

It was a ludicrous situation to say the least. Here we were in mid-December in wild seas in a small open boat that was leaking badly, the engine stalled and just one and a half oars to get us back to harbour and, of course, there were no other craft about in those stormy seas to whom we could signal for help. But with Leonard in charge I had no fear. Although then in his sixties, he was a fine-looking man with a sailor's far-seeing blue eyes. He had always taken a special interest in our welfare. He was of the opinion that we were too trusting. If so it stood me in good stead now for I had absolute faith in Leonard—all would be well with Leonard at the helm. It was all just a big adventure as far as I was concerned.

So when he asked if I was all right I replied, 'Well, all I can say is that this is better than queueing for a 77 bus in London.' Whenever I had wanted one they seemed to come in droves with a half-hour wait in between—or so it seemed to me. As in those far-off days I would often walk two miles rather than wait for a bus, it was no wonder that I though the present situation preferable—at least one had no chance of being bored. It just did not enter my head that if the boat filled up any more—and we had to pump really hard to stop the level from rising—the boat might well have sunk and we with it.

At last the rocks at Hannafore, exposed by the low tide, sheltered us from the worst of the seas running from the west. We now made good progress and eventually reached the harbour mouth, an hour or so after leaving the island. Leonard got me to row the last part in the river itself on the pretext of having another go at the engine. With hindsight I think he wanted to show me off to the many onlookers on the quayside, some of whom were those who had said that we would not last out on the island more than three months.

When shopping in Plymouth I had been given a gift box by a man demonstrating how to make them in one of the big stores. That evening after trying to make some for Christmas I took Toby for a walk and called on Leonard to see how he fared after our epic journey, but he was already in bed. By the time I went to bed I felt feverish and found that I was running a temperature of 102. So I stayed in bed until the following evening when I got up to make more gift boxes. I was convinced that I had caught a germ in that Plymouth store, for living in the pure air of the island one has no resistance against the germ-laden atmosphere of crowded places. I probably had, but it is only as I write this that I realize that it was much more likely that I had caught a chill from becoming heated from the exertion of rowing and pumping while I sat in freezing water as the icy seas sloshed over me, especially as I have, since early childhood, always been susceptible to sudden chills. It is only with hindsight, too, that I realize how lucky I was to escape with only a chill, for the following day it was discovered that the keel of the boat was fractured and we had been in very real danger of sinking in that winter sea.

Be that as it may, at the time I vowed that in future I would avoid crowded stores and go shopping as little as possible—a vow I have tried to keep from that day to this, although I must admit that I have never been keen on shopping anyway—I much prefer the hazards of island life.

However, it says something for Leonard's maritime expertise and the confidence that he inspired, that for all these years the only danger I felt I had been in on that weekend was from the germs of overcrowded stores!

The WINTER'S Tale

One of the questions we are most frequently asked, apart from 'Why don't you keep sheep and cows?' is 'What is it like in the winter?' or, as a variation, 'What do you *do* with yourselves in the winter?' The simple answer to the latter is 'Quite a lot.' What we do from day to day depends on the answer to the former, for the winter for us is a season of dramatic contrasts; storm-force winds will roar across the island to be interspersed with halycon summer-like days. Icy winds from the north will cut through one like a knife, while on the other side of the island, sheltered from the north, it may be possible to picnic in short sleeves; it is very easy to catch chills.

As our main interest is the cultivation of the land we are, like farmers, dependent on the weather and as we are entirely dependent on the state of the sea for obtaining our supplies, the services of the engineer, electrician, plumber and mason, and the delivery and collection of our all-important mail, we are obsessional about weather forecasts. We listen to the early morning shipping forecast and plan our day accordingly. The climate is exceptionally mild, similar we are told to that of the Isles of Scilly. Frost and snow are virtually unknown so the growing season is very long, and the growth of grass and weeds is continuous throughout the winter.

With the departure of summer visitors and voluntary helpers at the end of September our busy time, horticulturally, comes into its own. Harvesting which started in July, now reaches its peak, and goes well into November and even December. Now we gather the fruits of our labours: grapes, figs, sweetcorn, artichokes, apples, pears, plums, late tomatoes, marrows, courgettes, squashes, beans, main crop potatoes, late beetroot; other root vegetables, such as chicory, carrots, swedes, parsnips and Jerusalem artichokes, will be lifted as required throughout the winter. Blackberries grow in profusion; they start to ripen in July and some crops can be picked until December if the autumn rains have not ruined them. So on every fine day we climb around the island to garner them, making fresh tracks in the now crackling bramble. High up on the hill near the chapel site the berries are particularly large and luscious, like grapes, and give rise to our fancy that the monks may have cultivated them back in the twelfth century. There are apple trees in the daffodil fields as well as in the orchard, so in a bumper year we toil until nightfall to pick them before the gales hurl the fruit to the ground.

The autumnal equinox brings gales and with them a rich harvest of seaweed, so we drag up truckloads of this to spread on the land, which we are feverishly trying to clear and dig, before the rains come. This seaweed is invaluable and has a threefold use; not only is it a fertilizer and wonderful conditioner for the soil, but a thick layer will help suppress the weeds, which would otherwise be a foot or eighteen inches high by January. It also helps to feed the voracious appetite of our six compost heaps, together with a second growth of nettles which we cut. This is all hard physical work, often in less than ideal conditions, so it is almost a therapy to clear the two greenhouses to make way for winter salads, biennials and early crops, for our sowing season begins again in January. Now is the time, too, to plant trees, shrubs and bushes; each year we extend our range of fruits and have added nectarines, kiwi fruit, worcesterberries and tayberries to our black and red currants, raspberries, gooseberries etc. When we first came we started a plantation of conifers and they have grown into magnificent trees and provide us with our Christmas tree each year. The walnut tree we planted in 1976 is now a fine specimen but has yet to produce more than embryo walnuts. We have planted other nut trees as well as peach, apricot and almond and palm trees which are Babs' especial delight. In spite of the high winds they have grown tall and luxuriantly, and are a fine sight when they come into flower. We are gradually extending the vineyard too, and now that we have established an asparagus bed, the feathery foliage must be cut down and more seaweed brought up to spread here, for asparagus thrives on this treatment.

Beans are salted down, chicory and endive blanched, apples and potatoes graded and stored. The aroma of spices and the pungent smell of vinegar pervades the kitchen as produce is made into chutneys, pickles and relishes. Elderberries, blackberries and the fruit we have grown will now be made into jams, jellies, sweet pickles and wines. As November merges into December the heady scent of apples mingles with the warm smell of freshly baked bread. Wine ferments merrily in the kitchen as cheese-and yoghurt-making is in progress. The bees have been fed for the winter and now we label and store away the delectable jars of honey.

Somehow or other we must find time to deal with accounts and tax returns and answer the letters we receive with pleasure worldwide, for seemingly everyone loves an island. Time must be made, too, for printing our stationery and maps, and designing and printing our Christmas cards; cut stencils, duplicate leaflets and deal with correspondence connected with next year's conservation volunteers and would-be cottagers. We try to snatch time for our cherished crafts, for I have pots, chessmen and shire-horses to be decorated, glazed and fired in the pottery, and marquetry chess boards to be made. Babs has semi-precious stones from the sea-shore and innumerable shells awaiting her deft fingers. Wood is waiting to be carved and there are many more crafts that our itching, but too busy fingers are hoping, but often in vain, to make.

As autumn gales are succeeded by winter storms, we forage for drift-wood. Sometimes we alight with great triumph on timber that is fit for carpentry for making into benches, tables and shelving, or choice pieces that lend themselves to carving. Often tree trunks are thrown up by the sea and these can be chopped or sawn into logs for our fire. Storm-force winds scream through the woods, uprooting thirty-and forty-foot trees, toppling them like ninepins. Every possible day in the depth of winter we are up in the woods, dragging, sawing and chopping tree trunks and branches and hauling down truck-loads of logs. Several times we have had to hack and chop our way through fallen trees that have blocked our path before we could reach the beach to meet Tony Pengelly in the *Islander* when he brings supplies and our precious mail, and to reach the generator, which has to be tended daily. The winds are sometimes so strong that we have to stumble along the path in a crouching position for fear of being lifted bodily and hurled over the cliff. It can be dangerous, too, to lean against the wind for a gust that stops suddenly can send one sprawling headlong. It is in the winter that the freshwater pump down in the cliff face develops airlocks and other troubles, and slippery rocks and piles of seaweed sev-eral feet deep have to be traversed to tend it, often in biting winds and lashing rain.

The island now is as remote from Looe as though it were in mid-Atlan-tic; a jewel certainly, but set in turbulent seas. Giant rollers race past, spume flying in their wake, to break on the shore and rocks in towering cascades of spray. The screams of the gulls mingle with the howling of the wind and the thunder of the sea, and huge scuds of foam fly over the house and are driven from one end of the island to the other.

It was in such a day as this in 1974 that it was given out on the radio that owing to the conjunction of sun, moon and earth, the highest tides for 300 years were to be expected. This meant, on the mainland, the danger of widespread flooding and, on the island, the fear of losing the two boats we kept high up on the beach. These were tied up alongside the boathouse, tight up against the wooded cliff adjoining the path. We reckoned that the boathouse had been there close on a hundred years for we had been given pictures taken at the turn of the century showing it there then. It must, in that time, have withstood many onslaughts; it was large, some thirty feet by twelve feet, solidly built and housing several outboard motors, diesel drums, oars, rollocks and other impedimenta to do with boats. It should be safe enough.

The boats were another matter as they could be sucked out by the sea if it came up that high. One was a heavy clinker boat, with an inboard motor, which we had bought under Leonard's guidance so that Babs and I could ferry ourselves, and it replaced a metal boat that had been lost off our mooring in a gale; the other was an eight-foot, glass-fibre dinghy, a very light craft, used mainly as a tender for the *Islander*, which was moored in the river in Looe harbour. It was imperative that they were made as fast as possible. Knot-tying was not my forte—something about its intricacy eludes me—but I had had one unexpected success with a great-granny knot that I had once invented in an emergency, so I diligently tied the two boats to the trees at the foot of the cliffs, great-granny style, and hoped that they had a reasonable chance of withstanding the strain and pull of the sea if it encroached that far.

On the beach was an enormous barge. It was more like a flat-bottomed boat with four sides supported by substantial posts at each corner. It had been used in the past for towing heavy machinery and furniture and was very solid indeed, measuring some 25 feet long, 12 feet wide and 4 feet deep. It was half buried in the sand from the onslaught over the years of countless storms and, as it was absolutely immovable, had proved invaluable to us as a beach anchorage for securing our boats. Now, however, the boats stood a better chance from the encroaching sea high up under the cliff.

The morning of the highest tide I looked out of the bedroom window facing seaward and my mouth fell open, for mountainous seas towering higher than the cliffs were crashing on the cliff top itself, then sweeping from one side of the promontory to the other. The flagstaff was no longer

139

there. The tumultuous seas had uprooted the tabernacle supporting the flagstaff, and hurled it from the southern side of the promontory over to the cliff top on the eastern side. This was just a hundred yards or so from the house. Spray was driven across the lawn like a blizzard and great scuds of foam as large as one's fist clung to the branches of trees. What would it be like on the beach facing the mainland where the boats were? I raced down the path to the beach but to my relief all was still intact. The sea was swirling round the bows of the two boats and was actually lapping the side of the boathouse, but the moment of danger was past. Or was it? Sometimes after the highest spring tide, we have often, unpredictably, experienced an even higher one. This may be due to atmospheric pressure, for this can increase the height of the tide. Whatever the reason it can happen, so I tied some more knots in the ropes and dragged the boats tight up against the cliff. When I checked at high tide that night all was still secure.

The next morning, however, the sea was a scene of violent tumult: mountainous seas were still crashing over the cliff top at the back of the house and great breakers were thundering past Jetty Bay, the spume streaming behind in their wake for hundreds of yards. As I hurried down to the beach an incredible sight met my horrified gaze. Diesel drums were being tossed thirty feet in the air like ping-pong balls at a fair; a long line of debris swept at breakneck speed towards Rame Head—the contents of the boathouse—and before me was a scene of utter desolation, for of the boathouse, boats and barge there was no sign. Part of the path, too, had disappeared and left a six-foot drop to the beach below where the surf still sucked greedily. The raging seas beat against the cliff where once the boathouse had been. It and its contents were lost for ever, and nothing was seen again of the boats and the barge, although over the years the sea did give back the odd anchor, pulley, chain or other metal objects.

The only small consolation I had on that disastrous day was that I could have done no more to save the boats, for the frayed ropes still hung from the trees with the knots intact—it was the ropes themselves which had been torn apart by the force of the sea.

Every coast in the country suffered from those calamitous seas. Babs told me that the flooding in West Looe made the bridge impassable so that she could not get to school. At West Looe the swollen river overflowed its banks and cars were swept from the quayside over the road to the shops, and boats were dragged from their mooring on to the car park. She had heard that a man had swum in the streets in East Looe, another had rowed down the street in Fowey, and that fish had been caught in Boots, the chemists, there.

The winter takes its toll in other ways. Tiles fly off the roof every year—once thirteen went in one go leaving a gaping hole in the gable roof. Luckily this was over the hall and a row of buckets dealt with the continual stream of rain until Jack could get over to replace the tiles. On one never-to-be-forgotten occasion the bathroom flat roof took off and the rain seeped through and poured down in so many places that it was not possible to reach the wash-basin without an umbrella—except that we possessed no umbrella, for it is not standard equipment on windswept islands. We solved *that* problem by drilling a hole in the ceiling so that the rain would find its outlet in one steady stream and thus could be trapped in a dustbin. This we emptied at intervals until the gale subsided and Jack could get over to make a temporary repair, for this was a major replacement job, requiring, as it transpired, the services of a roofing expert experienced in the use of boiling pitch! Jack Tambling would come out in any possible weather, often braving stormy seas to replace tiles and make other emergency repairs. How we came to know him in the first place is a tale in itself.

Landslides are a common hazard around the coastline of Britain as the sea gradually erodes the coast. The island is no exception and there have been several falls since we have been here, making dangerous undercuts and leaving some of the cliff paths perilously close to the edge. One day after a series of severe south-west gales I heard a dull roar followed by an ominous thump. On investigation I found to my horror that there had been a landslide above the jetty beach, some twenty-five yards from the house and a bare two yards from the edge of the main path. Tons of earth and cliff had fallen and completely obliterated the pump-house in the cliff below.

This was a disaster indeed, for our only supply of fresh water was now inaccessible. When I told Babs on the radio telephone she went post-haste to the Council. Yes! they would do what they could to help, but it would be costly for us, as the rates did not cover this sort of contingency. When the weather calmed somewhat, out came a team of council workmen headed by their foreman, Jack Tambling. A shy, diffident Cornishman, he now showed his enormous courage. He hammered an iron stake into the daffodil field directly above the cliff fall, tied a rope to this, belayed himself, then casually stepped over the cliff edge as though he were stepping out side his front door, and climbed down the perpendicular precipice to the cliff fall some thirty feet below. The team now toiled away shifting the tons of earth and rock under Jack's direction and with his help. It seemed an impossible task, but after several days of navvying eventually the pump-house was excavated and the petrol pump lifted up out of the well where it had fallen, spilling oil and petrol into our precious spring water. The tunnel into the cliff now had to be cleared and the pump-house and the steps leading up to it completely rebuilt.

Unfortunately none of this was covered by insurance as a landslide was deemed an 'Act of God'. However, a tree trunk had fallen into the well from the cliff top, too, and for some technical reason God was not held responsible for this, and the assessor, over a glass or so of home-made wine—for I had no fresh water to offer tea or coffee—allowed us 25 per cent of the cost instead of nothing.

We had always had trouble with the petrol pump, and even when it functioned perfectly, it was no fun in the depth of winter to slither over piles of seaweed and rocks and clamber up the steps into the cliff face to start the engine. This entailed pulling a cord, similar to starting a motor-mower. If the engine was in a sullen mood and the tugs consequently became sharper, one was in danger of falling head-over-heels backwards down the steep steps on to the rocks below. Added to this was the ever present hazard of being drenched with icy water when the pipes jerked apart or split with the sudden force of water. We decided, therefore, that we would put the insurance money towards an electric pump. As this could be started from a switch in the house this would solve all our problems— or would it? Well not quite, as we were to discover. Air-locks and other non-events still necessitate winter visits to the pump-house, and, of course, all our eggs were now in one basket, for if the generator grinds to a halt, the pump is unusable. Not all can be perfect in an imperfect world, so we do our best to keep the water-storage tanks in the woods full to the brim, but this is not possible during a drought, which can often last from spring until autumn, the effects being felt until after Christmas. Paradise does have its problems!

When Jack left working for the Council he became self-employed and, as well as carrying out our emergency jobs, he became for a period the official postman, ferried the diesel oil and other supplies and transported Babs for her rare weekends and holidays on the island. During the Christmas holidays the big problem was when she should return to the mainland,

and it seemed that we spent most of the second week of her holiday with our ears glued to the radio listening to the shipping and weather forecasts in case her visit had to be suddenly curtailed.

One particular Christmas the weather turned foul almost as soon as Babs had landed. The gales continued the whole holiday period, at times reaching storm force. Luckily they abated towards the end of the holiday, but the aftermath left a great surge of wild seas breaking on the beaches. Jack had spoken on the radio telephone and it was arranged that he would come out and size up the situation to see if a landing were possible. It was a bright sunny day, so we felt optimistic as the white-crested rollers, crowned by the blue sky overhead, sparkled in the sunshine. Paradoxically it seems really menacing when those same seas rush at you from under leaden skies, the wind stinging your face with icy rain.

As we approached the surf we espied the *Islander*, a lone craft, gleaming white in the sunlight. It was bucking in the great troughs and at the helm stood the indomitable oilskin-clad figure of Jack. Babs, desperate to make it to the boat, now that Jack had braved the rough seas, reckoned that if she could wade out beyond the surf she could board the *Islander* there; it would prevent the danger of it going broadside on in the surf and getting smashed up on the rocks. Why we considered that she could withstand the raging breakers I do not recall, but ever prudent, we had thoughtfully brought a rope with us. Babs tied this round her waist and I belayed it round mine, in the best mountaineering manner. 'I am coming out beyond the surf on a rope,' yelled Babs above the sound of the crashing waves, as she ploughed into the sea, 'and you can pick me up from there.' Beneath his sou'wester we could see the look of horror on Jack's face. 'Don't you dare! You will be *drowned*!' he bellowed, and with that he turned the boat about and made for the harbour, the only way he knew to stop Babs from plunging further into the broiling sea. A receding breaker sucked round Babs' knees nearly toppling her over and dragging her back with it. I gave a tremendous tug and leaned back on the rope as though I was trying to land a fish and Babs staggered ashore to spend an extra day on the island.

The next day Jack was able to pick her up and take her ashore without incident as the sea, if not exactly calm, was manageable. Hazardous and unpredictable as the sea is, it was the only time Babs was adrift on the island in all the twelve years she was teaching in Looe, mainly because she usually curtailed her holidays as a precaution in case, as in this instance, the weather forecast was not a reliable enough guide. Paradoxically if she had lived up on Bodmin Moor on the mainland she would have been 'adrift' quite a number of times during those years, for staff who lived there were cut off by snowdrifts on a number of occasions during the winter months and were unable to make it to school.

Those Christmas holidays were very precious to us for it was, and still is, the only time we take a 'holiday'. We have the usual chores to do, the generator and water pump must be attended to, and Christmas cooking makes for busyness as for others, but we do relax mentally. We have this fantasy that from Christmas Eve until Twelfth Night we are cruising in a yacht to exotic places, and plot our 'course' according to the weather. We play Scrabble, read, listen to music, watch TV and enjoy the company of our pets. We cannot entertain our friends or relations; we are too remote and the danger of their being cut off is too great. Local friends have taken short trips out to see us but the possibilities are rare. The weather varies so much that we never know if we shall have to batten down the hatches, so to speak, or if the weather may be spring-like. Christmas 1983, for instance, we were able to have a barbecue and two picnics; we actually celebrated New Year's Day with a picnic high up on the hill in warm sunshine. When you live on the job it is difficult to take time off, and Christmastide with its special atmosphere is the only time when we can do this without the nagging thoughts of jobs to be done.

Christmas over, it is back to the land, and no more fine feasts at the Captain's table. Traditionally one can plant early potatoes on the island on Boxing Day. Afraid of compacting the soil we usually leave this for a few weeks, for the worst of the winter weather is still to come. Although it is only a matter of weeks before our spring, the storms can be so severe that the time seems incredibly long, possibly because we experience the winter in depth rather than in actual length. Now is the time for sowing and greenhouse work. Christmas or not, tree-clearing and log-sawing go on daily, if the storms are not wreaking havoc in the woods, for on those days it would be dangerous to venture there for fear of falling trees. Loads of seaweed are now brought up for potato planting as well as for the compost heaps. As soon as the soil is fit I dig hundreds of feet of trenches ready for the potatoes and later the runner beans. Babs and I then line them with comfrey, compost and seaweed. As soon as possible we start planting the early potatoes and rotavate the land that has gone back to nature over the winter. Daffodils start blooming in January, so soon we are feverishly alternating between daffodils, greenhouse and the land. If we do not cut the five lawns and many grass verges it must be done soon or a scythe will be necessary. In any case all the grass has to be raked up and added to the compost heaps.

In between Babs deals with a welter of correspondence about the working holidays; it is like a jigsaw puzzle as she tries to fit applicants in, knowing that some will cancel, and others alter dates; then the jigsaw will have to be started all over again. I print our headed paper and cut stencils for information sheets and the like, which we will both run off on our ancient and unreliable duplicator. Longingly we think of our neglected crafts, but now and again we take time to throw a pot, do some woodwork, shellcraft or whatever, if only as a refreshment for the spirit.

All too soon it will be spring and we are not quite ready, as we never are, as each season nudges into the next. The first visitors will soon appear and we must gear our thoughts and energies to our preparation for them. So the cycle goes on.

More than one visitor has said to us at the end of the summer season, 'I expect you will be glad when we all go and you can put your feet up,' little realizing that they are merely a pattern superimposed on the fabric of our island life, albeit with the passage of time they have become interwoven. Some with more perception have said, 'How do you put up with us, intruding on your lives?' Others ask 'What do you do for holidays?' and when we say we have none some will say, 'But you don't need holidays living in a beautiful place like this!' They would do anything, they say, to exchange their lives for ours. But would they? We understand their envy but doubt if they understand the responsibilities and hardships involved. When you live on the job it really is essential to get away for a break if only to recoup your vitality and recharge your mental and physical batteries. Not all understand this and think that if you live in a beautiful place, in some magical way you never get tired, never get worried, nor overwhelmed with day-to-day problems: that somehow it cannot be so bad. Why not? I have yet to hear of anyone who finds that a tooth aches any the less by a blue lagoon in the South Seas than in a crowded city—except of course that if you live in the latter a dentist is more accessible. An electricity cut, whether due to 'industrial action' or the breakdown of your own generator, plunges you into darkness as black on an island as in a city, except that if it is your own generator you have to go down at dead of night, perhaps in a howling gale and slashing rain, to try to do something about it—and there are no shops to fly to for candles or paraffin.

TALES FROM OUR CORNISH ISLAND

Many visitors who sit on top of the island in the hot summer sunshine, fanned by refreshing sea breezes or who stroll along the cliff paths admiring the magnificent views and the myriad colours of the translucent sea, do not realize when they envy us that no one will ever meet us there during the months of summer; that the only time we can enjoy a carefree jaunt or a casual stroll is during our hard-won Christmas holiday on our mythical cruise to faraway places. It is then that we also can appreciate the sheer joy of our island paradise. We feel, on those rare summer days in the depth of winter that sparkle like a jewel in the darkness, that we are on another planet; that we are privileged for a short spell to be part of the timeless universe, where there is no beginning, no end, only a magical limitless 'now'.

The AUTHOR'S Tale

'What made you want to write?' 'Had you written much before your book was published?' 'How do you find time to write *anything*?' The first two of these oft repeated questions I will attempt to answer here; the short answer to the third is by starting the day at 5 a.m.

Writing is a solitary occupation, but in my case it is not so. Lucky helps me. After we lost our splendid border collie, Kim, Babs heard that Lucky needed a home as his owner, a Marine Commando, was being posted to Malta. We were delighted, therefore, to welcome someone who was almost an exact replica of Toby, even to his tightly curled and jaunty tail. Partly a smooth-haired terrier, partly labrador, he is golden brown with an immaculate white front, paws and tail-tip. He has the same gentlemanly manners as Toby, too, allowing ladies through doors first, and letting his adorable but greedy young friend Emma, a black collie/labrador cross, share his meals and have the best place by the fireside. He does not sing as Toby did, but he speaks and most eloquently too. He has a repertoire of notes and tones that express a comprehensive range of emotions and comments—he has been known to make a downright condemnation if a politician on TV appears to act churlishly. A born actor, he will freely give encores if any clever action of his is applauded. He thinks things out for himself too. Obviously trained by the Marine Commando to attend to the calls of nature in the garden border, although only nine months old when he came here, he soon made other arrangements. He marches the quarter of a mile or so down the path to the beach, heads for the far eastern corner of the shore and uses the point where waves from the east and west meet and will thus obliterate all traces of doggy visits. He then marches home again. Visitors have noticed these expeditions and are amazed to learn that this contribution to a pollution-free island is entirely his own idea.

It is his own idea, too, to sit with me here while I write—here in Jetty Cottage. Sue, the silver-grey cat, who took over from Joan, has decided that she is going to help me write the book, too, and Emma sometimes wants to be in on the act. My table is beautifully crafted from driftwood by

Andrew Giles and Adam Kelly, two of our most stalwart and regular helpers, who spent many hours fining and polishing it to perfection. By contrast the chair on which I sit is an elegant antique. As well as the impedimenta of writing I have a camera nearby, for early on a summer's morning the view across the bay, through the window opposite, is one of ever-changing beauty; the rising sun pierces the morning mist and the limpid sea, stirred by a slight breeze, ripples in the sunlight. With luck a fishing-boat will sail across the sparkling pathway of the sun and, framed by a dark hanging bough of a tree on the cliff top a few yards from the window, it is like a Japanese painting and I will capture the moment on film. If only I were an artist!

But I must write. Lucky sitting beside me will see to that. He joined us when *We Bought An Island* was published and he appeared in the first TV programme made to launch the book here on the island. This was only a matter of days after he took up residence. He was determined, therefore, that this, the sequel, should be written and he nudges me down here if I should falter. But he has other duties to perform too; there is the whole island to be policed—he and Emma know instantly if anyone lands. He must keep a watchful eye on Emma, too, help Babs and encourage the helpers then, handsome and charming, he will accompany Babs and Emma to greet the visitors. Tilly, our magnificent long-haired light tortoise-shell cat, runs her own escort service, meeting and seeing guests off the boat and accompanying them on walks up the hill and over the rocks. Samantha, the dark tortoise-shell one, truly splendid with emerald jewels for eyes, is too languid to take an interest in people, or the book, and is often referred to as Samantha, Lady Bertram. Later Lucky will return to keep me informed of any events that require my presence.

It is said that everyone has a book in them, and countless people will tell you that they could write a book about their experiences—if only they had the time. When I first decided to be a writer I did not have a book in me, nor had I much in the way of experiences, although there was an enormous amount of time ahead to write about them, for I was just six years old. There was no doubt about my future career. When asked at school what we wanted to be when we grew up, among the would-be nurses, ballerinas, actresses and circus riders, I declared grandiously: 'I am going to be an author.' No 'want' about it—just a declaration of intent. It may seem odd, therefore, that I had retired more years than I care to acknowledge before I actually became one. Why this lengthy interval? To explain it is necessary to go back a bit—almost a lifetime, in fact.

Although I never gave up the idea of being a writer, other pursuits claimed my attention too. Reading was obsessional. Photography had caught me in its magic spell since the age of four, inspiring me to make my own camera around the age of ten. With a cricket-loving father and brothers, games became a creed. Classes in gymnastics, dancing and eurhythmics were part of the fabric of early childhood and music became an enduring passion. One could escape at the piano into a solitary enchanted world. Mother encouraged me in all these pursuits, especially music—the music teacher did too, and when she said I was her best pupil, I considered the idea that perhaps, as well as becoming an author, I would be a concert pianist, too. The world was certainly my oyster. It was early days yet, however, for I had not yet reached double figures in age.

As a first step towards authorship, my friend Ethel and I produced a magazine, written entirely by ourselves, apart from one story which we accepted from her brother. This magazine did not go down at all well with the Principal of our private school where we were flogging it at one penny a copy. Endeavouring as she was, with indifferent success, to instil in her charges ladylike qualities and accomplishments, she disapproved of Bessie Bunter, who was the heroine of most of our stories. She, according to her, was no lady. The magazine was banned.

Showing the determination that is essential if one is to become a genius, Ethel and I now turned our creative urge to play-writing. We wrote, produced and acted the main parts in all our plays, auditioning among our favoured friends for the lesser roles. These were open-air productions performed in our garden. This was not popular with those who had been turned down for bit parts, especially when we draped the end of the garden with sheets, to prevent gatecrashers or prying eyes from enjoying free entertainment. Babs, who now appeared on the scene for the first time, but was still a toddler, was considered too young to pay and was allowed in free. Nepotism is not only practised in high places! Our stunning performances were then given to the accompaniment of jeers, boos and cat-calls from the young ladies and gentlemen who had taken up their stance on the other side of the barricade, and who far outnumbered the paying members of the audience. In spite of their mixed reception these open-air plays were a regular feature until, at the age of thirteen, Ethel left the district and I moved to another school.

Here my literary efforts, which had graduated from episodes in the life of Bessie Bunter, became more officially acceptable. Prizes were won, and the editorship of the school magazine conducted with much pride. As far as homework was concerned I wrote unceasingly on subjects such as history, geography and literature, happily giving up much of my leisure and holidays to them, but neglecting other subjects. It seemed a waste of time to compose in Latin and French when there was so much to be said in English. Consequently my scholastic achievements were somewhat lop-sided and school reports appeared to be written about two different pupils. Nevertheless our austere Headmistress, eagle-like with her aristocratic nose and flowing black gown, inspiring awe and admiration in both pupils and parents, ordained that I was destined for Oxford and an academic career. At that time a university education was not the general passport to careers as it is today, and was not generally pursued by girls unless, as I thought, they were bluestockings. I viewed with horror the prospect of a narrow academic life. In any case I had already made up my mind that I was going to be a journalist. This decision had a frozen reception. Anything less than a Bursarship, Exhibition, or Scholarship, with an Hons. Degree at Oxbridge and a fine string of letters after one's name, to be embellished in gold on the Scroll of Honour in the School Entrance Hall, was considered, one felt, fit only for the compost heap.

I was more than agreeably surprised therefore, when the school advanced me the fee to take a correspondence course in journalism when I left. It was a well-known School of Journalism with a good reputation, but I did not care for the lessons at all. At that time I fancied myself as an amalgam of Robert Louis Stevenson, Thomas Hardy, J.M. Barrie, with a dash of the Charles Lamb, and Hazlitt, plus, in my finer moments, a touch of the Beaumont and Fletcher; I was also inclined sometimes, like Walter de la Mare's Traveller knocking on moonlit doors, to ask if 'anyone was there?' and giving my own fanciful answers. The course did not cater for these literary aspirations. The lessons were full of useful tips on salesmanship, how to aim at particular markets, and a realistic attitude, that with all the ignorance and arrogance of youth I despised. So I sent the money back.

I would get a job in a newspaper office. But it was the time of the depression, and there were no jobs of any kind. I bombarded editorial offices, but to no avail. Desperate for a job I even applied for that of telephonist, but was turned down on account of the fact that I could not pronounce the letter 'R', a defect that had given me a poor showing in French, and was probably due to the time when I travelled by pram and my brothers, fighting over who should have the honour of pushing me, let the pram roll away—a split tongue being the consequence.

150

Then unexpectedly came a reply from the Editor of *Pearson's Weekly*. They had no job, but would be pleased to interview me to give advice. There were two other people as well as the Editor at the interview. They said that the best thing was for me to write free-lance along the lines they specified and then to submit the articles to them. They outlined their market requirements, and the kind of material they wanted, and kindly gave me a great deal of advice and encouragement.

Thrilled beyond belief I spent all my time scribbling away. Meantime I still needed a job. Here again the school helped. The Headmistress arranged an interview for me with the Headmistresses' Association for a post with the newly formed and prestigious I.C.I. and I became an invoice clerk at 25s. per week. We were very busy and, over a long period worked overtime. In those days there was no payment for overtime, but we were allowed to claim for a meal. Usually we had Welsh rarebit costing 1s. for we did not want to overcharge the firm, but sometimes, greatly daring, we had buck rarebit—i.e., with an egg on it, and this, with a cup of tea cost 1s. 6d. I used to get very tired and after a time my music began to suffer and memorizing became more difficult. I continued to write, however, on the lines suggested by the Editor of *Pearson's Weekly*. Somewhere I had read that it was a mistake to send off anything one had written, red-hot; it should be put aside for an interval, then brought out for later appraisal. I wanted to produce my very best for the revered Editor of *Pearson's Weekly*, so I decided that my masterpieces should be put on ice for six months.

Six months later I had the shock of my life. The sage, whoever it was, who had suggested this idea, had given the most salutary advice that could help a young aspiring writer. I was appalled at what I had written. It was immature, schoolgirlish, self-concious, pompous even. No one at *Pearson's* would want to read or publish that rubbish. I tore the whole lot up. Whether it was wise to be my own mentor I shall never know, but I do remember deciding that the world must await the flowering of my genius for a few more years yet. I needed, I decided, experience of Life with a capital 'L' before I put pen to paper again, for publication that is.

So at the age of nineteen I made the momentous decision that I would not write again until the age of thirty. Why thirty, one wonders? When I was very young my ambition was to reach the age of eleven, mainly because a pair of twins in a favourite magazine had the most fantastic adventures at that age. Having reached the age of eleven the next leap forwards was the desire to be thirty. This because a glamourous lady detective of that age spent her time, in the pages of a film magazine, solving the most amazing crimes. From then on thirty years old had an alluring image. By that age, I now thought, I would have shed my gawkish schoolgirl outlook and emerged a *soignée femme fatale*, endowed, of course, with penetrating powers of detection and the ability to write with a pen dipped in liquid gold.

One might conjecture from all this fantasizing that I should find my niche as a lady writer of detective stories. Not so. Life with a capital 'L' did in fact take over, culminating, before I reached that magical age, with the outbreak of the Second World War. Well, the sort of life that appealed to me anyway. Some time after the age of twenty I regretfully gave up thoughts of becoming a concert pianist; partly because, with continuing overtime, I could not memorize whole sonatas and partly because even I, with my grandiose ideas, realized it was not something one could become in one's spare time, especially when that was in short supply.

Photography was a different matter; although exacting, it was flexible in its demands on one's time. I joined a Camera Club, later attended photographic classes at Morley College with my brother Trevor, and for good measure classes at Regent Street Polytechnic where my enthusiasm land-ed me with the job of Secretary of the Group. All these involved photographic expeditions and I worked far into the night in my dark-room at home. I had work exhibited, won some prizes and awards and hoped that eventually I might become a photo-journalist.

The drawback to becoming anything at all was the diversity of interests that took my fancy. Mountaineering lured me to the Alps and I have to this day my ice-axe notched with the number of peaks climbed that were over 10,000 feet. Brief weekend visits were made to the Lake District to climb there and take photographs. Weekends that were not devoted to hiking round different parts of the country with the Mountaineering Club were spent on other outdoor activities: Youth Hostelling, playing hockey, tennis, cricket and cycling. I went on lone cycling jaunts; once for a whole week. There was a purpose, apart from exploring the countryside and taking photographs; I was compiling a dossier of literary associations in Surrey. Fanny Burney's residence in the county, William Cobbett's *Rural Rides*, George Meredith's and Keats' association with Box Hill—Jane Austen's famous picnic there in *Emma*. These and many more were investigated, visited and written up in a large alphabetically indexed book I was keeping.

Box Hill had other attractions, too. My schoolgirl friend Tommy and I knew a group of young men who were involved in a Red Indian cult. This meant sleeping out on Box Hill and living a pure and wholesome life. We were made honorary members and I was given the appellation 'Minnehaha' and we partook of Indian-type food under the stars.

Working in London had many advantages and we were able to attend performances of *Hiawatha* at the Albert Hall, as well as the *Proms* and many other concerts, for which we queued happily. Theatre going in the 'gods' was a regular pursuit, and Babs, who had now caught up a bit age-wise, and I were devotees of Sadler's Wells and the Old Vic.

There was no subject that could not be studied at evening classes. Musical Appreciation conducted by a Professor of Music was particularly enjoyed, for as I now acknowledged that I should not be gracing the concert platforms of the world, I wished to applaud with informed intelligence those who did. Spanish was tried to roll out the elusive 'R's but was soon given up as a disaster; bookkeeping, to help my career, was found to be incredibly boring when there were so many more exciting things to do. I joined a Language Circle to refurbish my neglected French, but as all the other members were foreigners trying to learn English this proved to be stalemate, and I retired to be taught German by a linguist friend. This proved a much easier language to learn, as unlike the excitable Latins, the Germans seemed to pronounce each word and did not run streams of words into each other in a cacophony of unintelligible gibberish. Perhaps unexpectedly, cookery classes were attended with great enthusiasm. There seemed to be something creative and magical in transforming an assortment of ordinary, everyday ingredients into something, delectable both to eye and palate, that could give pleasure to others. Furthermore it had been no part of the curriculum at my schools—apparently future ladies or academics were not expected to eat unless someone else prepared and set the food before them. Elocution classes were joined partly because prizes had been gained for this in the past but also with the idea of dealing with the troublesome 'R's and to help with Amateur Dramatics. I belonged to the I.C.I. Players, the Sutton and Cheam Amateur Dramatic Society and later attended Evening Drama Classes run by Babs, who had a great flair for acting and was an Adjudicator for Drama Festivals.

Sacrosanct, however, were the classes held at the City Literary Institute on The Craft of Writing. I attended courses over several years, did the exercises set and meticulously filled many notebooks. These I still have and they are valid today. It was possible to fit in yet another Photographic class on the same evening and in the coffee interval I met a lady who earned her living sticking labels on wine bottles. She gave me the benefit of her expertise which later came in very useful when I took up wine-making.

With promotion came the move to IC House, where there was a fine gymnasium and indoor sports facilities. Here I took up badminton (and later squash), rifle shooting and fencing. Foreign travel became important. Europe was explored by buying a ticket at Victoria, then once across the Channel, sleeping on the luggage rack of the third-class compartment, as the seats were so hard, until we reached Italy, Bavaria or wherever. When cruises became available for other than the wealthy and quite cheap cruising holidays were possible, I persuaded Tommy to try one with me. Our senior secretary lent me the money to buy several evening outfits which she said I would need, and off we set on our big adventure in the *Doric*, bound for Lisbon, Gibraltar and Algiers. It was a bitter disappointment. Too many people everywhere and too little time to explore faraway places, it seemed to me. We danced the night away, but I could do that at home, and the trips ashore, which were the *raison d'être* as far as I was concerned, were all too short and one was surrounded by other tourists. There was only one adventure. A doctor and his patient became our escorts for the cruise. They went to a belly dance in Algiers but would not take us as they considered it unsuitable. Furious, we decided we would explore Algiers ourselves that evening. It soon became obvious that this was not approved of by the local male population who tried to chase us away with loud cries of indignation. Soon we were pursued by hundreds of white-robed Arabs and, breathless, we only just made it back to the ship.

The following year I took to the mountains having been lured there by the *National Geographical Magazine* which had on one of its front covers a picture of a mountain in Austria crowned by a fairytale castle; but Tommy, who had become an addict, goes cruising still whenever she can.

Life was becoming crowded. Lunch-times were allocated very carefully. Mondays were spent in the Westminister Library; Tuesdays at chamber music concerts given in Christ Church; Wednesdays, browsing in a bookshop or a work-out in the gym, according to the weather; Thursdays were given up to exploring any part of London within reach. The idea was to walk in a different direction each time going as far afield as possible. The places ranged from as far apart as Blackfriars and the Tate Gallery.

This last became a favourite port of call, as there was just time to study one picture in detail on each visit. Friday I graciously joined my friends for lunch. They lunched together every day and were inclined to think that I was anti-social. Nevertheless the bonds remained firm and one came to the island recently to see me.

Evenings were even more crowded. Immediately after leaving the office I would play badminton, or take part in some other activity in the bowels of IC House, have a shower, go on to an evening class or concert and finish up at a dance or party—arriving home around 1 a.m. where a rather sad-looking dinner awaited me in the oven. To fit in the obsessive reading I would on occasion, with my season ticket, board a train on a newly formed loop line and travel round and round to London and back until my book was finished, that way avoiding distractions of any kind.

Perhaps the biggest problem was fitting in various boy friends without becoming too committed. One had given me his course on Pelmanism, but that did not provide a solution; another gave me a pack of fortune telling cards, which, though they gave me the reputation for being clairvoyant, did not predict the outcome or advise me. The fact was that although romance was essential to me, my idea of it was based on Sir Thomas Malory's *Le Morte d'Arthur* and Spenser's *The Faerie Queen*. Diet of this sort of literary fare had inculcated in me, early on, high-flown ideas that were not compatible with those of young men, however personable and indeed chivalrous, whose aim was the altar, children and the quiet domestic scene, or prospective mothers-in-law who would ply me with articles 'for your bottom drawer'. I viewed with alarm the domestic constrictions of marriage and was of the opinion that some people were more suitable for the wedded state than others—and I did not feel so suited. I wished, too, for a more exciting life, and yearned to explore faraway places. Once when I read in the newspaper about a forthcoming expedition to the Antarctic I wrote offering my services as a cook/photographer. The courteous reply said that unfortunately the expedition was not recruiting ladies. It was just as well for I never could stand the cold.

When I reached the magical age of thirty I found that the complexity of reconciling these problems with multifarious pursuits and earning a living left little time for the sedentary occupation of writing, but in addition, I had a war on my hands.

Although this is by no means intended as a potted autobiography of those stirring times, for that would take a tome or two, there are some aspects that do have a bearing on the long dormant period of authorship that, like a volcano, erupted from time to time.

As I was fortunate enough to have a straight eye and a steady hand, rifle shooting had produced gold medals, silver cups, an assortment of awards, the honour of shooting for Surrey at Bisley and the accolade of 'Master Shot'. On the outbreak of war my ladies' team and I were in fact engaged in a postal match with the Polish ladies' team. That we had not received their return set of target-cards struck us with a chill of foreboding as we hastily packed our gear to move from our London Office to offices in huts on the factory site of I.C.I. Plastics Factory at Welwyn, Herts. Here we were tracked down by a photographer sent by the *Daily Mirror*, for we had recently won a National Competition. As a result of this publicity a 'friendly' match—could it have been otherwise with those lethal weapons in our hands?—was arranged with a regiment stationed nearby and awaiting embarkation for France. I do not recall who did the challenging, but I do remember the Colonel showing me how to use a .303 rifle as I had never used one of this calibre before I did not care for it very much for the recoil thumped one's shoulder painfully. However, much to my consternation, we won.

I was convinced by this that we should now lose the war. In any case I thought, our superior marksmanship was being wasted in the country's hour of need. So now at long last I put pen to paper, hopefully for publication, and wrote a blazing article which I sent to the Editor of the *Evening News*. I chose the *Evening News* as this was the newspaper that had published a picture of me on its front page. This showed me being bowled at in the nets of my brother's cricket school by members of the England cricket team who were about to tour Australia for the forthcoming Tests. The gist of the article was that we ladies should be armed so that while the men were away fighting we could defend the homeland. 'We already had a group six strong,' I said. 'Arm us and form similar detachments throughout the land,' I pleaded. The editor replied very courteously and said that he could not publish the article, for although he applauded our patriotism he did not think that his readers would approve of ladies going about killing people. His reply brought me up short. Infused as I was with all this white-hot patriotism I had never actually visualized shooting anyone *dead*—even a Nazi, although it was obvious that we were not about to be invaded by a horde of target-cards. That I was not the type to go killing anything living was soon to be proved.

Among other activities to help with the war effort I had become a part-time land girl. This resulted in my becoming very friendly with a handsome young farmer and, what was more, *he knew Cary Grant*. He was also a keen croquet player. He, I and four other young farmers used to repair to the local hostelry and spent many a pleasant summer evening playing croquet. Sometimes Babs came to stay with me for the weekend and she joined us in the croquet playing. We played darts as well and Babs showed that she could be a marksman too, for once, when it was her turn to play, she turned round on the bar stool on which she was sitting, and without getting up, nonchantly threw her dart from there, to hit double-top, to go right out and win the game for her side.

One weekend my farmer friend invited us both to a shoot. There were ten men as beaters, and it was all very exciting until someone emerged triumphantly from the wood with a dead hare slung over his arm. Its head was lolling sideways and blood poured on to the ground. I not only retired immediately from the shoot. I gave up my farmer, eating meat, my digs, and took up residence forthwith in a vegetarian guest-house. In any case I had decided that milking cows at 5 a.m. and threading one's way through cowpats was surely no way of fulfilling one's destiny.

The other guests at the vegetarian establishment were interesting to say the least. One was a Russian Jew, another a lady pacifist who showed me how to make and play a recorder, and for some incomprehensible reason, how to drop dead in seven different ways—one hoped that it was for histrionic purposes and not in anticipation of the expected invasion. I now composed music and played it on the recorder for the delectation of my fellow-guests. One of these was a girl of slant eyes and ethnic origins. She claimed that she came from Yugoslavia, but it transpired that she originated from Bethnal Green. She had a hang-up that she was a reincarnation of an Indian princess, and she spent much of her time clad in a sari, performing Indian dances for us, with much swaying and wafting of chiffon scarves. I had shared my former digs with two young research chemists. We became bosom pals, cycled the countryside and as a trio had great times together. One was Philip from Somerset, the other Sundra, a Buddhist and a Hindu of high caste, who was writing a book on comparative religions of the world. He decided to join me at the vegetarian guest-house. Although we still remained a threesome Philip stayed in the digs as he preferred a carnivorous habitat.

Sundra invited me to visit some friends of his who had a flat in London, and many an interesting evening was spent with compatriots of his from their far continent. Sometimes we took along our friend of the sari so that she could live out her reincarnation. As I was the only English member of the company and was not knowingly a reincarnation of anybody, I was the odd one, but I enjoyed the companionship of my new set of friends, their cultured conversation and their many-flavoured foods.

Another resident of the guest-house was a middle-aged Hungarian of imposing stature and obvious erudition. The books she had written, she said, had forewords by Freud himself, for she was a psychologist. When she found out that I worked at I.C.I. she made a play at me. In the long and immensely interesting conversations we had, she slipped in the odd leading question. 'Where', she once asked me, almost as an aside 'do I.C.I. store their explosives?' Her eyes pierced mine hypnotically. Without any hesitation and zombie-like, as though the words were being dragged out of me, I answered; 'THEY ARE ALL BURIED UNDER THE TURNIP FIELD ON OUR FACTORY SITE HERE.' Of course it was a complete fabrication. Our explosives' factories were all up north, which was common knowledge, and of course I had no idea if or where the explosives were stored. We had tunnels under the turnip fields on the factory site but they were air-raid shelters, and where we slept when on fire duty. I rushed off to warn the powers-that-be before she had time to signal to the Luftwaffe to blow our sleeping quarters and us with them to smithereens, if indeed she were a Fifth Columnist. Apparently the authorities had their suspicions also and not very long after this our psychologist was interned for the duration. As she was escorted away, she turned to me with her compelling eyes full of reproach. 'I am very disappointed in you,' she said. 'You have let me down.' I felt most uncomfortable.

I made other unusual contacts through my fellow-guests. One day I found myself high up in a flat in Tottenham Court Road, in almost pitch darkness because of the black-out and almost curtainless windows, learning how to make Molotov Cocktails—home-made bombs—and how to put sugar in enemy petrol tanks when the invasion came. Babs was a bit worried about this assignation and took me there by car the first time, so that she could inform the police if I were spirited away without trace, to have I.C.I.'s secrets ferreted out of me. The fact that I worked in Treasurer's Department where salaries, cash payments and monthly statements were the order of the day and details of which, if divulged to the enemy, could have little effect on the course of the war, was beside the point. But all the others there appeared to be patriots from various parts of north-west London. I did, however, over a Molotov Cocktail, become friendly with a lady who was closely connected with the Free French. So henceforth I spent spirited evenings with the Free French at their particular rendezvous in Soho. Afterwards I would stay the night with my new friend at her flat, joined rather mysteriously by her son, a Ph. D., for he never showed up if the Free French were around and disappeared if ever they were.

Once, after a merry evening with the Free French at their Soho pub, she persuaded me to speak to a gathering of ladies at a Kensington hotel. I cannot remember the details, for having agreed when in a carefree mood, I needed some fortifying when it came to keeping my promise. She was determined to get me there for she had some 300 ladies awaiting my words of wisdom. Why I was qualified to speak or on what subject I cannot recall, if indeed I ever knew. However, I do remember being asked in question time: 'Is it true what the Nazis are supposed to be doing to the French women over there?' I replied in ringing tones, with a great deal of emotion and emphasis—for I had learned that trick of oratory from politicians' speeches—that 'I was sure that our boys would take care of *that*.' This drew vigorous rounds of applause and cheers. The meeting was declared a great success and my friend plied me with more drinks to recover.

I also found myself one evening in the flat of another patriot from the Molotov Cocktail set. This time I was entertained by a gentleman who was so much like a caricature of a Colonel in the British Army, but who, significantly was not serving, that he must surely be a fifth columnist, I thought, or at least a phoney. He kept persuading me to stay on, as his son, he said, was most anxious to meet me and was due home any moment. I wondered *why* his son should be so anxious to meet me, especially as so far he had not seemed keen to turn up. In spite of constant cajoling to stay I insisted that I must catch my last train, and eventually managed to leave with a certain amount of relief, because nobody knew where I was *that* time. The whole evening had seemed highly suspicious so I took no chances and reported the incident to the police. There was no opportunity of following up this bit of detection, as the glamour lady of the film weekly would have done, for the bombs started to rain down on London and visits there became more hazardous and less frequent.

No long after this the vegetarian guest-house closed down—ostensibly for lack of food, which had been delicious. I.C.I. had taken over Digswell

Park Conference House in old Welwyn to accommodate some of its Head Office employees and, when we were evacuated, I had opted out of living there as I did not relish the idea of communal life, but now, finding no other digs that appealed, I decided that I would give it a try.

I therefore indicated to Miss Buist, the Lady Supervisor of Head Office who lived there, that I would be pleased to join them at Digswell if anywhere could be made available for me to set up my dark-room. Relieved, no doubt, to get all her charges into the fold, she overlooked the effrontery of this request, and placed at my disposal the whole of the East Wing which was considered too damp for sleeping quarters. As photography interested many of the young men, they now came to help me. This led to a lot of unfounded gossip about the 'goings on' in the East Wing, but happily this stigma on my character was removed as the young men were called up.

Members of our sex could not be called up as ours was designated a reserved occupation, for we now took over the men's jobs and our work became much more responsible. However, some of us felt that we were not contributing enough to the war effort. True I had the Amazons at the ready should the need arise, but nobody wanted us so far. I was captain of a Fire Squad. This entailed being in charge of a small mobile fire engine and sleeping in the tunnel under the turnip field when on night duty; practising the fireman's lift, directing members of staff to crawl under tarpaulins of smoke—a most satisfactory operation when the victims were the bosses—and being trained by the Fire Chief in climbing up steep ladders and over the roofs at Digswell. When on night duty at the factory I used to load up my truck ready for any eventuality; photographic equipment and lamps to set up a studio for portraiture and still life while waiting for incendiary bombs to drop; books, boiler suit and tin helmet; food and the two half pints of beer allocated, whatever one's sex and—just in case— my .22 rifle. Sometimes, when we were in our bunks under the turnip field, I would blow the whistle for an emergency practice. We would then run out the fire engine, climb the fire escape, hose over shoulder, to the top of the factory roof and start the pump to put out non-existent fires. No incendiary bombs came our way, however, and we felt particularly ineffectual, for we could see the red glare in the sky, twenty-five miles away, as London burned. Sick with frustration, two of us went up to London to try to enrol in the Auxiliary Fire Service, but we were turned down: they did not think that it was a good idea for us to travel fifty miles each day, nor was it feasible as it was uncertain that we should reach our destination. In any case, they added, we were needed where we were.

Some of us were doing part-time Land Army work, but hoeing miles and miles of mangel-wurzels did not seem dramatic enough when lives were being lost. We were allowed to join the Home Guard, referred to now as 'Dad's Army', but as auxiliaries only, to do the cooking and generally help behind the scenes. Our Unit, which consisted of men whose jobs were reserved and those awaiting call-up, was in charge of a section of the Great North Road. Here in a strategic position high above the road we awaited the Nazi hordes to come rumbling along in their tanks, so that we could hurl them back across the Channel. Although there were only some half a dozen rifles distributed among the men, the enormity of the task did not seem to daunt anyone and optimism ran high. I had the satisfaction of building a field kitchen—'just like Churchill' I thought proudly, as I smacked cement and bricks together—and I had the added pleasure of doing some cooking.

As the imminent danger of invasion receded some of us wanted to take a more active part in winning the war and constantly lobbied the powers-that-be to be allowed to join the Women's Services. Meantime, in addition to these spare time contributions to the war effort, communal life lent it-self to many recreational activities. We had musical evenings, organised parties and snowball fights in winter, attended WEA classes and went on cycling expeditions and long walks in the surrounding countryside. When I had practised at my brother's cricket school before the war, Jean Much had often accompanied me. She and I now arranged ladies' cricket matches and tried to put our expert coaching into practice. Peter, a friend who was awaiting call-up, and I managed to get up to the Lake District for some climbing and were able to visit London frequently for concerts. Once when we were at the Albert Hall, Myra Hess was the soloist and little did I know that one day I should come to live where once she had practised, for where I write adjoins the one-time barn which became a music room. She may even have slept in this very room, for Jetty Cottage was once used as an annexe for sleeping house guests, as it sometimes is now. Peter and I once organized a memorable skiing expedition by moonlight on the slopes of a cabbage field adjoining Digswell. An Austrian refugee, a Digswellian room neighbour, lent me her skis with the dire warning that skiing on two inches of snow in a cabbage field was a highly dangerous thing to attempt and could prove fatal. Certainly there were many falls, but luckily there was more laughter than groans.

Now that the Great North Road had not become congested with the Nazi hordes another friend and I used it for lorry-hops. We would, on occasion, book seats at the theatre at Stratford-on-Avon for the Saturday night performance, take up our stance in the morning on the Great North Road and arrive just in time for curtain up. Once after the performance and before travelling around the countryside the next day, Cecilia and I stayed the night in the first class compartment of a train in a siding, having been conducted there by a porter, who in the morning kindly brought us cups of tea.

These lorry-hopping expeditions became quite a feature when we had a spare Saturday and Sunday. We had several inviolate rules: we would only travel by lorry—private cars were allowed only in exceptional circumstances; trains were absolutely forbidden and we would take with us just 10s. apiece to supplement our picnic fare and for use in emergencies. I remember only breaking these rules twice; once finding ourselves in Somerset at dawn we allowed a BBC car to pick us up on its way to Bristol, our destination, as its speed would get us there more quickly and we had a crowded itinerary for the rest of Sunday. The second time was when we decided to visit my parents, who had evacuated themselves to join my sister-in-law and children in Aberdare in South Wales, after all the windows in our house in Surrey had been blasted out. We made good going on the Saturday and actually arrived in the valley below our destination just before dusk. As we wanted to reach Aberdare by nightfall we decided to take a bus. It was full of workers and shoppers returning home and although it was only a short ride it was an experience I shall never forget. A red sun was setting over the misty Welsh mountains and flooded the bus with a ruby red light; the whole busload of passengers suddenly burst into song and sang as only the Welsh can, as we climbed the valley into the westering sun. We arrived in Aberdare by twilight, and intoxicated by the heady delights of our musical ride, we descended on my unsuspecting and astonished parents.

The next morning we travelled high over the Brecon Beacons and were finally deposited at a milk depot somewhere in Buckinghamshire shortly after midnight. Here we were given the choice of the 1 a.m. or 3 a.m. London-bound milk-tanker. We chose the 3 a.m. run so that we could be shown over the depot—a fortunate choice, for not only did we have a most interesting tour but we were regaled with glasses of milk and cream. We arrived at Digswell at 8 a.m. just in time for a bath and the second sitting at breakfast, before walking across the fields for our day's work and a short sleep before the evening's activities.

During the waits for the lorries of our choice I read for the first time *War and Peace* and was so enthralled with it that it became my No. 1 in the literary charts and I read it again in more comfortable circumstances. Some of our lorry drivers became our regulars and looked out for us. They all warned us of the dire perils of our mode of transport. Nevertheless, without exception, we found them to be true 'knights of the road'. In any case it was all just an adventure to us. To keep my hand in at writing I wrote up accounts of all these expeditions at great length and Cecilia, who was a secretary, typed them. They are apparently lost to posterity, for Cecilia who, with Jean, came to visit us last year, said that she no longer had them in her possession. So these epic tales are 'Missing presumed lost'.

She and I also took up tomato growing. We had two packet of seeds and experimented by growing them under different conditions: in the un-heated conservatory at Digswell, in rich soil in the walled garden of the grounds there, on virgin soil near the turnip field on the factory site and, lastly, in a flower border beside our offices in the wooden huts. Two ferti-lizers were used: dried blood and cow manure and, as a control, we had a 'no fertilizer' group. I kept a progress chart showing the number of trusses per plant, the number and weight of fruit on each truss, and so on, to show the yield from the two different packets of seeds. Surplus fruit was bottled, for, by kind permission of the chief cook, we were allowed the use of the enormous kitchens at Digswell when she was off duty. As the permuta-tions were numerous to say the least, this chart became about two yards long and was kept meticulously. In spite of its size, at the crucial moment at the end of the season I lost it, so our findings were never published. However I do remember that the virgin soil produced the biggest tomatoes but the skins were tough; the walled garden produced lush plants that grew like lofty trees and bore numerous fruit the size of marbles, and the cowpats as a fertilizer were a runaway success. The office border plants were the envy of all the men and we were persuaded to sell them at 6d. each, which was the going rate at the time, as they were considered superior to the commercially grown ones.

This gave us the idea that we would put the money aside for a trip round the world when the war was over. I added my mangel-wurzeling wages, which had recently been increased from 1s. 4d. per hour to the top rate of 1s. 8d. All this amassed to the satisfying sum, for those days, of

£11 6s. 7d. which I put into National Savings Certificates for the duration. By that time Cecilia had moved to the US with her husband, and I was far too involved in this country to spare the time for a world trip. My savings, which had accumulated to a nice sum, went towards buying one of the earlier TV sets so that dad could watch the first Olympics Games to be televised, so enabling him to re-live his active and adventurous younger days when he sailed the Seven Seas, rounding Cape Horn under sail on passage to Valparaiso. By now at the age of seventy-five he was confined to a wheelchair having had both his legs amputated.

The tomato growing became an abiding interest. Here on the island they have become one of our main crops. Local folk come here especially to buy plants and the fruit, for they find the flavour delicious. With the long season and the wonderfully mild climate one can experiment endlessly to produce bumper crops, and I have the charts to prove it!

Literary efforts now turned to yet another magazine. A friend, Jane Lygo and I, together with Bill Bristowe, the Head of Central Staff Department, all three residents of Digswell, brought out a *Digswell Magazine*. This was considered a great success, especially by the three of us, and it became a regular feature of life there, and some of us have copies we have kept as a memento of those times we shared together.

Then at last came my big chance to fulfil my life's ambition. An advertisement appeared in the press for the job of sub-editor on *Woman's Journal*. Excited beyond measure I was called for an interview. This was conducted by the Managing Editor and the lady Editor. I explained that I was in fact in a reserved occupation, but I thought that I could arrange to get myself unreserved. While we were discussing this the Picture Editor came in and said that if they did not want me on the editorial side she would have me in the Photographic Department. Their depletion of staff due to call-up was giving me the chance of a lifetime. It was left that I should sort out the reserved occupation position.

Head in the clouds, I raced back to Digswell and almost hurled myself at Miss Buist, the Supervisor. She was a very kindly Scottish lady who was always most helpful to her 'girls', making us all feel like a family. Yes, she would do her best to get me released, for she knew of my ambitions. She was also a very clever lady. She pointed out that I ran the risk of being one of the first to go when their own staff returned at the end of the war, and somehow or other she implied, without actually putting it into words, that I should be deserting I.C.I. in their hour of need. She would do her very best for me, but I was to think about it and let her know. Of course I felt I would be an absolute heel to leave and decided I must remain loyal to I.C.I.

In the course of time, after continued lobbying, those who wished were allowed to join the Women's Services and we were actually paid a retainer so that our jobs would be secure when we returned after the war. A farewell party was thrown for Cecilia, Jean and me, and paper sailor hats were made for each of us. We all three were joining the WRNS on the same day, but were destined not to meet together again until the summer of 1983 here on the island, forty years later.

My career in the WRNS, although full of exciting incidents, as could only be expected of one so incident prone, is not strictly part of 'The Author's Tale' for I did no writing at all.

An impressive looking Naval Officer, dripping with gold braid, addressed our gathering of newly recruited Wrens. He told us we were not, absolutely *not*, to keep a diary, in case it should fall into enemy hands. So I did not. By the same token I reckoned that I should not write letters either; so none were written except for guarded ones home. This gave rise to an item in the *Digswell Magazine* that Admiral 'Attie' had been sunk without trace, and to recriminations from all my friends that I had not answered a single letter throughout the war. In any case I had had a very busy war. Ever willing to help the Allied Cause I became very friendly with a contingent of Norwegian Naval Officers in Scotland and, but for my fortuitous posting *en route* for a commission at Greenwich Naval College, might have found myself spending the rest of my life in 'civvy street' in Norway.

After the war, responsibilities at home and I.C.I. grew enormously, and with new interests and friends life became very crowded indeed. It became even more so when Di Sorby, she of the abortive treasure-hunting expedition to the island flagstaff, took a hand in my photographic career. Di, who had been a member of the Fire Brigade at Welwyn, and a leading light in the I.C.I. Players, was a member of Publicity Department and took a great interest in my photography. My camera accompanied me, as usual, on all activities and post-war wanderings at home and abroad. Hours spent in the dark-room at the *Camera Club* in London and in my blacked-out bedroom at home produced exhibition prints, and Di showed some of my collection to the Art Editor. As a result he published many of these on the front and back covers of the I.C.I. Magazine for which I was handsomely paid. He then commissioned me to take photographs on a regular basis and I became official photographer of the *Head Office News*, covering all kinds of subjects: Sporting events, amateur theatricals at the Fortune Theatre, office parties, presentations, bell-ringing in Southwark Cathedral, portraits of Heads of Departments and architecture to name a few. Others now commissioned me to take photographs, including portraits of people, babies, animals, weddings at Caxton Hall and elsewhere and receptions in Soho and fashionable hotels. With the fees that continued to be paid for the cover pictures photography was proving most lucrative. All these earnings were, of course, subject to income tax and I found making the returns complicated and a bit beyond me. Here it must be said that I found the Tax Officials most helpful. I would go along to the Tax Office with my scrappy bits of paper showing expenses; the Tax Officer would then work them all out for me and actually fill in the form. I was most surprised and gratified, especially as I was given advice that would benefit me and save me tax.

Now I was so busy with deadlines and dark-room work as well as working overtime in my Staff Department post that I scarcely had time to sleep, certainly not to write. Di, however, did write although not in a professional capacity. She inaugurated a Past and Present Club for lady members of I.C.I. Head Office which is still flourishing. Now retired, in spite of ill-health, each year she writes a Newsletter, which entails much research and editing of her enormous correspondence, so that up-to-date news can be circulated to all members, some of whom are in hospital or housebound. Having launched me into professional photography Di now keeps everyone informed, in her Newsletters, of all our island activities and of my progress in authorship.

How then, after a lifetime of abortive attempts, did I at last come to write a book, and am even now finishing a second? I can take no credit for this myself.

When we first came to the island, after my early retirement, it was my dream that, in the sequestered calm of this splendid solitude I would at last be able to fulfil my childhood ambition of becoming an author; here, where there would be no people to distract me nor any pursuits to tempt me to dilly-dally along enticing side-tracks. That this dream was shattered is obvious from the foregoing *Tales*. Who or what was the catalysis? It was Babs!

Babs, who had started off as a toddler applauding my plays, and who seemingly graduated in no time at all to helping or guarding me at crucial moments in my life, now became directly responsible. Many books have been dedicated: 'To . . . without whose help and encouragement this book would never have been written.' I can and do so dedicate this book most wholeheartedly to Babs, but it would be more accurate to add that but for her it would have never been started.

A few years after we came to the island, Babs, in the course of her duties at school, was speaking to Terence Hanson, the rep. from Harrap, the publishers, about the educational books they were supplying to the school. The fact cropped up that she lived on an island. Terence Hanson pricked up his ears. 'Tell me more,' he said. Babs tossed him a few details about how we came to own an island in the first place. Intrigued, he said 'That sounds like the making of a book. Do you mind if I discuss it with Harrap staff in London?' 'Not at all', said Babs politely, little knowing that that innocuous phrase would light the fuse to a time bomb.

Shortly after this she received a letter from Paull Harrap, the Managing Director of Harrap, the gist of which was that they were interested in a book, and said that he would like to send his Senior Initiating Editor, Frank Waters, to discuss the matter.

Subsequently Frank Waters and his wife Denise came down to Looe with the intention of coming over here to the island with Babs to discuss the matter with us both. Somewhat to my relief, for by now I was quaking in my shoes—or rather gumboots—it was a wild wet day, with a forecast of worse to come. There was no possibility of getting over to the island, so Frank Waters took Babs to dinner at the Portbyhan Hotel, where she regaled him with tales of some of our adventures. He said that definitely they would like a book. After some general discussion Babs pin-pointed a major problem. 'How do *two* people write a book,' she asked, 'especially as I am on the mainland and my sister is on the island?' 'You have a point there,' said Frank Waters. 'Leave it with me.' Not long after his return to London he telephoned Babs. 'It has been decided', he said, 'that as your sister is living on the island all the time, she should write the book.'

Babs called me on the radio telephone. 'You are writing a book!' she said. Just like that.

I will not say that the idea did not appal me—it did. The sheer enormity of the task overwhelmed me. I was already like a demented being running

the island—single-handed most of the time; coping with daffodils, cultivating the land, tending two greenhouses, printing, typing and doing the
daily accounts, baking for day visitors and meeting them, coping with the
cottagers, feeding the students, and attending to the generator and water-
pump, as well as incidentals like feeding five pets, the goat and hens as
well as myself, and trying to keep my hand in at pottery and assorted
crafts—as a kind of relaxation. I felt, however, when I had recovered from
the initial shock, that Fate had once again got me in its grasp. Just as it
had brought us to the island, so now its finger pointed inexorably towards
authorship. Was it not perhaps written in the stars? How else should I have
known at the age of six that one day I would become an author, albeit a
lifetime away. Or is it perhaps that if one wishes hard enough and long
enough, the wish will one day be granted? Paull Harrap and Frank Waters
gave me the initial stimulus for the first book. Now Simon Scott, the present
Editorial Director of Harrap, has entered the field and his very real encouragement has helped me when I have faltered on the way to finishing
this sequel.

Little did I know when Babs announced 'You are writing a book!' that
I would be writing two books; that I would have enough material for a
third, a fourth or even a fifth. But would I have the time?

What a pity that I did not start at the age of six.